D1087409

GOOD GOVERNMENT AND LAW

Good Government and Law

Legal and Institutional Reform in Developing Countries

Edited by

Julio Faundez

Professor of Law
and Director of the International Economy Law Programme
University of Warwick

in association with
THE BRITISH COUNCIL

First published in Great Britain 1997 by
MACMILLAN PRESS LTD
Houndmills, Basingstoke, Hampshire RG21 6XS and London
Companies and representatives throughout the world

A catalogue record for this book is available from the British Library.

ISBN 0–333–66996–7 hardcover
ISBN 0–333–66997–5 paperback

First published in the United States of America 1997 by
ST. MARTIN'S PRESS, INC.,
Scholarly and Reference Division,
175 Fifth Avenue, New York, N.Y. 10010

ISBN 0–312–16473–4

Library of Congress Cataloging-in-Publication Data
Good government and law : legal and institutional reform in developing
countries / edited by Julio Faundez.
p.   cm.
Includes bibliographical references and index.
ISBN 0–312–16473–4 (cloth)
1. Law reform—Developing countries.   2. Rule of law—Developing
countries.   3. Developing countries—Politics and government.
4. Law and politics.   Faundez, Julio.
K561.G66   1996
340.3'09172'4—dc20
96–9724
CIP

This book is printed on paper suitable for recycling and made from fully managed and
sustained forest sources.

10   9   8   7   6   5   4   3   2   1
06   05   04   03   02   01   00   99   98   97

Printed in Great Britain by
The Ipswich Book Company Ltd
Ipswich, Suffolk

Contents

CASE STUDIES

Contributors

Ama Annan, Journalist and aid worker, Christian Aid, London

Robert Annibale, Vice-President, Citibank N A

Nancy Bermeo, Associate Professor of Politics, Princeton University

Alberto de Capitani, World Bank

Ross Cranston, Professor of Commercial Law, London School of Economics and Political Science

Luis José Diez-Canseco Núñez, UNCTAD

Julio Faundez, Professor of Law, University of Warwick

Leila Frischtak, Consultant, World Bank

Reginald Green, Professorial Fellow, Institute for Development Studies, University of Sussex

Ann Matear, Lecturer, School of Languages and Area Studies, University of Portsmouth

Maria Luiza Vianna Pessoa de Mendonca, Federal Judge, Brazil

Patrick McAuslan, Professor of Law, Birkbeck College, London

John McEldowney, Reader in Law, University of Warwick

Shirin Rai, Senior Lecturer, Politics and International Studies, Warwick University

Malcolm Rowat, World Bank

Joseph Thome, Professor of Law, Univeristy of Wisconsin, Madison

Lawrence Tshuma, Programme Legal Counsel, International Development Law Institute

Good Government and Law seminar

British Council, 27-28 March 1995

Participants

AnnLis Aberg, Swedish International Development Authority
Robert Annibale, Vice-President, Citibank N A
Nancy Bermeo, Associate Professor of Politics, Princeton University
Anne Bruzelius, Swedish International Development Authority
Karin Buhmann, DANIDA, Copenhagen, Denmark
Alberto de Capitani, The World Bank
Fernando Carrillo-Florez, Inter-American Development Bank
Ross Cranston, Professor of Commercial Law, London School of Economics
Sital Dhillon, British Council
Ben Dickinson, British Council, Kenya
Mamadou Dia, World Bank
Friedrika Diaby-Pentzlin, Deutsche Gessellschaft fur Technische Zusammenarbeit (GTZ) Gmbtt, Eschborn, Germany
Luis José Diez-Canseco Núñez, UNCTAD
Julio Faundez, Professor of Law, University of Warwick
Leila Frischtak, World Bank
Reginald Green, Professorial Fellow, Institute of Development Studies, University of Sussex
Michael J. Greaves, Overseas Development Adminsitration (ODA), London
Ann Keeling, British Council, Manchester
Patrick McAuslan, Professor of Law, Birkbeck College, University of London
John McEldowney, Reader in Law, University of Warwick
Claire McVeigh, British Council, Chile
Nena Manley, World Bank
Helen Meixner, British Council, Manchester
Shirin Rai, Senior Lecturer, Politics and International Studies Department, University of Warwick
Lindsey Russell, British Council, Manchester
Malcolm D. Rowat, World Bank
Joseph Thome, Professor of Law, University of Wisconsin
Margit Tveiten, Royal Norwegian Ministry of Foreign Affairs, Oslo

Foreword

A clear commitment to the practices of good government by recipient countries is an important criterion for many aid donors, including Britain's Overseas Development Administration, in deciding how resources are allocated. An essential characteristic of good government is promotion of the rule of law.

The Council has traditionally played a key role in bringing together expertise from both the public and private sectors. It was in this context that the Council decided to organize an international seminar on the theme of good government and law, and asked Professor Julio Faundez of Warwick University to act as the seminar's director. The seminar was held at the Council's London headquarters 27-28 March, 1995. Its objective was to initiate a dialogue between practitioners in the field of legal technical assistance and law specialists in the private sector and in academic institutions.

The establishment of a viable democracy in developing countries and in countries of the former socialist bloc will depend on the existence of legal systems which protect individual rights and enable enterprise to flourish. Governments must also be capable of managing the complex transformation required for the liberalization of their national economies and of responding to the demands of their citizens so that potential is fully realised. This will not be easy to achieve, but the seminar and the papers which it is now publishing are a contribution to that goal.

Sir John Hanson KCMG, CBE
Director General, The British Council

Acknowledgements

I am grateful to the British Council for inviting me to direct the Seminar on Good Government and Law. I am especially indebted to Sital Dhillon from the Council who supported this project with enthusiasm and commitment. Paula Horgan and Deborah Hall provided excellent administrative support both before and during the Seminar. I am also grateful to Angela Dewsbury who copy-edited the text and prepared the camera-ready copy and to Mayura Baweja who compiled the index.

Julio Faundez

Abbreviations and acronyms

ACLA	Advisory Commission on Land Allocation (South Africa)
ADR	Alternative Dispute Resolution
BCCI	Bank of Credit and Commerce International
BIS	Bank for International Settlements
CIA	Central Intelligence Agency (USA)
CIS	Commonwealth of Independent States
CIDA	Canadian International Development Agency
DANIDA	Danish International Development Agency
EU	European Union
FILMUP	Financial and Legal Management Upgrading Project of Tanzania
IADB	Inter-American Development Bank
ICSID	International Centre for Settlement of Investment Disputes
IMF	International Monetary Fund
MERCOSUR	Mercado Común del Sur, Regional Integration Agreement based on the Treaty of Asunción of 1991. Its members are Argentina, Brazil, Paraguay and Uruguay.
MMC	Monopolies and Mergers Commission (UK)
NAFTA	North American Free Trade Agreement
NGO	Non-Governmental Organisation
NORAD	Norwegian Agency for International Development
ODA	Overseas Development Administration (UK)
OECD	Organization for Economic Cooperation and Development
PIL	Public Interest Litigation
SADT	South African Development Trust
SERNAM	Servicio Nacional de la Mujer (National Women's Office, Chile)
SIDA	Swedish International Development Authority
UNCTAD	United Nations Conference on Trade and Development
UNDP	United Nations Development Programme
USAID	Unted States Agency for International Development

INTRODUCTION

1 Legal technical assistance

Julio Faundez

The widespread process of economic and political liberalization currently taking place in developing countries and in countries in Eastern and Central Europe has brought about a renewed interest in the role of law and legal institutions. The introduction of policies of economic liberalization, deregulation and privatization is generally accompanied by major changes to the legal framework. Likewise, the process of political liberalization is often combined with constitutional reform. While the primary responsibility for developing a new legal framework rests with national governments, multilateral banks and bilateral donor agencies have become increasingly concerned with it. Thus, over the past eight years, legal technical assistance has become a major component of both multilateral and bilateral aid programmes.

The phrase 'legal technical assistance' describes a range of activities which include: drafting constitutions and legislation; advising on institutional reform; establishing new institutional frameworks; providing technical support for the development of parliamentary procedures and practices; advising on judicial reform; offering short training courses on specific legal topics, and providing advise and guidance on legal education generally. Although most multilateral banks and bilateral donor agencies are involved in programmes which fall within the broad notion of legal technical assistance, the intellectual and practical leadership is provided largely by the World Bank, through its numerous publications and the projects in which it is involved.

The activities described above suggest that the phrase 'legal technical assistance' is little more than a new phrase to describe an old practice. Indeed, the importation, transplantation or imposition of laws and legal institutions has been a permanent feature in world history, both ancient and modern. Law as an instrument of social domination and subjugation has been an essential tool in the establishment of empires. In recent decades, the end of colonialism and the emergence of a large number of newly independent states led to a flurry of activities which, today, would be described as legal technical assistance. More recently, in the 1960s, United States foreign-aid agencies explicitly incorporated law into their programmes. Although the US aid agencies' interest in law was short-lived, it prompted the emergence of an important body of literature which

1

has greatly contributed towards furthering our understanding of the role of law in the process of modernization.

The practical concern of international financial institutions and bilateral aid agencies with the role of law in the process of development, combined with the continuous academic interest in this topic, prompted the British Council to organize a seminar on Good Government and Law. One of the main objectives of the seminar was to promote a dialogue between practitioners in the field of legal technical assistance and academics from various disciplines.

This volume consists of revised versions of the papers presented at the seminar together with written comments on each paper. It does not represent an agreed position. It does, however, offer a variety of critical perspectives for the evaluation of legal technical assistance projects and contains concrete proposals for action and research. The selection of topics covered in this volume does not purport to be comprehensive. The contributions to this volume do, however, illustrate the problems and issues arising out of the process of legal and institutional reform in developing countries.

This Introduction consists of two parts. Part I examines some of the arguments for and against legal technical assistance, describes how law came to be a part of the development aid agenda, explains the World Bank's approach to law and compares it with that of the law and development movement of the United States. Part II offers an overview of selected themes discussed by the contributors to this volume.

I. LAW: A MOBILE TOOL?

Since law in a modern state is generally regarded as the supreme manifestation of national sovereignty, it is pertinent to ask whether, and if so how, multilateral banks and bilateral donor agencies should be involved in the provision of legal technical assistance. Copying, borrowing and drawing inspiration from foreign institutional and legal models is, of course, neither new nor mainly brought about by external legal technical assistance. It is a process which takes place in different countries at a different pace and with different degrees of success and is often, though not always, associated with changes in the economic and social structures. This process, often referred to by comparative lawyers as 'reception of foreign laws', involves the migration and cross-fertilization of legal institutions, often aided by conscious efforts toward the harmonization and unification of rules and procedures in various areas of the law.[1]

---

1   See generally, Konrad Zweigert and Hein Koltz, *Introduction to Comparative Law*, Vol. I (Oxford, Clarendon Press, 1987).

The World Bank is aware that the provision of legal technical assistance is a sensitive issue. In one of its recent publications, it clearly states that the political decision about the choice and direction of legal reform is one which has to be made by each country: "before launching comprehensive legal reform, each society has to make fundamental choices about the structure of its legal system".[2] Consistent with this approach, the Bank defines the role of external advisors narrowly as assisting in the decision-taking process, but not deciding which specific legal model should be adopted.[3]

Sceptics would probably argue that by making the disbursement of loans conditional to the adoption of specific legal reforms, the World Bank is, in practice, contradicting the principle that the choice and direction of legal reform rests with each country. This is not the place to go over the debate about conditionality. It must be noted, however, that, in practice, the distinction between the direction of legal reform – a political choice – and the role of external legal advisers – a technical function – is not always easy to make.

Indeed, the distinction between policymaking and legal advice in general is a difficult one. It could well be that, in some cases, where the project is very technical – such as drafting legislation on securities regulation – and where there is no body of local rules or practices upon which the legal reformer can draw, the external legal consultant not merely advises, but actually formulates policy. The foreign legal advisor's role may also become paramount when unrealistically short deadlines are set to complete a given project.

The boundary between the roles of advisor and policymaker is not always easy to draw, is not of great concern if law is regarded as a mere technical artefact. From this perspective, once the critical decision to modernize the legal system has been taken, the drafting process can be regarded as purely technical; if not mechanical, since often there is only a limited number of models from which to draw inspiration. An argument along this line was made some thirty years ago by René David, a leading French comparative law specialist, in connection with the Ethiopian Civil Code which he had drafted.

According to David, once Ethiopia had opted for the path of legal modernization, it would not have been practical to wait for a law to emerge from within the indigenous culture. The adoption of a civil code, based on the French model, would according to David "assure as quick as possible a minimal security of social relations".[4]

---

2   The World Bank Legal Department, *The World Bank and Legal Technical Assistance*, (Policy Research Working Paper 1414, 1995) p9. Hereinafter LTA.
3   Ibid.
4   René David, 'A Civil Code for Ethiopia: Considerations on the Codification of the Civil Law in African Countries', <u>Tulane Law Review</u> Vol. 37 (1963) p189.

David's remarks on Ethiopia's Civil Code could be seen simply as a legal consultant's rationalization of the assignment that he had undertaken. It could be argued that David misrepresents the choice confronting an external legal consultant, for in the statement quoted above he appears to suggest that the choice was between either waiting for a modern indigenous legal culture to emerge, or introducing an imported civil code. An alternative course of action would have been to ensure that the new legislation was as far as possible consistent with local practices.[5]

David's remarks on the drafting of Ethiopia's Civil Code raise, however, an important point about the role of external legal advisors in the process of legal reform. Given that for technical and practical reasons the process of legal reform generally involves a certain amount of borrowing from other legal systems, doesn't this further blur the line which purports to distinguish between policymakers and external legal advisors?

If law and legislation are mere technical artefacts, then the fact that external legal advisors have a controlling role in the process of legal reform is of no great concern. This approach to legal reform has a respectable pedigree. As Hannah Arendt reminds us, the ancient Greeks did not regard law-making as a political activity. The legislator's task was seen by the Greeks as equivalent to that of the architect who builds the city's walls and whose job has to be completed before politics in the city can begin. Hence, the legislator – as architect – did not have to be a citizen and could therefore be recruited from abroad. While only citizens were allowed to engage in politics, the task of making laws, that is, defining the space in which politics would be carried out, could be entrusted to a foreigner, albeit an enlightened one.[6]

The ancient Greeks' conception of law-making does not fit with contemporary conceptions about national law and sovereignty. Law-making – preferably through democratic processes – is an expression of a state's sovereignty. Under this conception, law is seen as special to each country and expressing and determining its people's political, social and economic identity. This situation is, however, paradoxical, for, as Alan Watson has pointed out, law is highly

---

5   In fact, as David explains, he actually tried to incorporate elements of local customary law into the code, but because of the diversity of regional customs, only some could be incorporated. Hence his statement that Ethiopia could not afford to wait 300 years to have a modern system of private law. Ibid., pp193-196. For a general evaluation of Ethiopia's legal transplants, see John H. Beckstrom, 'Transplantation of Legal Systems: An early Report on the Reception of Western Laws in Ethiopia', American Journal of Comparative Law Vol. 21 (1973) p557.
6   Hannah Arendt, *The Human Condition* (Chicago: University of Chicago Press, 1958) pp194-5.

mobile. As Watson explains, "legal transplants – the moving of a rule or of a system of law from one country to another, or from one people to another – have been common since the earliest recorded history".[7]

Based on his own extensive research in legal history, Watson goes on to argue that transplanting legal rules – that is, taking a system of rules from one environment into quite a different environment – is a relatively easy task. The fact that this process often involves the application of rules which were not designed for that particular society is, in his view, not important.[8] According to Watson, successful borrowing can be achieved even if the legal reformers know nothing about the political, social or economic context of the place where the law originates.[9] Following this line of reasoning, an external legal advisor does not need to know anything about the context of the recipient country. Thus, what emerges from this analysis is a conception of the external legal advisor which comes close to the Greek notion of the law-maker as architect. As such, foreign legal experts not only advise on policy options, but may also determine the content and direction of the legal development in a particular area of the law.

Watson's interpretation of the process of legal transplants, though controversial, is a helpful reminder that the evolution of law and the development of legal traditions are complex processes which cannot be adequately explained by focusing exclusively on national legal systems. From a historical perspective, national legal systems are indeed a recent and perhaps transient phenomenon.[10] Acknowledging, however, the fact that law is a highly mobile, cosmopolitan artefact does not endorse the view that national legal systems are empty shells waiting to be filled. Because law both legitimizes and controls the use of force, its form as well as its content are not matters of indifference. In order to understand the role of law and to make meaningful recommendations about its reform, it is necessary to understand the political (state) and social (society) context in which it operates. Conversely, an adequate understanding of a particular state and society cannot ignore its laws and legal system.

---

7   Alan Watson, *Legal Transplants* (Edinburgh: Scottish Academic Press, 1974) p21. Watson's notion of legal transplants is broad and includes a whole range of possibilities such as imposed reception, solicited imposition, penetration, infiltration, crypto-reception and inoculation. Ibid., p 30.
8   Ibid., p96.
9   Alan Watson, 'Legal Transplants and Law Reform', Law Quarterly Review Vol. 92 (1976) p79. Watson, however, does not regard legal transplants as a purely mechanical operation. Because legal rules or even the whole system of rules transplanted generally change after the transplant, Watson points out that the specificity of a legal system is not found in the overall system, but in those aspects where it differs from other systems; that is, in its details. Ibid., p97.
10   R. C. Van Caenegem, *An Historical Introduction to Private Law* (Cambridge: Cambridge University Press, 1992) p11.

A new approach to development

The provision of legal technical assistance is generally seen as part of the broader objective of improving the governance capacity of recipient governments. The concern of multilateral banks and bilateral aid agencies with governance issues stems largely from their awareness that, increasingly, economic and social development projects fail to achieve their objectives because of inadequate, or even lack of, institutional and legal frameworks.

Because of the nature of its mandate, the World Bank prefers to use the notion of governance rather than good government. Under its Charter, the Bank is not allowed to introduce political reforms or even question the political regime of the recipient country.[11] Accordingly, the World Bank uses the concept of governance to refer to the capacity of governments to formulate and implement policies and the processes by which authority is exercised in the management of a country's economic and social resources. It explicitly distinguishes this aspect of governance from that which refers to the form of political regime.[12] Bilateral donors, for their part unconstrained by the restrictions which the Articles of Agreement place on the World Bank, generally prefer to use the concept of good government. The practical consequence of this difference in approach is that bilateral donors are able to add to the World Bank's governance agenda an explicit democratic and political component. Thus, bilateral donors are concerned with issues such as the promotion of multi-party democracy, freedom of the press, penal reform and, in some cases, the promotion of certain social rights.[13] While aid agencies define governance capacity in different ways, most of them regard improved public sector management, accountability of public officials, transparency in policymaking and a suitable legal system as essential components.

The transition to a market economy in the countries of Central and Eastern Europe has undoubtedly contributed towards stimulating the interest of the World Bank and other international agencies in the role of law and legal institutions. For there, the absence of a suitable institutional framework, rather

---

11 The two relevant charters are the Articles of Agreement of the International Bank for Reconstruction and Development and the Articles of Agreement of the International Development Association. For a detailed and authoritative discussion of this issue, see, Ibrahim Shihata, *The World Bank in a Changing World* (Dordrecht: Martinus Nijhoff, 1991) pp61-65.
12 World Bank, *Governance and Development* (Washington: 1992) p58. Hereinafter *Governance*.
13 See, for example, The British Council, *Development Priorities Guidelines* (London: 1993); ODA, *Taking Account of Good Government* (London: 1993); Royal Norwegian Ministry of Foreign Affairs, *Support for Democratic Development* (Oslo, 1994); SIDA, *Making Government Work* (Stockholm: 1991); OECD, *DAC Orientations on Participatory Development and Good Governance* (Paris: 1993); Commission of the European Communities, *Report from the Commission to the Council on the Implementation of the Resolution of the Council and of the Member States Meeting in the Council on Human Rights, Democracy and Development* (COM (94) 42 final).

than its inadequacy, made the task of drafting laws and designing new institutions both urgent and, in the first instance, almost uncontested.[14] Thus, not surprisingly, some of the publications on the role of law in the Eastern and Central European transition process read almost as a handbook on the legal steps required to establish a market economy. The five main areas of law identified in this process are: property, contract, company, bankruptcy and competition.[15]

The involvement of the World Bank and other multilateral agencies in projects in Eastern and Central European countries has undoubtedly contributed towards reinforcing the awareness and interest of international aid agencies in the role of law in the economy. The World Bank's interest in governance and law in developing countries, however, is based on its – and the IMF's – new approach to development which began to take shape in the mid- to late-seventies and which was reinforced by the shift to neo-liberalism in the leading industrialized countries. While in the past, underdevelopment was seen largely as a consequence of a series of structural constraints which called for a massive increase in domestic investment relying largely on the state, under the new approach both the diagnosis and prescription changed. Structural constraints came to be regarded as distorted consequences of misguided state intervention which could only be overcome by greater reliance on the market.[16] The policy reform process thus advocated was aimed at freeing market forces from excessive state intervention so as to ensure an efficient use of resources.

This shift in focus involved a new interpretation of the role of the state in the process of development. The political implications for the state of this new approach is concisely summarized in the World Bank's call for a new type of state: one that is market-friendly.[17] The Bank's new focus on a market-friendly state as the means to promote growth policies was combined, in the aftermath of the debt crisis of the early 1980s, with closer co-ordination with the IMF. The stabilization policies traditionally advocated by the IMF to deal with balance of payments problems were combined with policy-based lending by the World

---

14 For an interesting assessment of legal technical assistance in the Commonwealth of Independent States, see, Thomas Waelde and James L. Gunderson, 'Legislative Reform in Transition Economies: Western Transplants – A Short-Cut to Social Market Economy Status', International and Comparative Law Quarterly Vol. 43 (1994) p347.
15 See, for example, European Bank for Reconstruction and Development, *Transition Report* (London: 1994) pp69-77; Cheryl W. Gray (et.al.) *Evolving Legal Frameworks for Private Sector Development in Central and Eastern Europe* (The World Bank: Washington 1993); Michele Balfour and Cameron Crise, 'A Privitization Test: The Czech Republic, Slovakia and Poland' Fordham International Law Journal Vol. 17 (1993) p84.
16 Montek S. Ahluwalia, 'Structural Adjustment and Reform in Developing Countries', in UNCTAD, *International Monetary and Financial Issues for the 1990s* Vol.4 (New York:1994) p129.
17 World Bank, *World Development Report 1991: The Challenge of Development* (Oxford: Oxford University Press, 1992) p6.

Bank which called for the implementation of a comprehensive programme of structural reforms. This programme of reform involved: deregulation of investment, prices and production; liberalization of trade and the financial sectors; privatization of public enterprises; labour market reforms; and changes to tax laws and systems of tax administration.[18] The market-friendly approach to economic policy reform in developing countries is also known as the Washington consensus.[19]

The implementation of the new policy reform agenda, carried out largely under structural adjustment programmes, generated considerable interest, as well as controversy.[20] Given the nature and scope of the new reform agenda, it is not surprising that the prevailing institutional frameworks soon became a major focus of concern. In some cases this concern was prompted by the apparent failure of the structural adjustment programmes to achieve their objectives; in other cases, it was prompted by the strong popular resistance brought about by the implementation of the adjustment programmes.[21] Thus, concern with institutions in the narrow context of individual projects gave way to the more general concern of governance. The failure of some international funded projects to achieve their objectives was attributed to the overall weakness of the institutional framework of the countries concerned.

Governance and law
The introduction of governance into the reform agenda brought with it concern with law and the legal system. Even under the World Bank's narrow definition of governance, law figures prominently as one of its four main components. As the World Bank publications explain, the Bank's concern with law is restricted only to those legal aspects which are connected with the efficient use of resources and productive investment. The legal framework should thus be expected to create a stable environment so that economic actors can carry out business transactions without the threat of arbitrary political interference. To achieve such an environment, the legal framework must fulfil five requirements: "(a) There is a set of rules known in advance; (b) the rules are actually in force;

---

18 For a recent re-evaluation of the roles of the World Bank and the IMF see Bretton Woods Commission, *Bretton Woods: Looking to the Future* (Washington: 1995).

19 This phrase was introduced by John Williamson and was originally intended to describe the policy reforms in Latin American countries. See John Williamson, 'What Washington Means by Policy Reform', in John Williamson (ed.), *Latin American Adjustment: How Much Has Happened* (Washington: Institute for International Economics, 1990) pp5-20.

20 See, for example, Renee Prendergast and Frances Stewart (eds.), *Market Forces and World Development* (London: Macmillan Press, 1994); John Cavanagh, Daphyne Wysham and Marcos Arruda (eds.), *Beyond Bretton Woods: Alternatives to the Global Economic Order* (London: Pluto Press, 1994).

21 Leila Frischtak, *Governance Capacity and Economic Reform in Developing Countries* (Washington: The World Bank, 1994).

(c) there are mechanisms ensuring application of the rules; (d) conflicts are decided through binding decisions of an independent body; and (e) there are procedures for amending the rules when they no longer serve their purpose."[22]

These five requirements, though apparently formal, presuppose the existence of a complex institutional framework, one which is generally associated with modern states. The enactment of abstract rules of behaviour presupposes the existence of a body of legal experts who elaborate the rules. The effective enforcement of these rules requires an effective administrative apparatus made up of professional civil servants and backed by a professional police force. Conflict resolution by an independent body – independent of the government and of the parties to the dispute – presupposes the existence of a state within which its different organs perform clearly defined functions within a stable constitutional framework. Finally, the requirement that procedures should be in place to amend laws when they no longer serve their purpose also presupposes a specialized branch of the state, generally a legislature which is distinct and independent from the organ in charge of administration. It must be noted however, that the World Bank, because of the restrictions imposed by its Charter and because it recognises that this is a matter for each state to decide, does not prescribe how the legislative process should be organized or whether it should be democratic.[23]

The World Bank's approach to law and governance recognises that successful law reform requires adequate implementation. Thus, the Bank is not only concerned with the enactment of specific legal rules, but it is also concerned with the processes which lead to the enactment, implementation and enforcement of the rules; and with the institutions which make these processes function.[24] But the Bank does not regard law solely as an enforcement machinery which can serve any purpose. Such a conception could easily lead to the emergence of the very practices that the Washington consensus is seeking to eradicate; that is, state practices which are not market-friendly. Accordingly, the legal system must have a minimum content – it must also be market-friendly and conducive to balanced development.[25]

The Bank's concern with the content of legal rules is, according to Ibrahim Shihata, appropriate, so long as it is based on considerations of efficiency.[26] A legal system which satisfies the minimum requirements of form and substance is described in one of the Bank's publications as 'a fair legal system'.[27] It is this

---

22 *Governance*, p30.
23 Ibid., p38.
24 *LTA*, p7.
25 *Governance*, p30.
26 Shihata, op.cit., p86.
27 *Governance*, p30.

concern with the substance of the rules of law which has opened up the area of legal conditionality; that is, adjustment loans conditioned to the implementation of specific legal reforms such as the enactment of commercial codes, modernization of the judiciary, or the establishment of debt collection systems.[28]

The Bank has not yet developed in detail the notion of a fair legal system. Yet, a comparison with the notion of law held by the law and development movement in the United States will help clarify its meaning.

Law and development

As the last wave of decolonization was about to come to an end in the 1960s, the US Government, through its international aid agencies, began to take a special interest in the modernization of both the new and the old states in the Third World. Accordingly, academic lawyers from leading law schools in the United States were recruited by the Government to work on legal technical assistance projects.[29] In addition to their work as consultants, legal academics also received generous grants from the US Government and from private foundations – mainly the Ford Foundation – which further stimulated their practical research interests in the role of law in developing countries.[30] By the late 1960s the number of academic lawyers with knowledge and direct experience of developing countries had increased and the group was soon seen as forming part of a new trend within American legal education: that of the law and development movement.

The law and development movement was, however, short-lived. By the early 1970s it was declared, if not dead, at least terminally ill by two of its leading figures.[31] One of the factors which contributed to the early demise of the movement was financial. As Government agencies and private foundations began to lose interest in law in the development process, academics were left without the necessary financial support to carry out research which requiring extensive and expensive field work. But there were also intellectual reasons to account for its collapse.

The main reason for the crisis of the law and development movement was –

28 LTA, p4-7.
29 On the law and development movement, see Elliot M. Burg, 'Law and Development: A Review of the Literature & a Critique of "Scholars in Self-Estrangement"', American Journal of Comparative Law Vol. 25 (1977) p492 and John Henry Merryman, 'Comparative Law and Social Change: On the Origins, Style, Decline & Revival of the Law and Development Movement', American Journal of Comparative Law Vol. 25 (1977) p457.
30 For a critical assessment of the role of the Ford Foundation in these activities, written by one of its former senior officials, see, James Gardner, *Legal Imperialism: American Lawyers and Foreign Aid in Latin America* (Madison: University of Wisconsin Press, 1980).
31 David M. Trubek and Marc Galanter, 'Scholars in Self-Estrangement: Some Reflections on the Crisis in Law and Development Studies in the United States', Wisconsin Law Review (1974) p1062.

according to David Trubek and Marc Galanter – the misguided notion that the American model, which they call liberal legalism, could be exported to and take root in developing countries.[32] Liberal legalism, as described by Trubek and Galanter, assigns a crucial role to law in the process of development. It sees law both as a mechanism to curb arbitrary powers of the government and as an instrument to achieve social and economic objectives.[33] This instrumentalist conception of law led the movement to place special emphasis on legal education on the assumption that the development goals of the state would be facilitated if lawyers were trained to use law as an instrument for change.[34] The expectation that a different approach to law would contribute to development was, however, not fulfilled. As Trubek and Galanter point out, the instrumentalist approach had failed to take into account that a more effective system of law would not necessarily bring about economic and social development or greater respect for the right of citizens. In the hands of an authoritarian regime, legal instrumentalism might further economic growth at the expense of the rights of individuals. The development of instrumental skills of lawyers could have the effect of reinforcing social and economic inequalities as the élites – those with a vested interest in the *status quo* – would hire them to undermine and resist the implementation of development programmes.[35]

The law and development movement, according to Trubek and Galanter, failed to understand that the formal legal system – the main focus of liberal legalism – only reaches a small section of the population in most developing countries. Thus, by focusing largely on the formal legal system the movement went astray, as it ignored customary law and other informal systems of legality.[36] The crisis of the law and development movement was further deepened when their practitioners became aware that sometimes law either has no effect on social and economic conditions, or, worse still, often has a negative effect as it reinforces existing inequalities.[37] Liberal legalism – according to Trubek and Galanter – was, not, however, a cynical sham designed to deceive the poor in developing countries. It was perfectly consistent with the view held by legal élites in the United States about the relationship between law and society in their country. Accordingly, the law and development movement practitioners who shared this view were not being dishonest; they were simply mistaken: "liberal legalism may have been ingenuous, but it was not insincere."[38] Trubek and

---

32 Ibid.
33 Ibid., p1074.
34 Ibid., p1075.
35 Ibid., p1076
36 Ibid., p1079
37 Ibid., p1080

Galanter's scepticism about the possibility of successfully exporting the American model of liberal legalism is ultimately based on the view that perhaps the history of the United States is unique and therefore its institutions and other features of its society cannot be easily copied.[39]

Disenchantment with liberal legalism, combined with a reduction of the US aid budget, led to the removal of law from the agenda of development assistance programmes and to a marked decline of academic interest in law and development.[40] Interestingly, however, the failure of the movement had a significant impact on the academic legal community in the United States. For, as Trubek and Galanter note, the unease which members of the law and development movement felt about the model of liberal legalism in developing countries was extended to the role of law generally. Hence, they started to question whether the paradigm that they were exporting was valid even in the United States.[41]

Bringing law back in

Given the experience of the law and development movement it is necessary to ask whether the current efforts of legal technical assistance might not meet the same fate. Is it not likely that the enthusiasm for legal technical assistance will soon give way to disappointment and that law will again be quietly withdrawn from the development agenda? It is, of course, too early to answer this question, as the current interest in law is only recent. It must be noted, however, that despite their obvious affinities, there are some important differences between the old and the more recent interest in the role of law in the process of development.

On the surface, the similarities between the US sponsored law and development movement and the World Bank's model of a fair legal system are quite obvious. They are both based on a concept of law which corresponds to that of law in modern liberal societies: general rules, known in advance, enacted and interpreted by specialized institutions and applied equally to all. Thus, on the surface, they are both based on the paradigm of liberal legalism. There is, however, an

---

38 Ibid., p1088

39 Ibid., p1092. For a recent statement of this view see, Seymour Lipset, *American Exceptionalism*, New York: Norton, 1996.

40 In the United Kingdom, academic lawyers have continued to work in law and development. See for example, Sammy Adelman and Abdul Paliwala, (eds.), *Law and Development in Crisis* (Oxford: Hans Zell, 1993).

41 Trubek and Galanter, op.cit., p. 1083-4. The disenchantment with the legal theory of liberalism later became more widespread and soon led to the establishment of a new movement, critical legal theory, which challenges the claim of law under liberalism as a form of rationality. On critical legal theory see, Roberto Unger, 'The Critical Legal Studies Movement', Harvard Law Review Vol. 96 p561.

important difference between the two, in their conception of the role of the state in the process of development. While the law and development movement regarded law as a mechanism indispensable for taming and controlling political power and protecting individual freedom, it continued to regard the state as the centre which would initiate and promote the process of economic development. Hence the emphasis on legal instrumentalism: socially and politically aware lawyers would be at the forefront of the development effort orchestrated by the state.[42] From this perspective it appears that the law and development movement was exporting the legal techniques for designing a liberal welfare state, rather than a liberal state.

The World Bank's approach to law is quite different. Consistent with its endorsement of the new market-friendly conception of development, the Bank does not advocate the establishment of welfare states. In a market-friendly state, law is not an all purpose tool at the service of an interventionist state, whether of the welfare, mild authoritarian or despotic variety. Instead, law, provides rules to facilitate market transactions mainly by defining property rights, guaranteeing the enforcement of contracts and maintaining law and order. Law is no longer a protagonist of social and economic change. Its role, though indispensable, is largely passive. Under this conception, there is no room for lawyers reared in legal instrumentalism as they might either support those with a vested interest in supporting policies which distort market relations or, worse still, use law to expand the role of the state in the management of the economy.

The foregoing might give the impression that the World Bank's approach to law is little more than a crude restatement of old *laissez-faire* liberalism according to which individuals are free to pursue their economic interests while the role of the government is limited to ensuring the smooth operation of the market. This however, is not the case. The market-friendly state, as conceived by the World Bank, does not regard state intervention as necessarily undesirable. The problem is that the form of state intervention prevalent in developing countries often aggravates rather than resolves the problems it addresses. Government intervention in the economy is often economically harmful and generally tends to create vested interests which make it difficult to change the policy after the policy has fulfilled its objectives.[43] State intervention thus has to be carried out with great caution so as to further rather than undermine the market process. "To justify state intervention it is not enough to know that the market is failing; it is also necessary to be confident that the government can do better."[44] If intervention

---

42 Trubek and Galanter, op.cit., p1079.
43 World Development Report 1991, op.cit., p131.
44 Ibid.

is to be carried out properly it is thus necessary to reform the state. Hence the inclusion of institutional reform as a vital part of the governance agenda.

The market-friendly state requires institutional structures that facilitate rather than obstruct the operation of the market. Institutional reform is thus a key component of the World Bank's governance agenda and in this area it is greatly influenced by the work of Douglass North and other Neo-Institutional economists.[45] Under this approach the state is not necessarily the minimalist state of classical liberal theory, but a dynamic and economically aware entity – an indispensable complement to the market. Within this conception of institutional reform, law plays an important, though still passive role. Although it is no longer a mere guardian of negative freedoms, it is subordinated to the logic of economic analysis. Law is thus not an autonomous force to be used indiscriminately to further social and economic objectives of interest groups or of individuals.

The World Bank's approach to the study of law and legal institutions is, of course, not new. In recent decades it has enjoyed considerable popularity in academic and policymaking circles in the United States.[46] The application of this methodology to developing countries is, however, a new and intriguing development. Because this new approach to change in developing countries has not yet been fully developed it cannot be properly assessed. It is unlikely, however, that simply by shifting the focus of attention from legal institutions to economic analysis this new approach will manage to avoid the problems which so frustrated and disappointed members of the law and development movement. For the factors which Trubek and Galanter identified as the cause of the crisis of the law and development movement are not new. Is a formal legal system indispensable for the development of a market economy? Does law promote economic activity by providing essential legal concepts and techniques? Are these concepts and techniques always consistent with the needs of business? How does law relate to the political process in a market economy? What impact does the decentralization of economic activity have on governments in developing countries? Does the establishment of a market economy in developing countries require strong authoritarian executives to steer the process? Will the market economy contribute to the transformation of strong authoritarian governments into strong democratic governments?

---

45 Douglass North, *Institutions, Institutional Change and Economic Performance* (Cambridge: Cambridge University Press, 1990). See also, Thráinn Eggertsson, *Economic Behaviour and Institutions* (Cambridge: Cambridge University Press, 1990).
46 The seminal work in this area is Ronal Coase's essay 'The Problem of Social Cost', Journal of Law and Economics Vol. 3 (1990) p1. The most prolific exponent of this approach is Richard Posner. See his *Economic Analysis of Law* 2nd edition (Boston: Little Brown, 1977).

II. OVERVIEW OF SELECTED THEMES

As pointed out above, an adequate understanding of local conditions is generally regarded as essential for the success of legal technical assistance projects. The World Bank acknowledges this: "countries undergoing legal reform benefit from in-depth assessment or diagnostic analyses and studies of their legal system (both legal and regulatory frameworks and institutional set-ups) prior to implementing legal technical assistance projects."[47] The Bank admits that occasionally, because of lack of time, such diagnostic studies are not carried out.[48] It would be interesting to know whether, in the studies that have been carried out, but not yet published, local conditions have been taken into account. The evidence in the case studies contained in this volume suggests that not enough attention is being paid to the specific circumstances of the recipient countries.

The liberalization of the financial sector in Africa illustrates how important it is to take into account the specific context in which policies are applied. As Robert Annibale's paper shows, financial liberalization cannot be achieved merely through deregulation. The prevailing regulatory system in Africa is undoubtedly less than perfect, as borne out by the cases of Kenya and Nigeria. While in Kenya, a single banking scandal wiped out 10 per cent of the country's GDP, in Nigeria, the growth in the sheer number of banks that have to be regulated has led to placing some banks under the supervision of the Ministry of Public Works. Financial liberalization, Annibale argues, requires effective and comprehensive regulation, not less regulation. As he points out, an effective regulatory system requires training which cannot be acquired instantly or through distance learning methods. Many countries in Africa liberalized their financial sectors before the banking regulators were prepared for the task. Had the financial sector reformers paid more attention to local conditions, perhaps the pace of liberalization would have been slower.

Recent banking scandals, such as the collapse of Barings Bank and BCCI, confirm that banking regulation in an increasingly global market is by no means simple.[49] Banking regulation, however, is not the only case which illustrates how difficult and painful institutional change can be. The design of a legal framework for the regulation of public utilities has generated considerable technical and political controversy in the United Kingdom. As John McEldowney points out, the framework introduced in the aftermath of the privatization of public utilities

---

47 *LTA*, p10.
48 Ibid., p11.
49 See Ethan B. Kapstein, *Governing the Global Economy: International Finance and the State* (Cambridge: Harvard University Press, 1994).

in the UK was an afterthought, rather than a well-planned strategy. According to him, neither the issue of accountability nor competition were properly addressed and new legislation had to be enacted to correct these omissions. Some may find McEldowney's assessment of the regulatory framework for public utilities in the UK unduly pessimistic. From the perspective of developing countries, however, McEldowney's contribution to this volume is a sobering reminder that even countries with an institutional capacity light years ahead of that in most developing countries have great difficulties designing new institutions.

It could well be argued that the design of a regulatory framework in a high profile area such as public utilities inevitably gives rise to controversy and difficulty. By contrast, in areas of policy which do not enjoy such high political profile the design of an institutional framework would appear to be easier and less controversial. Such, for example, is the case of competition policy. Indeed, as Malcolm Rowat's chapter shows, in recent years most countries in Latin America have enacted comprehensive legislation introducing a modern approach to competition policy inspired by either the US or the EU model. This process of legal reform has not been controversial. In fact, it has hardly been noticed. With the possible exception of Colombia where – as Rowat explains – the new competition law was enacted by Presidential Decree in order to avoid opposition from the Congress, in the rest of Latin America the new competition laws have only attracted the attention of a handful of technical experts. Local competition law experts, with the support of external advisers, have thus been left free to draft legislation consistent with best practice in this area. Yet, as Rowat points out, the new competition laws in Latin America have some serious shortcomings, such as the extreme centralization of their enforcement agencies and the absence of adequate procedures to review the decisions of these agencies. It is undeniable that a highly centralized system of enforcement, which in addition is not subject to judicial control, could easily subvert the objectives of competition law. It must be borne in mind, however, that the two shortcomings noted above are also typical features of Latin American states and legal systems: a high level of centralization and a weak and often discredited judiciary. Thus, from this perspective what appears to be a shortcoming may become a virtue, for it could well be seen as an attempt to adapt the new competition laws to the institutional realities of Latin American states.

The case study of competition law in Latin America illustrates a characteristic dilemma for legal reformers: either they create a structure which in all respects is consistent with best practice elsewhere or they adapt the new structure to local conditions. If they take the first route they run the risk that the law will not be effectively enforced. If they take the second, they may undermine the very objectives sought by the new legislation. It is too early to evaluate the effect of the new competition laws in Latin America. It could well be that in practice, the institutional shortcoming identified above are no obstacle to their implementation.

It is essential to take into account technical considerations when undertaking major law reform. It is, though, an open question whether all factors which are regarded as technical do in fact have that status. The ostensibly technical arguments over the reform of land tenure systems in sub-Saharan Africa illustrate the difficulty of regarding some issues as purely technical. Some experts regard communal land ownership in sub-Saharan Africa as an obstacle to development and advocate either direct intervention to transform communal rights over land into individual property rights or indirect intervention to support the process of individualization of property rights brought about by economic factors beyond the control of the state. Others, however, point out that the assignment of individual property rights over land do not always have the desired effect and hence call for solutions which assign a greater role to indigenous land arrangements.[50]

In addition to the uncertainty as to what constitutes – at a technical level – the best option for land reform, political and social factors cannot be ignored. As Joseph Thome points out, in South Africa, where the white minority controls 87 per cent of the best agricultural land and blacks have access to only eight per cent of the land, agrarian reform is an imperative, both on technical and political grounds. Arguments about the inviolability of property rights are unlikely to carry much weight among those who were directly or indirectly dispossessed of their land by the apartheid regime.

Achieving a balance between the demands of technical efficiency and broader political considerations is not an easy task. The agrarian reform process in Chile is a good illustration of this and a useful reminder to those in South Africa who will have the responsibility of deciding upon a land reform policy. As Thome argues, in the mid-1960s Chile enacted an agrarian reform law explicitly designed to ensure both an increase in productivity in the agricultural sector and greater social and political rights for agricultural workers. In the event, however, the agrarian reform process ran out of control largely because the political system was unable to satisfy the demands and expectations of agricultural workers who, until then, had been virtually excluded from it. A stronger leadership, together with a suitable institutional framework, will, hopefully, spare South Africa of the problems encountered in Chile.

---

50 For an excellent recent summary of this debate see Jean Phillippe Platteau, 'The Evolutionary Theory of Land Rights as Applied to Sub-Saharan Africa: A Critical Assessment', <u>Development and Change</u> Vol.27 (1996) p29. See also, John Quiggin, 'Common Property, Equality and Development', <u>World Development</u>, Vol. 21 (1993) p1123.

The variety of strategies which countries may adopt to develop their institutions is illustrated by Ross Cranston in his chapter on access to justice in South and South-east Asia. While developing countries have similar problems in the area of administration of justice – courts are slow, inadequately funded, too close to the government of the day and far too removed from the daily lives of ordinary people – the specific strategies which they have adopted to improve access to justice are varied. Some involve strengthening the existing system of courts while others involve developing alternative mechanisms of dispute resolution in order to speed up judicial proceedings while reducing litigation costs.

As Cranston explains, countries in South and South-east Asia have used different strategies with varying degrees of success. His case study illustrates problems which most developing countries confront; that is, the choice between strengthening the prevailing system of courts or developing alternatives to them. If courts are hostile to business or if court procedures drag on indefinitely it seems reasonable to opt for alternative mechanisms, such as arbitration, for the resolution of conflicts. Yet, too much emphasis on arbitration may have the effect of marginalizing ordinary courts from involvement in important social and economic issues and hence their standing within the political system will be affected. It is necessary to ask whether the absence of an efficient system of, say, commercial courts has a negative effect on business. Although World Bank publications on governance appear to assume that courts are indispensable for fostering a good business environment, other Bank publications suggest otherwise. Thus, for example, a recent World Bank study on the Brazilian and Chilean garment industries suggests that the absence of an effective system of courts does not have a major effect on business. Although in both countries the garment trade is heavily dependent on credit, the proportion of customers that fail to pay on time is very small: eight per cent in Brazil and three per cent in Chile. Such relatively good records are remarkable given the fact that resort to courts in both countries is expensive and time consuming – two features which in this context would appear to benefit debtors. The relative efficiency of debt collection in these two countries is, however, attributed to the use of flexible debt instruments and a variety of institutional mechanisms, formal and informal, which circumvent the court system.[51]

Mechanisms for the resolution of conflicts outside the system of state courts are favoured in most societies because of their speed and their relative low costs. In addition, informal mechanisms are supposed to be less intimidating and hence more acceptable to the population. The popularity of Lok Adalats (people's

---

51   Andrew Stone, Brian Levy and Ricardo Paredes, *Public Institutions and Private Transactions* (The World Bank: WPS 891, 1992) pp19-22.

courts) in India appears to confirm the benefits of informal justice. Yet, as Cranston reminds us, these informal mechanisms for the resolution of disputes raise important questions for which there are no easy answers. How do these informal systems of justice relate to the formal system? Do they contain safeguards adequate to protecting the rights of individuals? In addition, as the Lok Adalats demonstrate, informal courts have a tendency to expand their jurisdiction to areas which are not traditionally regarded as proper for court activity. Thus, the Lok Adalats in India, apart from having a considerable case load, perform a variety of functions such as controlling the behaviour of public officials at the local level and acting as a focal point for popular mobilization against injustice.

The Lok Adalats' popularity is very likely based on the fact that they are successful in performing functions other than those normally expected from a court. In other words, the informal systems of justice often perform functions which the state is unable, or unwilling to take on. Such is the case also of peasant organizations in Perú (*rondas campesinas*) and of popular tribunals in some Brazilian shanty towns, where the absence of state courts has prompted local communities to establish informal mechanisms to administer justice. These informal courts, apart from resolving local disputes and dealing with petty criminal offences, also perform political functions in the immediate community, which the state has failed to perform.[52] Not surprisingly, informal courts tend to have an uneasy relationship with the state. As they are *de facto* exercising state functions the state cannot afford to ignore them. If, successful, there will be pressure either to incorporate them into the formal institutional framework or to replace them with newly-created state agencies.

The popularity of institutions such as the Lok Adalats seems to confirm Reginald Green's view that law and order is not a matter to be decided upon by armchair philosophers, but by the people themselves – the experts from below, as he describes them. He defines law and order as providing ordinary people with the ability to go about their daily business without fear of violent intervention. Personal security and the efficient delivery of social services are public goods valued by people. As he explains, the relative efficiency of the police force in Tanzania and the delivery of milk to pregnant women in Mozambique are greatly appreciated by the people. Few would disagree with Green's insistence that bureaucracy and law and order are there to serve the people and not the other way around. The chances of social policy programmes being successfully implemented

---

52 On Brazil, see Edesio Fernandes, *Law and Urban Change in Brazil* (London: Avebury, 1995); on Perú, see Inter-American Development Bank, *Challenges for Peace: Towards Sustainable Social Development in Perú* (Washington: 1995).

naturally increase if the end-users are consulted and their views taken into account. Efficient administration and popular government are desirable objectives. The problem is, of course, how to achieve these objectives in settings where states are weak and often do not even exercise effective control over the whole of their territory. One solution is to give priority to the building of a strong political centre, even if this involves adopting undemocratic methods of government. This approach has been favoured in the past by a variety of theorists who base their argument either on historical interpretations of the development of modern states or on sociological interpretations about the prerequisites for democracy.[53] An alternative solution would be to turn to civil society as a means of both supporting and counter-balancing the power of the government.

If economic decisions are taken through the decentralized mechanism of the market, then it is natural that civil society organizations – that is, those intermediary groups that occupy the space between the family and the state – should assume greater prominence. Current interest in civil society, Nancy Bermeo points out, derives precisely from the generalized disenchantment with the state as an agent of social and economic change. Accordingly today, she argues, some attribute heroic qualities to civil society and see the state as the source of major problems. However, as Bermeo points out, this conception of civil society contrasts sharply with another view of civil society, one which until recently was held by most political theorists. This negative view stems from the perception of civil society as a potential spoiler of public policies and de-stabilizer of governments. While sharing the objective of strengthening civil society, Bermeo warns about the dangers of having misplaced illusions about it, for, she declares, the violence and disorder that undermines good government is often brought about by interactions within civil society.

Channelling and processing the often contradictory demands of civil society is one of the main tests of a sound political system. It is not, however, an easy test, as shown by Shirin Rai in her case study on the political representation of women in India and Chile. In both countries, the issue of representation of women's interests became part of the political agenda as a consequence of pressure resulting from the activity of civil society organizations dedicated to the defence and promotion of women's interests. In both countries also, the political system bowed to the pressure and responded by establishing a special agency within the government to deal with women's issues. Yet, as Rai notes, the institutionalization of women's demands raises serious strategic questions

---

53 See, for example, Samuel P. Huntington, *Political Order in Changing Societies* (New Haven: Yale University Press, 1968); see also, Seymour Lipset, 'Some Social Requisites of Democracy: Economic Development and Political Legitimacy', <u>American Political Science Review</u> Vol 53 (1959) p69.

within the women's movement. Does institutionalization amount to a state take-over of the women's movement? Does it create further divisions within the movement? Will the party system – which is strong in both countries – allow for greater representation of women within the political system?

Rai's case study on the representation of women illustrates how difficult it is to formulate policies and establish institutions that can effectively bring about a reconciliation between the state and civil society. Moreover, as Bermeo notes in her contribution, the rigidity of the economic model embodied in the Washington consensus makes the task of reconciling the demands of civil society with state policies even more difficult. For the market-friendly economic policy as currently prescribed does not allow much scope for political debate. According to John Williamson, the economist who coined the phrase Washington consensus, this is not a bad thing as otherwise demagogues and populists would hijack the policy reform process and re-introduce the discredited policies of the past.[54] Since popular discontent with structural adjustment policies provides a fertile ground for the emergence of demagogues and populist leaders, the solution is to rely on strong executives. Yet as Bermeo notes, strong executives both suffocate civil society and undermine the ideal of good government.

The legitimacy of the economic and legal reform process cannot be taken for granted. The mandate for change, as Leila Frischtak argues, needs to be periodically renewed. The programme of reforms should not be treated as a rigid formula subject to an inflexible timetable. In this respect, it is useful to recall the case of privatization in the UK. Although, as McEldowney points out, the regulatory framework for the privatized utilities may not have been carefully prepared, the actual process of privatization was introduced gradually. Indeed, although privatization was a key component of Margaret Thatcher's programme, the actual privatization of public utilities only began several years after her government had been in office. This delay was not only because of the technical complexity of the enterprise, but because public opinion had to be prepared and its support secured for the introduction of an initiative which involved a major departure from a policy which had hitherto been considered an essential component of the British welfare state and, as such, had enjoyed considerable popular support.[55] Few would find the Thatcher administration's concern with public opinion surprising, as this is a normal characteristic of a democracy. Yet, such concern is often lacking in developing countries where the expectation of

---

54 John Williamson, 'Democracy and the "Washington Consensus"', World Development Vol. 21 (1993) p1330.
55 On this point see William H. Riker and David L. Weimer, 'The political economy of transformation: liberalization and property rights', in Jeffrey S. Banks and Eric A. Hanushek, *Modern Political Economy* (Cambridge: Cambridge University Press, 1995) p85.

international financial institutions is often that liberalization and privatization should take place within an unrealistically short period of time, thus giving little time for the government to consult widely and to prepare public opinion. This undemocratic approach to the reform process works against the ideals of good government.

The case studies in this volume show that there is no magic formula that will guarantee the successful implementation of legal and institutional reform. Experience suggests, however, that chances of success are greater if local conditions are taken into account. This is an especially important factor when legal reform is introduced as a condition for the disbursement of loans. The methodology employed by the Financial and Legal Management Upgrading Project of Tanzania (FILMUP) is an example of good practice which deserves careful consideration. The project, Patrick McAuslan explains, involved the establishment of a Legal Task Force consisting of senior Tanzanian lawyers and academics. Ten areas of legal interest were identified and studies were commissioned for each area. The studies were carried out by teams of experts appointed by the Task Force which included both Tanzanian lawyers and foreign legal consultants. The studies were discussed in a workshop, whose conclusions and recommendations were submitted to the Tanzanian Government. The Government decided then which recommendations should be implemented. Donor agencies can, of course, refuse to fund the projects chosen by the government. As McAuslan points out, the methodology employed by this project ensures that those projects that secure external funding have a reasonable chance of implementation. More important, the approach taken by this project shows that it is possible to reconcile the political and the technical components of the legal reform process. The selection of projects by the government is not a mere formality as it is based on detailed studies carried out by local lawyers and other specialists. Foreign experts participate in this process, but as consultants to teams made up mainly of nationals who, apart from having the technical qualifications, are familiar with the local environment. Thus, extensive consultation may generate genuine national ownership of the project and ensure its long term sustainability.

CONCLUDING REMARKS

If legal technical assistance projects, such as Tanzania's FILMUP, are to be successful, foreign legal experts must be capable and willing to learn about local conditions. This is not easy as the reaction of lawyers to foreign legal systems often tends to be parochial. Anything not done in the same way as it is done at home is often regarded as imperfect, inferior and exotic. This attitude colours not only the perspective that western-trained lawyers have of Third World legal systems, it also affects the way they regard the legal systems traditions of other developed countries.

The World Bank is aware of the importance of selecting suitably qualified external legal consultants to work in legal technical assistance projects. So far, however, most of the external legal consultants working on such projects come from large law firms based either in the United States or the United Kingdom. According to the Bank, the reason for this is that most of the bids for these projects come from such firms. The Bank acknowledges that this often results in bias towards the United States or British legal models.[56] This is indeed a major problem as the legal systems of a large proportion of countries are not based on the common law.

Another problem concerning the selection of foreign legal experts is whether they should be academics or practitioners. Legal practitioners, according to the Bank, often do not have the policy perspective required to prepare comprehensive legal reforms, while academics are not always familiar with the practical issues involved in implementation.[57] The way the Bank characterizes academic and practising lawyers corresponds to stereotype images. While legal practitioners regard legal academics as interesting but with no grasp of the real world, the latter regard practitioners as competent but narrow in focus. In the present context, however, this stereotypical characterization, though not entirely inaccurate, is misleading. There are many academics who have a better feel for practical issues than most practitioners, just as there are practitioners who have a more profound understanding of law and society than academics. Whether the foreign legal expert is an academic or a practitioner is unimportant, provided that the individual is technically competent and has the capacity to understand the intellectual and policy framework surrounding the specific reform programme.

Law is neither an unqualified human good nor is it always a benign instrument of power. Where laws are made by elected representatives, administered by a responsible and accountable executive and interpreted by an independent judiciary, then they may be regarded as a humane instrument of power. But when any of these elements are missing and law loses its capacity to discipline power it can easily become an instrument of domination which powerful groups in society may use to exploit and oppress weaker groups.

It must be noted, however, that even in its ideal humane democratic form, law presupposes the existence of a state which has the monopoly of the use of force. This well-known fact is often forgotten by legal and economic consultants who

---

56 *LTA*, p24.
57 Ibid.

live in countries where the democratic rule of law prevails and where law and order are largely taken for granted. Thus, an essential prerequisite for successful legal reform – whether or not it involves the importation or transplantation of legal rules – is the existence of an effective and well-organized political centre with the power to enforce the law. This essential prerequisite is often missing in many developing countries. Moreover, since legal reform does not take place in a vacuum, but in societies where structures of authority and legal relations are already in place, the new legal order, or the new system of rules, if successful, will displace, replace or restructure the rules of the prevailing system. The success or failure of comprehensive legal reform will thus depend largely on the central authorities' capacity to use the power of the state to overcome obstacles created by those with an interest in maintaining the *status quo*. Thus, while failure of comprehensive legal reform may often be caused by the weakness of the political system, success is always accompanied by a significant reallocation of resources and legal entitlements which will benefit some and hurt others.

Legal and institutional reform in developing countries is both urgent and desirable. I hope that this volume contributes towards reviving and broadening the intellectual debate on this issue. I also hope that it serves to persuade those responsible for managing legal technical assistance projects that the participation of those directly affected by the reform process is essential both to ensure the success of the specific project and to further good government.

2 Law, governance and the development of the market: practical problems and possible solutions

Patrick McAuslan

The legal framework in a country is as vital for economic development as for political and social development. Creating wealth through the cumulative commitment of human, technological and capital resources depends greatly on a set of rules securing property rights, governing civil and commercial behaviour, and limiting the power of the state... The legal framework also affects the lives of the poor and, as such, has become an important dimension of strategies for poverty alleviation. In the struggle against discrimination, in the protection of the socially weak, and in the distribution of opportunities in society, the law can make an important contribution to a just and equitable society and thus to prospects for social development and poverty alleviation. (World Bank, 1994)

INTRODUCTION

This ambitious and optimistic statement from the World Bank is a useful reference point for a discussion of the role of law in development. This is because it comes from the major player on the world development stage and not from some academic legal observer of development activity.

It cannot be dismissed either as the statement of a person who is biased in favour of a major role for law or as a theoretical proposition which is unsupported by practical experience. Here is the major actor telling us what is happening and what ought to happen in the front line. Whether legal development as outlined in the above statement can achieve good governance and can develop the market economy in both developing and transitional countries is a different matter.

While law reform as aid and the idea that law has a major role to play in development is a new concept to the present World Bank and most donors, we have been here before. Leaving aside the use of the law by colonial powers to achieve their economic and social ends, often as not the development of a market economy, the Law and Development movement which emerged in the 1960s did not start off in the classrooms of the North or in the academic journals; it started in the field, in the South.

When the late and great Wolfgang Friedmann was brought out to the Law Faculty at Dar es Salaam, Tanzania in 1963, it was to develop a programme of instruction in law for development purposes for senior civil servants in the newly independent or about-to-be independent states in East and Central Africa. The support of USAID (and the CIA, because certain Americans involved in developing legal resources in East Africa were mixed up with that agency) in funding staff and resources for law schools in Africa and Asia in the 1960s was avowedly because this was seen as an important contribution to those countries' development. Lawyers were needed to develop the laws which would empower the state to force the pace of development.

Similarly, the Alliance for Progress in Latin America in the early 1960s gave many North American lawyers their first introduction to Law and Development studies. Later on, their experience in the field fed into early writings and theorizing about law and development.

The teachers, researchers, consultants and practitioners who were on the Research Advisory Committee on Law and Development of the International Legal Center between them provided extensive experience of developing countries – indeed one third of the Committee's membership came from developing countries. Even twenty years on some of the views contained in the Committee's 1974 seminal report on *Law and Development* are worth noting. The following passage taken from the report illustrates its usefulness in this discussion:

> [Law and Development] researchers will be concerned with understanding the actual structure of decision-making in a society and in evaluating the impact of this structure on developmental goals and processes. LD scholars will want to know who has access to legal processes and how decisions are actually made. They will want to look beyond the formal rules of the legal procedure and formal doctrinal argument to identify any systematic structural features of legal process which may affect a citizen's access to courts and administrative agencies and influence the decisions reached by those bodies... LD scholars might, for example wish to ask whether the language, costs, location or other features of official legal process make courts more accessible to some social classes or ethnic groups than to others... These studies may as easily lead the researcher to identify law and legal process as one of the obstacles to the achievement of development goals as it will show law's positive potential in the developmental effort. Thus, such research could demonstrate the many ways in which legal processes can be used to distort development goals, delay the implementation of development programs, and mask inaction and the maintenance of privilege behind a formal facade of change and legal equality. (International Legal Contract, 1974)

Today, these suggestions are almost platitudes even if not all legal scholars and practitioners observe them when undertaking research. Even official agencies and programmes of law reform in many countries now use the techniques of socio-legal research in developing their practical proposals for reform. However, I question whether this is the approach which is taken when law reform is part of an aid package.

CONCEPT OF GOVERNANCE

We need to understand what is the agenda behind the notion of governance or good governance. I support attempts to use governance as a tool both of analysis and of aid conditionality.[1]

The use of governance as a term of analysis and a tool of action in aid circles has developed alongside a heavy emphasis on 'downsizing' the role and reach of governments and increasing the role and reach of markets as the only way for a developing country to progress. The progress implied is for its economy to grow and for the benefits of that growth to be spread throughout society.

The concepts associated with good governance – accountability, transparency, probity, the rule of law – have tended to be developed in the context of making markets work more efficiently rather than, for example, making governments more accountable to their citizens. Making markets work more efficiently has been taken to mean reducing or eliminating 'controls' rather than developing more appropriate controls to curb the excesses of the market.

In practice, despite the rhetoric of the World Bank, the emphasis given in the law reform programmes has been on the areas of: commercial law; laws supporting private property rights; reorganization of the court systems, and management of case loads to improve efficiency in the settlement of commercial disputes via speed and predictability. In a recent publication the World Bank specifically states that:

> ...the Bank may not be involved in financing legal reform activities that do not
> have a direct and obvious link to economic development.

---

1 At the annual meeting of the Urban Management Programme (UMP) in July 1992 I organized a workshop with colleagues from the World Bank and United Nations Development Programme for about 40 senior persons from donor agencies, the Bank, UN agencies and several developing countries. (This was in the capacity of my work for the United Nations Centre for Human Settlements [Habitat] in the UMP.) I wished to use the term 'Governance' in the title to the workshop and was prevented from doing so by the World Bank official co-ordinating the programme. Governance, he said, implies involvement with politics which was forbidden to the Bank. He was right on both scores but wrong on the implications of what he said. It is not irrelevant that he came from a developing country.

It goes on to explain that its support for advancing the rule of law is derived from an interpretation of that concept which emphasizes:

> ... the objectives of stability, predictability and elimination of governmental
> arbitrariness, which are preconditions to economic development... An essential
> element of the rule of law concept is the existence of an independent dispute
> resolution body that resolves conflicts in the application of the rules or addresses
> instances of non-compliance with the rules. This element has a direct relevance to
> the proper functioning of the economy and the conduct of economic activities... In
> that sense, reform of the judiciary and the establishment and strengthening of
> arbitral and other dispute settlement mechanisms which help achieve efficient and
> expedient enforcement of agreements between private parties, resolution of disputes and
> enforcement of laws and regulations is intrinsically tied to economic progress.
> (World Bank, 1995)

That these matters are important is not disputed. However, it is too easy to take these legal mechanisms for granted once they are part of our system. One of my most consistent messages as a consultant on urban land management is the importance of a clear framework of land law – coherent, comprehensive, simply drafted – together with specialist dispute-settlement mechanisms to speed up the resolution of disputes and increase their acceptability. There are other factors which also need to be considered.

ROLE OF LAW IN DEVELOPMENT

Two issues need to be addressed: the assumed central role of law, and the areas, apart from the market, where law reform could and should be deployed. To begin with the first, there is an assumption behind the law reform agenda that law matters and formal law reform will produce beneficial results. The Law and Development movement of the 1960s was set up on these assumptions and one reason why it subsequently declined was that they proved, if not false, then at least, questionable. Von Mehren and Sawers make the point well in their article on 'Revitalising the Law and Development Movement: A Case Study of Title in Thailand':

> A major problem with Law and Development literature has been its failure to state
> explicitly the casual interaction between law and development. Indeed, few case
> study authors directly address this fundamental issue. Yet, if the law and
> development movement is to influence the literature on social change, the law
> needs to be cast as at least an important reinforcing variable in the process of
> change. If law is merely a product of social change, then analysis of legal
> development loses all normative implications for policy-making...Our case study

has shown the law cannot be seen as an entirely independent variable. Law plays a modest, though important reinforcing role in the process of social change... The implication of our case study is that while overstating the importance of law leads to absurd practical results and academic scorn, students of law can still contribute to the understanding of social change provided they remain sensitive to the inherent limits of their field. (Von Mehren and Sawers, 1992: 67)

A project which overstated the importance of law is the UNDP funded legislative drafting project for the People's Republic of China. The project set out to train Chinese legislative draftspersons to become legal theorists and comparative Law and Development scholars with a knowledge of research methodology (all in English). This was based on the beliefs that: law constitutes the government's principal tool for changing institutions; China's weak legal sector persists because its system for drafting laws lacked the capacity to draft them properly; the project would enable them to produce statute laws which would allow China's market-orientated reforms to rest on a firm legal basis. The evidence for these far-reaching assumptions was tenuous.

Philip von Mehren and Tim Sawers adopt a midway position on the role of law in development, stressing the need for evidence of the connection between the two. The UNDP China project is closer to the approach adopted in developing law reform aid projects because these projects are competing for funds and therefore doubts cannot be admitted. No donor is going to fund a project that provides little or no evidence that it will yield both economic and social development. (This is not to say that donors do not in practice fund such projects; see, for one example, R v Secretary of State for Foreign Affairs, *ex parte* World Development Movement Ltd, [1995] 1 All ER 611, the Pergau Dam case).

Where there is a midway position, there are also two polar positions, which need to be considered. A good example of what may be called the China Syndrome – formal law as the foundation of a modern market economy – is contained in the paper by Sherwood, Shepherd and De Souza (Shepherd being from the World Bank) on *Judicial Systems and Economic Performance* which "examines the importance of judicial systems to economic performance, particularly in the countries of Latin America which are attempting economic liberalization". The authors are in no doubt as to the importance of the role of the judicial system and therefore of its reform:

It is our thesis that in a liberalizing economy with a weak judicial system, far less happens than in a country where the judicial system works well. Although we can offer no support for the figure, we suspect it would not be surprising to eventually find that countries attempting economic reform suffer at least a 15 percent penalty in their growth momentum if their judicial system is weak. That is to say, if GDP growth were otherwise capable of reaching something like 3 percent, a weak judicial system would restrain growth to perhaps 2.6 percent.

Judicial reform is on the modernization agenda of many countries. Demands for reform, however, are not founded on an acknowledgement that a more effective judicial process is needed to facilitate economic performance. The rationale for reform needs to be strengthened in order to sustain reform efforts in the face of strongly entrenched interests which will oppose all but superficial reform. (Sherwood, 1994)

The statement in the first paragraph is just the type of 'evidence' that donors need: a precise quantification of the benefits to be obtained from reform. It is, however, rather undermined by the second paragraph which admits the need to strengthen the case for reform by providing better evidence that judicial reform will yield economic benefits.

Interestingly, a sharp attack on the notion that courts are in any way useful as agencies for implementing development programmes is contained in *State and Law in the Development Process* by Robert and Ann Seidman. They argue that courts cannot make the type of polycentric decisions required for development. The Seidmans are the driving force behind the UNDP China legislative drafting project so they are clearly committed to a high profile for formal law as a tool of development to facilitate the operation of a market economy. How commercial disputes will be settled in such an economy is not clear in their work. It is unlikely that the laws can be drafted so perfectly that disputes will not arise, however well trained the draftspersons.

The lack of hard evidence about the benefits of legal reform is not deterring donor agencies. The Financial and Legal Management Upgrading Project of Tanzania (FILMUP) is just one example. Masterminded by the World Bank with funds contributed by no less than five bilateral donors – Overseas Development Administration (UK), Norwegian Agency for International Development, Swedish International Development Authority, Canadian International Development Agency and Danish International Development Agency – the project has put the whole of the legal system under scrutiny. This includes courts, tribunals, legal personnel in the public and private sectors, legal education and training, legal records and library facilities, legal aid and public education.

The project is firmly set in the context of Tanzania's "far reaching economic and political reform programme, focusing on broadening the role of market forces as well as human rights, democracy and good governance and environmental protection considerations in guiding economic decisions and improving or strengthening major policy instruments and institutions that would support markets and private economic activity". The legal sector is "ill-equipped to meet the challenges of the market economy" and the studies that are being undertaken will, it is hoped, lead on to a programme of legal system reform which donors will buy into.

As one of the participants in this project, I would have to say that the enterprise is based on an act of faith. None of the specific studies commissioned were required to produce evidence that reform would contribute to economic regeneration and good governance. While law reform does have a positive contribution to play in Tanzania's political, social and economic regeneration, it could also work against it.

Even those who support law reform as an essential input into economic liberalization believe that the necessary evidence for the connection is lacking and there is disagreement as to what needs reform. The challenge to law reform at the other end of the scale is more serious. This is because it is, *au fond*, a challenge not just to law reform, but to the whole enterprise of attempting to introduce a modern market economy by formal mechanisms, legal and otherwise, into a society which lacks the necessary cultural and social infrastructure to operate such an economy. These arguments are most persuasively put by Jean-Philippe Platteau. They are also evident in two works which have clearly influenced Platteau's thinking: Douglass North's development of the idea of the path-dependent character of change in institutions in *Institutions, Institutional Change and Economic Performance*, and Robert Putnam's study of civic traditions in Italy, *Making Democracy Work*.

To avoid oversimplifying what is such a rich argument, I will try to summarize Platteau's argument using his own words. He starts from the perspective that:

> ...the market appears as a delicate mechanism which may fail to generate powerful effects (in the sense of giving rise to efficient trade) if it is embedded in a uncongenial cultural fabric. Policy-makers concerned with reforming poor countries' economies entrapped in relative stagnation... ought therefore to question the appropriateness of abruptly imposing market mechanisms and rules (for example, private property rights) on these countries. Things may indeed turn out as though the latter's social structure would vengefully react to this 'institutional rape' by actually subverting the market and thereby causing unintended effects to arise not only on the plane of equity but also on that of efficiency. (Platteau, 1994: 536)

Platteau draws attention to two crucial aspects of the development of an effectively working market. First: "Private and public order institutions are required and recourse to coercive power cannot be escaped." Following North, he notes that the state was 'a major player' or a 'crucial actor in the process of economic specialisation' that took place in Europe during modern times. The second aspect is:

> the development of generalized morality in which abstract principles or rules of conduct are considered equally applicable to a vast range of social relations beyond the narrow circle of personal acquaintances... [I]nasmuch as they act as a substitute for, or as a reinforcement of, state-engineered rules or control mechanisms, such norms allow a society to reduce enforcement costs and the mistakes unavoidable (given asymmetric information) in any process of (central) law implementation. Unfortunately, generalized morality is not a commodity which can be easily called for as the need arises. It is actually embedded in the historically-determined cultural endowment of a society... In the absence of norms of generalized morality, a strong state is needed not only to give an impetus to investment and production through direct and indirect involvement... but also to support a rapid development of labour division and concomitant expansion of exchange transactions. (ibid.: 802)

Such a state, Platteau points out, might be more or less authoritarian and bureaucratic depending not only on the preferences of the state establishment but also on the historical trajectory of a particular society; the less the morality is generalized, the greater the need for a strong interventionist state:

> There is nevertheless the risk that by following the second (more interventionist) approach the state will reinforce negative aspects of the social fabric over which it rules, such as happens when it creates distrust rather than trust to reduce policing costs. Also, the situation becomes hopeless when the state itself is partial and corrupt... [O]bstacles to expansion of complex exchange in contemporary developing countries [and as Platteau makes clear, some at least of the transitional countries of East, and Central Europe and Central Asia] can arise from two distinct sources (at least). In some countries, the individual does not get emancipated from old allegiance ties and the state remains weak, or else it consists of a theocracy. In other countries, where such generalized emancipation is under way but no shift from limited-group to generalized morality takes place, the state is not sufficiently impartial, wise and effective to create the trust required for thriving exchanges... [S]tate intervention aimed at correcting the 'trust failure' is required. (ibid.: 803)

However, following Putnam, Platteau suggests that in states with unfavourable civic endowments "even if formal institutional changes are adequate, history will move slowly and the efficiency of the economic exchanges will improve only over decades".

Thus, law reform aimed at facilitating the operation of a market economy may, at best, only produce beneficial results in the long run, and at worse, a much more likely scenario, worsen matters in many countries. A clear implication of this thesis is that much careful research and preparation is needed before reformers plunge in with their legal panaceas. This point was a major thrust of the International Legal Centre report on Law and Development, where it was strongly emphasized from two perspectives: those from the North who had been engaged in law and legal institutional reform in the South and were looking back in something approaching horror at their naivety in assuming that the import of laws would change the way the importing society would work; and those from the South whose countries had been the objects of this reforming zeal. It has also been reiterated by Cheryl Gray who states:

> The way legal processes are handled in developing countries such as Indonesia
> has little to do with the way the formal legal system operates. Studying the formal
> legal system alone will provide little insight into the nature of the actual legal
> system. (Gray, 1991: 763)

While there is evidence from the publication *Governance: the World Bank's experience* that the World Bank is aware of the difficulties attendant on law reform and of the need to try and form some view of its effectiveness, the pressures on multilateral and bilateral donors to produce 'results' militate against the slow incremental approach to law reform. Under this approach formal reform and societal change interact with each other and help each other to develop in the desired direction.

It is with Platteau's explicit message that we ought, however, to be more concerned. Is there a role for law and legal institutional reform directed to facilitating a market economy in those societies where the appropriate cultural endowments do not exist? Platteau draws attention to their absence or inadequacy in many sub-Saharan African and South Asian countries and Russia. The fact that taking this line would be to adopt a counsel of despair should not deter us from doing so if the evidence points in this direction. The evidence from many African countries, and from Russia certainly, would not seem to inspire confidence that law reform has much of a role to play in either developing a market economy or good governance.

However, this is too extreme a conclusion to adopt. Within Europe, the fact that Albania is not very promising territory for the development of a modern law-led market economy does not lead to the conclusion that the Czech Republic is similarly not very promising. *A fortiori* with, for example, Rwanda and Botswana, Liberia and Ghana, although the fragility of the institutions and the extent of corruption in states such as Botswana and Ghana, which on the surface appear to be making a good fist of developing a market economy, are worrying. An agenda which concentrates on the development of a market economy and uses that perspective to advance the cause of good governance is misguided. This model of economic development assumes that a market economy means less government so that the thrust of law reform is on less regulation, more rules facilitating transactions in the market, the acquisition of private property (where market forces are assumed to take care of any inequities in development) and judicial reform aimed at facilitating the settlement of commercial disputes. Inevitably, too, the models of law offered for use in developing and transitional market economies are those which are thought to have been successful in the creation and operation of market economies in the west, usually, as Moore has pointed out, Anglo-American models. Good governance *per se* is not addressed, neither is the alleviation of poverty. Both are necessary preconditions for the efficient and equitable operation of market-orientated economies and societies, wherever they are. Good governance involves not less, but differently structured, empowered and accountable government. More attention needs to be paid to: the experience of law reform in all developed countries, in other words to comparative law; the nature of law and its development in developing and transitional countries; indigenous institutions which should be assisted to evolve and adapt to modern functions.

I want to elaborate on these points with reference to urban land issues and administrative justice. With the first area, I will discuss general matters of law reform, drawing on my article (see McAuslan,1994); with the second, I will draw on my work for FILMUP.

LAND LAW REFORM

Preconditions for successful land reform include firstly a government which has a collective belief in the benefits of an efficient and effective state and at least a passive acceptance by its citizens that such a state exists. The government must be legitimate, and legitimacy incorporates the same notions embraced within good governance: accountability, transparency, probity, equity and efficiency. If these attributes are present in government, reforms can be introduced which will benefit society as a whole and will be accepted by society.

Another precondition is that the necessary social conditions are in place; without this the laws, whether related to a state-administered land allocation system or a market allocation system, are unlikely to work. Any legal framework

---

1 See David Sahn and Alexander Sarris's instructive article 'The Evolution of States, Markets and Civil Institutions in Rural Africa' in <u>Journal of Modern African Studies</u>, Vol. 32, 1994, p279.)

for urban land management (or any other area of a modern economy) assumes the existence of a system of public administration and a civil society. In other words the existence of: persons with some familiarity with modern government and market processes; institutions with financial independence; sources of capital accumulation other than, or in addition to, access to land; a range of professions to operate land management processes; a variety of media outlets where matters of concern to the public can be openly discussed and information disseminated; and as a consequence, governments which recognize some social limitations on their powers. These social conditions do not exist in most countries in Africa, nor in those countries in South Asia where access to land is still an important means of accumulating wealth. While some of those countries with political power may be willing to introduce laws which read as if a transparent market economy is being introduced, numerous studies have shown that they will not allow them to be implemented in any way which might threaten their traditional source of wealth or political power, that is, land. In such countries, law reform must be allied to political and governance reform.

Leaving aside these problems, there are several legal factors which need to be present for the successful use of law to bring about change in land management policies and practices. First, there is the issue of indigenous versus imported law. It is highly significant that the more successful instances of land law reform to improve land management have taken place in those countries which have, or have created out of disparate sources of law, an indigenous legal framework for their land management. Botswana in Africa, Thailand and Malaysia in Asia may be instanced among current developing countries. In contrast, most sub-Saharan African countries still operate a dual system of land law with the modern statute law a replica of the metropolitan law. In Tanzania, to give one example, the basic law on title registration enacted in 1953, "borrowed heavily", in the words of the draftsman, from the English Land Registration Act 1925. This Act was intimately related to substantive English land law which was being reformed at the same time, itself closely bound up with the evolution of English society. Again, in the Indian sub-continent, although there is a mass of legislation on land, the basic legislation governing land transactions and land use planning still relies heavily on English models.

In any country contemplating land reform, there has to be in existence land-related professionals sufficiently experienced and able and willing to take the lead in developing proposals for reform. Just as laws cannot be imposed from outside, the drive for reform cannot come from outside. Outsiders – consultants, visiting academics, an international conference – can all be helpful but only as subordinate contributors to a national effort. Law reform as conditionality is of limited utility.

An interesting contrast is provided by two World Bank projects involving urban land programmes in, respectively, Zambia in the early 1970s and Lesotho in the late 1970s. In the first, involving squatter upgrading, a group inside Zambia developed draft legislation to provide a legal framework for the programme including a simplified system of land titling. This draft law was part of the report produced by Zambia which led to a World Bank loan for the programme, one of the conditions of which was the enactment of the law. The law was duly enacted and its implementation has been successful. In Lesotho, the World Bank imposed as a condition of the loan for its land management programme that a new land law be enacted which would make land transactions easier. The law was enacted but never seriously implemented. While working in Lesotho I came across a valedictory memorandum written by an expatriate official seconded to work on implementing the law. This memorandum revealed that the government had never had any intention of applying the law because it regarded it as being designed to make it easier for foreigners, such as South Africans, to buy up choice sites in Maseru and elsewhere. The law also disturbed the fundamental ground rules of land rights in the country, the balance between the power of the King, the chiefs and the government, and contributed to the breakdown of relations between the King and the government and ensuing constitutional and political upheavals.

If a country is to secure land-related professionals with the necessary experience to implement the land reform there has to be in existence, or at least in development, a national legal literature of depth and maturity. Without this a country cannot hope to educate and produce lawyers and other land-based professionals with an understanding of the national land laws and the relationship between those laws and economic and social development. Land reform has to be accompanied by the development of literature on the new law and a training programme 'selling' the new law. A good example of the development of the literature alongside the creation of the new law is provided by *The Land Laws of Trinidad and Tobago*, a major text written by John Wylie as part of his work as draftsman of the legislation "to explain the operation of the new laws". Regrettably, the new laws are not yet in operation. This is partly due to a failure to associate sufficiently the legal and other land-related professions with the process of reform.

When considering the actual process of reform it is relevant to refer to the English experience of land law reform. The following aspects stand out:
• the time it took – the package of land law reforms known as the 1925 Property Law reform was the culmination of a century of debate and of various packages of reform;
• the process of reform was highly political; landowners had to be convinced.

The lawyers were constantly at odds with each other. The Houses of Parliament had to be persuaded. As the century wore on, new actors entered the arena and had to be accommodated. The upshot was, inevitably, a compromise. The ideology of land law literature has always portrayed the reforms of 1925 as a seamless web of intellectual coherence. They were not, although they do hang together pretty well and they meet the principal aim of the reforms, to make transactions in land simpler and cheaper;

• the 'final' version of the reforms was built on earlier attempts that had not always worked. Title registration is a case in point. The Land Registration Act of 1925 built on two previous attempts at introducing title registration, in 1862 and 1897. It learned from past errors but these were as much political as technical.

Land law reform is not a one-off process; it never ends. Even a major piece of legislation will need constant review and amendment. One year after the Law of Property Act 1925 – the corner-stone of the English reforms – was enacted, it had to be amended to correct mistakes. The English Law Commission has, in almost 30 years of its existence, produced a stream of reports and draft Bills, several of them enacted, to reform, update and clarify the legislation of 1925. A better example perhaps is the National Land Code of Malaysia, enacted in 1965 (and based on legislation going back to the 1890s) yet amended and added to no less than 22 times since then, with some amendments being quite significant. The basic statutory code of land law in Kenya, enacted in 1963, has never been formally reviewed and revised in its 32 years of existence. However, it may be significant that while there is some good legal writing on Malaysian land law, legal writing on Kenyan land law is poor in both quality and quantity. Also, there is a much closer correspondence between the practice of land dealings and the law in Malaysia than in Kenya.

From this discussion the following conclusions can be drawn:
• any significant programme of externally funded and technically assisted law reform has, and will be seen inside any recipient country to have, a political dimension; law reform is part of the process of changing or reforming policies so it cannot be left to technical experts;
• a national constituency for law reform has to exist; it can neither be manufactured nor led from outside;
• while relevant laws, practices and processes of reform from other countries can and should be assessed during the reform programme, the output has to be seen to be national, dovetailing into the existing corpus of law and appropriate to local circumstances; off-the-peg imports don't work;
• a programme of law reform has to prepare for the long haul; it cannot be expected to produce measurable results in a few years. Nor can all the results be expected to be as predicted at the outset.

Overall then, involvement in law reform means involvement in politics and the lessons derived from externally inspired law reform programmes of two and three decades ago are still valid; law reform is not a quick fix and if not approached in a sensitive manner is as likely to do damage as to succeed.

REFORM OF ADMINISTRATIVE JUSTICE

To turn now to the FILMUP exercise. I want first to discuss the manner in which the exercise has been structured, since this offers lessons to other donor-funded and technical-assistance-provided law reform programmes. I will then look at the importance of administrative justice as an element in a law reform programme directed to achieving good governance, particularly in respect of assistance to the poor.

FILMUP was structured as follows: a Legal Task Force was established consisting of senior Tanzanian lawyers from the bench, the profession, public sector lawyers and academics. The task force broke down the legal system into ten separate areas of study and determined the terms of reference for the ten studies that were to take place. It was involved in the selection of the consultants, both external and national, although the degree to which they worked as a team varied from study to study. Study teams submitted a draft report to the task force. A workshop was held on the draft report with inputs from principal participants in each field of the study; the report was then revised in the light of the workshop and submitted to the task force. The task force's function was to prepare an overall report to submit to the government of Tanzania. It was then up to the government to decide how much of the report and its proposals to accept and put to donors for support in implementation.

This might seem a bureaucratic and long-winded process, and some donors were not too happy with it, but it did allow a proper balance to be maintained between the donor and external consultant input and national ownership of the output. Donors, and the consultants they funded, were confined to individual studies; Tanzanians were responsible for developing the overall package of proposals to put to donors. Donors will have the last word for they can reject all or any of the proposals but those that they accept would have a reasonable chance of implementation because the political input would be present; the constituency would have been created for the reforms, and comparative and national perspectives would have been included in the original studies and so would be available for use in developing the specific legislative or institutional reforms. The project, therefore, has national ownership.

While the following points on administrative justice are made in reference to Tanzania, they also apply to the majority of developing and transitional countries. The administrative process in Tanzania has hitherto been characterized by an absence of a legal culture. What mattered was to get things done; the manner and procedures by which things were achieved were much less important. No more graphic illustration of this approach to administration and its effect on ordinary people is provided than in the Report of the Presidential Commission of Inquiry into Land Matters. The report clearly showed that while the many administrative processes were inefficient and time-wasting, abuses of power allowed the élites to bypass the processes while bearing heavily on the poor in rural and urban areas. This was confirmed by the work of the team (of which I was a member) on specific tribunals and administrative processes.

A rapid move towards a market economy which concentrates on the development of private property rights and significantly reduces regulation but which also leaves the administrative process untouched, will undoubtedly hurt the poor. An un- or poorly regulated market economy, as we are now rather belatedly rediscovering in the UK, increases economic and social inequality and can lead to political instability through the growth of an underclass with no stake in and therefore no commitment to the prevailing constitutional and political system. In Tanzania, income differentials have markedly widened in the last few years as has access to and acquisition of capital resources, usually land, obtained at the expense of peasants and the urban poor. As a result an unregulated market is rapidly developing.

The unequal application of the administrative process in the new market economy is neatly illustrated by contrasting the differential approach taken to malversation in the issue of tax exemption certificates in respect of foreign investors, and in the refusal of business licenses to some of the unorthodox shops – container shops – and to the hawkers springing up in the commercial centre of Dar es Salaam. With respect to the tax exemption certificates, after pressure from the World Bank and donors who withdrew aid, the relevant Minister was moved from his post. Here the views of consumers – foreign investors – backed by powerful financial organizations prevailed. In the second case, attempts to chase hawkers away and close down container shops led to urban disturbances. The ban was relaxed but licences have still not been granted, leaving these commercial outlets, vital to the urban poor, at the continued mercy of unscrupulous officials and police. Part of the problem with the business licensing laws and their administration is that there is a lack of a clear policy behind the law: it is questionable whether it is a revenue-raising measure, in which case the more shops that are licensed the better, or a measure to control the type of shops to be permitted in different parts of the urban areas, in which case it could be seen as a quasi-townplanning measure. This lack of a clear policy facilitates abuse of power in the application of the law.

An approach to developing a fairer system of administrative justice can be placed four-square within the overall notion of good governance. Embraced within that notion, as we have seen, are the concepts of transparency, equity, probity, and accountability. These modern terms, however, have an older formulation, familiar to lawyers and others acquainted with British administrative law. These concepts are simply new names for the old principles of openness, fairness and impartiality in administrative decision-making and an opportunity for such decisions to be reviewed by some authority outside the administrative process, in other words to provide accountability.

Many countries within the Commonwealth have during the last 30 years made conscious efforts to develop their systems of administrative justice on the basis of these principles. Some have used statutory reforms, for instance in Australia and Barbados with their development of a national Administrative Appeal Tribunal and their simplification of practice and procedures for judicial review. Many countries have created an Ombudsman, and in yet other countries, a more creative judicial approach to the courts' powers to curb administrative wrong-doing has been developed. These reforms have benefited all sections of society and are based on an approach to governance which does not put the values of the market first.

With regard to Australia where a more managerial market-orientated approach to the administrative process is considered by some to undermine the justice approach on grounds of cost, the comment by Ernst Willheim is worth noting:

> Perhaps part of the answer is that concern for the rights of the individual is one of the values we cherish in a fair and free society. There is another perspective. Every decision-making process involves difficult cases and disputes. A satisfactory mechanism for their resolution is part of the overall cost of that process. In a democratic society a proper opportunity for the citizen to challenge the lawfulness of government decision making is a right that cannot be evaluated solely in terms of the cost of an individual case. (Willheim, 1990: 125)

This is relevant to the ideological thrust of law reform aid packages. Law reform designed solely to facilitate the development and operation of the market involves a reduction in the regulatory framework and the costs of administrative decision-making. Law reform designed also to improve the justice of the administrative process may well involve an increase in the regulatory framework and the costs of administrative decision-making. Decisions where previously there was no appeal will become appealable. Activities which previously took place in the public sector and were regulated, if at all, by administrative means will, if transferred to the private sector, be subjected to legal regulation which may well involve hearings and appeals. Above all, a concern to improve dispute-settlement mechanisms to facilitate market transactions will concentrate on improving the quality of the upper levels of the judiciary and court systems. A concern to improve administrative justice will concentrate on access to justice for all and improving the total judicial system. This will inevitably involve looking at integrating into any reformed system dispute-settlement mechanisms known to and understood by the citizenry. A concern to improve the settlement of commercial disputes will be more likely to put the import of western judicial systems above the need to understand and build on existing national, including traditional, systems.

CONCLUSIONS

Three decades on from the early years of the Law and Development movement, the wheel has come full circle. In the 1960s, the aim, or at least the assumption behind the drive to use law as a tool for development, was that the continued use of law and legal concepts derived from the west – the old and new colonial powers – would play a vital role in rapid economic and social development. Within developing countries, law as a tool of development then went out of fashion among donors and even among legal scholars. Now, under the rubric of 'governance', the use of law to stimulate economic and social development has made a comeback among the donors and therefore among the donees.

Two general comments on this renewed faith in law reform must be made. Firstly, we are far more aware now of the difficulties of using law – principally law based on western ideas and concepts – to bring about economic and social change. However, this understanding does not seem to have penetrated through to the official aid community or, if it has, it is being resolutely put on one side in the higher interests of advancing the global market economy. To put it more bluntly, multilateral lending agencies and some donors have taken a political decision that their concern should be with that part of the economy of a developing country which can be integrated into the global market economy and to that end should pursue global market facilitating law reform. Governance is seen as being that form and process of government which facilitates the operation of the market. Rhetoric might hint at a wider meaning of the term and a wider use of law as a tool of social and political development but little is being done to that end in practice. On this basis, law reformers can afford to ignore Platteau et al., since they do not have a concern with the wider society. So long as a reasonably efficient enclave of a market economy, replete with its normal institutions, can be put together and helped into operation, the side effects can be largely ignored or left for national action.

In the debate on governance in developing countries and how aid can and should be used to improve the quality of governance, the voice of the lawyers has been muted. It is World Bank publications, economists, political scientists and policy analysts that have developed the concept and explored its practical and theoretical implications. It is aid officials which have used the concept to justify law reform aid packages. Similarly, with the rule of law; it is being redefined to emphasize its role in facilitating the enforcement of private contracts so that law reform to advance the rule of law is the same as law reform to advance the market economy. It is hardly surprising that the type of concerns of law and development lawyers – access to justice, land reform, controls over abuses of power in government, regulatory arrangements for a privatized economy, gender and development – are not central to the governance agenda. They are not there because there is no pressure to put them on the agenda. It is not because they are 'political' issues; all matters of law reform are political. You could argue that it is because they have not been made explicitly part of the political agenda of law reform as aid that they are not seen as part of governance.

Similarly, with the actual agenda for law reform and the approach being taken in implementing that agenda. If, as I believe, there is a real danger that the old mistakes of the 1960s will be repeated, this is in part due to the lack of communication between the academic law and development community, and the development community, both academic and practitioners. The development practitioners tend to go to the private legal practitioners for their law reformers. Such persons, with rare exceptions, know nothing of the practical problems of law and development and do not have time to grapple with them. The development academics, with rare exceptions, tend not to take law on board as one of their concerns. In that respect, if in no other, nothing has changed since the International Legal Centre's report on *Law and Development* twenty years ago.

These are not mere academic concerns nor is my criticism of the present position fuelled by sour grapes, for I have been fortunate enough to be involved in law and development as teacher, consultant, scholar and UN technical co-operation administrator. My concern is to try and ensure that the present commitment to law reform and to improving the quality of governance through law and legal institution reform does not, once again, peter out in mutual incomprehension and recriminations a few years down the road. I have the following suggestions to make.

On the practical side, the FILMUP model of managing a donor-funded law reform aid programme is one which could with advantage be used more widely. The kernel of usefulness in the UNDP China law reform project – involving local lawyers as equal partners in the practical aspects of a law reform programme – should be common practice in all such donor-funded projects. The need for a careful study of the existing situation and possible options for reform, conducted in equal association with local legal and other consultants and scholars, elements of both the FILMUP and China projects, should be a *sine qua non* of any law reform project as should a follow-up study or continuing assessment of the project. Training to understand and implement new laws must be an integral part of any law reform programme. In these two respects, I am at one with the World Bank which also emphasizes national ownership of any law reform programme and training as an essential part of a law reform programme. Finally, there is a strong case for donor support to be given to a major international programme devoted to governance in all its aspects and not just as an aid to facilitating a market economy, along the lines of the Urban Management Programme whose donors include the UNCHS (Habitat) (United Nations Centre for Human Settlements), World Bank and UNDP. The establishment of the Management Development and Governance Division in UNDP is a significant step forward. The Division's responsibilities go beyond capacity-building for a market-based economy to embrace capacity-building "for elections and other democratic processes, legislative and judicial systems, human rights initiatives, and broader participation of civil society in governance" (UNDP, 1995: 4).

On the academic and research side there is a great need to foster closer links between the academic and practitioner community in respect of law reform as a contribution to better governance. An annual forum similar to those which the World Bank hosts on development economics or sustainable development bringing the two sides together would be a significant contribution. The development of training programmes, materials and courses – not Masters' Programmes, though they have their place – on aspects of law and development in academic centres and between academic centres and the United Nations Institute for Training and Research and the Economic Development Institute needs to be prosecuted with vigour. More research could be undertaken on the impact of law on development; compared with economic and policy impact studies, there is a paucity of legal impact studies. There is also a strong case for considering the creation of a Centre for Law and Governance which could be a focal point for developing the programmes suggested here. It could also work closely with any international programme for governance that may be created.

Virtually every year there is a major UN Conference, mandated by the General Assembly on some issue thought to be of significant international concern. In 1994, the Conference was on Population; in 1995, there was one on Social Policy and one on Women; in 1996, one on Human Settlements, Habitat II. These major events focus national and international attention on the particular subject matter and advance our thinking and practical commitment to the issues raised by and agreed to at the Conference. Would there not be a case for a UN

Conference on Governance to advance our knowledge, understanding and commitment on the subject? In some respects, the preconditions for such a major conference are in place. There is widespread agreement for the principle that good governance is the foundation of development but considerable disagreement as to what constitutes good governance and how to bring it about both in developing and developed countries. While a major UN Conference would not solve these issues, it might serve to highlight and clarify them and set the stage for governance to make an important contribution to a just and equitable society and thus to prospects for social development and poverty alleviation.

REFERENCES

Gray, Cheryl W, 'Legal Process and Economic Development: A Case Study of Indonesia', World Development, Vol. 19 (1991) p763.

International Legal Centre Research Advisory Committee on Law and Development, *Law and Development: The Future of Law and Development Research* (Uppsala: ILC and the Scandinavian Institute of African Studies, 1974).

McAuslan, Patrick, 'Law and Urban Development: Impediments to Reform', Cities, Vol. 11 (1994) p402.

McAuslan, Patrick, Meela, Damian, S., Mgullu and Francis, P., *Administrative Justice in Tanzania; the Report of the FILMUP Study: Quasi-Judicial Institutions and Other Alternative Dispute Settlement Mechanisms* (Dar es Salaam: 1994).

Moore, Mick, 'Declining to Learn from the East? The World Bank on Governance and Development', Institute of Development Studies 24 Bulletin 39 (1993).

North, Douglass C, *Institutions, Institutional Change and Economic Performance* (New York: Cambridge UP, 1990).

Platteau, Jean-Philippe, 'Behind the Market Stage Where Real Societies Exist; Part I: The Role of Public and Private Institutions', Journal of Development Studies, Vol. 30 (1994) p533; 'Part II: The Role of Moral Norms', ibid., p753.

Putnam, Robert D, *Making Democracy Work: Civic Traditions in Modern Italy* (Princeton: Princeton UP, 1993).

Sahn, David E and Sarris, Alexander, 'The Evolution of States, Markets and Civil Institutions in Rural Africa', Journal of Modern African Studies, Vol. 32 (1994) p279.

Seidman, Ann and Seidman, Robert B, *State and Law in the Development Process: Problem Solving and Institutional Change in the Third World* (London: Macmillan, 1994).

Sherwood, Robert M, Shepherd, Geoffrey and De Souza, Celso Marcos, 'Judicial Systems and Economic Performance', The Quarterly Review of Economics and Finance, Vol. 34 (1994) p101.

von Mehren, Philip and Sawers, Tim, 'Revitalising the Law and Development Movement: A Case Study of Title in Thailand', Harvard International Law Journal, Vol. 33 (1992) p 67.

UNDP, 'Management Development in Progress', MDG UNDP, Vol. 3/1 (1995).

Willheim, Ernst, 'Ten Years of the ADJR Act: from a Government Perspective', Federal Law Review, Vol. 20 (1990) p111.

World Bank, *Governance: The World Bank's Experience* (Washington DC: The World Bank, 1994).

World Bank, 'The World Bank and Legal Technical Assistance; Initial Lessons' Policy Research Working Paper 1414, (Washington DC: January 1995).

Wylie, John, *The Land Laws of Trinidad and Tobago* (Port-of-Spain: Government of Trinidad and Tobago, 1986).

COMMENT

Joseph R. Thome

McAuslan's paper wastes no time in getting to the nub of his arguments. The very first paragraph consists of a direct quotation from an "ambitious and optimistic statement from the World Bank". Because of its centrality to McAuslan's critique of the premises and orientations of current law and development projects being pushed by western donors, I set it out in its entirety.

> The legal framework in a country is as vital for economic development as for
> political and social development. Creating wealth through the cumulative
> commitment of human, technological and capital resources depends greatly on a
> set of rules securing property rights, governing civil and commercial behavior,
> and limiting the power of the state... The legal framework also affects the lives of
> the poor and, as such, has become an important dimension of strategies for
> poverty alleviation. In the struggle against discrimination, in the protection of the
> socially weak, and in the distribution of opportunities in society, the law can make
> an important contribution to a just and equitable society and thus to prospects for
> social development and poverty alleviation.

However, McAuslan says of this statement: "Here is the major actor telling us what is happening and what ought to happen in the front line. Whether legal development as outlined in this statement can achieve good governance and develop the market economy in developing and transitional countries is a different matter".

He expresses surprise at the recent 'discovery' by the World Bank and other donors of the idea that law can play an important role in the process of development. As McAuslan says, "we have been here before", referring to the Law and Development programmes of the 1960s and 1970s. That movement also was premised on the centrality of western law for promoting development in the less developed countries, but its lack of success seems to be ignored by current donors. We could ask, if 'law' didn't lead to 'development' then, why should it now?

McAuslan points to the 1974 seminal report on *Law and Development* prepared by the Research Advisory Committee on Law and Development of the International Legal Center, one third of whose members came from developing countries. This report recognized the flawed focus of the Law and Development movement and called for a more realistic view of the role of law, emphasizing the need to go beyond formal rules to determine who has access to legal processes and how decisions are made, and the need for thorough socio-legal research that goes beyond the premise that law plays a positive role but rather recognizes that it can distort or even be an obstacle to development, while hiding behind the facade of change and legal equality.

While, as McAuslan says, these ideas are almost platitudes to today's legal scholars,[1] he questions whether they are reflected in current law reform aid packages (ibid.) Apparently, then, western donors haven't learned from the Law and Development experience and seem determined to repeat the mistakes of the past. The images that come to mind are those of a bad movie sequel, something like 'Law and Development II: the Empire Strikes Back'; or the Yogi Bear adage 'It's Deja Vu All Over Again'.

McAuslan does recognize that the current law reform approach is now somewhat different from the original fixation on legal education. International aid circles, for instance, are currently focusing on 'governance' as an instrument of action. However, their understanding of 'governance' emphasizes that the only road to development is to downsize the role and reach of government while increasing the role and reach of markets. The classic governance concepts – accountability, transparency, probity, the rule of law – are now developed in the context of making markets work rather than making governments more accountable to their citizens.

While downsizing the role of the state and improving market transactions are legitimate concerns, McAuslan finds them too narrow. He sets out two important issues that require examination: whether the assumed centrality of law in the process of development really matters and whether there are areas other than facilitating the market where law reform could and should be deployed.

As regards the first issue, he sets out three positions. The dominant position as espoused by the current law and development missionaries is that law, particularly judicial reform, can and does play a central role in the process of development. At least three of the premises of this position, however, are questionable. First, that development requires a 'modern' legal framework,[2] meaning one just like in the United States; second, that in the USA this 'formal' model establishes clear and predictable rules and processes which channel and promote efficient economic behaviour; and third, that this legal model is easily transferable to other societies operating within sometimes radically different contexts. Sociology of Law and Legal Anthropology scholars would largely

---

1   The preface of a recent comparative law text, for example, tells us that "...it is seldom the rules of law that are truly significant or interesting about a foreign legal system; it is the social and intellectual climate, the institutional structures, and the procedures characteristic of the legal system that are instructive". (Merryman, John Henry, David S. Clark, and John O. Haley *The Civil Law Tradition: Europe, Latin America and East Asia* [Charlottesville: The Michie Company, 1994] page viii).

2   As stated in Merryman et al., op. cit., p18, "There are no universally accepted measures of legal development that are independent of specific social, economic and political objectives."

refute these assumptions with empirical and field studies, notable by their absence in most law and development proposals.[3]

At the other extreme is the position that law hardly matters; that it is a reflexive institution, subject to more important social, economic and political forces.

McAuslan adopts a middle position, a 'Goldilocks' type approach probably held by most of us who have field research experience: law does matter, in the proper context. For those in this middle position, however, and even for some of the strong protagonists of law reform, there is a nagging concern over the lack of evidence connecting law reform with economic liberalization, and disagreement as to what it is that needs reform. McAuslan, citing several seminal works, questions the enterprise of attempting to introduce a modern market economy by formal legal and other mechanisms into a society lacking the cultural and social infrastructure to operate such an economy. In this context these efforts may actually subvert the market and produce both inequity and inefficiency.

So what does McAuslan suggest as the agenda for legal missionaries and 'goldilockeans' alike? He begins by calling for a cautious approach. Noting the wide diversity among developing or transitional societies, he rejects the extreme conclusion that law reform has no role whatsoever in helping to establish a market economy or good governance. On the other hand, he calls for "...careful research and preparation ... before reformers plunge in with their legal panaceas". If nothing else, scholars and reformers must go beyond the formal legal process if they are to understand the nature of the actual legal system.

Beyond this, he contends that the current market model for law reform is misguided. It's not less government *per se* that is the problem, but the lack of good government and of programmes that alleviate poverty; these, to him, are the necessary pre-conditions for the efficient and equitable operation of market-orientated economies. "Good governance involves not less but differently structured, empowered and accountable government."

He suggests as starters, a renewed focus on: comparative law studies; the use of law and reform in developed countries; the nature of law and its development in developed and transitional countries; indigenous institutions which should be assisted to adapt to modern functions (ibid.). He then provides analyses of appropriate law reform projects, many based on his own field studies. From these, he arrives at conclusions worth the attention of international donors:

• any law reform project will have a political dimension; as such, it cannot be left to technical experts alone;

---

3 A particularly egregious example is an excerpt from the Sherwood, Shepherd and De Souza paper on Judicial Systems and Economic Performance quoted by McAuslan: "Although we can offer no support for the figure, we suspect it would not be surprising to eventually find that countries attempting economic reform suffer at least a 15 percent penalty in their growth momentum if their judicial system is weak."

• a national constituency for law reform has to be in place before its initiation; it cannot be manufactured from outside;
• while relevant institutions from outside should be considered, the output has to be national; that is, it must fit into local institutions and circumstances. As he puts it, "off-the-peg imports don't work";
• law reform is a long-term project; there are no quick fixes nor can all the results be predicted from the outset.

Throughout, he warns us about potentially adverse side effects from law reform projects; current pure market approaches, for instance, will inevitably lead to a concentration of resources to a privileged few. If the poor are to participate more evenly from economic growth, they must be provided with effective access to the allocation of goods and services, including justice.[4] This in turn requires state action, and not less government, through regulation, and affirmative action (such as land reform) and empowerment programmes.

As McAuslan points out in his conclusions, there is at present a much better understanding of the problems in using law, particularly when based on formal western models, to bring about economic and social change. Unfortunately, international donors seem to either reject or to ignore this accumulated knowledge and understanding. Bound as they are to their goal of advancing the integration of developing nations into the global economy, their legal reform projects are limited to pursuing a market facilitating legal framework.

Lawyers, moreover, are playing a minor role in this process; it is the economists, political scientists, policy analysts and World Bank and other aid officials who are largely responsible for designing, implementing, and justifying the new law reform projects. Not surprisingly, for they have little if any exposure to the messy arena of the law in action, these policymakers tend to have greater faith in the behaviour-inducement power of legal prescriptions than lawyers do. They seem oblivious to the multiple ways in which legal processes can be subverted, bypassed, and manipulated, or frustrated by the lack of resources or the presence of a hostile legal-political culture. They ignore or reject the major concerns of law and development lawyers: access to justice, land reform, controlling abuses of power in government, regulating the excesses of a privatized economy.

Given these concerns, McAuslan makes some concrete suggestions, both practical and academic. On the practical side, he recommends that future law reform programmes adopt as a common practice the full involvement of local lawyers and other local consultants and scholars. This participation is especially

---

4   McAuslan, correctly in my view, emphasizes that the poor benefit more from access to 'administrative' justice, where most of their conflicts would be processed, than from access to the upper levels of the judiciary, which is the emphasis of the market-orientated legal reforms.

important as regards pre-implementation studies of existing situations and possible options for reform, as well as follow-up studies or continuing assessments of the projects in question. Training in preparing, understanding and implementing new legislation must also be an integral part of any law reform programme. As a final 'practical' suggestion, he re-asserts his earlier call for a focus on "...governance in all its aspects and not just as an aid to facilitating a market economy". On the academic and research side, he expresses the "need to foster closer links between the academic and practitioner community in respect of law reform as a contribution to better governance" through such mechanisms as annual workshops involving both communities; the collaboration of academic and donor and other relevant institutions in creating and organizing non-degree training programmes and teaching materials on aspects of law and development; and, perhaps, the creation of a Centre for Law and Governance which would develop programmes along the lines already suggested and work closely with international governance programmes that may be created.

McAuslan does perhaps undervalue some of the local involvement and participation in the procedural and judicial re-organization programmes that form an important part of the law reform process in Latin America.

On the one hand, it does appear that the initial USAID justification and support for judicial reform in Latin America was linked to an either naive belief or cleverly diversionary position that the unresolved political murders in El Salvador during its civil war was the result of obsolete penal processes and an inefficient judicial organization. On the other hand, it is equally as true that many leading Latin American legal scholars and activists had long been espousing drastic and basic reforms of legal processes and judicial reform, and had indeed initiated reforms on their own, as was the case in various states or provinces in Argentina and Brazil, as well as in smaller countries such as Costa Rica and Uruguay. To them, the new sources of funding was most welcome, although they also had to include some of the market-orientated reforms pushed by the western donors, whether relevant or not.

Somewhat surprisingly, McAuslan doesn't pay much attention to the growing phenomenon of 'legal pluralism' throughout both the 'developed' and 'underdeveloped' world, as demonstrated by the current manifestations of, and demands within, different nations of the world, for ethnic and regional recognition in both the law and in political organization. At the same time, the global economy is producing a push toward supra-national law and judicial review. In the process, as Merryman puts it, "The state is losing power in both directions", as we are witnessing a "redistribution of sovereignty".[5] This is a problem area

---

5 Merryman et al., op. cit., p24.

that is also ignored by the new neo-liberal law reformers; given its importance for the process of development, it should be added to McAuslan's list of areas to study and explore.

On the whole, however, few experienced law and development academics and practitioners would quibble with McAuslan's analysis and recommendations – at least not those familiar with the literature if not having actually been involved in the 'law and development' programmes of the 1960s and 1970s. He incisively points out the lack of any empirical basis for most of the premises that underlie the current law reform programmes. It would seem that neo-liberal ideology rather than a careful assessment of regional differences, local problems, social reality and institutional processes form the basis for the international donors' almost dogmatic belief in the centrality of formal 'western' law in promoting development. Even a fairly quick review of the law and social science literature would have revealed the problems in using formal legal reforms as the major instrument for carrying out drastic social and economic reforms. The ex-Soviet Union, after all, provides some of the best examples of the problems and failures of such attempts.

McAuslan's recommendations also reveal a deep understanding of the complexity and difficulties involved in any process of social change, and of the means that should be followed in this process, not least of which is paying attention to and involving those that would bear the 'benefits' of the reforms. It is to be hoped that this paper and other similar critiques begin to be heard and have some impact on the planning and funding of current and future law reform projects funded by international donors.

3 Bureaucracy and law and order

Reginald Herbold Green

"I could not believe it would ever happen. I filled the form. Now I can feed my children."
Destitute Maputo female household head on receiving Supplement Alimentaire

"We cannot understand people who are so violent to each other. We had to call out the *sungu sungu* every night."
Ngara (Tanzania) village leader on Rwandan refugees and response.

EXPERTS FROM BELOW?

These are voices of two very ordinary Africans: one in a war-ravaged land vying with Afghanistan and Angola for the most devastated and with Ethiopia for the poorest titles; the other in a poor, isolated (the end of beyond even in most Tanzanian perspectives) district overrun by refugees who outnumber residents. These are two people who have seen only too much of ineffective government and violence even if the philosophical debate on good governance might seem confusing and confused from their – necessarily – temporally and spatially limited perspectives.

These two voices both praise state bureaucracy and state-managed, community-run law and order. If the Mozambican lady was told that this system of Weberian, referral, checking, rostering, payment delivery disempowered her and violated her culture, she would either not understand or would disagree emphatically. For her, and 75,000 other households, the test is whether it delivers something relevant to her needs, as perceived by her, and does so in a non-demeaning way. If the Tanzanian village leader was told law and order was merely a shield for oppressive state power he would probably understand but doubt the speaker's sanity; to him the *sungu sungu* (community recruited and managed auxiliary police force), the backup regular police and the army are what makes his village a world away from the horror of Rwanda even if in distance terms it is only 100 metres from him across an unmarked patch of bush.

These two examples suggest that much of the good governance debate on Africa appears to be simplistic, using bureaucracy and law and order as caricaturized terms of abuse rather than as working concepts of key elements in good governance, even if both are inadequate by themselves and subject to abuse. They also illustrate how the dialogue is usually top down and carried on at a philosophical level far removed from the man in the street or woman in the

51

field (reversed in the cases cited) who are asserted to be the intended subjects, beneficiaries, and judges of good governance, but whose opinions are rarely requested or listened to in any detail.

It would be easy to find equally lucid African condemnations of bad or non-governance, not least in Mozambique and Tanzania. However, many of these condemnations would be the converse of the affirmative arguments, citing absence of ability to ensure and enforce law and order and lack of administrative structures and procedures (bureaucracies) capable of delivering the desired services with the given resources. Officials who do not act, or act only on side payments, and police who steal, take bribes or use random violence are condemned, but the former are the opposite of Weberian bureaucracy and the latter are the corruption of the forces of law and order into the agents of disorder and of the unlawful.

This paper will explore briefly the accepted elements of good governance as intermediated through bureaucracy and the law and order apparatus to the experience and perceptions of ordinary women and men in urban and peri-urban neighbourhoods and rural villages and homesteads. In this context bureaucracy is defined in neo-Weberian terms as a system to facilitate rapid decision-taking and implementation at all levels of the public service with procedures for referring complex cases and those which raise policy issues upwards while ensuring that the routine cases are dealt with at initial field contact level. Similarly, law and order is defined as the ability of ordinary people to go about their daily business without fear of violent intervention by anyone (bandit, policeman, corrupt official, civil enemy) and with the assurance that breaches of that peace will be acted against reasonably promptly, impartially and effectively. While this does not constitute the full rule of law, it is a large part of it, just as bureaucracy alone cannot bear the full weight of policy implementation, let alone of formulation and articulation. To assert that law and order and bureaucracy form a significant part of the answers to good governance questions – especially to ordinary people who are far from levers of power – is not to assert that they are answers to all questions or to all aspects of any.

The concluding section of this paper explores the policy implications of strengthening state capacity to deliver basic services – including law and order – in a user-friendly way. It suggests that interim approaches need not wait on elaborate overall reviews and restructurings. Efficiency wages (which are high enough to allow public servants to be full-time and to act in the public interest) and adequate related resources (including institutional operating procedures) are both necessary and, together with basic performance tests such as attendance, are sufficient conditions for achieving radical progress towards this aspect of good governance. The problem lies in resource mobilization and allocation. Reallocation alone is unlikely to work because both core staff levels and ratios of supporting resource to staff are too low for efficient service provision. However, bureaucracy properly designed can make a significant, low cost contribution by increasing the efficiency of use of whatever resources are available through reducing uncertainty, time lags and waste.

THE MACRO DIALOGUE

In about 1990, external prescriptions for good governance in Africa appeared simple – not to say simplistic. Donors demanded free, competitive, multi-party elections with the clear belief that these would end corruption and bring 'market-friendly' governments to power. The World Bank more or less concurred, but its key theme was civil service reform. By that it meant, oddly enough, rather random across-the-board 'redeployment'. In reality, for most 'redeployees' this meant termination of employment with little chance of alternative livelihoods to replace the lost public service jobs . This approach was based on a non-factual belief that public service totals were high relative to needs and that pay was also high. The latter misperception seems to have been based on generalizing the cases of Cote d'Ivoire, Senegal, Cameroon, Gabon, Congo (Brazza) where, until the 1993/1994 devaluations and inflation, the salary side of the argument had a good deal of validity. Even there, in basic service areas (health, education, water, extension services, rural and peri-urban infrastructure, civil and police) professional and para-professional levels were too low if a dynamic towards universal access was to be sustained.

Today the intellectual discourse by external actors has become more complex. The donor record suggests no evident adherence to any consistent principle, for example, acceptance of the overthrow of a popular government with more than a third of a century of contested elections (Gambia); backing of a president who is a last ditch opponent of any electoral role for political parties (Uganda); acceptance of results of a election in which 55 to 60 per cent voted the government to be illegitimate but the system returned it to office (Kenya); acquiescence in fraudulent parliamentary and presidential elections, in the presence of international troops and observers who did report the 'election' to be unfree and unfair (Togo). The World Bank has moved more positively to stress accountability, more efficient public services – which alters parameters of civil service reform – and participation – at least where functionally useful and not too time-consuming. However, it still tends to concentrate on those aspects of governance which most directly affect World Bank staff and are based on somewhat simplistic macro-economic formulae or rules of thumb.

Intellectual debates by African officials have been complicated by some self-interested *status quo* backers and by a difficulty in sorting out responses to external agendas from attempts to articulate African ones. The following basic elements are common to the African and to the external actor discourse: accountable governance; transparency; honesty; capacity to deliver (and to prioritize what to deliver to whom); greater use of markets; rule of law; human rights; role of civil society and the domestic social sector, and bringing government nearer people. (The aspect of greater use of markets is often driven by a greater desire to manage or rig the markets than has hitherto been typical of donors, World Bank/IMF or many external intellectuals and most businesspersons, who are just as keen to back certain interventions but less eager to say so.)

However, the African participants often stress particular socio-economic-historical contexts to query or reject straight import substitution at institutional and policy levels. For example, with regional or sub-national parties frequently dominant, many seek to ensure that no substantial geographical area, or sub-national socio-political-cultural group, is totally excluded from governance. Some of the non-party and single party approaches do relate genuinely to this concern. Examples include the sunset coalition in South Africa and the incorporation of Ministers from Renamo – but not Renamo as a party – in the new Mozambican government and the allocation of the Prime Ministership and nearly half of the Cabinet seats to parties with less than 20 per cent of the vote in Burundi. Curiously, proportional representation by province or region, or even nationally, is rare – it was a transitory provision in Zimbabwe and was the electoral approach in the 1994 elections in Mozambique, South Africa and for regional government in Namibia.

A quick review of key elements in the intellectual dialogues may be useful as the themes – if not the form of discourse – relevant to and present in the concerns of 'ordinary' people such as the two initially quoted.

Accountability/transparency

The issue of accountability/transparency includes the publication of accurate intelligible accounts and the means of holding someone responsible for key decisions. The importance of Public Accounts Committees is stressed, initially more by Anglophone Africans than outsiders, as is openness in publishing the decisions and the administrative and legal rules governing them. The dialogue has to date centred on how this could be achieved for MPs, journalists, academics and other intellectuals with much less attention on how it could be related 'down' to village and neighbourhood levels, where both the content and format would need to be different. For example, a university or donor economist's ability to analyse and use a government or corporate audit report is not the same as a co-op or village members' ability to tackle financial reports and decisions of their bodies, let alone the complete texts of Auditor Generals' reports.

Predictability
Predictability of state action is perhaps more a 'grass-roots' or dusty peri-urban squares' concern, with the exception of the World Bank and businessmen in respect to contracts and tax regimes. However, it relates to accountability both with reference to the identification of decision-takers and the ability to gain redress for 'out-of-line' actions or, perhaps more commonly, inaction or grievously delayed action via elected officials, ombudspersons or the courts. It also relates to bureaucracy and to the rule of law which are intended to cause similar results in similar cases.

Competence and capacity
Competence and capacity are sometimes debated in the abstract and in respect to strategic goals, in terms of what action the state should take and what it should leave to civil society, enterprises and/or regulated or free markets, and also in respect to institutional structures (public service reform writ more broadly). To users, the issues are real and concrete. They relate largely to effective access to basic services, such as primary and adult education, preventive and primary curative healthcare, agricultural and veterinary extension services, a peaceful climate to go about daily life and a police and courts system to protect it, and non-exploitative markets without an extortionate, inequitable or brutally collected tax and fee burden.

Power to select, remove or retain leaders
The power to select, remove or retain leaders, including those from the domestic social sector, by effective procedures with predictable results is a goal which multi-party competitive elections may be unable to deliver at macro or micro level.

Decentralization and participation
The distinction between decentralization and broader participation in decisions as well as in their execution and review, at macro and micro level, is often conflated. Decentralization brings power closer to people but not necessarily more accessible to them. Local participation does require decentralization but the inverse is not true.

Human and peoples rights and responsibilities
The debate on human rights has become an expanded title of 'Human and peoples rights and responsibilities' largely in response to the African contribution to the dialogue. However, the World Bank does also stress user and community

responsibilities to provide resources and, less clearly, rights to inform and influence actions. Human and peoples rights and responsibilities are in principle not disagreed upon (*vide* the African Charter). However, this sometimes reflects more the injudiciousness of opposing them publicly than a deep commitment to enforce or in many cases even allow them. It also conceals or overlooks real resource problems even for the 'traditional' western core rights: effective police investigation costs more than beating out confessions; freedom of the press is not a reality to most citizens unless there are accessible public service media at all levels; political parties without state support or a sub-national cultural core tend to be 'bought up' as do underpaid decision-takers such as magistrates, constables, tax officers. It is specific issues which most concern people who are far from levers of power, not the presence, or absence, of bills of rights and other legal provisions even if it can be argued that these are at least facilitative to concrete micro results. That local level perceptions are inadequate is not in doubt. Beating out confessions can be popular if it does halt crime waves (as is not unknown); freedom of the press and of verbal expression of views beyond immediate micro issues may not be backed broadly or with fervour. A wide remit for accepted comment, including the freedom to criticize officials and service delivery, but with some areas and persons known to be 'out of bounds' is not necessarily unpopular. However, these limitations need to be analysed to understand why they exist. They need to be seen as requiring ordinary person and specialist inputs, including lawyer, journalist, academic, opposition politician, to relax them, rather than limiting the discussion on rights to élite circles.

This swift *tour d' horizon* does not suggest the good governance dialogue is irrelevant to, or discordant with, the concerns of most Africans. It does suggest that this dialogue is now at a philosophical and general level which is far removed from most Africans. The implicit assumption that there exists an educated citizenry who understands and has access to legal recourse is incorrect. This throws into question the accessibility of the existing legal system, not least the magistracy and police. The macro nature of the poor user's collective perspective has recently been well expressed in UN Secretary General Boutros Boutros Ghali's Herald Tribune article on the World Summit for Social Development as:

> ... a crisis that would have been unimaginable a decade ago; the unravelling of society. ...Social services are eroding. Crime, terrorism, drug trafficking and abuse have become everyday features of modern life. ...What is now under siege is something different [from cross-border invasions]; the security of people in homes, jobs and communities.

> This erosion of personal security is making people profoundly pessimistic. Many
> no longer see the prospect of better times. There is a rising sense of cynicism not
> only about political processes but about the efficacy of democracy itself. For the
> poor, in particular, there is rising bitterness and frustration...
>
> Governments alone cannot control the causes of social dislocation and alienation.
> Yet they have to face the consequences. Ordinary people hold governments
> responsible...

The article highlights how the delivery of social services and of personal
security is closer to the concerns of poor and middle income Africans (or indeed
Asians, Latin Americans, Europeans or North Americans) than to most of the
macro issues in the governance debate. It also shows up the lack of livelihoods,
but this issue is beyond the scope of this paper.

BUREAUCRACY, LAW AND ORDER – DESERVEDLY LOW PROFILE?

Bureaucracy and law and order have not figured prominently in the governance
debate or at least not in any serious fashion. This is surprising given the stress
on capacity and civil service reform, on markets as a means to livelihood
improvement and on predictability.

Bureaucracy has figured but as a catch-all epithet for governmental
incompetence, inertia and ill-judged interference with markets. This approach
is unhelpful since it takes misuse of bureaucracy or bad bureaucracy or, rather
frequently, the total absence of bureaucracy as formally defined and then lumps
them together as a term of abuse to apply to bad and/or too widely present, or
absent, governance.

Bureaucracy is a system to ensure that routine decisions and actions, which
make up between 90 to 95 per cent of all decisions, can be taken uniformly and
promptly by field land personnel. The other decisions can then be referred
upwards for more detailed examination with only the most complex or policy-
related ones reaching senior officials and political personnel. Both procedural
and policy reviews start at middle or top level but they usually review lower
level experience.

The mechanism for such a system is a set of guidelines or standing orders to
allow all officials to know what to do, how and what to refer to whom and why.
Only genuinely emergency and policy alteration decisions fall outside the
guidelines, which should indicate the criteria for making such exceptions.

There is no implication that front-line personnel act as automata or without
professional judgement. For example, a Tanzania medical officer trained to
handle about 90 per cent of all cases and to refer the other identified 10 per cent

is expected to use professional judgement and skills when dealing with those 90 per cent. The same should hold for agricultural extension personnel, although this is often not the case because of inadequate training.

The 'post-bureaucratic' critique of bureaucracy assumes a functioning bureaucracy for the 90 to 95 per cent of all decisions. Nobody, or no rational governance analyst, wishes that, for example, deliveries of primary school texts to schools be a one-off since creative exercises vary from officer to officer, or that petrol purchase chits for ministry pool vehicles go up to the senior official in the ministry. Both often happen in Africa today and in that way lies disaster – the books are not delivered, the chief secretary has no time to act effectively on policy issues because of the clutter of routine micro decisions piling up on his or her desk. This is not because of bureaucracy (good or bad) but because of the absence of bureaucracy.

Similarly, if two of the main problems of public service capacity are absence from work place and inadequate training, then enforceable regulations on attendance and training course participation are part of the answer. (To be enforceable they may well need to be paralleled by pay bearing some relation to minimum household living costs.)

The 'post-bureaucratic' critique focuses on three risks: non-routine decisions and actions will be dealt with as if routine; routine (or repetitive) decisions and actions will be handled mechanically and not professionally; officials will not respond to service users' or applicants' needs and concerns.

All are real problems, but in each case good bureaucracy can be at least part of the answer – just as bad bureaucracy can be part of the problem. In the first case clear guidelines should help ensure referral; in the second, proper training should lead to professional front-line services – it is badly trained personnel who most frequently use guidelines as excuses for inappropriate actions; in the third, participation by a junior official is largely 'accepted' when and how guidelines call for it and user complaints and requests outside his empowerment to act should be among the items he refers for possible procedural or policy review- this then poses a secondary problem, that of participation within hierarchical public services.

Even the most in-depth civil service reform studies seem to underestimate how much the extent of what a user 'out there' receives, or does not receive, depends on a bureaucratic system which functions smoothly within appropriate guidelines. Intellectually, standing orders are not very interesting, but to a villager looking for improved seed, school texts, vaccines, or maintenance of a borehole they well may make the difference between prompt delivery and hopelessly delayed or non-delivery and in extreme cases this could be the difference between life and death.

The argument that Weber was not an African and that orderly processes are inherently un- or anti-African requires attention but does not appear cogent. Weber was indeed north-west European but many of his predecessors in bureaucratic promulgation and analysis, such as Hamurabi of the Code and Confucius of the Analects, assuredly were not.

Most African states before the European conquest had limited basic service delivery systems and therefore little need for an extensive civil service to operate them in an orderly fashion. This also characterized pre-18th century Europe. What African states often did have were hierarchical military, governance and role allocation (for example, to age groups and to women's groups) systems which did lay down guidelines for action, spheres of competence and referral procedures. Not all states were characterized in this way – personal dictatorships existed then, as now, as did broken-backed, low capacity states, in Africa as in Europe. Equally, few systems worked perfectly and most probably had periods of serious deterioration and abuse. Dr K. A. Busia's historic analysis of the Wenchi Omanheneship (kingdom) doubtless is slightly roseate if read as a literal account of governance in a typical Akan state. However, it does illuminate an 'ideal type construct' and demonstrates that orderly governance and participation has historic roots and present appeal in Africa as much as anywhere else. Taken literally, any innovation – especially if practised elsewhere – is initially non-African; that is as true of 'quality control circles' and 'participatory rural appraisal' as of bureaucracy. The relevant questions turn on whether the principles behind the form are compatible with those of the Africans expected to employ it and whether serious domestication and integration, rather than artefactual off-the-shelf importation, is practised.

The difficulties of transplantation are probably greater for western-style non-governmental organizations (NGOs) than for bureaucracy, excepting perhaps some religious related organizations and, oddly, the Red Cross. Western-style NGOs are, under certain conditions, useful vehicles for supporters of social action groups, such as in the Philippines and in sub-Saharan Africa, and for a handful of continental NGOs and national councils such as women's, church or, less frequently, youth, trade union and co-operative groups. They are unlikely to be optimal local level community programme operational bodies. Detached élite membership groups of well-wishers (usually professionals) working for, but not accountable to and often not in close day-to-day human contact with, those they serve are not notably 'traditional' in Africa (or perhaps anywhere else). They may have a future but are not a very speedy or sure route to local level participation and to raising the capacity of ordinary people.

What are historically and currently common in Africa are groups which link households or persons with common operational as well as representational issues. Women, small farmers, youth, religious, water users, road users and parent groups are among the commoner examples. These are generally local and rarely include the whole of a geographic community and people may well be members of more than one. Even at provincial or national level, confederations or apex representatives of such groups have more of a historic base and, surely, more organic accountability than the western and Philippine model NGO.

Law and order has been an unloved stepchild in development dialogue – especially in Africa – for more than forty years. The initial cause was a critique of colonial states as 'law and order' or 'night-watchmen' entities with few policy or domestic developmental concerns addressed.

This was something of a misunderstanding of most colonial states, which were very interventionist in respect to economic policy and sometimes, subject to limited personnel, to social policy as well. What they did not do was to provide broad access to basic social and human investment services, nor a physical infrastructure beyond that needed to serve the needs of selected constituencies (not all of which were foreign settlers or enterprises). The basic thrust of the development argument was logically not against law and order but against assuming it to be adequate in the absence of social-human investment-infrastructure services, and of accountable governance to shape the laws.

The result was that for many years law and order was given a low priority – not least by donors. This has not in most fora or at macro intellectual level changed even now.

Both police and the magistracy (law and order as perceived by most people) are also often part of the problem, in a number of ways. These are through: being instruments of macro or local repression and/or corruption; being personally corrupt in ways which distort or destroy basic security and predictability; engaging in privatized user fee collection (notably from chargeable motorists in lieu of taking them in to be charged) – in the case of some police forces this is because of need and these forces do not necessarily act unprofessionally in respect of their other responsibilities; withdrawing into 'safe' inaction driven by fear of ordinary people and politicians (most common in holdover police after the fall of an oppressive regime, such as Zimbabwe, Namibia, South Africa, Malawi). Each case is evidence of a failure of law and order and not evidence that law and order is unimportant; quite the contrary.

Analysis by legal functionalists may also have contributed to law and order being a low priority by virtually equating the Rule of Law to a Rule of Laws, which is distinctly different, by asserting freedom from external normative baggage but in fact tending to defend any *status quo* careful enough to enact laws covering whatever policies it intends to pursue and to follow them to the letter. (An irony in South Africa is that virtually none of the offences committed against its laws were necessary. Virtually all the apartheid regime's aims could have been carried out pursuant to its laws.) To the non-lawyer this approach to law tends to lessen respect for it.

Without law and order there is unlikely to be much else. Ordinary people give high priority to being able to go about their daily lives without the fear of violence from any source. They want to know what acts are unlawful (transparency) to avoid clashes with the police (predictability). They wish to know that breaches of the law affecting their peace and order will be dealt with expeditiously, honestly and efficiently enough to deter repetition. In many cases their complaint about police and magistrates is that they are too few and are not active enough and hence fail to deliver predictable security and to deter those who break the law. When police (and even army) perform, they are likely to be held in high regard, for example by residents of Tanzania's border Districts with Rwanda as of 1994/95.

Ombudspersons and higher courts have a much lower profile because, with the exception of felony criminal cases, they are irrelevant and inaccessible in the view of ordinary Africans. This is particularly true in the absence either of a tradition of class actions (or of one making general human rights provisions quasi-justiciable – as in India) or of legal aid beyond limited provision to indigent felony defendants.

As noted above law and order as defined here is not identical to nor as broad as the rule of law. For example, freedom of speech (especially critical speech) and of the press and the absence of a stifling climate of self-censorship beyond state promulgated boundaries of 'acceptable discourse' are important, as are procedural safeguards and a judiciary which is independent in politically sensitive as well as ordinary cases. This is clearer from the centre than at grassroots and probably clearer once law and order, as defined here, is attained. In the context of real security dangers, as in Tanzania's Kagera Region, the crippling of opposition party campaigning or deportation of 'inconvenient incomers' (including foreign traders and those from other regions) could have been made popular under the cover of 'law, order, security first' or even in response to public hysteria. In fact, neither was practised.

FROM USER THROUGH PROCESS TO SYSTEM

The mother in Maputo certainly sees herself as the beneficiary of government capacity to deliver a service. She was vaguely aware a 'food supplement' was available to women whose children were underweight and showed no growth in weight on monthly mother and child clinic visits. However, until a nurse told her she was eligible and gave her forms she had never supposed it related to her despite radio and – less relevantly – press coverage. She is the beneficiary of the deliberate creation of a simple, functional bureaucracy as much as of the political will to relieve urban destitution.

The political decision was to provide an income supplement to urban households below the absolute poverty line. Primarily for food, this was very modest because of resource constraints. The initial analysis – checked with local government, local councillors and women's groups – was to identify usable proxy categories. Three of these categories appeared to cover 90 per cent of absolutely poor households: female-headed households with no formal sector wage-earner; elder person headed households; disabled person headed households. Initial attempts to identify these categories directly were suspended because of pressure to act rapidly.

The initial interim method, still dominant, is referral of pregnant women and mothers by mother and child health clinics. The criteria for selection are underweight and no weight gain. Given 75 to 90 per cent coverage (and no fee to bar poor women's access, although there may be opportunity cost obstacles) the potential coverage is good.

The nurses inform the poverty supplement office which also receives papers, given to the applicant by the nurse, from either the local government, neighbourhood administrator or liaison officer, certifying she lives there and is not known to be non-poor. (Income is not checked because of the delay this would cause with little reliable data gained.) The office then contacts the woman and issues her a card which she can then present monthly at a stated bank branch to receive payment.

The system works. Since its present form was adopted 30 months ago, 80,000 households have become eligible (5,000 have completed eligibility which is 12 months in the case of pregnant women). An admittedly small survey of those eligible suggested that five per cent were relatively poor, 25 to 30 per cent absolutely poor, and 60 to 65 per cent destitute and that more than 80 per cent of receipts were spent on food, with fuel, clothing and soap accounting for the bulk of the remainder. The latter point may relate to payment being made to women, a decision taken on the basis that the clinic referral system named women and that women were responsible for providing and preparing food and meeting other expenses in relation to children. Administration costs (excluding technical assistance advice on bureaucratic system redesign and one professional officer) have been about four per cent of total costs.

The contrast with most Mozambican service delivery is stark. There is a simple, clear-cut set of procedures with stages and a workable delivery system as well as a reasonable and workable means of determining eligibility promptly, even if it is by proxy. The strategic frame was designed by a macro-economist and a doctor; the details by a bureaucratic systems specialist and a professional social worker (in each pair one an expatriate and one a Mozambican). The staff, one to four administrators/bookkeepers in each of a dozen cities plus the referring nurses, were trained by the central director (then associate director) on field visits; the local government certifiers were informed in a simple circular and by brief staff visits.

The only comparable delivery systems – and they do not require pre-identification of users – are primary healthcare and rural and peri-urban water supply. Each has a functioning system and rulebook and has used small clusters of Mozambicans, and foreign advisers from health, water and administration fields to update and streamline them. Each has benefited from a political climate which clearly prioritizes universal access to basic services. However, primary education has the same favourable political climate but no bureaucratic system or procedures and is a disaster area even by Mozambican standards.

The link to law and order in the Tanzanian case is more evident, but again there is a more complex institutional structure than the citation itself reveals. Tanzania is relatively under-policed – less than one per thousand persons concentrated in urban areas though each district town and most other small towns have police posts. The service is further limited because for a decade and a half, fiscal constraints have limited mobility (vehicles, spares, petrol), communications and equipment.

Grossly inadequate pay – only partly offset by quarters and meals – has led to what can be termed privatized fees or petty corruption, for example vehicles are charged 'fees' (usually of $1 to $5) to avoid being taken to a station and charged with a violation. However, the force on the whole is honest and professional in investigating major crimes and, by global standards, it is relatively user-friendly.

In an attempt to broaden coverage the *sungu sungu* have been evolved from local militias (created in response to border threats, in the case of the Kagera Region from Amin's Uganda) themselves loosely descended from traditional age groups which had specific duties. These groups have received some training, limited equipment and a less than optimally specified delegation of local law and order responsibilities. In many rural areas, including Ngara and Karagwe, they function well as do ten house cells (initially a Party group but in rural areas seen as governmental) and village para-judicial dispute resolution bodies. These are necessary because magistrates (and lawyers) are even scarcer than police and – rightly or wrongly – the magistracy has a far poorer reputation for competence and probity than the police.

When Rwanda exploded following the 1994 assassination of its President and – beginning 14 hours later – its Prime Minister and cabinet majority, followed by descent into genocide led by elements in the rump of the cabinet, the army and the militia, causing the invading Rwanda Patriotic Front to resume its conquest, the Tanzanian border area was at grave risk. The experience of raids in both directions across Burundi/Rwanda and Zaire/Rwanda borders demonstrates that neither border villages, District and Regional authorities, nor the central government were wrong to believe they faced a major security crisis.

Troops initially numbering 5,000 were rapidly, and with publicity, sent to the border and were then quartered out of sight. Police were reinforced in the two most affected Districts from about 50 to more than 500 with colonels, not lieutenants, in command. Two retired Brigadiers became District Commissioners to ensure liaison between security and local governance. Local governance was otherwise unchanged; martial law was never considered let alone imposed. No cross-border incursions took place in the face of this show of force.

The police and *sungu sungu* have focused on security in respect to Rwanda refugees. This is crucial to residents in border and near border villages who bore the brunt when the initial waves rolled in. Now both camps and transit points near the border have regular police who almost completely prevent spill-out crime and police the camps by day as well as ensuring that the continuing refugee flow no longer generates insecurity. Again, the show of force has worked – refugee violence against each other has been fearsome (at least in Tanzanian terms), but neither Tanzanians nor expatriates are attacked. While nobody would assert that there are no arms in the camps, no firearms are visible, and – in contrast to Zaire and the Central African Republic – there is no drilling of irredentists for reinvasion.

A parallel case – from the domestic social sector acting with village governance – arises on the capacity and bureaucracy side. Two of the most serious disasters inflicted on border and transit villages were the premature filling of their public pit latrines (crucial in rocky hillside country) and the literal consumption in a few days of their whole maize crop while still green. As maize is secondary to plantains and these were in season, no immediate food crisis resulted, but there was no seed for late 1994 planting.

In many villages the most effective response has been by churches (domestic social sector) at congregational, diocesan and national levels. For example, the development unit of the Anglican Diocese of Kagera has systematically raised funds to help villagers pay for pit digging labour, pole foundations and wood superstructures for latrines (the previous wood having being used for refugee cooking fires). In addition, the Canon responsible (a senior police and large enterprise security officer before ordination) systematically collected data on seed needs of ten villages via Village Executive Officers. The seed was then procured domestically and donated by the Christian Council of Tanzania. The Diocese delivered; the VEOs placed the seed in reasonably secure store rooms and then handed out ten kilos to the senior woman in each household on a queue and roster check-off system. (The Canon has monitored the operation but the VEOs appear quite used to that form of orderly delivery.) Again, common sense decided who in the household should receive it: women plant and grow household grain and then store and prepare it.

This system may be bureaucratic and formal but, in the eyes of the women happily lugging off their ten kilos of seed or chatting in the queue assured they would reach its head and that seed would be there, it is not considered delaying or decapacitating.

TOWARDS FUNCTIONAL, USER-FRIENDLY BUREAUCRACY? PROBLEMATICS

To argue that well-written standing orders and procedural guidelines would by themselves revolutionize capacity of public services in sub-Saharan Africa is inaccurate. They are facilitative not sufficient.

Seven problems interlock:
• most key public service cadres (from nurses and primary school teachers, water technicians and constables through tax inspectors and magistrates to accountants and engineers) are under-staffed relative to targeted delivery levels much less to the reasonable medium-term goals set;
• many post-holders have not been adequately trained (two-thirds of Mozambican primary school teachers are not qualified) and there is insufficient, or no, refresher or retraining on offer, which is required by at least half of all Tanzanian primary level teachers and health workers, in their own assessment;
• other cadres – petty administrators, cleaners and messengers, clerks, domestic service employees, drivers and secretaries – are seriously over-staffed with most 'surplus' personnel not obvious candidates for retraining to fill vacancies;
• wages are so low that absenteeism, refusal to spend out-of-hours time on retraining, self-designed and pocketed user fees and misuse or misacquisition of job facilities and materials are inevitable and uncontrollable because the failings occur at almost all levels so few are in any position to exert discipline;
• key complementary inputs, from bicycle spares and petrol through pump spares and desks to functioning telephone systems and decent condition buildings, are inadequate both in relation to intended delivery level and to actual numbers of key cadres in post;
• high and middle level personnel time is wasted because lack of guidelines results in referral up of decisions on actions which could and should be done by basic level staff;
• weak management of funds and physical resources related to unclear or unknown procedures wastes both.

Only in respect to the last two can bureaucratic recreation or reform make a major contribution, albeit that it could reduce the present scarcity of senior personnel time by improving backup and reducing time spent on needless referrals or correction of accounting and stock management errors. In the context of co-ordinated public service reform this can be of major importance – to ignore what is often 25 per cent and sometimes 50 per cent of the problem (as many civil service reform exercises appear to do) is hardly efficient in respect to local level service delivery.

However, new guidelines take time to learn and make unofficial acquisition and use of public goods more difficult. Therefore, while better bureaucratic structures, as illustrated in Mozambique by the supplement programme, can achieve selective breakthroughs and, as illustrated by the health and water services in Mozambique and Kagera region in Tanzania, can help to hold together institutions which on personnel and resource availability levels might be expected to collapse, their ability to yield large sustainable, across-the-board gains depends on better paid, better trained personnel and more adequate supplies of complementary goods. These improved structures can reduce the additional financial, personnel and physical allocations, but cannot be a substitute for larger allocations.

African governments could use resources more efficiently (partly a bureaucratic and partly a system design issue) and could reallocate to some extent; but in most cases these measures need to be taken in the context of greater resources in all areas. To argue that preventive and primary medicine do not receive large enough allocations relative to full service hospitals may not mean that the latter can be cut if, as in Mozambique, one such hospital designed to serve 100,000 to 150,000 now seeks with few additional resources to serve 1,400,000 and a city of 250,000 which has, until completion of an ongoing project, no hospital at all.

LAW AND ORDER – WHAT BASIC PROBLEMS?

Just as the weight of corruption proper in public service capacity constraints varies widely from country to country and sub-region to sub-region (with West Africa 'worse' than eastern and southern) so too do the different components of the law and order problem.

If the police and lower courts are perceived to be tools of oppression clearly they are part of the problem. Equally clearly the problem is unlikely to be answered without a sweeping, macro political change. While a majority government is not a sufficient condition for a user-friendly, community-backed police force capable of increasing order and reducing crime – as illustrated by Namibia and South Africa – it is a precondition.

Corruption is often a greater problem at the magisterial than the police level, partly because user fees on vehicle operations are less corrupting than user fees on court case outcomes. The problems of public service numbers, training and complementary resource and apparent inadequacy or ignorance of procedures arise at both magisterial and police levels.

Perceived user-friendliness varies for police, in ways which do not appear closely correlated to numbers or pay and only moderately more so to complementary resources (especially mobility). For example, Ghana's force is perceived as better on these counts than Nigeria's, and Tanzania's as better than Kenya's. There are macro political elements – poor Tanzanians are much more likely than poor Kenyans to view police favourably partly because the Tanzanian Force is much less politicized in the sense of riot control and 'non-approved' person surveillance; it is also less inclined to resort to violence because both public and politicians expect it to be a civil police force in both senses of civil.

Formal courts in sub-Saharan Africa are not user-friendly for the woman in the field or the man in the street. Their procedures are opaque and access to them is complicated and expensive, at least from the perspective of the ordinary person. (Hardly a problem unique to Africa.) 'Traditional' courts and para-judicial or para-conflict resolution bodies are sometimes user-friendly and accessible and sometimes very much the reverse, usually depending on local as well as national political power configurations. Those seen to be predictable, fair and user-friendly do reduce the overload of magistrates by providing a preferred alternative for minor or potentially criminal cases and most civil incidents.

Higher courts and ombudspersons are light years (or education years), many miles (literally) and a cultural *Weltanschauung* removed from ordinary people. (Again, hardly unique to sub-Saharan Africa.) They may be respected, but are not understood nor widely seen as an accessible resource. It is unclear whether more public service lawyers and more opportunities for class actions and for justiciability of constitutional principles would alter this pattern of perspectives, and if so, how widely and how fast. The future experience of Namibian and South African should be illuminating in this respect, albeit the degree of urbanization and education probably render South Africa a non-generalizable case.

Defects in laws are often serious but at grassroots level more often the immediate problem is non-operationality of laws or, in the case of 'traditional' laws, considerable uncertainty about what they are, especially at provincial and national levels. This is not a reason not to prioritize law reform but a warning that such a process needs to involve the following:

• to ask ordinary people (the woman in the Ngara kibanja analogue to the 'man on the Clapham omnibus') what they believe the substance of laws and of procedures should be; this procedure is rare in urban and virtually unknown in rural Africa (with Botswana's integration of 'traditional' and 'court' law a partial exception);

- to consider giving priority to para-judicial dispute resolution and minor offence resolution systems (such as elders' councils – but including women which is frequently not traditional);
- to examine how wide is the gap between the statute book and what actually happens and how this gap can be narrowed;
- to review training and retraining of magistrates and of police (basic prosecutorial service) and of ways of achieving effective access to courts (especially lower courts) as well as the potential for class actions and quasi-justiciable links between the provision of constitutional rights and basic goals and state policy;
- to treat standing orders and similar government procedural regulations seriously as a branch of administrative law subject to some type of review (possibly by an ombudsperson and linked to class actions and/or by direct reporting to a parliamentary committee).

There is no reason why such an exercise could not be conducted over a three year period in most sub-Saharan Africa economies in which the rule of law is now operational to a significant degree. However, there is good reason not to hold up the improving operation of the present systems – existing laws and existing magisterial level courts – while awaiting its report.

A CHECKLIST OF ACTIONS

For reasons cited in the last two sections, bureaucratic and law and order reforms can be more effective if they form part of a broader package. From the perspective of user-friendliness it is also desirable that they be conducted after a review of user perceptions of delivery limitations and of the effectiveness and acceptability of law and order.

In respect to capacity, action is needed on five fronts: identification of priority functions; immediate and five and ten year target levels of deliveries; sufficient and trained personnel and complementary resources to meet targets; efficiency pay levels for basic service provision cadres combined with effective attendance and retraining regulations and general and function specific standing orders/procedural guidelines to improve the efficiency and predictability of service delivery.

The initial steps of such an exercise can in cases of weak but functioning systems, such as Ghana, Tanzania, Mozambique, Ethiopia, be carried out in 15 to 18 months as the first stage of a longer process. This can then go into more detail and depth, as well as look at secondary problems, once a forward momentum has been attained. To take three to five years to map a 20-year course of action following on from five to seven years of rather random individual actions outside any strategic frame – only a slight caricature of the mid-1980s to mid-1990s experience of Ghana and of Tanzania – is grossly inefficient as can be seen only too clearly in retrospect.

The remuneration scale, for example, needs to begin at or near two-thirds the absolute poverty line for a household and have a ceiling of ten times this, in other words $50 to $500 a month in many sub-Saharan African countries. Fringe benefits, other than those related to housing or to transport to and from work, need to be consolidated and incorporated into that pay level. (Housing and transport to work benefits require the resolution of specific interim problems requiring more time to overcome.) Related to this could be:

• agreed community contributions in cash or goods and services paid to local level operating units and used at that level either as part of the basic remuneration package or as an incentive fund to supplement pay and complementary resources;

• 'buying out' *de facto* privatized user fees within the community contribution approach;

• tying new remuneration scales to effective attendance and, within a limited time-scale, satisfactory completion of training or retraining courses.

This approach has rather stronger incentive elements than are immediately apparent. Agreed community and user contributions and, *a fortiori*, actual collections will depend on user perceptions of quantity and quality of service delivery and of the user-friendliness of personnel. Keeping these revenue sources at local unit level – not remitting to the centre – will create *de facto* accountability to users and incentives for staff to perform.

The bureaucratic system rehabilitation/recreation actions can be most effective in the context of a broader reform package of the type partially sketched. Two new elements to be built in could be user consultation before decisions on and participation in service delivery provisions (as part of the annual budgetary process defined) and operation of regular, simple monitoring of actual versus target quantity of deliveries and of user perceptions as to quality. In both cases the initial goals would be simplicity and functionality, not long-term optimality.

The general public service reform points apply *pari passu* to law and order. However, as with other functional areas, additional service specific issues arise.

One is that the user perception side is better carried out by bodies independent of, but having credibility with, the police and magistracy. Unless either the present system works moderately well, or is perceived as well-intentioned but ineffective primarily because of inadequate resources, a police and magistracy run review of user perceptions is likely to produce results inversely correlated to the severity of the underlying problems. Identifying such review bases is a contextual issue: village and neighbourhood governance, elected local councils, domestic social sector bodies (usually churches and mosques) and – in respect to gender issues in particular – women's groups, are all potentially viable in some contexts and less than promising in others.

The need to 'buy out' privatized user fees is especially great in the law and order sector. The division between small charges based on ability to pay by health or education workers and corruption proper is less cloudy and the results less harmful than for police or *a fortiori* magistrates – or tax collectors in the bureaucracy proper. The potential for community support in food, building materials and labour (including assisting spouses in self-provision of agricultural activities as well as building maintenance and cleaning) and cash as part of an accounted budgetary process is no less great for law and order than for other sectors – perhaps greater given more general provision of housing and rations or messes.

As noted earlier, para-professional and para-community auxiliary law and order provision and dispute resolution procedures can increase actual delivery of the facilitating and sustaining functions of law and order. This is in one sense resource mobilization and service reallocation in the context of extreme central budget resource scarcity (and consequential paucity of personnel and mobility). However, a broader justification can be made on user-friendliness and community involvement grounds: regular police and courts are never ideal for settling quarrels not resulting in serious injury, genuinely petty theft and civil law disagreements which are complex, important to the parties but financially trivial. The inherent problems are devising user-intelligible forms, ensuring rough congruence of outcomes in similar cases and avoiding abuse.

A framework linking law and order provided by the formal sector to that provided by communities is required. Even in Tanzania anecdotal evidence suggests some *sungu sungu* units and ten house cell dispute resolution bodies operate as unaccountable arms of certain political office-holders, administrators or 'big men'. If this channel between formal and community law and order was in place then this link could be monitored, achieving accountability.

Mobility is a problem for all service delivery – and not only in rural areas. However, it is especially crucial in respect to law and order. Delayed delivery in most services is manageable, at least where it is within a week or fortnight, but in respect to policing it is gravely prejudicial to providing prevention, cure and deterrence at micro level and more generally. At one extreme a teacher at his school with basic supplies such as books and chalk delivered within a fortnight of target dates can carry out up to 95 per cent of the service he intended to deliver, whereas a rural police constable equally isolated and late supplied could be reduced to only performing five per cent of the service he intended to deliver. It is no accident that the districts of Ngara and Karagwe now have the most mobile police forces in Tanzania – priority to policing there has included priority access to vehicles, spares and fuel even if not generally to the mobile telephone systems omnipresent among foreign official and NGO vehicles and operating bases.

The fiscal backdrop to both bureaucratic and law and order improvement is beyond the scope of this paper. However, two observations may be appropriate.

To yield major results, procedural reforms need more resources if they are to be processed. Savings from better use of existing flows within functions and reallocations among functions will in most cases be inadequate (Mauritius and Botswana are exceptions as perhaps are Namibia, South Africa and Cape Verde).

There is no inherent reason that more basic reallocations and additional mobilization be unattainable. Most, but not all, technical assistance replicates or replaces domestic personnel and institutions debilitated by resource constraints and/or weak procedures. If the latter were addressed, a shift of up to half of all technical assistance (up to 20 per cent of bilateral aid in much of sub-Saharan Africa where 40 per cent technical assistance to total aid ratios are not uncommon) would become possible and logical on both capacitation and economic efficiency criteria. Another reason why this need not be unattainable is the relaxation of the pre-1980 canon that aid should go only to physical capital creation projects and an increased acceptance that technical assistance should be extended more generally to include agreed 'efficiency pay scales' (not selective donor payments to individuals) as it already has been to maintenance, key complementary resources (such as pharmaceuticals and textbooks), training and mobility. The rising proportion of programme assistance – especially import and fiscal support – means that few technical barriers to such a shift exist. The fungibility (re-deploying generally usable resources to priority uses) and quasi-market (incremental benefit/cost ratios of alternative uses) arguments for such relaxation are very strong – the main barriers appear to be psychological and inertial. At point of delivery levels, communities demonstrably can and will participate in paying, if payments relate to actual deliveries in a reasonably transparent and predictable way and are at levels sustainable from actual community cash, kind and labour resources. User fees set by and paid to the centre usually fail both tests. Cash is not necessarily the optimal sole resource nor the most available one to users. Agreed community resource inputs would provide incentives for the service providers to deliver.

These notes are not by themselves a plan for overcoming or loosening real resource constraints. They are reasons to perceive such a strategy as attainable and as having structural as well as marginal potential. The resource which will unlock the exercise's first steps of action needs to be part of the package including bureaucratic and law and order strengthening and reform, on which this paper centres.

'In conclusion' returns to 'in the beginning'. To the woman in the field and the man on the street good governance centres on desired basic service delivery and a peaceful context in which to carry on life and livelihood. Good governance – including participation, elections, the rule of law – is largely (not entirely) perceived in and judged by these tests. 'Bureaucracy' and 'law and order' have a great deal to be said for them as key contributory means to those ends, but in order to achieve that potential they need to be viewed from the perspective of the micro user as well as from that of the macro philosopher or administrator and political leader.

COMMENT

Ama Annan

Professor Green's paper attempts an analysis of the latest phase in the question asked since Roman times (and probably before), 'What to do about Africa?' Good governance is a concept that has been on the lips of donors, bureaucrats and diplomats since it was announced as a solution by the then Foreign Minister of Britain, Douglas Hurd. Once again those who know best wag a finger at the direction of African leaders, and this time the admonishment is to do better at democracy and human rights and to follow the advice of the World Bank and International Monetary Fund. This is absolutely in keeping with African post-colonial history which has been a string of instructions from the ex-colonialists to their erstwhile subjects.

This is all well and good – it looks great on paper and sounds simple enough to follow. However, as Professor Green points out early on, 'the test is whether it delivers something relevant to her (their; being Africans) needs as perceived by her (them)'. As Africans are so seldom consulted as to what is for their own good, the chances of this happening are remote. And, Professor Green himself misses out the vital matter of power relationships. Both power between Africa and the larger international world, and the balance of power between African rulers and their constituencies.

While all ideologies require an intellectual underpinning which Professor Green so fully explains in the case of good governance, in Africa these ideologies would be more credible if they were more consistently applied, and with less blatant self-interest on the part of those imparting pearls of administrative and political wisdom.

Further, the instructions from north to south would have even more credibility if they were not so irrelevant to the vast majority of the populations of African countries. Good governance has the ring of yet another set of rhetorical rules to wash over Africa.

There have been many other good ideas dreamed up elsewhere to be enacted in Africa. In spite of the increase in the hegemony of the World Bank and related agencies, the impact of the end of the cold war, the metamorphosis of generals to politicians, living standards for the vast majority of Africans continue to fall. The five poorest countries in the world, according to the United Nations, are all African. So the continent gets poorer and is reduced to providing raw materials for rich nations, while being hampered by the hangover of the last generation's good idea: debt. And then came good governance, forgive my weariness.

The concept of good governance is addressed to the handful of Africans who are engaged in the modern practice of running a nation state. Where communications are so weak some Africans do not even know who their leaders are. In Cabo Delgado, Mozambique, I came across villagers who did not know who President Chissano was, he had been in power for three years. Mozambique is an extreme example, but the principal holds true, that many Africans know little and care less about central government. Their only contact with it is associated with the humbug of taxes and the failure of services. Sadly, Professor Green's Mozambique example is a rare case of international co-operation having the desired effect. The theory of good governance has an even more hollow ring than other waves of rhetoric that wash over African heads. It could be taken more seriously and even be a cause for optimism if it were more evenly applied.

Professor Green has in his two examples pointed out a truism that is very often ignored. Good governance if it is to work at all, will work best if it serves the needs of those who have to live with it. Identifying and acting on those needs is often a problem for the simple reason that Africans are not for the most part important enough to consult.

There are basically three ways that the international community responds to Africa. On the level of trade the relationship is increasingly extractive. A good bureaucracy assists in this process. Diplomatically Africa counts for nothing, except maybe in the Commonwealth. Where Africa really takes centre stage is when there is an emergency; a famine, war or genocide is what catches international attention, and this can be responded to by gifts from the well-fed to the worthy poor and dying. In this scenario Africa is so powerless it does not even have the ability to say whether good governance is what it wants. This is not to say that there need to be some improvement in the African condition, and a breakaway from the monopoly of power held by a handful of the population, but this should at least be a semblance of genuine feeling, and not the self-interest of the donors dressed up as what's best for Africa (once again). If governments are not seen to be enacting elements of this idea, they don't get the resources they need to offer even the most basic services. There is nothing wrong with this abject bullying of Africa by the international community. It is called conditionality and is very fashionable.

However, although there is great donor agreement that good governance is a good thing for Africa, this idea is not consistently applied. Where strategic interests are affected, donors turn a blind eye to some of the less perfect elements of good governance as interpreted by governments with something to offer them. There is a blatant lack of consistency in donors' reactions to, say, elections. The Kenyan elections were damned by international observers and

President Moi closed the government when the opposition went against him. There is a *de facto* one-party state in Zimbabwe, and an interesting no-party system in another donor favourite, Uganda. Even President Mobutu of Zaire has found an international niche for himself since the arrival of the Hutu refugees, and his skilful manipulation of the balance of power in his sub-region. Ghana, the blue-eyed boy of the international community, managed a 'free and fair' election even though the opposition withdrew.

When governments realise what they can get away with under the system of 'good governance' it seems likely that they will realise they are playing yet another game of cat and mouse with the international community. Governments will go as far as they can to protect their hard-won internal power bases on the one hand, whilst juggling the meddlesome needs of the international community on the other.

In my travels as a journalist and aid worker, I am constantly amazed at the double speak between what beneficiaries are willing to tell one of 'their own', and the smiling face presented to a man or woman with the money. Talking to a recipient of European aid in Malawi, I was told 'Ah, you know these white people, they come with all these questions and papers, we just answer them to get the money, then we do what we need to for ourselves'. This was not a declaration of corruption, in fact the project was extremely successful, but just not run in the politically correct northern European way that was expected of the beneficiaries. Aid work can be seen as political interplay between 'the haves and the have not', writ small. Of course, donors must know, mustn't they, of the many Africans who harbour a deep cynicism to outside prescriptions to their problems, even though so many Africans collaborate with outside agencies to make a living or sometimes even out of conviction, until the time comes round for their ideas to be discredited.

The Tanzanian example seemed to illustrate the point, that when it is African interests it is possible to find solutions to problems using an unremarkable mixture of common sense and disciplines learned from outside just like everywhere else. In fact, the Tanzanian response to the Rwandan tragedy demonstrates many important points, but one that stands out is that the Tanzanians took in the Rwandans at the height of the crisis, whilst the international community has yet to bring any but the most superficial semblance of good governance to the situation. Underpinning the tenet of good governance must be justice, but justice only applies, so it would seem, to those who harbour something the donors want, be it minerals or some other more nebulous commodity, the rest are free to do their wicked best with no bothersome imported ideals to live up to. As a British diplomat said to me in the aftermath of the genocide 'Rwanda doesn't matter, we have no interests here'. Exactly.

4 Civil society, good government and neo-liberal reforms

Nancy Bermeo

Many scholars concerned with the quality of democracy have associated good government with strong civil societies. Indeed, civil society has been endowed with nearly heroic qualities of late. Although initially cast as the helpless victim of the oppressive authoritarian state, civil society eventually became the noble "celebrity" of the "third wave" democratic transitions.[1] Today civil society has become, for many, the key to democratic deepening and consolidation. As Francisco Weffort said of his native Brazil, "We need to build civil society because we want freedom."[2]

This essay is about the interaction between civil society, economic liberalization and that set of "freedoms" embodied in the term liberal democracy. After setting out a working definition of the term civil society, I will look at why and how civil society has come to play such a positive role in our current thinking about democracy. I will then illustrate that civil society was cast in a much more ambiguous role in our recent past and that the legacies of this more negative vision remain highly relevant to the politics of neo-liberal economic reform. I will then conclude by discussing how economic liberalizers might reconcile these two visions and maximize the likelihood that civil society will play a positive role in the construction of good government in the future.

CAUSE FOR CELEBRATION

Civil society is a shorthand term for the collection of intermediary groups and voluntary organizations that occupy the space between the family and the state. The celebration of civil society has deep roots in western political theory, but the intensity of our interest in civil society today derives from two sources. The first is the generalized disenchantment with "the state" as an agent of social and material change. As Jean Cohen and Andrew Arato properly point out, theorists from all over the world have turned to civil society in a 'search for a post-statist politics'.[3] With the state discredited, it makes sense that we would look to its 'opposite' with renewed interest.

---

1   Alfred Stepan, 1988, p5.
2   Francisco Weffort, 1989, p349.
3   Jean Cohen and Andrew Arato, 1992.

A second explanation for our renewed interest comes from the revolution in communications. Television now allows us to witness the drama of democratization as it unfolds. Viewing thousands of unarmed demonstrators confronting tanks and soldiers in struggles for democracy throughout the world, we see civil society today as we have never seen it before: wholly humanized and unambiguously heroic. The positive visions of civil society so prominent in our scholarly work reflect the literal visions projected by our media.

The positive vision of civil society has many elements. Charles Taylor portrays civil society as a space which provides "the taste and habit of self-rule".[4] Edward Shils sees it as the place where citizens learn the civic manners that "make opposition less rancorous".[5] Philippe Schmitter argues that civil society provides "reservoirs of resistance to arbitrary and tyrannical action"[6]; and hosts of other scholars associate strong civil society with just and effective government. Civil society is thought to provide state élites with "clear counsel" on "authentic" rather than contrived needs,[7] It is thought to present "authorities with more aggregated, reliable and actionable information"[8] and thereby to play "a central role in resolving problems of successful governance".[9] Strong civil societies "support progress towards ... greater social and economic equality".[10] Robert Putnam goes as far as to argue that strong civil societies "expect better government" and then "get it (in part because of their own efforts)".[11]

ANOTHER VISION OF CIVIL SOCIETY

Despite the fact that a positive, even laudatory vision of civil society seems widely shared, there are reasons to be cautious about interactions between the state and civil society in the future. High praise should not lead us to high expectations because, only a short while ago, scholars cast civil society in a dramatically different role. Rather than being the saviour of democracy, in the 1960s and 1970s it was cast in the role of spoiler. The term civil society itself was not fashionable then – scholars wrote of interest groups, class associations and popular movements instead. However, the message in this older literature was clear: an overly active civil society can harm our chances for good government. Almond and Verba's vision of the "civic culture" – the culture best suited to

---

4   Charles Taylor, 1990, p115.
5   Edward Shils, 1991, p13.
6   Philippe Schmitter 1993, p24.
7   Michael Bernard, 1993, p314.
8   Schmitter, 1993, p24.
9   Joshua Cohen and Joel Rogers, 1992, p394.
10 Reuschmeyer, Stephens and Stephens, 1992, pp10-11.
11 Robert Putnam, 1993, p182.

democracy – was "a *blend* of activity and passivity".[12] Samuel Huntington's theory of praetorian society warned us that disorder was inevitable when participation expanded to those who had failed to cultivate the "art of associating together".[13] Juan Linz wrote that "those identified with specific social interests" such as the "working class", "trade unions" or "the church" were "least able to give foremost consideration to the persistence of institutions" and therefore were "extremely unlikely" to make an "unwavering commitment" to democracy *per se*.[14]

Even Guillermo O'Donnell – who wrote from a neo-Marxist perspective at the time – cast civil society in a negative role in his seminal work on the origins of bureaucratic authoritarianism. Explicitly adopting Huntington's theory of praetorianism[15] he argued that when "the consumption and power participation preferences of the popular sector are high and are articulated with continuity and important organizational support," elected politicians in dependent economies face "a barely manageable schedule of political demands".[16] Attempting to respond to the "very real" threats from the mobilized citizenry, governments tended "to adopt whatever policies best satisfied the sector that was most threatening at a given time". This responsiveness only made things worse because "zero-sum conditions meant that each such policy decision raised new threats from other powerful sectors".[18] In much of the literature of the 1960s and 1970s, strong civic organizations were not associated with 'good' government but with bad policies.

This older literature gives us the impression that civil society is most likely to play the role of spoiler in conditions of scarcity. The theme of this older literature is that politicized people confronted with scarcity don't just get mad, they go mad. They act against their own long-term interests. They threaten the interests of the social whole. They ask too much and finally put democracy itself at risk. The sequence of events depicted in figure 1 (page 80) summarizes the more negative visions appearing in scholars' earlier work.

CIVIL SOCIETY AND ECONOMIC LIBERALIZATION

Although praetorian visions of civil society are no longer in vogue, this line of reasoning is still very much alive in our contemporary work on new democracies in economic crisis. When Linz, O'Donnell, Stepan and others argue that citizens in new democracies must lower their expectations they are essentially trying to break the praetorian policy cycle at Stage 1 (see figure 1). When Williamson and

---

12 Gabriel Almond and Sidney Verba, 1963, p369; emphasis mine.
13 Samuel Huntington, 1968, p5.
14 Juan Linz, 1978, p53.
15 Guillermo O'Donnell, 1979, pp143-144 and p74.
16 ibid., p192.
17 ibid., pp143-144.

Figure 1: The Praetorian Policy Cycle

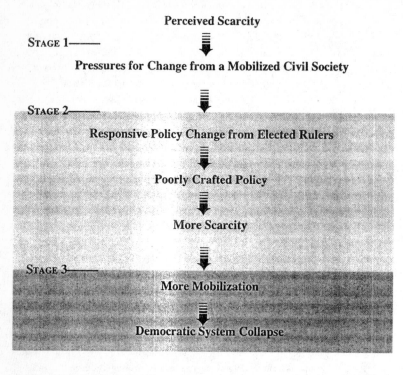

Haggard argue that the "ability to sustain viable reforms" may "depend on... mechanisms to bypass the legislature," they are trying to break the praetorian policy cycle at Stage 2.[18]

The desire to distance policymakers from civil society and to break the praetorian policy cycle is especially evident in researchundertaken on the political barriers to neo-liberal reforms. Our whole discourse regarding the need to "insulate" policymakers from "special interests" draws on the more negative vision of civil mobilization. The view that "bad policy choices and weak economic performance" are the result of "intense political pressure to use macro-economic policies to raise the incomes of lower-income groups"[19] is a tacit admission that good governance and strong interest associations may not go together at all.[20]

---

18 See the essays by Jeffrey Sachs and by Stephen Haggard and John Williamson in *The Political Economy of Policy Reform*.

19 Jeffrey Sachs, *Social Conflict and Populist Policies in Latin America*, p10.

Thus, at least two visions of civil society are alive and well today and the simultaneous tasks of democratic consolidation and economic liberalization have brought them into direct conflict. What can policymakers do to help to ensure that civil society will not play the role of spoiler in the future? How can policymakers maximize the likelihood that civil society will be the foundation of good government instead? As agencies such as the Inter-American Development Bank begin to argue, in official documents, that "the promotion of sound government and governance can be strengthened only if civil society is also strengthened",[21] the practical and pressing nature of these questions quickly becomes evident.

Fortunately, the drive for economic liberalization has coincided with the drive for the expansion of civil society for some time now, and we are thus able to extract some lessons from experience. I shall focus on three intertwined lessons which might be summarized under the following headings: Beware of strong executives; De-romanticize civil society, and Rethink equality.

BEWARE OF STRONG EXECUTIVES

The first lesson regards the use and abuse of executive power. There is an undeniable association between the successful initiation of structural adjustment programmes and the presence of strong executive authority. The authors of the 1990 World Development Report were on firm ground when they argued that "strong executives with a mandate seem best placed to pursue reform"[22], but there are indications that we are relying on executive power too heavily and too often.

The creation of what might be called an 'elevated executive' has become our primary means of blocking the praetorian policy cycle. Under an elevated executive, formal democracy remains intact but parties and legislatures no longer serve as the vital organs of the body politic. Chief executives and their teams of advisers come to elevate themselves "above politics" convinced that they have the obligation to rule above parties, trade unions and other representative institutions. They distance themselves from petitioners in an elevated safety net woven of "economic necessity" and anchored by periodic electoral mandate.

Economic liberalization requires that the state retreat from certain roles in the economy but this retreat should not be mistaken for a weakening of the state as a whole. The policy imperatives associated with structural adjustment actually encourage the strengthening of certain parts of the state because, as Hojman and

---

20 Mancur Olson has written in a similar vein in *The Rise and Decline of Nations*.

21 Inter-American Development Bank, *Relatória General de la Conferencia Sobre el Fortalecimiento de la Sociedad Civil*, pp1 and 4.

22 World Bank, 1990, p115.

others have pointed out, "it takes a strong government to take the government" out of the economy.[23] Concentrating power in the executive, avoiding legislative delays and ruling by decree are the hallmarks of an elevated executive and the quickest route to government strength.

Not surprisingly, the literature on the political economy in Latin America is replete with references to autocratic executives. In a diverse range of nations – including Argentina, Venezuela, Peru, Bolivia and Brazil – the executive proponents of liberalization programmes seem to have distanced themselves not only from interest groups but from legislatures and even from their own political parties.[24] *Decretismo* – that is, rule by executive decree – has become extremely widespread.

Decretismo exists in governments with all sorts of economic programmes but for economic liberalizers it may seem to be a particularly attractive formula for rule. Structural adjustment programmes involve a wide range of policy changes including the lifting of trade barriers, deregulation, fiscal reform, dramatic cuts in government spending and a flexible labour market. Although the sequencing and timing of these changes are the subject of much debate, their interrelationship is thought to be so strong that we often refer to them as a 'package'. José Martínez de Hoz, a former minister of finance and a long-standing proponent of adjustment in Argentina, expressed this sense of interconnectedness when he likened the components of a structural adjustment programme to the pieces of a clock. "If just one of them breaks or is poorly made, the whole program is in danger."[25] The idea that these programmes might function like clockwork if properly crafted implies that they cannot be compromised. If the margin for debate is narrow, why not use executive autonomy to ensure uncompromised craftsmanship?

First and most obviously, there is no guarantee that executive autonomy will be used for any particular sort of policy. Insulated executives might be useful for the swift implementation of liberalization programmes but they may also be

---

23 David Hojman 'The Political Economy of Recent Conversions to Market Economies in Latin America', p218.
24 For English language evidence of executive elevation in Argentina see: Scott Mainwaring 'Democracy in Brazil and the Southern Cone: Achievements and Problems' (unpublished manuscript, Kellogg Center, Notre Dame University, Notre Dame, Indiana, 1994) p36; Di Tella (1990) p97; James McGuire, *Peronism without Perón* and Marcello Cavarozzi, 'Politics: A Key for the Long Term in South America' in William Smith, Carlos Acuña and Eduardo Gamarra eds., *Latin American Political Economy in the Age of Neoliberal Reform.*, (New Brunswick: Transaction Publishers, 1994). For Bolivia see: James Malloy, (Summer 1991) and Eduardo Gamarra, 'Crafting Political Support for Stabilization: Political Pacts and the New Economic Policy in Bolivia' in William Smith et. al. eds., *Democracy, Markets and Structural Reform in Latin America*, and James Malloy and Eduardo Gamarra, *Revolution and Reaction*, (New Brunswick: Transaction Publishers, 1988). For Peru see: Manuel Pastor and Carol Wise, 1992, and Maxwell Cameron, 1994. For Brazil under Collor see: Kurt Weyland, 1993, and Ben Ross Schneider 'Brazil Under Collor: Anatomy of a Crisis', World Policy Journal, Vol. VIII/2 (Spring 1991). For the Andean Region as a whole, see: Catherine Conaghan and James Malloy, 1995.
25 José Martínez de Hoz, *Quince Años Después*, (Buenos Aires: Emecé Editores, 1991) p243.

used for their swift repeal. Peruvian President Alan García's decidedly non-liberal economic policies were crafted in a highly insulated environment and they fell short of anyone's vision of good government.

A second problem with this form of rule emerges from the fact that there is no guarantee that executives who seek autonomy from legislatures will not seek autonomy from their judiciaries as well, or from the rule of law in general. The sad coincidence of executive strength and rampant corruption under Fernando Collor in Brazil and Carlos Menem in Argentina are a cause for serious concern. Insulation keeps out good forces as well as bad.

The third and most serious problem with having the elevated executive as a form of rule emerges if we analyse how a strong executive affects the role of legislatures and political parties. If executive strength is gained at the expense of a weakened legislature, that is, if legislatures no longer function as representative institutions, the incentives to join or even vote for political parties decrease dramatically. This matters greatly for state-civil society relations because parties are thought to be the only means available for combating praetorianism. As Samuel Huntington wrote in 1968, strong parties are "the buckle that binds one social force to another". They create regularized procedures for leadership succession, "for the assimilation of new groups" and thus for "the basis for stability and orderly change".[26]

We still today rely on political parties as the single political institution capable of binding civil society's many associations together. After extensive historical and cross-national research, Seymour Lipset recently concluded that political parties "must be viewed as the most important mediating institution between the citizenry and the state" and that "having at least two parties with an uncritically loyal mass base comes close to being a necessary condition" for stable and democratic government.[27] Fernando Henrique Cardoso (who has dealt with the problems of policymaking as both a theorist and a practitioner) cautions us that civil society cannot "consolidate liberalism" alone and that "the Latin American democratic spirit cannot do without parties."[28]

Creating and maintaining strong parties is far more difficult than creating organizations in civil society. As Cardoso wisely reminds us, the primary relations between base and leadership in social movements and civic organizations are often much stronger than comparable links within political parties. "Parties can seem too weak to express the whole."[29] Yet, being unable to express "the whole" means being unable to bond the disparate groups of civil society together.

---

26 Huntington, 1968, p405.
27 Lipset, 1993, pp34-35.
28 Cardoso, 1986, p37.
29 ibid.,p37.

Creating strong political parties is difficult under any circumstances but under current conditions – as legislatures are weakened by strong executives – the challenge is especially great. Citizens will not join or become active in parties unless they are likely to gain something from doing so. If people come to believe that political parties have little or no effect on the allocation of key resources, one of the prime incentives for structured participation declines. Psychological rewards will remain, but even these may be adversely affected by the perception that party petitions are merely symbolic.

DE-ROMANTICIZING CIVIL SOCIETY

The need to think critically and early about how praetorianism might be avoided is especially important as policymakers take an increased interest in civil society's development. Those who seek the rapid expansion of civil society must beware of romanticizing a phenomenon that is much more multi-faceted and problematic than our current social science literature might lead us to believe. Two powerful but mythical conceptions are particularly dangerous. The first might be called the myth of singularity; the second might be called the myth of density.

The fact that civil society is so often defined as the opposite of the state means that it is usually discussed in the singular. Yet, neither the state, nor civil society are unitary actors. We have to unpack the concept of civil society. We have to recognize that it is a composite of often competing groups and that the success of economic liberalization will depend as much on how these groups interact with one another as upon how they interact with the state.

Those who design economic liberalization programmes are aware that their policies will provoke resistance from the groups that pay the (hopefully) short-term costs that liberalization inevitably incurs. Policymakers have given thought to the relationship between these groups and the state. The whole argument for executive insulation is an outcome of this awareness, but it is time to turn our attention to how elements of civil society will interact *with one another* under the conditions of scarcity that programmes of liberalization inevitably produce.

The violence and disorder that work against both good government and the continuity of economic reform programmes are often brought about by interactions within civil society. The riots that followed Alfonsin's attempt to halt hyperinflation in Argentina began as a struggle between consumers and shopkeepers. The riots that followed Andres Perez's attempt at structural adjustment in Venezuela began as a conflict between bus drivers and students. These disturbances soon attracted participants of all sorts but their catalysts were struggles within civil society itself. So long as policymakers fall prey to the myth of singularity they will not be able to anticipate or avoid civic conflict. Insulating executives (and policymakers in general) may temporarily deflect conflict but it will not end it. Displaced conflict – conflict which manifests itself outside of legislatures and structured political arenas – is very likely to end in the streets.

As burdensome as legislative conflict might be, civic conflict can be even more costly. The costs in terms of lives and property are obvious and the ones we should take most seriously, but civic conflict also exerts high costs on economic liberalization programmes themselves. Even the most stalwart liberalization teams seem to make costly concessions when threatened with real or promised violence.[30]

Whether scarcity causes actors in civil society to turn against one another or the state, there is a strong probability that the liberalizing government will pick up the costs of restoring order. Since government insulation is never complete, we get the worst of two scenarios; an overly muscular executive who weakens legislatures and political parties, and a government that eventually gives in to political pressures of the most destructive and least predictable kind.

Creating an environment with a greater number of civic associations is not the solution for the problem detailed above. Policymakers should not be misled by the myth of density – that is, the belief that increasing the density of civil society increases the likelihood of either good civic behaviour or good government.

A great many social scientists are under the impression that if voluntary associations are sufficiently numerous, individuals will elevate and improve their political vision and moderate their political behaviour. Unfortunately, there is little evidence to suggest that density actually leads to moderation or to good government. In fact, it is not difficult to make the counter-argument. Neither Weimar Germany, pre-fascist Italy nor Spain's Second Republic suffered from a bleak associational landscape. The problem with associational life in these regimes was not one of structure but one of content. Civil society was densely organized but many of its strongest associational units were anti-democratic themselves.

Policymakers can assist in creating an environment with a greater number of civic associations. They can certainly guarantee freedom of association but they cannot guarantee that associations will work in the interest of freedom, or indeed in the interests of anything in particular. We are wrong to prevent civil society's

---

30 Miguel Boyer and Felipe González had to backtrack on a massive pension reform plan when they met with resistance in Spain in the mid-1980s. Carlos Andrés Pérez changed his whole cabinet, reinstated price controls and reinstituted supports for small businesses after violence and a *coup* attempt in February 1992. Domingo Cavallo and Carlos Menem were forced into raising wages and implementing massive public job creation schemes because of violence in the north of Argentina in 1993 and 1994. The Bolivian government reversed its decision to privatize the state-owned mining company COMIBOL after a chaotic 18-day strike in Spring 1990.

many groups from gaining access to representative institutions but we are equally wrong to romanticize civil society itself. The existence of associational life does not in itself prevent conflict or lead to good government. Associations of consumers, merchants, students and drivers all existed long before the outbreak of the riots mentioned above. The problem was not the absence of associational life but the fact that the associations that existed did not play the roles that liberalizing policymakers found desirable.

Until policymakers debunk the myths of civil society – recognizing its plural and highly conflictual nature – they will be unable to create the political arenas in which competing interests can interact and formulate mutually acceptable responses to the problems of scarcity that liberalization will inevitably create.

RETHINKING EQUALITY AND THE WELL-BEHAVED CIVIL SOCIETY

If policymakers are to assist in creating an environment with a greater number of civic associations they must grapple with the question of how the more desirable civil society emerges and maintains itself. Despite an enormous literature on the origins of democracy, the origins of the well-behaved civil society remain surprisingly obscure. What we know, or think we know, can easily be questioned. Many believe, for example, that a denser, stronger and more democratic civil society will be a 'by-product' of capitalist development. Two types of argument sustain this belief. An explicitly materialist argument holds that capitalist development will provide the urbanization, communication, literacy and labour structure that facilitates voluntary association.[31] A slightly different, more institutional argument holds that a market economy with diversity of ownership will create sufficient pluralism "to permit the autonomous group activity" that a democratic civil society requires.[32] This second argument lies at the root of the widely accepted notion that market-orientated policies will aid the emergence of a democratic society in the former communist regimes.

Unfortunately, the association between capitalist development and pro-democratic civil societies is not nearly as robust as we might hope. The democracies that fell to bureaucratic authoritarianism in South America in the 1960s and 1970s were among the most urbanized, literate and "middle class" states on the continent, yet large sectors of civil society welcomed the initial installation of military rule. Similarly, the democracies that fell to fascism in Europe in the interwar years were not easily distinguishable – in terms of urbanization, literacy and class structure – from those that did not, yet large

---

31 Reuschmeyer, Stephens and Stephens, 1992, p6.
32 Juan Linz and Alfred Stepan Chapter 3: 'Democratic Transitions and Consolidation in Southern Europe (With Reflections on Latin America and Eastern Europe)', n.d., p9.

sectors of civil society embraced non-democratic groups anyway. The 'by-products' of capitalism may or may not be essential ingredients for the making of well-behaved civil societies but they are certainly not sufficient for the task. What else is required?

Political scientists have not addressed this question directly, but two related themes in the general literature on democratic theory provide us with the basics of a working hypothesis. The first theme relates to the connection between democracy and community. A broad range of theorists have argued that democracy depends on some sense of common identity. The concept of "We the people...", for example, is predicated on the idea that "the people" have a shared identity, shared purposes, and even a shared will.[33] In order for various individual people to conceive of themselves as singular people, they must share some sense of community. They must, despite their sometimes obvious differences, feel part of some meaningful larger collective. Without this, the compromise and patience required for the establishment and maintenance of democracy is not possible. As Edward Shils reminds us, "A democratic civil society requires civility and this means regarding other persons including one's adversaries as members of the same inclusive collectivity."[34]

If adversaries see one another exclusively as representatives of antagonistic collectivities, there is a strong likelihood that collective action will take anti-democratic forms. What produces this stabilizing sense of community? The literature on democratic theory suggests that equality should figure prominently in our response.

Tocqueville's arguments connecting democracy and civil society were developed in the context of a broader argument connecting democracy and equality. This seems to have been forgotten by some, but the text is unambiguous. Tocqueville writes:

> In the United States, nothing struck me more forcibly than the general equality of condition among the people. I readily discovered the prodigious influence that this primary fact exercises on the whole course of society... This equality of condition is the fundamental fact from which all others seem to be derived...[35]

It is not coincidental that Tocqueville finds a relatively pro-democratic civil society in a nation where equality was perceived to be relatively high. Perceptions of equality matter because they are the foundation of that minimal sense of community that a democratic civil society requires. Individuals will not feel part of the same community unless they can see themselves as equals along some

---

33 Charles Taylor, 1990, p111.
34 Edward Shils, 1991, pp12-13.
35 de Tocqueville, 1945, p3; emphasis added.

dimension that can be used to define community. If political adversaries are consistently seen as representing another community, the compromise intrinsic to democracy is impossible. Fear will dominate all political relationships and politics will become war.

How can policymakers who seek to advance both economic liberalization and good government promote that sense of equality that the more desirable face of civil society seems to require? The challenge is enormous for at lease two reasons: first, because our oldest formulas for community – nationalism and sub-nationalism – carry all sorts of dangers and are ill-suited to economic liberalization and openness anyway; second, because economic liberalization seems to be associated with dramatic increases in *inequality*, at least in the short run.

In the currently marketizing countries of Eastern Europe, for example, inequalities have been exacerbated by the growth of a highly ostentatious (often criminal) *nouveau riche*. Throughout the world, attempts to control inflation through de-indexation have often led to both a decline in real wages and a growing gap between those who live on fixed incomes and those who do not. Likewise, cuts in government spending, cuts in government employment and privatization in general lead inevitably to increases in unemployment and a widening gap between those who work and those who do not. Finally, trade liberalization inevitably drives less efficient industries into bankruptcy; it also rewards larger firms and leads to the impression that capital is becoming much more concentrated.

Governments can lessen these new inequalities through the provision of safety nets and compensatory programmes but these are costly. If carried out with enthusiasm – as they were in Spain, for example, under the PSOE (Spanish Socialist Party) – they can contribute to the deficit spending that the structural adjustment programme sought to reverse in the first place.

Room for manoeuvre is highly restricted but liberalizing policymakers who seek to strengthen pro-democratic civil society might combine compensatory programmes with other measures that strengthen non-material equality. Equal access to legal protection and to the benefits of the rule of law can greatly enhance that sense of community that the 'civil' civil society requires. Legal equality is probably less costly than social equality but it is of great (possibly paramount) importance in binding an otherwise diverse citizenry together. Historically, large sectors of civil society have sided with fascism and dictatorship only after a perceived breakdown in the rule of law. Citizens become easier to mobilize for extra-legal actions when they are convinced that the legal system serves only a sector of society or when they perceive that many of their fellow citizens live above the law.

The material scarcity that fuels the praetorian policy cycle cannot be corrected quickly but we can make faster progress at correcting the scarcity of fairness. Ensuring that all citizens are subject to and protected by the rule of law would do much to enhance the sense of community that civil society requires. It would also enhance the transparency and predictability required for investment.

CONCLUSIONS

Executive elevation and autonomy may seem to be efficient means of launching liberalization programmes. Devaluations and the freeing of prices are among several initiatives that are suited to swift and unilateral action. But the later stages of structural adjustment require a different type of policymaking environment. We can privatize by decree but we cannot attract buyers or investment by the same means. Likewise, we can decree the retraction of the state but we cannot force other societal actors to fill the voids that the state leaves behind. When voids in the provision of services and employment increase the perceived inequalities in a society and erode the norms and behaviours that were the basis of community in the past, the chances of praetorianism increase dramatically. Radical economic liberalization programmes have succeeded in ending hyperinflation in nations as diverse as Argentina and Bolivia. However, if these programmes are to fulfil their promises of growth and employment, their proponents must turn their attention towards political as well as economic reforms. Strengthening civil society is an adjustment of great value. However, without comparable adjustments in the strength of political parties, in the strength of legal systems and in the strengthening of all types of inclusive political arenas, the challenge of combining liberalization with good government will prove impossible.

REFERENCES

Almond, Gabriel and Verba, Sidney, *The Civic Culture*, (New York: Little Brown, 1963).

Banco Interamericano de Desarrollo, *Relatoria de la Conferencia Sobre el Fortalecimiento de la Sociedad Civil* (Washington DC: 1994).

Bernard, Michael, 'Civil Society and Democratic Transition in East Central Europe', Political Science Quarterly Vol. 108/2 (1993).

Cameron, Maxwell *Democracy and Authoritarianism in Peru* (New York: St. Martin's Press, 1994).

Cardoso, Fernando Henrique, 'Democracy in Latin America', Politics and Society, Vol. 15/1 (1986).

Cohen, Jean and Arato, Andrew, *Civil Society and Political Theory* (Cambridge, MA: MIT Press, 1992).

Cohen, Joshua and Rogers, Joel, 'Secondary Associations and Democratic Governance', Politics and Society Special Issue Vol. 20/4 (1992).

Conaghan, Catherine and Malloy, James, *Unsettling Statecraft* (Pittsburgh: University of Pittsburgh Press, 1995).

Di Tella, Guido and Braun, Carlos Rodriguez, eds., *Argentina, 1946-1983: The Economic Ministers Speak* (New York: St. Martin's Press, 1990).

Haggard, Stephen and Williamson, John 'The Political conditions for Economic Reform', in Williamson, John, ed., *The Political Economy of Policy Reform* (Washington DC: Institute for International Economics, 1994).

Hojman, David E., 'The Political Economy of Recent Conversions to Market Economies in Latin America', Journal of Latin American Studies Vol. 26 (Fall 1994).

Huntington, Samuel, *Political Order in Changing Societies* (New Haven: Yale University Press, 1968).

Linz, Juan, *The Breakdown of Democratic Regimes* (Baltimore: Johns Hopkins University Press, 1978).

Linz, Juan and Stepan, Alfred, 'Democratic Transitions and Consolidation in Southern Europe (With Reflections on Latin America and Eastern Europe)' (unpublished manuscript, 1993).

Lipset, Seymour Martin, 'The Social Requisites of Democracy Revisited', (unpublished presidential address, American Sociological Association, 1993).

Malloy, James, 'Democracy, Economic Crisis and the Problem of Governance: the Case of Bolivia', Studies in Comparative International Development Vol. 26/2 (Summer 1991).

McGuire, James, *Peronism Without Perón* (Palo Alto, CA: Stanford University Press, 1994).

O'Donnell, Guillermo, *Modernization and Bureaucratic Authoritarianism* (Berkeley, CA: University of California Press, 1979).

Olson, Mancur, *The Rise and Decline of Nations: Economic Growth, Stagflation, and Social Rigidities* (New Haven: Yale University Press, 1982).

Pastor, Manuel and Wise, Carol, 'Peruvian Economic Policy in the 1990s', Latin American Research Review XXVII/2 (1992).

Putnam, Robert, *Making Democracy Work* (Princeton, NJ: Princeton University Press, 1993).

Reuschmeyer, Dietrich, Stephens, Evelyne Huber, and Stephens, John D., *Capitalist Development and Democracy* (Chicago: University of Chicago Press, 1992).

Sachs, Jeffrey, 'Life in the Economic Emergency Room', in Williamson, John, ed., *The Political Economy of Policy Reform* (Washington DC: Institute for International Economics, 1994).

Sachs, Jeffrey, *Social Conflict and Populist Policies in Latin America* (San Francisco: ICS Press, 1990).

Schmitter, Philippe, 'Some Propositions About Civil Society and the Consolidation of Democracy' (unpublished manuscript, 1993).

Shils, Edward, 'The Virtues of Civil Society', Government and Opposition Vol. 26/1 (1991).

Smith, William, Acuña, Carlos, Gamarra, Eduardo, eds, *Democracy, Markets, and Structural Reform in Latin America* (New Brunswick, NJ: Transaction Publishers, 1993).

Schneider, Ben Ross, 'Brazil Under Collor: Anatomy of a Crisis', World Policy Journal Vol. 8/2 (Spring 1991).

Stepan, Alfred, *Rethinking Military Politics: Brazil and the Southern Cone* (Princeton, NJ: Princeton University Press, 1988).

Taylor, Charles, 'Modes of Civil Society' Public Culture Vol. 3/1 (Fall 1990).

Tester, Keith, *Civil Society* (New York: Routledge, 1992).

de Tocqueville, Alexis, *Democracy in America - Volume I* (New York: Vintage Books, 1945).

Weffort, Francisco, 'Why Democracy?' in Stepan, ed. *Democratizing Brazil*, (New York: Oxford University Press, 1989).

Weyland, Kurt, 'The Rise and Fall of President Collor and Its Impact on Brazilian Democracy', Journal of Inter-American Studies and World Affairs Vol. 35/1 (1993).

World Bank, *World Development Report* (Washington DC: World Bank, 1990).

COMMENT

Alberto de Capitani

The interaction between political process, civil society and economic reforms – the topic of Nancy Bermeo's paper – is a central theme of discussions on the political and economic sustainability of adjustment programmes in developing countries. When Douglass North (1993) and other representatives of the New Institutional Economics say that it is the admixture of formal rules, informal norms and the enforcement characteristics of both that determines economic performance, they allude precisely to this interaction. Similarly, the emphasis in economic development literature on the importance of participation in the design and implementation of economic reform programmes (World Bank, 1994) is another way of highlighting the role that civil society can play in improving both the quality of governance and the sustainability of economic reforms. Robert Putnam (1993) has shown that how effectively this role is played by civil society is partly a function of 'social capital', defined as the degree of trust and co-operation existing in a given society as a result of norms of reciprocity and networks of civic engagement.

The current paradigm of civil society – which has its roots in the classics of political liberalism and found eloquent expression in Alexis de Tocqueville in *Democracy in America* – celebrates intermediate groups and voluntary organizations as the cradle of democracy. Yet, as Professor Bermeo's paper reminds us, there is a darker side to it. A number of political scientists in the 1960s and the 1970s and a substantial body of contemporary economic literature have stressed the role of special interest groups in shaping or distorting collective decisions. Milton Friedman (1984) talks about the role of the 'Iron Triangle' of special interests, bureaucrats, and politicians in preserving the *status quo*. Oliver Williamson (1985) has argued that the concept of 'opportunism', defined as self-interest seeking with guile, is essential to understanding the economic institutions of capitalism. James Buchanan (1991) has referred to politics as a struggle between the 'rent-seekers' who try to secure private profits through the authority of government, and the 'constitutionalists' who seek to constrain this authority.

A de-romanticized view of civil society – which is the view Nancy Bermeo leans towards – acknowledges the risk of the 'praetorian policy cycle', essentially a vicious circle of demagogic policy decisions which worsen resource scarcity, which in turn leads to even worse policy choices, all for the sake of appeasing those groups in society who scream louder. A key concept in Professor Bermeo's paper is the idea of 'unpacking' civil society – recognizing the variety of groups which make up civil society and being aware of the complexity of interactions that this can generate. Depending on how these interactions work, democracy and economic development may flourish or society can 'get stuck' (to use Douglass North's metaphor).

Whether these interactions can be socially engineered to produce the results we want (and if so, how) is one of the challenges of development. Professor Bermeo is right in advising scepticism against such standard prescriptions as increased reliance on executive power to push reforms or the idea of trying to create more associational life in order to increase 'social capital'. As for the relationship between economic development and democratic institutions, I would not disagree that the causality links are complex and in many respects still obscure. Yet, I would point to a growing body of empirical evidence (Klitgaard, 1993) that suggests significant correlations between rule of law and economic performance. I would also refer to an economic historian of the stature of Douglass North (1993) who has asserted that "while economic growth can occur in the short run with autocratic regimes, long run economic growth entails the development of the rule of law and the protection of civil and political freedoms".

Professor Bermeo's conclusions are not too dissimilar, but the reasoning is different. She posits that democracy depends on some sense of common identity, and that this sense of identity requires that individuals see themselves as equal along some dimensions that can be used to define community. What values can serve this function is an open question. Professor Bermeo leans towards non-material equality, defined as equal access to legal protection and to the benefits of the rule of law. I disagree with some of the arguments she uses, for example, that "cuts in government spending, cuts in government employment and privatization in general lead inevitably to increases in unemployment and a widening gap between those who work and those who do not" – she clearly has in mind more efficient uses of economic resources by the government than I observe in many countries. Nevertheless, there is considerable empirical evidence (World Bank, 1993) that the rule of law is a necessary ingredient in making government policies and commitments 'credible'. This in turn is a key condition for creating an 'enabling environment' for production and investment, in other words for economic growth.

The hypothesis Professor Bermeo proposes goes beyond that, namely that the rule of law is also crucial in binding together an otherwise diverse citizenry into a cohesive community. How this process works in practice in different institutional settings and what other conditions may need to be satisfied in order to achieve the goals referred to by Professor Bermeo, are important empirical questions that deserve further study.

In *Democracy in America* de Tocqueville wrote that when free individuals attend to the affairs of a community, they are "drawn from the circle of their own interest" and begin to perceive that they are not so independent of their fellow men as they had at first imagined and that in order to obtain their support they must often lend them their co-operation. New "habits of the heart" are thus shaped that are conducive to the emergence of a democratic society. The important question raised by Professor Bermeo's paper is how the rule of law can be instrumental to this process, so that economic reforms can be fully compatible with democratic governance.

REFERENCES

Buchanan, James, M., *Constitutional economics* (Cambridge, MA: Blackwell, 1991).

Friedman, Milton & Friedman, Rose D., *Tyranny of the status quo* (San Diego, CA: Harcourt Brace Jovanovich, 1984).

Klitgaard, R., 'Better states, better markets', paper presented at the South African Economics Society Biennial Conference, Pretoria, 11-12 October 1993.

North, Douglass, C., 'The New Institutional Economics and development', paper prepared for the conference on Public Choice Theories and Third World Experiences. London School of Economic and Political Science, 17-19 September 1993.

Putnam, Robert, D., (with Leonardi, R., and Nanetti, R. Y.) *Making Democracy Work: Civil Traditions in Modern Italy* (Princeton: Princeton University Press, 1993).

Tocqueville Alexis de, *Democracy in America* 2 vols., translated by Lawrence, G., edited by Mayer, J. P. with an introductory essay by Max Lerner (New York: Harper, 1966).

Williamson, Oliver, *The Economic Institutions of Capitalism* (New York: The Free Press, 1985).

World Bank, *The East Asian Miracle – Economic Growth and Public Policy* (New York: Oxford University Press, 1993).

World Bank *The World Bank and Participation* (Operations Policy Department, September 1994).

5 Political mandate, institutional change and economic reform

Leila Frischtak

INTRODUCTION

During the 1980s the economic picture in much of the developing world looked rather dismal. Many governments either resisted adjustment at ever-increasing costs of macro imbalances and income foregone, or tried at varying degrees of ambivalence to promote it, facing rising political opposition to the unpopular austerity policies. Even in those countries which eventually moved to a stronger commitment to economic reform, it was difficult to detect unequivocal achievements.

By the end of the decade the accumulated impact of adjustment loans and agreements negotiated by the international institutions with willing and resource hungry governments was hardly reassuring. Although technical opinion increasingly espoused the soundness and urgency of the adjustment measures, there were barriers of a political and institutional nature limiting their implementation and effectiveness which governments were often too weak or incapable of overcoming. The political economy of unsuccessful adjustment gained increased salience in policy analysis.

The persistence of economic crisis or stagnation led to mounting pressures on the governments to deliver or in some cases to vocal demands for a change of regime. Many governments, caught in a process of political and institutional desegregation, were even failing to guarantee law and order, let alone show an ability to promote reform. Many developing countries were diagnosed as suffering from a crisis of governance.

By the mid-1990s, the monotone picture of economic failures and political pessimism of the previous decade has faded. The African governments have not for the most part collapsed, even though their capacity to govern has not dramatically improved, and there has been little progress towards achieving economic reform. In Latin America, almost every country has ventured on the reform path, with varying but considerable initial success. In Eastern Europe and elsewhere, while results are mixed, the commitment to reform has not been abandoned.

Nevertheless, achievements in the introduction of short-term stabilization measures have not been matched by headway in structural reforms, where progress has been slower and more inconsistent across the different policy components. Initial public support for many reform processes has lost steam, just when it was needed to allow governments to address what proved to be the most politically sensitive and divisive problems of privatization and state reform. In a few but telling cases, early reform achievements have been reversed due to lack of political support, or to a radical change in the coalitions in power. Attention has now switched to the politics of sustained adjustment.

It seems clear that the conditions that allow reform to be initiated are not necessarily the same as those which can make reform efforts endure and prosper. There have been many valuable hypotheses put forward to explain this trend of increasing difficulties and diminishing popular appeal which challenge the sustainability of the reform processes. Some appeal to common sense, such as the 'honeymoon' proposition, according to which new governments would enjoy a limited grace period, and momentarily suspended opposition, to initiate reform (Williamson, 1993). This seems to be particularly the case when, prior to reform, the perception of economic crisis is acute and widespread, such as in scenarios of high and spiralling inflation.[1] However, even when governments are successful in restoring stability, the memories of the past crisis seem to fade in time whereas the continuing costs of the reform measures, such as severe fiscal discipline, austere monetary policies, and removal of subsidies remain vivid.

Another popular explanation highlights the relative ease and speed of successfully promoting stabilization measures, which would require no more than committed and credible leadership supported by a small team of capable technocrats and specialists, compared to other structural reforms, which involve complex co-ordination among several government ministries and agencies, as well as the positive response and participation of key economic players.

This paper will explore an additional explanation to the underlying difficulties in sustaining reform. These difficulties lie partly in the over expansion of the reform agenda, which is often presented and adopted in such a way as to obscure the different nature of its components, and the different requirements of the changes involved. The purpose is not to question the ultimate validity of the reform goals, but to desegregate this agenda to identify these differences and their political and

---

1 The positive impact of crisis in facilitating the launching of reform efforts in may different contexts cannot be denied; typically, the significant costs and risks associated with overall economic reform will be avoided if other less disruptive alternatives are perceived to be available. Nevertheless, most of the political economy literature has embraced rather uncritically the postulate that crises are necessary for reform, greatly overstating the explanatory potential of crises. (See, among others, Drazen and Hill, 1990, who sustain that high and prolonged inflation are instrumental in leading to welfare enhancing reforms, and Ann Krueger, 1993, who puts forward the argument that sufficiently deteriorated economic conditions generate political imperatives for reform). Although crises, or the generalized public perception of crises, create potential conditions for change, they cannot by themselves explain the direction and nature of changes. In addition, it is much easier to establish ex-post when a crisis had reached its limit, producing imperatives for change, than to detect and predict this condition ex-ante.

institutional implications for adequate and realistic policy intervention. The next section will characterize the dual route of expansion of the reform agenda, as it moved simultaneously from the initial need to address an acute macroeconomic crisis to the promotion of structural reforms geared to the development of stronger markets, and from the diagnosis of ongoing governance problems and crisis to the promotion of democratic governance. The problem of governance capacity will then be considered, identifying some of its main determinants. Finally, I will focus on the different political nature and implications of the processes which lead to enhanced governance capacity, on the one hand, and to markets and democracies, on the other.

The paper is an analytical exercise, mainly concerned with the problems affecting the political sustainability of reform. It treats the development of markets and democratization as reform goals at an abstract level. It does not intend to discuss the economic constraints of reform nor to characterize democratic systems.

THE EXPANSION OF THE REFORM AGENDA

Structural adjustment was originally conceived as a solution to address the severe balance of payments problems afflicting many developing countries in the late seventies and early eighties. It basically consisted of a set of austere policy measures to establish monetary and fiscal discipline and exchange rate realignments. From the very beginning the international financing institutions, supported by private lenders and the donor community, assumed a leading position in the articulation and the advancement of this policy agenda, which was clearly inspired by the orthodox economics prominent in the policy thinking of the 1980s. Although the 'orthodox' orientation of these policies would gradually lose ideological and political significance as the decade went by, the central role of external actors in promoting and pressuring for the adoption of reform policies would only increase, especially in the African and other lower income developing countries.

Paradoxically, even while the reality of adjustment was proving harder than anticipated, the agenda of policy reforms in the structural adjustment package kept expanding.[2] What had begun as a 'quick fix' for the macroeconomic disequilibria precipitated or revealed by the onset of the debt crisis, soon turned into a general remedy to correct the distortions of the previous development strategies pursued by most Third World countries. Structural reforms aimed at

---

2 For the changes in the conception of structural adjustment reform, see Nelson (1989) and Frischtak (1994); and for an account of the origins and progression of adjustment lending at the World Bank, see Shihata (1991).

trade liberalization, privatization, deregulation, and other related measures designed to reduce the degree of state intervention in the economy became integral components of changes to be introduced if countries were to overcome economic instability and decline.

The addition of structural reforms to the adjustment package was not merely an incremental change. Together, these stabilization measures and structural changes amounted to a new market-based development model to displace the import substitution policies pervasive in developing countries for at least three decades. Admittedly, by the 1980s these policies had clearly outrun their value, and had become virtually non-performing even where they had been reasonably successful before; there was much room and need for policy change. It is also undeniable that there was strong affinity between these policies and the counter-cyclical expansionary measures adopted by most developing countries in response to the oil shocks of the 1970s, which caused greater vulnerability to the crisis to come in the early 1980s. However, it is also true, as Rodrik has put it, that import substitution policies were rather imprecisely lumped together with unsustainable fiscal and exchange rate practices in taking the blame for the debt crisis and its aftermath (Rodrik, 1994).[3] Indeed, if unsustainable macroeconomic policies rendered the ailing 'import substitution model' irreversibly exhausted, they can be equally damaging to the 'market' or 'neo-liberal' model as well, as recent developments in Mexico suggest.

The political economy side of the reform agenda was similarly expanded. Concern over governance capacity to promote reform arose out of the realization that the political and institutional environment in which policy decisions were made and implemented was a crucial determinant of their success.[4] If structural adjustment was economically convincing it proved to be less palatable politically.

---

3 In the author's words, "... the crisis became an opportunity for orthodox economists who had the ear of policy makers to wipe the slate clean and discredit the whole range of policies in use" (op. cit., p 9).
4 By the end of the 1980s there was already a small but growing body of literature focusing on the institutional and political constraints underlying economic policymaking. Part of this literature was concerned in mapping out these constraints through comparative analyses of diverse country experiences in the attempt to explain governmental policy choices to reject, delay, or implement economic reform (in addition to Nelson, op. cit., see also Nelson, 1990; Haggard and Kaufman, 1992; Bates and Krueger, 1993). Another strand of literature, less empirical in orientation, and not exclusively concerned with developing countries, focused more specifically on identifying the dynamics of institutional constraints on collective decision-making which prevented economically superior, welfare-enhancing policy choices from being adopted (see Alesina and Drazen, 1991; and Fernandez and Rodrik, 1991). However, it was probably from within the international financing institutions that the earliest and strongest emphasis was given to governance issues as a major source of constraints to economic reform. After the release of a landmark World Bank report on the extreme shortages of governance prevailing throughout the African region, which comprised any serious attempts to promote economic policy changes (World Bank 1989), there followed a series of other studies similarly highlighting the prominence of the governance problem (see Hyden, 1990; Landell-Mills and Seragaldin, 1991; World Bank 1992; and Frischtak, op. cit., among many others).

It implied the displacement of entrenched interests, possible harsher short-term costs to vulnerable sectors of the population, and therefore a sizeable political risk for governments to undertake. Governments which enjoyed reputations of weakness and corruption could not be expected to generate credibility for economic reform programmes which implied immediate costs and sacrifices for society. Even if committed and credible leadership was available it was reasonably assumed that this leadership would need to have access to basic political and institutional resources – such as a capable and motivated bureaucracy – to implement reform.

Political resistance and general shortages of governance capacity were the major reasons for the postponement of the adjustment programme in the 1980s. Admittedly, this was reversed in the early 1990s not just because of improvements in overall governance capacity; prolonged economic crisis was also a factor. As shall be discussed below, prolonged economic crisis typically generates natural domestic constituencies for change, as even those groups privileged by the economic regime in place see their rents progressively decline. By the end of the 1980s the options available to developing countries had steadily narrowed: the flow of external financial resources for crucial investments had not resumed, and those governments which resisted reform faced an increasingly hostile world economic environment.

Despite this, recent experience seems to confirm the strategic importance of governance capacity in the sustainability of reform programmes. Without this capacity, the host of other factors which may have contributed to the launching of reform will not make it possible for reforms to endure. Governance is increasingly seen as a pivotal feature of the recent East Asian economic successes (Rodrik, 1994). In Venezuela, key governance failures are associated with its dramatic reversal of the reform process. The Venezuelan government found itself increasingly alienated from Congress and the public which could not understand or attach positive value to the policy changes introduced, in spite of their undeniable economic achievements (Naim, 1984, and 1993; Navarro, 1994). Similar failures can be related to the difficulties emerging across the reform path in Egypt, Bolivia and Mexico. Only able governments can use, and not waste, the political capital accumulated with the initial stabilization achievements to discredit alternatives other than the furthering of the reform efforts. Only they can provide the co-ordinating skills and necessary credibility to induce co-operation and to adequately manage the new policies, both politically and technically. Most importantly, governance is essential if the changes introduced are to be institutionalized, although, as this paper will argue, governments can neither substitute for society's role in this process, nor control its ultimate results.

More recently, the emphasis attributed to the role of the state in economic reform by most of the agenda setters in the international financing institutions, and by many 'local' policymakers, has extended beyond the concern with the need for governance capacity to focus on the specific features the state has to acquire to develop strong market-oriented economies. In this process, the necessary input of society was curiously downplayed or bypassed, despite awareness of the need for 'ownership' of the reforms by the public. There is a tendency to treat all obstacles to developing strong markets as institutional inefficiencies to be overcome by state reforms (the design of which could supposedly come from abroad, or at best, from above, with societal ownership coming hopefully later).

This tendency can be illustrated with reference to what is so far the most troubling challenge to economic reform, namely, the realization that the expected vigorous investment response to the reforms may either be slow in coming or fail to materialize at all. Even countries which managed to stay the course of the reforms have often not been rewarded by the significant growth rates necessary to accommodate development needs. This anaemic or absent growth response which has placed a growing political burden on the governments in question has only recently been acknowledged by policy analysts (World Bank, 1992). Its impact is not negligible. The whole issue of welfare or equity enhancing development had been subsumed, or put on hold, under the reasonable assumption that no equity or distribution concerns could be realistically addressed in the absence of growth. While short-term costs to the most vulnerable sectors of the population could be temporarily cushioned through mechanisms of 'social safety nets', ultimately only the resumption of growth could politically justify the structural adjustment reforms.

The lack of a strong supply response generated an opportunity for a critical reassessment of the reforms proposed, and for readjusting, or qualifying the scope of their promises; even if the reforms were still a necessary condition for the resumption of growth, they could not in themselves deliver it, at least not everywhere. Yet, the no-growth challenge seems to have led only to calls for increased governance. The policy environment, and not the policies themselves, was exclusively deemed to be the source of failures. Investments could not be attracted, and strong markets could not develop in the absence of an 'enabling environment' with clearly established property rights and contract enforcing mechanisms, and a 'level playing field' for competition.[5]

As developing countries' states are often poorly equipped to provide such enabling environments, they became a logical target of reform. Previously,

---

5 This paper takes no issues with these reforms. The point is only that a greater balance in the distillation of the lesson (or in the distribution of blame) would be desirable.

emphasis was given to the removal of cumbersome and distorting regulatory barriers, subsidies, and incentives. However, more recent analyses have focused on the role of governments in establishing and in guaranteeing the functioning of crucial institutional arrangements and the necessary legal framework for the operation of markets, and therefore, for the promotion of growth and development.

Significantly, the more detailed and inclusive blueprints of state reform which have emerged began to display the full set of operating principles of western liberal democracies. Greater transparency and accountability in governmental decision-making, increased political competition and freedom of the press, and better and more open institutional channels for interest representation, are commonly included as requirements which the states of developing countries have to conform to so that economic reform can be sustained and will succeed.

The conception of the reform treatment developing countries should undergo has expanded considerably from stabilization measures, to structural reforms geared to the development of market-driven economies, to the need to enhance governance capacity and, finally, to the establishment of democratic governance mechanisms. As it has been established, this conception of reform has become a 'meaningful whole', its components not easily distinguishable, or even intelligible on their own, bearing reciprocal interrelations of causal necessity.

From an epistemological standpoint, the historical affinity between markets and democracy that characterized the developed West was transformed into a historical necessity for the developing Rest. Strangely enough, however, any real sense of history was deleted in this transformation, since it abstracts from the centuries long processes of change, conflict and adaptation which resulted in the western model of development, in the assumption that the latter can be synchronously mimicked through capable policy intervention alone.

On a practical and more immediate level, the effect of this expanded conception of reform was an overloading of the policy agenda of many developing countries. While struggling to structurally adjust, these countries are in reality aiming at many different things at the same time. Whether governments were pressured into this agenda by their dependency on foreign aid and loans, or have become independently committed to it to address domestic demands for political change and to solve economic crisis, it is not entirely clear that the overloaded reform agenda is either politically feasible in the short run, or necessarily the most efficient way to introduce the changes everywhere. Even if all the reform goals, once achieved, are mutually reinforcing, there is no evidence to support the claim that the simultaneous promotion of these goals makes the process any more viable.[6]

---

6 For the complex interactions of the dual transition processes see, for instance, Haggard and Webb (1994); Nelson (1994); and Nelson et al. (1994).

This holistic approach to reform is of most concern for the purposes of this paper in so far as it has obscured the nature, implications and requirements of the reform's components. In this context, holistic is intended to imply the way that once the whole is established, the components cease to have distinguishable individual identities, and therefore their discrete merits, performance, and pre-conditions cannot be easily assessed. The failure of policymakers to identify these differences while promoting reform may be one important reason why reform processes slow down, stall, or are even reversed, in spite of initial successes. Accordingly, a few discriminating propositions can be advanced.

The first is that the problem of stabilization is fundamentally distinct from that of the greater reliance on markets at the expense of state intervention to promote economic development. The need to maintain macroeconomic equilibrium is pertinent to all economies, regardless of their developing strategies. It concerns the control and management of society's resources, the provision of order and stability so that any form of economic activity and exchange can take place on a predictable basis, and constitutes the proper domain of action, and a primary attribution of any government. The ability to avoid prolonged macroeconomic imbalances is a test and condition of governance capacity.

Likewise, the problem of governance capacity cannot be reduced to that of the establishment of democratic governments, since it is more general and may equally concern any political regime. As both democratic and authoritarian regimes can be afflicted by governance shortages or crises, governance capacity should refer to some basic minimum conditions all effectively functioning governments have to address regardless of the nature and form of decision-making and interest representation mechanisms in place. All governments have an intrinsic mandate to maintain order and enforce the law, and no government can last if it systematically fails to perform these functions.

By contrast, market-driven economies and democratic systems of government refer to specific choices societies may make in response to their perceived problems. Societies are likely to vary in their perceptions of their needs, and the solutions chosen to address them, and will often have internal disagreement over these choices. Governments are not passive in this choice-taking, and whether democratic or autocratic, governmental input and leadership plays a large role in shaping the outcomes. Nevertheless, governments do not have an intrinsic or automatic mandate over these choices independent of societies; these mandates have to be politically built and renewed to maintain public support.

Effectively operative markets and democratic systems comprise of a complex set of institutions, which must be grounded on culture and behaviour, and be consistently linked with other areas of social experience. These constraints also apply to governments, which are institutions as well. Nevertheless, the nature of the processes and changes required for the development of markets and democracies is much more demanding and subject to dispute, and therefore differs considerably from those of stabilization and the re-establishment of governance capacity, where this capacity was previously lacking.

Admittedly, the dividing lines are not always clear cut. For instance, there may be considerable overlapping in the policy instruments necessary to promote stabilization and the development of market driven economies (for example, privatization is high on the list of the most important structural reforms but some degree of privatization may also be essential for the purposes of fiscal balance). Also, governance shortages or crises are often manifest in crises of the political regime, or may precipitate demands for a change of regime. Nevertheless, there are important distinctions which should be identified in the nature and orientation of the changes and policies in process.

Markets may work better in resource allocation than states in most circumstances, and few would challenge the precept that democracies are superior and more desirable than authoritarian forms of government. However, not distinguishing the components of the expanded reform agenda may lead to inadequate policy choices and strategies. The holistic approach to reform may lead governments mistakenly to assume that the public support obtained in the promotion of stabilization measures automatically translates into a mandate to introduce other policy changes which political constituencies may be unable to accept.[7] Alternatively, this approach may steer ongoing demands for political change to focus exclusively on the issues of greater access to participation and representation in governmental decision-making, putting into the background those issues related to capacity proper (such as the ability to enforce the existing laws or exercise control over an undisciplined or corrupt bureaucracy).[8] In both cases, the strategies can backfire, leading to delays, deadlocks or reversals in the reform process, ultimately compromising the attainment of its goals.

The tendency to discount the importance of construing a mandate for structural reforms, and to underestimate the complexity of the institution building processes that these reforms entail, particularly in reference to the constraints of culture and past experience, has unfortunately become a trademark of many recent reform experiences (Navarro, op. cit.; Ibrahim, 1994; and Morales, op. cit.). Modern technocrats and policymakers in several developing countries seem to expect that these reforms can be endorsed at their face-value, and that

---

7 Morales (1994) has recently argued this case to explain the current difficulties in the reform process in Bolivia.
8 I have previously identified this trend in the transition to democracy in Brazil in the 1980s (Frischtak, 1994-b).

their benefits are self-evident; they also seem to believe that the new institutions will spring from the ground, in ready-to-wear fashion, as a result of top-down expert design alone.

I have argued before (Frischtak, 1994-b) that this tendency can be partly explained as a contemporary distaste of the grand development plans of the 1960s and 1970s and also as a need to product differentiate the current reform-oriented governments from the populist and manipulative political practices of the past. However, this approach to reform suffers from serious communication failures, generating political, institutional and symbolic gaps which eventually exert their toll in the form of increasing apathy, alienation, or overt opposition to reform processes. As an overall strategy, the holistic approach to reform may be curiously shallow and not nearly comprehensive enough.

However, governance capacity seems to be a crucial, even if not the only, precondition of these processes if they are to lead to effectively operative markets and democracies. Without, or with little governance capacity, institutional choices and changes which are contingent on particular political mandates and extended political support do not stand a realistic chance of success. Although the process of enhancing or exercising capacity may not be easy or even feasible in many circumstances, this process does not seem to require any mandate or support in addition to that granted any government. There are two things, then, which need to be identified: to what the different components of reform relate, and the nature of the problems afflicting developing countries which this reform is designed to address.

Governance is potentially a broad notion. The next section will address the problem of governance capacity without any claim to exhaust its relevant meanings. It will also attempt to avoid referring to the many specific features along which governments can be classified (such as the nature of political regimes), and will focus instead on a few attributes of governance that can be relevant to the performance of most contemporary governments in general.[9] The underlying premise is that there are such basic attributes of governance which relate to the constitutive nature of governments qua governments, even if they can only be analysed in an abstract and restrictive way.[10]

---

9 On an earlier occasion I have argued that attributing to governance capacity the same meaning as that of a democratic political system, as some proponents of the 'good governance' approach will have it, amounts to sheer conceptual redundancy (Frischtak, 1994). Moreover, neither the supply of governance capacity, nor the form of political regime, include all the defining dimensions of governments. The fact that in any given concrete situation all these dimensions – and other political and non-political circumstances – will be naturally interacting, does not provide a reason for not distinguishing them analytically.

10 No understanding of governance could reasonably be ahistorical; although some of its attributes relate to very early and enduring features of governments, others reflect the changes the very notion of governing has gone through.

GOVERNANCE CAPACITY: BASIC ATTRIBUTES

Governance capacity relates to the need to distinguish the physical existence of governments from their effective functioning at any given time. The reason why it is pertinent to ask whether a government can govern, or how well it can govern, lies in the fact that the formal structure of a government does not necessarily account for the manner in which it manages society's resources, and exercises control and discipline over its own power and policy instruments. The description of the formal organization of a government, of its composing bodies, agencies and their respective attributions, the enunciation of its rules and of the scope and forms of the intervening and regulatory presence of the government in society, do not necessarily explain the extent to which this same government can enforce its laws and decisions, or its capacity to effectively lead and co-ordinate the aggregation of social interests, managing both conflict and co-operation.

Although the size and inner structure of the government may remain constant over a given period, there may be wide variations in the ability of the government to generate the belief that its policy decisions are consonant with the public interest. The capacity of the government to perform its role of agenda setter, and to gather enough support for this agenda from society may vary, even though the rules and mechanisms that orientate this process remain the same. It is therefore reasonable to assume that capacity may be more volatile than governments themselves.

The word governance is not new. It was rescued from earlier and mostly forgotten usages, when it seems to have had the same meaning as 'government'. It is a useful tool for addressing the possible gap between existing governments and their capacity to discharge the governing function, as defined by the existing rules and arrangements. In this sense, the contemporary concept of governance capacity refers to a qualitative and dynamic dimension of governments.

Effectively-functioning governing institutions go a long way in explaining this dimension. Institutions are norms, rules and values, written or unwritten, that actually guide behaviour.[11] They can be thought of as any form of patterned meaningful interaction in society. Although they can be encapsulated in formal laws and organizations, the latter become hollow abstractions once the behaviour connection is severed. For governing institutions to be *de facto* established and operative, they must be grounded on shared principles or perceptions of the social order. Because institutions can substantially bridge the gap between the formal organization of governments and their actual governing capacity, it is frequently understood that the quality of governments is equal to that of its effective institutions.

---

11 There is a sizable and ever growing literature on institutions, which could not be adequately cited here. For usages of the concept which are pertinent to the meaning used in this paper, see North, 1990 and Rowe, 1989.

Institutions may be elusive to measurement but they can be identified and analysed, allowing for some degree of predictability of governance capacity in specific circumstances.[12] Nevertheless, a central proposition of this paper is that governance capacity is also a function of some much less tangible factors, not captured by the institutional content of governments. It is to those factors, largely unpredictable, that capacity owes much of its relative volatility. Intangible elements are at play in most of the defining institutional attributes and dimensions of capacity, although in varying proportions. Before their impact can be discussed, it is useful to identify some of these institutional attributes.

The rule of law

Organized society and some form of government are virtual synonymous. As far back as history has recorded, the hypothesis of no government has been the same as that of unlimited war and chaos, or, the very extinction of society as we understand it. This helps to explain why many governments can survive in a state of degeneration with almost exhausted capacity. The generalized crisis of governance in Africa, diagnosed in the last decade, very seldom led to the collapse of the state. In the few instances where it did, society collapsed alongside it.

Consequently, the prime function of governments, and the very first institutional determinant of capacity, is the ability to maintain order, or bound and regulate conflict in society. Order cannot be logically conceived without some established parameters, or reasonably known rules. Some notion of law, even if rudimentary, has always been intrinsic to the feasibility of order.[13] Tension between the government or ruler and those bounded to obedience has always been intrinsic to society. Many different arrangements to bound and limit arbitrariness in the exercise of authority must have been devised to accommodate this tension, and increase predictability in the social order. The western principle of the rule of law, as we know it, is the result of the historical development of one such particular institutional arrangement. However, as it came to constitute one of the central pillars of the modern nation state, and as this state, in form even if not wholly in essence, became the hegemonic and compulsory form of political organization of societies worldwide, it is pertinent to represent it as a defining feature of governance capacity in general.

As a concept, the rule of law stands first and foremost for the notion of the supremacy of the law over state, government or ruler. Institutionally, the rule of

---

12 Some attempts have been made at measuring institutions. See, for instance, Clague et al (1994).
13 According to Watson, there is evidence that, as early as 451 BC, a group of Roman citizens demanded and obtained a written code of law (known as the Twelve Tables) which was binding upon the consuls in their exercise of judicial power (Watson, 1991, p11).

law necessarily implied some enforcing mechanism. In accounting for the Western European development of the rule of law, Berman (1983) describes this mechanism in terms of the division of power, which originally was made possible by the Church and the feudal barons, as "concurrent polities within the same territory"; in the modern manifestation of the rule of law, the division of power mechanism assumed the more familiar form of the system of checks and balances among the legislative, judiciary and executive, as "concurrent branches of the same polity".[14]

The rule of law, both as a procedural concept and as a set of institutions, is compatible with many different political regimes, although these institutions may assume varied shapes and attributions in different national contexts.[15] Whatever the division of attributions among the various branches of government, and whatever the scope of the judicial function in different countries, an independent and well functioning judiciary is considered to be the most fundamental institutional guarantee that the rule of law is to prevail. The judiciary is not only the "arbiter of legal disputes and the provider of criminal justice in society" (Shihata, 1993, p279), but also the key enforcing mechanism of the principle of the supremacy of the law. If the judiciary is subject to the control of those exercising political power, or to the pressures of particular interests, or is otherwise unable and under-qualified to perform its enforcing role, stability, predictability and lack of arbitrariness in the social order are extensively undermined.[16]

An independent and effective judiciary is far from being the norm in the developing world, and considerable efforts and resources have been spent by international agencies to assist governments in reforming and equipping this pivotal institution. Notwithstanding the undeniable value of these initiatives, their limitations are also obviously clear. To be effective – and fair – a judiciary

---

14 Berman actually compares the early institutional form of the European rule of law, around the 12-13th centuries and its legal principles, embodies in such documents as the 1215 English Magna Carta and the 1222 Hungarian Golden Bull, with the latest shape and content of this institution in contemporary times. In addition to the enforcing mechanism of the division of power, the author argues that supremacy of the law also entailed, then as now, a principle of law which transcended the structure of power; originally based on natural and divine justice, this principle has then been replaced by human or individual rights, or democratic values.

15 This rather broad conception is admittedly controversial, as there are those who will maintain that the rule of law is necessarily associated with democratic systems of government. Nevertheless, there are other governing systems, including those prevailing in some Islamic states, where the ruler can be no less bound by the rule of law than in many western democracies, no matter how difference and authoritarian that conception of law can appear to western eyes.

16 See Shihata, op. cit., for an argument on the importance of judicial reform in developing countries. In this same article the author states that even when the role of the judiciary is relatively restricted, that is, in those legal systems where it is intended merely to 'declare' the law issued by the legislative, the latitude, and the importance, of the courts in interpreting and filling gaps in existing law is considerable. But Shihata also calls attention to the increasing number of countries where the judiciary is legally given the role of guardian of the constitution and promoter of its principles, extending its law-making attributions.

needs a clientele who are not only committed, but also politically able, to exercise a reasonable degree of control, ensuring legitimacy to the judicial process. The difficulties in manufacturing truly enforcing institutional mechanisms by top-down policy intervention highlight the insufficiencies of any approach to governance which places more emphasis on institutional design than on the degree to which institutions are embedded in politics and culture. There remains, nevertheless, a not-easily-resolvable tension within the very notion of independence.

A professional civil service

The principle of the need to distinguish the administrative from the political function of government is historically much more recent than the principle of the rule of law. It evolved as a reflection of the overall pattern of societal changes in the direction of greater specialization in economic activities and differentiation of interests, leading to an increased number of interactions and externalities that had to be managed and regulated. The consequent growth in size and complexity of the managing function of governments – including its technical, regulatory and enforcing aspects – was not the only outcome; it also became necessary to ensure some continuity and objectivity for governmental management beyond the volatile contingencies of the exercise of power.

An early and most valuable analytical exposition of this principle and of its institutional implications can be found in the Weberian construct of the rational-legal "ideal -type" of public administration as the main pillar of the modem capitalist state. It has since become standard to expect that a technically qualified, professional, meritocratic, career-oriented governmental bureaucracy should respond to the more complex management functions of this state and provide the basis for insulating the policy implementation from the policy formulation activities of governments.

A professional civil service in the terms described above is a critical institutional asset of governments, and thus a major determinant of capacity. However, the task of generating and maintaining such an asset has proved difficult; the reality of most governmental bureaucracies would fall somewhat short of the principles of professional management and political insulation. As with the principle of an independent judiciary, insulation in this area is problematic since it does not refer exclusively to the need to protect the public bureaucracy from the short-run policy inclinations or from the whims and ambitions of the political authorities in charge. There is also the need to protect the governmental administration and its resources from the game of politics, or from the pressures of conflicting social interests, simultaneously avoiding the alienation of these same interests.

The effective shape and content of institutions always reflect the form possible to accommodate the principles and needs they were intended to address and the major tensions and conflicts in society. It is often possible to reach such an accommodation without major deviation from the original purposes. However, in the case of many governmental bureaucracies – particularly, but not exclusively, in developing countries – the principles of technical and professional management and of insulation have been overwhelmingly subverted. So has any commitment to the public interest. In those contexts the governmental administration is typically the locus of pervasive clientelism, patronage, rents and job distribution – or even corruption – which can simultaneously be promoted by public servants and bureaucrats independently and in complicity with the political (and elected) authorities. To the extent that these activities can characterize an specific form of political management, the governmental administration plays its institutional role. Nevertheless, public resources are inadequately appropriated and wasted, the quality, continuity and predictability of public management are undermined, and therefore governance capacity is vitally compromised.

Political control over state resources: Problem of capture revisited

The distorting and rent-seeking effects of most economic policy interventions have received wide attention in policy analysis. So did the patrimonialist state, with its emphasis on generating clienteles and privileges to groups with special ties to governmental officials. In all these analyses, governmental officials are characterized as the diametrical opposites of the Weberian career-minded public bureaucrat; they are self-interested and predatory, concerned primarily in trading in their special access to public resources for their own private advancement.

Leaving aside the issue of self-interest as the single rational behavioural motivation, to which this paper does not subscribe, it can be argued that not all rents, subsidies, and protection are predatory in nature, even if they do introduce market distortions. Rents can be legitimate instruments of policy, as elements of incentive structures designed to achieve specific policy goals; indeed there are such things as growth-enhancing rents. It is naive to suppose that all forms of political patronage, which constitute the main currency of the exercise of power, could be eliminated from any given polity. The fact is that states can – and most do – absorb a considerable amount of rent and patronage distribution without becoming captured.

The problem of capture relates to the lack of control in the management of the state's policy instruments and resources, be they political, institutional, administrative, fiscal or financial. Extensive penetration of the state by private interests, leading to the appropriation of resources by a few or several powerful groups, or extensive fragmentation of these resources within the various agencies and branches of government, implies that the government is unable to exercise control, co-ordination and discipline over policy decisions and their instruments. State resources then move from being governing assets to becoming the assets of the recipients, and the government becomes a hostage of these recipients.

The ability to exercise control over the state's resources in the political and economic management of society constitutes one other clear determinant of governance capacity. The larger the size of the state, in terms of its institutions, agencies, and bodies, the more complex and varied the policy instruments and processes, the larger the extent of its intervention in social and economic activity, then the more governance capacity is taxed in the exercise of political control, co-ordination and discipline. There is thus an intrinsic underlying tension between the scope of state action and governance capacity.

Most developing countries currently suffer from the dissonance of a state whose scope has overextended its capacity. Many governments have considerable difficulty in exercising political control over the policy processes. They may find themselves in varied situations of capture: unable to dislodge powerful groups from the control of public assets and sectors of the governmental bureaucracy; unable to co-ordinate and make consistent the activities of different regulatory agencies or financial institutions; incapable of disciplining state enterprises and even of enforcing its own decisions. These governments may find it especially difficult to revert subsidies, tax breaks and incentives, and above all to alter the overall direction of ongoing policies.

The sustained inability to revert situations of severe macroeconomic disequilibria is a clear manifestation of low governance capacity in the sense described above. Situations of capture may be particularly associated with the difficulties in re-establishing fiscal balance. Nevertheless, maintaining the value of a nation's money is the paramount attribution of the economic management function of the state. In so far as governments have an established, constitutive mandate for economic management, the commitment to provide macroeconomic stability is an intrinsic and defining feature of this mandate.

Intangible determinants of capacity

For all the many institutions which can guarantee the exercise of governance capacity, and of which just a few were identified, governance capacity can never be fully institutionalized.

The intangible dimensions of governance can affect and modify the performance of existing functioning institutions, but their impact is especially critical in those areas of governance where institutions are either weak or do not exist at all.

Governmental credibility may well be one such intangible. The problem of credibility has received considerable attention, especially in connection with its impact on economic reform processes.

Credibility refers to the ability of a government to generate the expectation that it will do what it says it will. It is therefore an important component of capacity, in that it can alter the behaviour of individuals ex-ante thus reducing the need for coercion and engaging the voluntary co-operation of society. Credibility can be grounded on reputation, on the accumulated experience of repeated interactions.

Alternatively, it can be evaluated through examining the implementation capacity and enforcing mechanisms available to the government. Ultimately, however, credibility hinges on its ability to be communicated, and there are strong and unpredictable elements of persuasion which cannot be extricated from it.

Credibility is closely associated to another major intangible dimension of governance, that of leadership. Governmental leadership need not necessarily be personal, although it often takes this form.

Leadership can be performed in an enduring form by institutions, such as congress or the executive, but it cannot be fully institutionalized and predictable.

Leadership is crucial for governing as it entails making decisions which may involve high political risks, providing the consistency and the general orientation of the governmental decision-making process at the various levels where it takes place, and giving an intelligible shape to the final policy agenda that is presented to society.

Leadership may be critical to the political co-ordination of the effective political interests which constrain the policy process. This is especially so when there are no established functioning institutions for interest representation and aggregation, such as a parliament, congress or other consultation-type processes; nevertheless, even the best aggregation rules and functioning institutional arrangements never entirely exhaust the tasks of managing conflict and co-operation.

The problem of leadership has long been approached with ambivalent suspicion by many political scientists and economists, who hesitate in attaching weight to such an uncontrollable factor. Arguably, reliance on leadership makes for an awkward and risky policy prescription. Nevertheless, leadership is increasingly being given more serious attention in the academic literature. Grindle and Thomas (1991) make an emphatic case for its importance in bringing about change: the characteristics and abilities of leaders and key policymakers are determinant in altering the existing constraints, and in creating and enlarging the "policy space".

Most importantly, there are undeniable links between leadership and legitimacy, or the ability to convincingly translate governmental policies and decisions as constitutive of the public interest. Legitimacy may well be the single most important determinant of governance. It is certainly much less dependent on the intangibles of leadership in those contexts where the institutional component of governance is high.

However, again there is always some latitude in the government's interpretation or 'construction' of the public interest. While private interests, even if adequately represented, tend to be fragmented, short-sighted, and even inconsistent over time, the public interest needs to be given consistency and endurance (Chubb and Peterson, 1989).[17]

Likewise, most institutions unavoidably enjoy some latitude in their functioning, by virtue of the need to endow them with some insularity from political and economic competition and conflict. How then to ensure that the public interest is legitimately interpreted and advanced by the government and by the existing institutions?

This paper cannot attempt any fully-fledged explanation of the problem of legitimacy, nor advance propositions on how to determine where, between being embedded or captured in society, the public interest should lie. It is doubtful that these issues can be usefully resolved through independent abstract reasoning. However, it is reasonable to conclude that the decisions and processes of the government and its institutions will be perceived to be more legitimate the more the latter appear to be consonant with the dominant political culture and shared acceptable values, even though there may be disputes over the nature of decisions and the results of the processes. Although culture and values may be not quite intangibles, there is no ruler to determine their ever-changing limits and possibilities.

The reason why there may be intangible governance dimensions at play even where institutions are strong and effective partially relates to the fact that much about governance capacity lies in the dynamics of political communication, or in the process of shaping and reshaping perceptions that constitute the essence of politics. There are explicit symbolic functions of the exercise of political power which cannot be neglected. According to Ibrahim, governance capacity relates to the effective deployment of both the means of coercion and the means of inspiration (Ibrahim, 1994). The latter may be critically important for governments attempting to mobilize political support to promote change in society.

---

17 The authors address the institutional role and the latitude of the American Executive in shaping the national interest. Thus, their argument does not explicitly hinge on intangibles.

PROMOTING GOVERNANCE AND INSTITUTIONAL CHANGE
IN DEVELOPING COUNTRIES

Enhancing governance capacity

Most developing countries are chronically deficient in their governance capacity. Although their institutional legacies may be as rich and varied as those of developed countries, their governing institutions are typically weaker and less effective. As argued above, effective institutions may not entirely account for the supply of governance capacity. Yet, they are valuable insurance against the volatility of the intangible governance attributes. In this respect, developing countries, to a much greater extent than their developed counterparts, are hostage to the eventual contingencies of credible, politically able and legitimate leadership.

At least in part, the structural governance deficiencies of developing countries may be rooted in some persistent underlying incongruence between the indigenous political culture and values as expressed in the existing institutional stock, and the structure of those governmental institutions which were mimicked from abroad. Considerable blending and selective adaptation may still be required before these institutions can become ingrained and effective.

Recent analyses have correctly emphasized the importance and urgency of improving the quality of the civil service in most developing countries. As with the problem of judicial reform, they have shown the need for extensive training for technical staff and a redesigning of the structure and attributions of the different organizations and agencies. In other analyses the focus has centred on altering the behavioural incentives of governmental officials and bureaucrats. Accordingly, Trebilcock has suggested that "...a focus on institutional development would view as of central importance the whole incentive structure of particular civil service regimes, starting with the process by which appointments are made, salary and benefit levels determined, and promotions and terminations decided. Over the long run, the structure of these decisions may have a more significant impact on the quality of the civil service than the provision of training programmes for a handful of present or prospective civil servants". (Trebilcock, 1994, p6)

All of the above is important, yet it is unlikely that better training, salaries and promotions alone can compensate for the opportunities available for engaging in patronage, rent distribution or corruption. As the same author has concluded, it is naive to suppose that bureaucrats can be required or induced to engage in collective decision-making using criteria that are strongly at variance with the criteria by which their political overseers make collective decisions." (Trebilcock, 1994, p7) Enhancing governance capacity may not be an easy political proposition. There are strong synergies along the whole spectrum of governance failures or shortages which conspire against the success of surgical reforms and interventions. In the absence of credible leadership to reduce uncertainty as to future compensation, stabilization attempts will find strong resistance from those benefiting from the *status quo*.

Typically, the stalemate of negative synergies that characterize governance crises can be broken with the timely, but unpredictable emergence of an able leadership that is capable of communicating credibility and legitimacy. The reversal of the crises may, but does not necessarily lead to enduring sources of governance. These may still then hinge on further institutional development and learning.

Nevertheless, the enhancement of governance, and the promotion of macroeconomic equilibria, do not need to be politically 'sold' as projects to society, as both concern the very constitutive mandate of governments. There are natural constituencies for the process of enhancing governance capacity; ultimately this process is supply, not demand constrained. Prolonged governance shortages introduce ever-increasing instability and uncertainty in the social and economic environment, and ultimately the costs of this uncertainty outweigh any other benefit or rent appropriated. As in any negative sum game, everyone stands to lose from further instability and lack of governance. Therefore, the possible political conflicts surrounding stabilization and governance enhancing policies and initiatives, once these are adopted, tend to be small and further decrease with time.

There seems to be discontinuity between pre- and post-reform resistance to stabilization measures. Game-theoretical explanations for delayed stabilization usually model environments for collective decision-making in which either the state is assumed away, or is pictured as another interest group responding to a similar set of incentives.[18] In these games it is the uncertainty over the distributional consequences, or over the identity of relative gainers and losers, which prevents all groups from choosing or voting for the adoption of stabilization measures, even though each will gain in absolute terms. However, in an alternative scenario where the state adopts these measures, the same groups which were previously unwilling to support the measures are now highly unlikely to oppose them. Similarly, stabilization could be regarded as a public good, which will typically not be the outcome of voluntary co-operation due to the impossibility of excluding free-riders.

---

18 See Rodrik, 1993, for a brief but useful review of several of these game models.
19 In analysing the results of several country experiences with reform, Bates and Kruegger conclude that "... perhaps the clearest pattern emerging from the case studies is that economic policy reform implies the strengthening of the executive branch of government and, within the executive branch, the financial – as opposed to the spending – ministries". (op.cit., p462)

Most of the reform trajectories to date seem to confirm these observations. In the Latin American region, for instance, which in the 1990s has moved towards substantive economic adjustment, there are no recorded experiences of outright significant resistance to the introduction of stabilization measures, notwithstanding their admittedly high costs in some specific contexts. This is so in spite of the fact that there seems to be a tendency in stabilization reforms for an initial concentration of governmental power in the executive at the expense of congress.[19] The fact that stabilization could still command support at a time when the region had returned almost *en masse* both to democracy and competitive politics is of no small significance.

These reform experiences are often associated with the emergence of a leadership with enough resolve to break away from the pattern of postponing reform, which dominated the previous decade in the region (with the notable exception of Chile which had ventured on the reform path much earlier). The past ideological origins and personal history of this crop of leaders bear no affinity to the orientation of the present economic reforms: the adjustment programme was launched in Bolivia under the presidency of Paz Estenssoro, who proceeded to rapidly dismantle the very state-oriented corporative system he had put in place decades before; Argentina's President Menen came to power through his Peronist party, which was one of the main opposers of the policies which were subsequently implemented.[20]

Institutional choices and change

Nowhere can institutions endure, prosper and perform unless they are based on shared values and beliefs. Governing institutions are generally supported by shared principles about the social order and the role of government in this order, or the nature and limits of contractual obligations binding state and society. Economic institutions are also grounded on shared principles and norms which ascribe positive values to the goods and benefits to be produced and inform on how they should be distributed.

Structural policies geared to the development of markets, and policy interventions designed to introduce democratic mechanisms in the structure and operation of the political system are not likely to succeed in the absence of a supporting value system that can make these changes intelligible and desirable. The economic institutions in place in many developing countries were orientated to the promotion of values of national autonomy and industrial self-sufficiency, and ascribed a prominent role for the state in the production and distribution of

---

20 A similar pattern can be detected elsewhere as well. Ghana's President Rawlings, whose popularity as a leader was associated to his socialist-inclined political views, has been in power since the beginning of the reform process in his country.

goods. To the extent that the underlying political culture and institutions may be at variance with the intended goals of democracy and markets, a complex process of institutional change is at stake. If effective, this process would entail the recharacterization of the social order on the basis of the collective understanding of the principle that the public interest and general welfare is best served by the free competition of private interests, both economically and politically, and by a reduced and better-targeted scope for state intervention.

The extent of existing cultural incongruence and of the institutional adaptation required varies considerably across the developing world. The Latin American region is by and large familiar with the institutions of the market and democracy and their underlying principles. The challenge there seems to be in strategically, and culturally, redefining the scope of attributions of the state, and of generating strong and effective institutional mechanisms to allow for greater economic and political 'inclusion'.[21] By contrast, Eastern Europe seems to face a much more complex institutional building challenge, as the sudden dismantling of most previously existing institutions left neither much time for, nor much ground on which to base processes of gradual adaptation and learning. Eastern European countries epitomize both the possibilities and the difficulties – and ultimately the uncertainties – of the dual transition to markets and democracies. Choices over the timing of the reforms and in what sequence they should run can have a determining impact on the fate of the transition process. In the words of Nelson: "Simultaneous economic and political liberalization, deliberately and rapidly introduced, is a largely new experiment on the world stage. (...) It is not at all clear that most simultaneous transitions will reach their objectives" (op. cit., 1994, p3).

Nevertheless, it is in the ongoing reform attempts in Africa where the sense of urgency is most compelling and the challenge most demanding. On the one hand, the severity of economic constraints leave only a dramatically narrow margin for error in strategic policy choices. On the other, the superimposition of class, racial, and tribal cleavages and the multiplicity of inherited political messages and collective identities make it extremely difficult (and risky) for policymakers to explicitly link their policies to any specific institutional and cultural stock which could provide the basis for a road map for social and economic change.

For all the recent growing emphasis on the importance of institutions, much less is known about the dynamics of institutional change (Clague et al, op. cit.). Nevertheless, it is clear that it cannot take place independently of the political

---

21 Brazilian President Cardoso has recently declared that his country is not poor, but simply unjust. This statement has since been quoted often by the Inter-American Development Bank President Iglesias, and although in different degrees, it can be related to many countries in the region.

processes evolving in society; rather it is the nature of these processes – messy and uncertain as they may be – and their patterns of interest conflict and alignment, which shape the course and the fate of the processes of institutional change. The promotion of markets and democracy are quite different propositions, and their implications can only be treated here together in a very generalised manner. Nevertheless, in so far as they both refer to specific choices for the direction and nature of institutional change, they are likely to entail considerable and lasting displacement of wealth, income, power and privileges, and thus acute political disputes.

The point argued here is twofold. First, governments do not have an intrinsic mandate over these institutional choices independent of societies. If governments are to lead the process of changes towards markets and democracies, this mandate will have to be construed through the dynamics of political interaction with the diverse interests of society. Second, there is no possible control over the process and its institutional results, and thus expertly designed blueprints for institutional reforms have limited effectiveness. If the process of changes towards democratization and a stronger role for markets is successful, the result, at any given point, will probably differ substantially from the original blueprint: it will be as much an accommodation of the main disputes among the politically effective interests -as they manifest themselves locally- as a synthesis of the new with the old elements of prevailing institutions and the general political culture.

This should not be surprising. Both market-driven economies and democratic political systems are concepts which are meaningful only at an abstract level. Western economies and polities that qualify under these concepts, display wide variety in the extent and forms of state intervention in the market, or in the division of attributions between state and market in resource allocation, as well as in the set of political institutions that compose governments, their nature, and *modus operandi.*

The historical development of these economic and political arrangements and institutions was shaped not only by the progress of ideas and values and the processes of economic change but to a great extent by the political conflicts and constraints of past experience and culture.

Leading the processes of change towards stronger markets and democracy in the context of the low governance capacity which characterizes many developing countries is likely to tax heavily the intangible determinants of this capacity. In the absence of an effective legal system that can bind policymakers to the rule of law, with a public bureaucracy prone to patronage, capture, or corruption, and given the probable widespread perceptions of governmental unfairness, arbitrariness and ineffectiveness, it may take very strong and able leadership to command trust, credibility and legitimacy for the reforms. Considerable political skills would be needed to craft strategic support coalitions and administer the conflict over the redistribution of gains and losses. Established institutions and value systems have a powerful grip on behaviour (van Arkadie, 1994), and are likely to prove resilient to strategies of change that discount the importance of the symbolic and inspirational aspects of policymaking. The mandate for reforms has to be construed, in an environment where the changes are generated and maintained, and the underlying principles and goals of the new institutions have to be made intelligible and consistent with past experience, as interpreted by the existing political culture.

Concluding remarks

This paper has attempted to distinguish the various goals of the reform agenda by focusing on their different nature and political requirements. It has thus tried to explain why reforms may fare better at achieving stabilization and reversal of governance crisis than at maintaining and generating political support for the longer, more complex and demanding processes of institutional change which lead to stronger market-orientated economies and democratic systems of government. The prospects for the latter are far from hopeless. However, they may hinge on the understanding that governmental mandates for these changes are not intrinsic or automatic, that their value is not self-evident and has to be made consistent with culture and experience, and that there will likely be considerable political dispute and adaptation shaping the course of these changes and their results.

References

Alesina, Alberto and Drazen, Allan, 'Why Are Stabilizations Delayed?', American Economic Review, Vol. 81 (1991) n.5.

Bates, Robert, and Krueger, Ann, (eds), *Political and Economic Interactions in Economic Policy Reform*, (Cambridge MA: Blackwell, 1993).

Berman, Harold J. , *Law and Revolution – The formation of the western legal tradition*, (Cambridge: Harvard University Press, 1983).

Clague, Christopher et al, 'Institutions and Economic Performance: Property Rights and Contract Enforcement', paper presented at the conference on 'Economic and Political Institutions for Sustainable Development', Washington DC (1994).

Chubb, John and Peterson, Paul, 'American Political Institutions and the Problem of Governance' in Chubb, John and Peterson, Paul (eds), *Can the Government Govern?*, (Washington DC: The Brookings Institution, 1989).

Drazen, Allan and Grilli, Victorio, 'The Benefit of Crises for Economic Reforms'', Working Paper n.3527, (Cambridge, MA: National Bureau of Economic Research, 1990).

Fernandez, Raquel, and Rodrik, Dani, 'Resistance to Reform: Status-quo Bias in the Presence of Individual-Specific Uncertainty', American Economic Review (1991) p81.

Frischtak, Leila, 'Governance Capacity and Economic Reform in Developing Countries'', World Bank Technical Paper 254 (Washington DC: The World Bank, 1994).

Frischtak, Leila, 'Governance and Adjustment in Brazil', paper presented at the Conference on Governance and Structural Adjustment (Washington DC: The World Bank, 1994-b).

Grindle, Merilee and Thomas, John, *Public Choices and Policy Change* (Baltimore: John Hopkins University Press, 1991).

Haggard, Stephan and Kaufman, Robert (eds), *The Politics of Economic Adjustment* (Princeton: Princeton University Press, 1992).

Haggard, Stephan and Webb, Steven (eds), *Voting for Reform* (New York: Oxford University Press for the World Bank, 1994).

Ibrahim, Saad Eddin, 'Governance and Structural Adjustment: the Egyptian Case', paper presented at the Conference on Governance and Successful Adjustment, Washington DC, The World Bank (1994).

Landell-Mills, P. and Seragaldin, I., 'Governance and the External Factor', Proceedings of the World Bank Annual Conference on Development Economics (1991).

Morales, Juan Antonio, 'Governance Capacity and Adjustment in Bolivia', paper presented at the Conference on Governance and Successful Adjustment, Washington DC, The World Bank (1994).

Naim, Moises, *Paper Tigers and Minotaurs: The Politics of Venezuelan Economic Reform* (Washington DC: Carnegie Endowment Books, 1993).

Naim, Moises, and Pinango, Y., *El caso Venezuela: Una ilusion de armonia* (Caracas: Ediciones IESA, 1984).

Navarro, Juan Carlos, 'Reversal of Fortune: the Ephemeral Success of Adjustment in Venezuela between 1989 and 1993', paper presented at the Conference on Governance and Successful Adjustment, Washington DC, The World Bank (1994).

Nelson, Joan (ed), *Fragile Coalitions: The Politics of Economic Adjustment* (Washington DC: The Overseas Development Council, 1989).

Nelson, Joan (ed), *Economic Crisis and Policy Choices* (Princeton: Princeton University Press, 1990).

Nelson, Joan (ed), *A Precarious Balance: Democracy and Economic Reforms* (California: The Institute for Contemporary Studies, 1994).

Nelson, Joan et al, *Intricate Links: Democratization and Market Reforms in Latin America and Eastern Europe* (New Brunswick: Transaction Publishers, 1994).

Rodrik, Dani, 'The Positive Economics of Successful Reform' in the <u>American Economics Association Pacers and Proceedings</u>, Vol. 83 (1993) n.2.

Rodrik, Dani, 'Understanding Economic Policy Reform', mimeo.

Rodrik, Dani, 'King Kong Meets Godzilla: The World Bank and The East Asian Miracle' in Wade, Robert et al (eds), *Miracle or Design? Lessons from the East Asian Experi*ence (Washington DC: Overseas Development Council, Policy Essay No 11, 1994).

Shihata, Ibrahim, *The World Bank in a Changing World* (Dordrecht: Martinus Nighoff, 1991).

Shihata, Ibrahim, 'Judicial Reform in Developing Countries and the Role of the World Bank' in *Justice and Development in Latin American and the Caribbean* (Washington DC, The Inter-American Development Bank, 1993).

Trebilcock, Michael, 'The Institutional Preconditions of Development: what do we know?', mimeo (1994).

Van Arkadie, Brian, 'Economic Strategy and Structural Adjustment in Tanzania', paper presented at the Conference on Governance and Successful Adjustment (1994), forthcoming.

Watson, Alan, *Roman Law and Comparative Law* (The University of Georgia Press, 1991).

Weber, Max *Economy and Society, Volume 2* (Berkley: University of California Press, 1978).

World Bank, *Sub-Saharan Africa – From Crisis to Sustainable Growth. A Long-Term Perspective* (Washington DC: World Bank, 1989).

World Bank, *Governance and Development* (Washington DC: World Bank, 1992).

World Bank, 'Adjustment Lending and Mobilization of Private and Public Resources for Growth', <u>Country Economics Department Policy and Research Series</u>, No 22 (1992).

COMMENT

Patrick McAuslan

This paper develops some important themes and in a sense, brings us back full circle to where we set out. I would like to draw attention to two important points in the paper, to try and summarise the most crucial issues arising from the paper and to offer reflections on how law and governance might develop in the future.

The first point to which we should pay close attention is her comment that by ignoring our own history of the evolution of markets and the connection between markets and democracy we are also ignoring the history of those societies on which we are seeking to impose the same kind of economic and social transformation. I would agree with this criticism of present policies. The evolution of societies in Western Europe to their present state was a slow, uneven and messy process yet we seem to imagine that with the 'correct' application of law, market-orientated economics and principles of governance, societies in the developing world and in Eastern Europe will be able to avoid the kind of historical process of development we have been through and arrive painlessly at the desired state of well-run free markets and democratic policies. The evidence does not support this assumption.

The second important point made in the paper is the need to separate out the components of the reform process so that they can be judged on their individual merits rather than adopt a holistic view and hence lose the identify of each. While agreeing with this I think Frischtak may be fighting a losing battle since the message coming through in statements by some World Bank official is that governance has moved from being concerned with stabilising macro-economic imbalances – that is from having specific components directed to an economic end – to being the organizing principle for the World Bank and therefore possibly for donor intervention in a country's management as a whole; in other words governance is seen in a holistic fashion. I will return to this point and its implications later.

Frischtak's paper expertly draws attention to three tensions in the governance/ law debate. These exist between: market reform and democratic reform; institutional change and the less than tangible factors of leadership; externally promoted and induced change and the traditional cultures and beliefs of society. While these tensions are important there are two other equally important tensions which Frischtak only hinted at. I will return to these below.

Frischtak states that these tensions have to be managed by governments and this creates overload problems for governments. So the process of reform itself for once they start from contributing to solutions to governance problems actually compounds the problems. The lack of skills and knowledge which reform is, *inter alia*, meant to address prevents the reforms from getting under way or being successful.

Another vital point which Frischtak makes, which has been made by many other commentators, is that there has to be internal momentum for change; without that, change is neither possible nor effective. An important issue then is: What can external pressure do to promote internal change? Can or should external pressure be used to promote internal change? Is there not some evidence that internal momentum for change can only be truly brought about by internal catastrophe or near catastrophe since it provides a window of opportunity for reform to take hold. In Africa, the following countries had all reached the point where there was nowhere to go but to introduce fundamental economic, social and political reforms: Uganda in East Africa; Ghana in West Africa and South Africa in Southern Africa (although the extent to which external efforts helped to provoke the reform process in South Africa is at issue). In each of these countries it is the presence and force of a charismatic leader which has been of crucial significance in the reform process. In Eastern Europe and the CIS, the old system ran out of steam and so provided the opportunity for reformers on the inside to begin the process of introducing market-orientated economic reforms and democratic-orientated political reforms.

So too with law reform. States have to be aware of their problems and see the need for reform before external assistance can be of use.

I want to turn now to the two missing tensions I referred to above:
• the tension between the whole state and the market enclave; that is tension between governance reform designed to legitimize the governing institutions in the eyes of the citizenry and governance reform designed to ensure the efficient operation of the market in those parts of the state where a market will benefit the global economy, or in other words the legitimization of the governing institutions in the eyes of the foreign investment community;
• the tension within the donor community arising out of the first 'missing' tension; between that is the Scandinavian, the Dutch and to some extent the German GTZ donors stressing human rights and administrative justice and the World Bank, ODA and USAID stressing efficient markets and governance.

This is where the hegemonic approach to governance espoused by on behalf of the World Bank by some of its officials poses real dangers for the developing world. This approach is designed to 'trump' or push to one side the Northern European approach to governance as a tool to pursue social and political justice. Governance as justification for policy and institutional intervention into developing countries is to be used to advance the imperatives of the market. Rather than social justice as the goal, it is law and order which is to be emphasized. Rather than administrative justice, it is deregulation and privatization which is to be advanced by accountability and transparency. Governance is to be used to advance the special approach to government which first came to prominence in the Reagan/Thatcher years in the USA and the UK, that of economic liberalism and social authoritarianism, which is also the approach taken by the more successful East Asian economies.

When applied from the outside, from the North, to developing countries in Africa, Asia and elsewhere in the South, we can see that this recipe for government has been used before: in the colonial experience where the mission of the North to bring modern government to the South was far more about enabling the North to exploit the resources of the South than to introduce the inhabitants of the South to the trappings of liberal democracy.

Here too then is where interest from forces in Latin America in World Bank involvement in criminal justice as an aspect of governance should be of concern to all those sceptical of the World Bank's approach to governance. For an important tenet of Anglo-American social authoritarianism is that there is no connection between the withdrawal of the state from social welfare and economic development programmes designed to boost employment and a rise in crime which begins to impinge on upper income groups. So if the World Bank and ODA and USAID do begin to put resources into criminal justice reform, and I think that this will come, these resources will not be directed to access to justice programmes – legal aid, popular legal education, neighbourhood law centres – designed to improve the quality of criminal justice as it impinges on the urban poor. Instead, these resources will go to what no doubt will be called 'correctional justice programmes' or the more efficient management and even privatization of 'public enforcement utilities' which will be aimed at punishing the poor and putting them in their place. This too was a part of the colonial experience for many indigenous peoples.

We are at a crossroad on governance and Frischtak's paper brings that out well. She concludes that economic reforms should concentrate on the shorter term efforts at stabilization and the reversal of governance crisis as the alternative to bringing about institutional changes which will "lead to stronger market-orientated market economies and democratic systems of government". However, this approach will, I believe, flounder on the incompatibility of trying to do both, with the inevitable result, if the World Bank continues to set the pace on governance reform, that market reforms will be emphasized at the expense of democratic reforms. A further consequence is that democratic reforms may even be reversed if the social authoritarianism in welfare and criminal justice, thought to be an essential component of market reforms in the UK and the USA, infects the World Bank's programmes and perspectives.

6 The need for a regulatory framework in the development and liberalization of financial markets in Africa

Robert A. Annibale*

The transition to a spontaneously functioning market economy cannot be initiated by market forces themselves. Indeed, the only force powerful enough to set the market forces in motion is the very state that is supposed to remove itself from the picture. And for a number of reasons, the state may be unable to accomplish this task. (Frydman and Rapaczynski, 1994, p 57)

INTRODUCTION

Economic reform and liberalization in Africa aimed at developing an open market economy will be the focus of this paper. The implications of such policies on the development and governance of the financial sector, especially the banking sector, will be given particular attention.

'Emerging markets' is the new buzz word in financial jargon. It is used by the international financial press and financial institutions to describe those financial markets, in developing countries, perceived to be in the process of liberalizing economic policies and opening up their economies to domestic and foreign private sector investors. There is the perception and, indeed, likelihood that once categorized as an emerging market these economies will attract significant, though not necessarily stable, foreign investment funds.

Privatization and the rapid deregulation and liberalization of the financial sector, at times within the policy framework of a structural adjustment programme, as is often the case in Africa, are commonly associated with emerging markets.

There are strong pressures for many of these governments to significantly and rapidly deregulate their financial markets as a prerequisite for attracting such investments. However, I would argue that the political decision to move from a centrally planned or managed economy to that of an open market economy necessitates a discussion as to what activities and groups are encompassed by the term 'market'.

* Vice-President, Citibank, NA. The views expressed in this paper are those of the author and do not necessarily correspond to those of Citibank, NA.

The implications of introducing appropriate restructuring and training programmes, as well as technical and legal mechanisms to ensure the good governance of the financial market, also needs to be discussed.[1]

To present my argument I will draw on my experiences of issues and opportunities which the transition to, and development of, a market economy in Africa have provided, and on my role of supervising treasury, capital markets and equity activities for an international financial institution with a local presence in many of these markets.

I will argue – perhaps to the surprise of some – that a precondition to the sustainable development of an 'emerging' and open market economy is not the rapid deregulation of the financial sector, marginalization of government regulators or greater self-regulation by the private sector. Governments must ensure that policies and laws supporting the development of an open market system are based on broad domestic support, including respect and the incorporation of aspects of customary law when possible, and not only that of international institutions, bilateral donors, economists and bankers. The policy and legal or regulatory changes associated with the development of the financial sector in an open economy should be implemented at such a pace that local financial institutions can participate in the inherent and changing opportunities and risks. The state must provide a fair, consistent, and transparent regulatory framework for those operating in such markets.[2]

I will not attempt to review the vast literature on the issues raised, but will share some observations and concerns on the liberalization and reform of financial markets in Africa, particularly the banking sector, from the perspective of being daily engaged with such markets. Recent experiences in Eastern and Central Europe also have something to offer to the argument since many countries in these regions have similar objectives for making the transition to a market economy and are similarly confronted with the issue of defining the role of the state in the transition and the development of the domestic financial markets, particularly the banking sector. [3]

Unless deregulation and liberalization are implemented and introduced in Africa's financial markets at a realistic pace, the anticipated economic benefits may be restricted to a small section of the banking sector.[4] As part of this implementation process domestic financial institutions and the regulatory agencies, professional associations and legislation that govern the market need to be reformed and strengthened.

---

1   I have discussed these views on market liberalization in Africa on a number of occasions; see Annibale (1993a; 1993b; 1994).
2   For a broader discussion on these issues, see Healey and Robinson (1992) and Przeworski (1991).
3   See Griffith-Jones and Drabek (1995).
4   For a detailed overview of recent economic trends and statistics for Sub-Saharan Africa, see Hadjimichael et al. (1995).

RELATING MARKET LIBERALIZATION TO THE 'MARKET' IN AFRICA

To discuss financial market reform in the broader context of the fundamental economic and political liberalization which has occurred in much of Africa during the last few years it is first important to define what is encompassed by the term 'market'. It is also necessary to verify whether the regulatory institutions involved are effectively empowered, competent and independent and are supported by a dynamic legal and regulatory framework which can provide the degree of supervision and intervention necessary to facilitate and sustain the development of a resilient and open market economy.[5]

The terms 'market reforms' and 'market liberalization' are bandied about in most discussions on economic deregulation or restructuring, but it is important to understand how fragile and thin many of the present formal sector financial markets are in Africa when applying them to the situation here. According to the World Bank, sub-Saharan African bank deposits represent just 15 per cent of its GDP and its financial systems have not grown in real terms in the past decade (World Bank, 1994, p110). While most adjustment policies are designed and evaluated on the basis of their impact on the formal sector of the economy, the banking, capital and equities markets, the informal sector is generally only mentioned when comparing official to 'black market' or 'parallel market' exchange rates. However, as Nissanke puts it, "While thriving forces are operating on a remarkably significant scale within some of the sub-sectors of the informal financial activities, this dynamism has hardly been transmitted to the formal financial sector though potential and complementary relationships" (Nissanke, 1994: 169).

While the informal sector has been a source of working capital and credit for many small enterprises, it is not unknown for larger enterprises to approach it for 'financial solutions', particularly relating to foreign exchange in highly regulated markets. Although this paper does not focus on the informal financial markets, the subject deserves more attention since it is often the only significant provider of financial services to some communities.[6] If the formal financial sector is to dominate policy considerations, then those institutions which will service the needs of these communities should be developed. The links between the formal and informal financial markets need to be understood and often strengthened. The development in an increasing number of countries of links between micro-finance institutions (which lend small amounts to the self-employed or to very small scale industries, usually on terms based on customary or community

---

5   See Colclough and Manor (1991), who examine the neo-liberal debate in development policy formulation between those who advocate primacy of states or markets.
6   See Roe (1992).

lending traditions) and formal sector financial institutions (banks) is encouraging. The latter are rarely significant direct lenders to small scale businesses. As observed by Johnson, "for many countries, particularly in Africa, bank credit has remained elusive for most of the population, particularly those in rural areas, the urban poor and women" (Johnson, 1994, p175).

In many countries, the formal financial 'market' is comprised of only a few banks, most of which are under-reserved for bad debts and have troubled balance sheets, low capitalization and liquidity (funding) problems, inadequate financial reporting, outdated technology, and a management lacking the experience and information systems to respond quickly to changing economic policies or increased market volatility and illiquidity. Many major economic policy and regulatory changes have been focused on this troubled sector, particularly in structural adjustment programmes in Africa, with the expectation that it will increasingly lead to an open market directed economy.

STATE OF THE BANKING SECTOR

The banking sector in most African countries is segmented into groupings – development institutions, public sector banks, local private sector banks and international banks, which do not necessarily actively interact or compete. With the liberalization of markets has come a proliferation of new banks and other, often virtually unregulated institutions such as finance and leasing houses, mortgage banks and bureaux de change. Although the banking sector in most of Africa is segmented and in need of restructuring and recapitalization, the role of the banks in an open market economy is pivotal. Their state and capabilities need to be reviewed carefully when developing plans to liberalize the sector, particularly with regard to the pacing of such programmes and to the redefinition of the roles of regulators in an open market economy.

In many countries, the central bank remains the dominant player in the banking sector. It controls interest rates and exchange rates, is the sole issuer of and agent for securities in the market (treasury bills and bonds), and the 'lender of last resort' for banks.

Interbank money markets (the lending of funds between banks) in most African countries are not active for maturities beyond three or six months. Many are still only overnight markets (when banks place or borrow funds from one another overnight), and even fewer have secondary securities markets (the active buying and selling of bills and bonds between institutions and/or investors). There are a number of explanations for this, but the lack of published standard financial information and audited accounts, has resulted in banks frequently restricting who they extend credit to, and trade with, to only short tenors. Instead of lending excess funds to one another, banks often choose to place these funds with the central bank or use them to purchase government treasury bills. This is particularly true of branches of international banks and foreign investors since they are more risk adverse to institutions which do not release adequate and timely financial information. In some countries where there have been significant bank failures, negative real interest rates and poor management of the economy by the government, the banking sector can become disintermediated by a parallel or black market economy, such as in Zaire.

These factors, combined with the existing segmentation of the banking sector and the absence of alternative capital and equity markets, have resulted in markets more characterized by restricted bank lending to a narrow section of the economy, little competition between banks, fewer innovative financial products or concern for customer service quality, than is usually the case in more developed markets.

Development institutions and directed lending

In addition to direct lending to the government, many banks have loan portfolios distorted by government-directed lending to specific sectors. This is often to public agencies, projects or institutions whose subsidies, market protection or state patronage are likely to be reduced or eliminated under liberalization or structural adjustment programmes. Such directed loans (for example, agricultural, housing, small business financing) are often for the medium term, usually over one or two years, but can be for a period of five years. They are also often below commercial lending rates and are primarily held by public sector and development banks.

Many of these institutions, however, do not have corresponding local currency medium-term liabilities (funding) or adequate capital. They therefore often fund such loans with foreign currency borrowings from bilateral or multilateral development institutions, exposing themselves or their customers to significant foreign exchange risks.

Development banks and public sector banks have found themselves with drastically reduced funding and difficulties in raising increased capital from governments which have introduced economic liberalization programmes. This means that economically fragile, though critical, sectors of the economy have reduced access to financing since private sector financial institutions are rarely interested in filling this financing gap. Instead, lending is generally focused on short-term trade, particularly to those importers or industries which can respond quickly to opportunities which have been created by reductions in import duties and other trade liberalization policies, which are often closely timed to financial liberalization.

Government shareholding in the banking sector

In some markets, the government represents the largest shareholder in the banking sector, both in specialized institutions, such as development and agricultural banks, and in the commercial banking sector. This inevitably results in management and directors of these financial institutions being appointed and acting as agents of government, or having specific political interests. Such shareholding and management structures, particularly in commercial and savings banks, make minority shareholders and foreign institutions wary, because the roles and independence of shareholders, boards of directors, management, and regulators become blurred. The benefits of a system of checks and balances between these groups is lost and good corporate governance proves more difficult. When the majority of shares are held by the government, political appointments for senior positions of management are common. This perception of political interference in the management of publicly-held banks has deterred many investors from pursuing potential joint banking ventures, between the public and private sector. This makes the role of banking regulators and supervisors difficult since they are likely to find their authority challenged by politically appointed and powerful managers and directors with vested interests.[7]

While some government equity holdings in banks date back to nationalizations during the independence era, others relate to more recent or ongoing government takeovers of troubled banks. The collapse of the Bank of Credit and Commerce International (BCCI) banking group, which had a presence in many African countries and which was one of the most sensational international bank failures, resulted in governments having to undertake local BCCI affiliated bank rescues. In most cases, governments decided to take over failed banks rather than to liquidate them, often merging them with other publicly controlled institutions. Other financial institutions, such as finance, mortgage and leasing companies have also had many failures. Governments in Africa, as in most other parts of the world, have found that national depositor insurance funds, when they exist, will lack the resources to cover fully depositors in the event of major bank failures. They have usually chosen to intervene and take over such institutions to protect depositors and stabilize already fragile banking systems.[8]

---

7   For a more detailed discussion of the issue of 'patrimonial character' of the state, see Dia (1993).
8   This is not dissimilar to the decision by the US government when faced with the collapse of dozens of savings and loan associations and banks in the late 1980s. The US government chose to establish the Resolution Trust Company, which would issue securities to the market, with the government's guarantee, and take over many of the troubled loan portfolios of these savings banks, so that they could be sold and often merged with larger banks. The recent French government bail-out of troubled Credit Lyonnais, a state-owned bank which in 1994 received more than $4. billion in support from the government, demonstrates that the decision by many African governments to take over or inject capital into troubled banks is not unfamiliar to governments in more developed financial capitals.

The necessary powers, training and resources which have been allocated to central bank regulators and supervisors by governments in Africa have frequently not been commensurate or introduced at the same pace as those of reform and liberalization of their financial sectors. Perhaps for the first time in many countries, including the United Kingdom, the collapse of the BCCI group raised public attention and concern for the solvency of major banking networks. The effectiveness of banking supervisors and independent external auditors in ensuring transparency and accuracy of financial information for shareholders and depositors was thrown into serious doubt. Subsequent investigations also highlighted the many close and inappropriate links which existed between BCCI directors and senior government officials in a number of countries, making it almost impossible for local banking regulators to intervene or publicly expose obvious irregularities. Consequently, public confidence in government banking supervision and in the banking system suffered in much of Africa, as well as in the UK. [9]

While banking frauds are common in many markets and often have a political dimension, the exposure of the so-called 'Goldenberg swindle' in Kenya raised the discussion of the 'crisis of government' to new levels, locally and internationally. Using two Kenyan firms, Goldenberg International and Exchange Bank, a well known Kenyan businessman and senior officials of the Central Bank and ministry of finance are alleged to have defrauded the Kenyan Government of more than 18 billion Kenyan shillings. They achieved this primarily through export compensation claims for fictitious gold and diamond exports. They now face charges for stealing more than Sh 40 billion in total from the government from 1990-1993. This is roughly the equivalent of $890 million which, as the 19-25 December 1994 issue of the Nairobi The Economic Review put it, is "slightly more than the $850 million new aid which the bilateral and multilateral donors committed to Kenya in November 1991. Even more significant, the amount is equivalent to 12.5 per cent of Kenya's gross domestic product (GDP) of Sh 320 billion (in 1993)".

The scale of these frauds and the seniority of government officials charged has resulted in a further loss in confidence in the integrity, independence and competence of banking regulators and the judiciary in Kenya. As stated well by Evans, "personalism and plundering at the top destroy any possibility of rule-governed behavior in the lower levels of the bureaucracy" (Evans, 1992, p150).

This scandal, which follows others in Kenya and the collapse of a number of financial institutions in the last few years, resulted in various demands being made by donors, opposition parties and the press. These were for increased

---

9   Many of these linkages were discussed in detail in the US Senate hearings on 'The BCCI Affair' (1992).

powers and independence for banking supervision and judicial enquiries, more transparency in the ownership and management of financial institutions, and public access to mandatory external auditors' reports prepared according to international standards.

Many regulators, bank managers or directors in Africa lack the training and experience in key areas. These include managing risks in floating foreign exchange or interest rate environments; open-market operations; securities and equities trading.

With the liberalization and internationalization of many previously closed financial markets, speculative and other pressures are likely to increase significantly the volatility of markets and rates, particularly exchange rates. Institutions, both public and private, will need specific training, technology and policies to limit and monitor such risks. Certainly, almost none of these institutions will have had any experience with derivative products, which are volatile, complicated to value and monitor, and the subject of significant recent media attention regarding cases involving Bankers Trust in the US and the failure of the Barings group.

Some of the north African countries (Tunisia, Morocco and Egypt) have liberalized and reformed their financial markets gradually, avoiding sudden policy changes and shocks. While they have caught the attention of emerging markets' fund managers, investment in them has been primarily restricted to privatization schemes, which have not usually included financial institutions, or through their small stock exchanges.

Some investment funds have invested relatively small amounts in Ghana, Zimbabwe, Mauritius and Botswana. However, sub-Saharan Africa has received virtually no net foreign investment in years, despite nearly a decade of structural adjustment and economic reform programmes which were intended to liberalize markets and to attract foreign investment. Even the World Bank estimates that for those countries with "large improvements in macro-economic policies" the median change in gross domestic investment as a share of gross domestic product only increased by 1.1 per cent – for the periods 1981-86 and 1987-91 (World Bank, 1994, p154-155).

Few governments, however, can claim to have consistently followed through with their adjustment programmes as agreed with the Bretton Woods institutions. This was usually because the programmes lacked broad political support and realistically-paced implementation. The liberalization of policies and markets in the banking sector often preceded essential restructuring and recapitalization of weak banks, and occurred before banking regulators and supervisors were prepared to regulate effectively and supervise financial institutions in increasingly volatile markets.

Action of foreign banks

The banking sector in most of Africa has experienced significant and visible disinvestment by international banking groups during the last few years. Several major international banking groups, represented in Africa since before independence, have sold their entire African networks. The sale of the French group BIAO, with its presence across Francophone Africa, to the pan-African Meridien group (the now in liquidation Meridien/BIAO Group), based in Luxembourg and managed from Lusaka, was perhaps the most significant signal to the financial markets that French banking groups and the French Government, which was the largest shareholder in BIAO, were reducing their commitment and exposure to Africa. Similarly, the decision by Anz Grindlays to sell its African franchise to Standard Bank of South Africa indicated to many that traditionally present international banking networks no longer viewed Africa as an important part of their global strategy. It was seen as confirmation that the expansion of South African institutions in the region would be cautious. Other foreign banks have recently reduced their presence, closing branches (Barclays in Francophone Africa) and representative offices, or reducing their equity holdings in subsidiaries or affiliates. Other than in South Africa, major international banking groups based in Japan, Germany, Switzerland and elsewhere have shown little interest in establishing a presence in Africa. Citibank is the only major international financial institution to continue to expand its already extensive branch network in Africa, and the sole American bank with a network across Africa.

Foreign-controlled banks play an important role in many African markets by introducing products, activities, and expertise acquired in other developed or emerging markets. This is despite usually being small in comparison with major national banks and being criticized for restricting their lending primarily to the largest and strongest corporate customers and for being primarily based in major cities. Inevitably, their local staff, usually very selectively recruited and often trained overseas, are hired away by local institutions for their skills. There is an enormous demand from local banks and regulators for training in areas such as foreign exchange and money market trading, primary and secondary securities markets and for technology to monitor new types of price and liquidity risks, as well as to meet accounting, tax and regulatory reporting requirements. While competitive factors limit how much of these needs can be directly addressed by foreign-controlled banks, there is usually a good flow of such information across markets primarily facilitated by staff moves, the introduction of new products which have been inspired by experiences in other markets, and information shared with local professional associations (such as forex associations and bankers associations).

Most foreign-controlled banks will have to fulfil the regulatory, accounting, and legal requirements not only of the local market, but also of the head office depending on its location. American bank branches overseas, for example, must apply US accounting standards to their financial accounts, as these are then consolidated with those of its parent group. It must also have processes in place to cover US legislation governing officers' conflicts of interest, insider-trading and bribery, as well as to demonstrate to US regulators that adequate regulatory and risk management controls are in place in each operation. Overseas branches of American banks are regularly inspected by US banking supervisors such as the Federal Reserve Bank and Office of the Controller of the Currency. They may be active advocates of, and players in, open-market economies, including that of the domestic US market itself, but they are also among the most heavily regulated, supervised and circumscribed banks in the world. Such institutions are likely to pressure governments to introduce many of these requirements and standards in their own markets, if only to ensure they do not have to operate at what might be seen as a competitive disadvantage to less regulated local competitors.

South African market

South Africa is the only country in Africa likely in the near future to further attract significant numbers of foreign commercial and merchant banks to participate in its domestic market. It has by far the most developed banking sector in terms of meeting international capital adequacy levels, credit and financial disclosure standards, technology and management information systems, a well-developed clearing system, a developed capital market and a management which has benefited from training and exposure to international markets. South Africa's banking sector is comprised of strong specialized institutions, such as merchant, commercial, savings and development banks, interbank and stock market brokers and research firms, the world's ten largest stock markets and a futures exchange. Since the Government of National Unity took office, foreign commercial and merchant banks, which have long been represented in South Africa, are increasing their presence. Many others have opened representative offices with the intention of expanding these to full service banks, while South African banks have expanded their international branch networks.

The financial press sometimes refers to the South African banking sector as being an 'overbanked market', because it has become a very competitive market with banks having to decrease margins and increase the sophistication of products and services to attract or retain customers. However, one must again ask what is being referred to by the term 'market' in this context. Who are the participants in this market, which institutions and individuals, and who is benefiting from such competition and services? Although the South African financial markets cannot be described as undeveloped, thin or fragile, they have largely ignored whole sections of the population. The African residents of many townships and rural areas, who combined represent the majority of the population, would be unlikely to argue that the 'market' is overbanked or that they are benefiting from competition in the market. This may also be true elsewhere but rarely with the extreme contrasts which characterize the South African market. In the case of South Africa, the market is divided and the majority of the population continues to have a limited relationship with a banking sector that has few branches in the areas where they live, employs few African managers, and which generally only offers savings products to these communities, as opposed to loans and mortgages.

PROCESS OF LIBERALIZATION

The process of liberalization and reform of the financial sector involves many agents, political as well as economic, whose interests and views need to be considered when designing and implementing an economic liberalization programme. Those agents primarily concerned with economic policy issues – technocrats, regulators and financial intermediaries, including external groups such as the World Bank and International Monetary Fund – need to co-operate with other political, civic, environmental and, in some countries, religious groups when developing and implementing an economic reform programme. After many years of debate, social and environmental implications and concerns are beginning to be at least discussed in the development of these programmes. While it is often argued that these reforms will be beneficial to the economy as a whole, the effects of policy and regulatory change on different groups and interests will not be the same. Special interest pressures will arise and, in a democratic system, will need to be addressed by those politicians that have delegated such powers to economic technocrats and regulators.

Liberalization has generally been introduced through structural adjustment programmes, whether IMF and/or World Bank inspired formal programmes with agreed actions and targets, usually tied to borrowings. Typical policy changes in structural adjustment programmes which directly affect financial markets include steps towards floating the local currency (commonly resulting in a devaluation), liberalization of interest rates (rate increases to achieve real interest rates), and control of the money supply and advances by the central bank to government entities and financial institutions (tightening liquidity in the market). Other common features include reduced government budget deficit targets, trade and payments liberalization, reduced government subsidies and price controls, fiscal reform, privatization and civil service reforms. While the effectiveness and social costs associated with structural adjustment programmes have been the subject of much debate, they are likely to continue to dominate economic policies in Africa. Bilateral and multilateral development aid flows, Paris club (official debt) and London club (private bank debt) restructuring and debt reduction schemes are usually conditional upon a country complying with agreed economic and policy targets detailed in the terms of a structural adjustment plan.[10] Because few countries have significant access to the international capital markets, such conditionality tends to dominate decisions on the pace and implementation of reform programmes.[11]

To reform and liberalize financial markets does not necessarily mean to deregulate them. On the contrary, it may imply the need for more comprehensive, innovative or flexible regulations applied by new or reinvigorated supervisory institutions with the resources and training to supervise complex and globally-integrated financial markets effectively and dynamically. According to Bates, "This is the essence of what Kahler has labelled the 'orthodox paradox': that the expansion of the role of markets requires a strengthening of the state and especially of its financial bureaucracy" (Bates, 1993: 426). Ideally, the strengthening of the financial bureaucracy and of the supervisors and regulators of financial markets, would be accompanied by a decrease in the powers and frequency in which these institutions intervene in an open market, other than to ensure adequate market liquidity, transparency and stability.[12]

While many economic reform programmes and structural adjustment programmes have included financial sector restructuring or recapitalization programmes, the sequencing and timing of fundamental macro-economic reforms should ensure that these institutions are prepared to participate professionally in an open market economy. The process of financial sector restructuring must not only take into consideration the banks and other financial institutions; it must also address the role of the central bank and other governmental agencies with responsibilities for the regulation of the market. While the World Bank has articulated many of the policy planning, management, institutional, legal and regulatory reforms necessary to support sustainable development, it is unfortunate that it does not stress the importance of the sequencing of these reforms and market liberalization taking into greater account the characteristics of each country's situation.[13]

---

10 See Kahler (1992) for a discussion on conditionality and the politics of adjustment.
11 For a comprehensive analysis of the World Bank's position on economic adjustment policies, reforming public sector institutions and so on, see World Bank (1994), and Husain and Faruquee (1994). For a discussion challenging many of the statistics and conclusions drawn by the World Bank on these issues in these publications, see Mosley and Weeks (1994). Also see Stewart (1992) for a number of well developed arguments calling for 'alternative development strategies for Africa'.
12 For an analytical framework for explaining the ways in which institutions and institutional change affect the performance of economies, see North (1990).

There is the assumption that with the development of an open-market economy financial institutions will play a greater role in determining the direction of market rates, such as foreign exchange and interest rates, based on competition and supply and demand. These institutions will determine whether to provide short-term or long-term financing at commercial rates and to whom, primarily based on the profitability of the particular transaction and the credit-standing of the customer. As these rates are increasingly determined by banks and their major customers in liberalized or open markets in most of Africa, the volatility of what were previously fixed foreign exchange and interest rates will rise and have significant effects on businesses and the economy. One would also assume that with the liberalization of these rates and greater convertibility of local currencies, banks will become more aggressive in trading foreign exchange and interest rate volatility, taking larger speculative positions. The activities of international speculators' positioning against a country's foreign exchange rate or in arbitrating its interest rates will further increase the volatility of these rates and will reduce the power of the state to manage previously fixed rates.

Even those who advocate that the adjustment of such rates should be left entirely to market forces are often concerned by the associated dramatic rate moves and significant speculative pressures. Not only do banks face new challenges based on their own positions and exposures to these markets, they will also be affected by the impact of volatile rate movements on their customers. While discussions on the role of, and limitations on, central banks to intervene and provide liquidity and stability to markets is beyond the scope of this paper, such interventions, individually or on a concerted front by various central banks, have become regular events in 'developed' markets and need to be considered when restructuring and strengthening the powers of Africa's central banks.[14]

REGULATING THE MARKET

The role of the central bank and banking regulators is perhaps most important when markets are in the process of liberalization since the transition to an open-market economy is likely to claim some financial institutions.[15] However, it is important to stress the supervisory role of central banks, or other banking regulators, in ensuring that the markets operate transparently and that institutions are adequately supervised, to minimize the risks of individual bank failures and

---

13 For a fuller understanding of the World Bank's view on some of these issues, see the World Bank document 'Governance and Development' (1992).
14 See Sobel (1994).
15 As Vos stated, "The experience in most reforming Latin American and East Asian countries has been that inadequate prudential regulation prevailed when initiating liberalisation policies and that banking crises were needed to pursue reforms in the system of bank supervision." (Vos, 1995, p192)

systemic risks regarding clearing and settlements systems. As Fisher stated, "Strong regulatory and supervisory policies are important to minimize moral hazards (including the corruption, fraud and excessive risk taking) in the banking system, to ensure the viability and health of the banking industry.... The ultimate objective of prudential regulation and supervision of the banking sector is to achieve stability (and public confidence in such stability) of the financial system, as well as to manage systemic risk and to protect clients" (Fisher, 1993, p126). He concluded that "as risks in the financial system increase as a result of greater competition, market volatility, and uncertainty after deregulation and liberalization, the authorities must strengthen prudential regulation, notably with respect to capital requirements and the range of bank supervision" (Fisher, 1993, p126).

The roles of different regulators must be clearly defined and consistent. This is even more important given the sudden increase in some countries in the number of new and small banks, many inadequately capitalized or staffed to respond to the rapid and volatile market movements which accompany reform. In Nigeria, for example, the number of banks increased mainly because banks had preferential access to foreign exchange from the central bank under an earlier foreign exchange allocation system. By mid-1993, there were about 125 commercial and investment banks, 100 mortgage banks and 600 finance houses and many bureaux de change. The regulators were left to keep up with the pressures of regulating so many institutions, under more complex and ever-changing regulations, in more volatile markets, with virtually no increase in resources or staff. Of particular concern was the growth in the number of finance houses, which, not being regulated by most banking acts, were under-supervised but still functioned much as banks. While the central bank was responsible for supervising most financial institutions, mortgage banks were, believe it or not, regulated by the Ministry of Public Works. Meanwhile, many senior and able central bank officials were offered attractive positions by these new or rapidly expanding financial institutions, further reducing the resources of the state to establish and implement policies, and to provide adequate supervision over this sector. With regulators paid much less than their counterparts in the private sector it is not surprising that there are regular allegations that some banking supervisors have been 'influenced' to look the other way at obvious regulatory infringements by some institutions.

There are those who advocate that self-regulatory bodies should play a greater role in regulating the financial markets in Africa. They usually refer to the UK, where self-regulatory bodies were the principal form of regulation for centuries in the banking and insurance markets. While these might have provided adequate supervision over the markets at one time, the corporate take-overs of many old and prominent partnerships and private banks in the 1980s and the entry into the market of many new players led to a significant increase in the powers of official regulatory bodies. Such self-regulatory bodies can play an important role, not as primary regulators, but in the form of professional associations. Groups, such as bankers associations, can be instrumental in developing 'codes of practice', as with the recent Code of Banking Practice in Britain. Such agreements provide a good basis for an ethical framework for market behaviour and are usually based on achieving a common position with the official regulators.[16] Such bodies, however, are not a substitute for independent and institutionalized regulatory oversight of banks and financial markets. These are needed to ensure that neither cartels nor monopolies have control over the fixing of interest rates, pricing or access to credit in the market.

Recommendations for prudential banking guidelines

Prudential banking guidelines and banking acts or legislation should provide for the following:
- the adoption and implementation, over a reasonable time frame, of risk-based bank capital adequacy guidelines as per the Basle Committee of Bank Supervisors recommendations, already a standard in most markets but still not introduced in a number of African markets[17];
- the establishment of standards and disclosures required for externally audited accounts, balance sheets and income statements, and other financial information to international norms;
- the introduction of standard requirements with regard to loan-loss reserves for non-performing debt;
- the guarantee of the collection and secure investment of adequate depositor insurance funds;
- the standardization and, to the extent that local technology permits, automation of daily and monthly reporting to the central bank, and co-ordination of reporting required by other government agencies or ministries, making as much information as possible available to the public;
- the standardization of market guidelines regarding insider trading, confidentiality, fiduciary activities, suspected fraud and money laundering;
- the regulation and supervision of bank holding companies, and bank holdings and activities in non-bank investments;

---

16 See McHugh (1995) for a fuller discussion on the issue of ethics and decision-making.
17 For a good description of the 1993 Basle Proposals, capital adequacy standards, harmonization of standards for banks and securities firms and, accounting and disclosure recommendations, see 'Developments in the Regulation of International Banking' in International Monetary Fund (September 1994).

- the encouragement of independent local credit ratings agencies to provide investors and depositors with the information necessary to differentiate institutions on the basis of both risk and returns;
- the monitoring of the activities of brokers and other financial intermediaries;
- the maintenance of appropriate bank statutory reserves but avoiding directed-credit requirements;
- liaison with legislators to ensure an adequate legal framework covering bankruptcy, foreclosure, registration and pledging of land and other assets;
- the regulation and supervision of the clearing system and any futures or options exchanges which are developed in the local market;
- the supporting of the establishment of professional bankers' associations which can improve the flow of market information and views between the banks and regulators, arbitrate on disputes between banks and establish 'rules of the game' or 'market practices' for some interbank activities;
- a guarantee to enact anti-trust legislation and regulations.[18]

One of the areas where regulators and supervisors must work with the banks in developing appropriate, accurate and timely information, especially if they are in the transition to an open economy, is foreign exchange positioning and other price risks associated with trading in increasingly volatile foreign exchange, securities or equities markets. Similarly, the monitoring of banks' interest rate and liquidity exposures needs to be done by both banks and by their regulators, who are most often their central bank and 'bank of last resort'. With the introduction of domestic and internationally traded derivative products (options, futures, swaps and so on), guidelines for the reporting and accounting of these activities need to be constantly reviewed, as this is an area under much discussion in virtually all markets where these products are traded. Regulators need to be able to review not only the technical models and systems used by banks engaged in derivatives products, but be equipped to make subjective judgements on bank managers' and directors' competence and understanding of the risks associated with these products.

CONCLUSIONS

> The market can reflect contrived or frivolous wants; it can be subject to
> monopoly, imperfect competition, or errors of information, but, apart from these,
> it is intrinsically perfect. (Galbraith, 1994, p107)

Regulatory institutions of the state have a fundamental role to play in a market economy, which does not preclude market participants and their collective

---

18 See Fisher (1993) who provides a more comprehensive list, which the author has extensively drawn upon and found very useful.

forces from exerting their influence and power. Market forces in even the most liberal *laissez-faire* economy represent particular vested interests. While these forces should be permitted to influence greatly and challenge the direction of financial markets, within a flexible framework of rules, they should not be a substitute for national economic policies developed for the collective interest of a broader spectrum of society.

The role and, perhaps, the political concept of the state is being challenged in much of Africa, as evidenced by the many democratically elected governments which have taken office in the last few years and by the demise of the role of the state in countries such as Liberia, Sudan, Rwanda, Somalia, Angola and Zaire. Institutional and regulatory restructuring is lagging, particularly in sub-Saharan Africa where political liberalization and economic liberalization are occurring simultaneously. This will inevitably affect the governments' ability to implement policy reforms. While there is wide support for the liberalization of the financial markets in Africa from many of the excessive and intrusive regulations, controls, and shareholding structures that existed between the state and financial institutions and markets, these objectives can be pursued and achieved without rejecting or substituting the role of the state for that of the market.

In recounting how, after the election of democratic governments in Eastern Europe, economists and others tried to find an economic theory with sufficient scope to tell them how to design a market economy, Frydman and Rapaczynski concluded that such a theory does not exist and that "we may never know enough, about markets themselves (and especially about the institutions embedded in a market economy) to make the East European transition a matter of applying proven economic theories to new material. Thus, it would be fatuous to expect that any design can be fail-proof; the only promising strategy is to try to set up an institutional arrangement that contains in itself some self-correcting mechanisms. Such mechanisms must, of necessity, be imperfect, in the sense that the achievement of an optimal solution cannot be assured" (Frydman and Rapacznski, 1994: 57).

The task before Africa's leadership is much the same. These leaders should be wary of any simple and standard solutions recommended by international financial institutions, advisors or, for that matter, bankers such as myself. As financial markets are liberalized in Africa they will quickly find themselves integrated into the international financial markets, an experience familiar to many of them with regard to global commodities markets. Their financial institutions will require the support, supervision, and representation in international forums of a flexible, knowledgeable and accountable central bank or banking regulator.

140 *Robert A. Annibale*

REFERENCES

Annibale, Robert, 'Will Africa Ever Become an Emerging Market', Euromoney, (May 1993a) p147-150.
Annibale, Robert, 'Bank Supervision Necessary Before Liberalisation', Africa Analysis, (August 1993b) p15.
Annibale, Robert, 'Investor Interest In Africa Outperforms Small Markets' in *Emerging Markets* (IMF/World Bank Daily Brief, October 1994) p34.
Bates, Robert H., 'The Politics of Economic Policy Reform: a Review Article', Journal of African Economies Vol. 2/3 (1993) p417-433.
Colclough, Christopher and Manor, James (eds.), *States or Markets?: Neo-liberalism and the Development Policy Debate* (Oxford: Clarendon Press, 1991).
Dia, Mamadou, 'A Governance Approach to Civil Service Reform in Sub-Saharan Africa, The World Bank' Technical Paper Number 225 (Washington, DC: World Bank, 1993).
Evans, Peter, 'The State as Problem and Solution: Predation, Embedded Autonomy, and Structural Change' in Haggard, Stephen, and Kaufman, Robert R. (eds.), *The Politics of Economic Adjustment* (New Jersey: Princeton University Press, 1992).
Fischer, Bernhard, 'Impediments in the Domestic Banking Sector to Financial Opening', in Reisen, Helmut and Fischer, Bernhard (eds.), *Financial Opening: Policy Issues and Experiences in Developing Countries* (Paris: OECD, 1993).
Frydman, Roman, and Rapaczynski, Andrzej, *Privatization in Eastern Europe: Is the State Withering Away?* (London: Central European University Press, 1994).
Galbraith, John Kenneth, *A Short History of Financial Euphoria*, (New York: Penguin Books, 1994).
Griffith-Jones, Stephany and Drabek, Zdenek (eds.), *Financial Reform in Central and Eastern Europe* (New York: St. Martin's Press, 1995).
Hadjimichael, Michael T. et al., *Sub-Saharan Africa: Growth, Savings, and Investment, 1986-93,* Occasional Paper 118, (Washington, DC: International Monetary Fund, 1995).
Healey, John, and Robinson, Mark, *Democracy, Governance and Economic Policy: Sub-Saharan Africa in Comparative Perspective* (London: Overseas Development Institute, 1992).
Husain, Ishrat and Faruquee, Rashid, *Adjustment in Africa: Lessons from Country Case Studies* (Washington, DC: World Bank, 1994).
International Monetary Fund, *International Capital Markets: Developments, Prospects, and Policy Issues* (Washington, DC: World Economic and Financial Surveys, International Monetary Fund, September 1994).
Johnson, Melanie, 'Financial Sector Reform in Structural Adjustment Programmes' in Van Der Geest, Willem (ed.), *Negotiating Structural Adjustment in Africa* (New York: United Nations Publications, 1994).
Kahler, Miles, 'External Influence, Conditionality, and the Politics of Adjustment,' in Haggard, Stephen, and Kaufman, Robert R. (eds.), *The Politics of Economic Adjustment* (New Jersey: Princeton University Press, 1992).
McHugh, Francis P., 'Proposal for an Ethic of Financial Decision-making' in Frowen, Stephen F. and McHugh, Francis P. (eds.) *Financial Decision-Making and Moral Responsibility* (New York: St. Martin's Press, 1995).
Mosley, Paul and Weeks, John, 'Adjustment in Africa', Development Policy Review Vol. 12/3 (1994) p319-327.
Nissanke, Machiko, 'Financial Policies & Intermediation Performance' in Van Der Geest, Willem (ed.), *Negotiating Structural Adjustment in Africa* (New York: United Nations Publications, 1994).
North, Douglass C., *Institutions, Institutional Change and Economic Performance* (Cambridge: Cambridge University Press, 1990).
Przeworski, Adam, *Democracy and the Market: Political and Economic Reforms in Eastern Europe and Latin America,* (Cambridge: Cambridge University Press, 1991).
Roe, Alan R., 'Africa's Experiences with Economic Policy Instruments' in Roe, Alan R. et al., *Instruments of Economic Policy in Africa* (London: African Centre for Monetary Policy and Association of Central Banks, 1992).
Sobel, Andrew C., *Domestic Choices, International Markets: Dismantling National Barriers & Liberalizing Securities Markets* (Ann Arbor: Michigan University Press, 1994).
Stewart, Francis et al. (eds.), *Alternative Development Strategies in Sub Saharan Africa* (London: Macmillan Press 1992).

Vos, Rob, 'Financial Liberalisation, Growth and Adjustment', in Griffith-Jones, Stephany and Drabek, Zdenek (eds.), *Financial Reform in Central and Eastern Europe* (New York: St. Martin's Press, 1995).

World Bank, *Adjustment in Africa: Reforms, Results, and the Road Ahead* (Oxford: Oxford University Press, 1994).

COMMENT

Reginald Herbold Green

FINANCIAL MARKETS AND STATES

Financial markets run by states tend to be sluggish and are likely to engage in unsound resource allocations in respect to other state entities whether budgetary or commercial. Financial markets regulated by procrustean regulations – and weakly staffed overseeing bodies – are likely to be just as sluggish and prone to catastrophic risk and fraud because the rules do not address innovative methods of asset dissipation as effectively as they hamper innovative methods of asset and risk management and because limited staff, procedures and experience lead to oversight in the sense of overlooking rather than looking over. Total deregulation – especially in respect to new and/or unsophisticated customers – leads to catastrophic risk both of asset misallocation by misjudgement and misappropriation by malfeasance.

What action in this environment should African states seeking to create enabling climates for serviceable, cost- and resource-use efficient, innovative, user-friendly honest financial systems be taking? What should users and honest financial institutions seek? These are the core questions addressed by Robert Annibale's paper.

On examination the call for less government turns out to be one for more disciplined and more focused government. Modern markets cannot function properly outside clear normative and prudential frameworks. Self-regulation – whatever its virtues – cannot be successful unless operated by substantial monitoring and investigatory bodies with legal powers in respect to non-members (or compelled members).

Regulation by wink, nod and nudge through state entities also concerned with supporting and promoting the financial sector tends to lead to a situation where lack of clarity, misplaced charity and inefficiency abound – as was only too clearly illustrated by the 1995 experiences of the Bank of England and the Japanese Ministry of Finance.

The case for autonomous regulatory bodies with legal powers to enforce rules and levy penalties for their breach and with personnel, procedures, plus rule and guideline books to enable them to spot probable violations and to act both predictably and consistently, is clear. Nor, as Annibale's paper demonstrates, do reputable financial institutions reject this proposition in principle; *au contraire*, even if they fret over particular requirements and sometimes lack insight into their own asset allocation and the asset misallocation failings and the errings of their siblings.

Annibale rightfully recognizes that there are no perfect answers; that industrial economies have faced similar problems and by no means with uniform success; that prevention is better than cure. Financial fraud – often to hide initial losses from financial misjudgement – is a global growth sector, cf., BCCI, Daiwa, and several domestic banks in Kenya, Nigeria and Zambia. This is also the case for gross miscalculation of risks leading to massive asset shortages, cf., US Savings and Loan Associations, the Japanese banking system and Meridian. Once the losses have happened, both responsibility to depositors (especially if there was purportedly effective regulation and/or deposit insurance on their behalf) and for keeping a viable, credible financial sector in being (as well as less illustrious motivations) exert compelling pressure for state bail-outs, cf., Credit Lyonnais, the Ghanaian and Tanzanian banking system reconstructions, the US savings and loan rescue operation, several African BCCI and Meridian branch reconstitutions.

These problems are compounded in sub-Saharan Africa (with South Africa only partly an exception) by five factors:
• the proportion of users (depositors as well as borrowers or service purchasers) of formal financial institutions is very low;
• risk limitation and macro-economic gain maximization (for example, Treasury bills versus medium-term fixed asset lending to domestic enterprises) are in greater tension than in most industrial economy markets;
• a higher proportion of formal financial sector transactions have foreign ramifications reducing access to information and raising risk for all domestic actors including regulators;
• both government regulatory and independent auditing capacity are limited;
• the informal (that is unrecorded and unregulated) financial market is large in respect to the formal in number of users and in terms of proportion of total funds available to small enterprises.

Given the imbalance between urgent needs and available resources, there is a need to prioritize. Commercial banking (including related investment and merchant banking) should come first when:
• restructuring and recapitalizing – or closing – present weak institutions;
• adopting – and enforcing – prudential guidelines such as thos earticulated in the paper;
• encouraging joint studies on ways and means of increasing user access – for depositors as well as borrowers – using approacheswhich are consistent with prudent banking;

- requiring higher – and more depositor and regulator friendly – standards of auditing from international as well as national auditors.[1]

It also suggests great prudence (overcaution because of a lack of information) in: licensing new banks – domestic or foreign; review of existing ones with a view to forcing reconstruction or closure of ones which present a high risk to clients for whatever reason; massive training – preferably funded and managed by all licensed banks – of personnel using expatriate as well as local trainers; encouraging major south African financial institutions to build up African specialist/wholesale branch, representative office and joint venture (in retail banking as well as wholesale and merchant) networks because they do have more expertise, are relatively prudent and well-resourced, are unlikely to have major fraud problems, and are almost the only established financial institutions likely (as Annibale notes) to be interested in expansion along these lines.

The informal market is a reality, a potential and a problem, but not one that can be tackled directly on a broad front today or tomorrow. A modest initial agenda might be:
- to undertake serious research on size, users, modalities, 'depositor' losses, types and frequencies of fraud;
- to offer an optional[2] registration system providing advice, access to commercial information and commercial banks, the right to give status as a 'regulated institution' in return for meeting certain prudential standards (such as those relating to unimpaired capital and liquid asset proportions) and timely, rigorous, independent audits;
- to encourage broader access to commercial banks so increasing competition (for depositors and borrowers), presumably with benefits to remaining informal sector clients both in terms of costs and, less certainly, honesty.

The regulation of insurance companies and pension funds is also a initial priority – albeit less fraught with reconstruction costs and traditions of mis- or-mal-management, but this is not certain because to date there has been less analysis and investigation of this sector.) Insurance is broadly analogous to

---

1 This is a global problem. BCCI demonstrates that split national regulation plus top level international auditors give no timely protection. Whether or not BCCI's auditors were or were not negligent and whether or not Cayman, Luxembourg, UK and Gulf regulatory authorities exchanged information according to best standard practice is irrelevant. The auditing and exchange were inadequate and need major augmentation. Either the Basle Group or the BIS or the IMF (or preferably all three) needs to take a lead in elaborating better safeguards. The role of sub-Saharan African central banks in such an exercise will be limited, but they should collectively press the need for it as a matter of urgency and urge that whatever system emerges is user-friendly to small, peripheral regulatory authorities.

2 Optional because for smaller institutions costs to them, and to regulators, might well outweigh benefits, because the regulators could not handle thousands to tens of thousands of clients and because take-up or otherwise – and discussion on the reasons for it – would be some guide as to how appropriate were the initial guidelines.

banking in respect to prudential guidelines (and problems). Pension fund regulation might begin with a study of South African and USA practice. Stock markets are a lower priority at present, beyond half a dozen countries. A quiet pre-emptive exercise to identify best practice for small markets and unit trust funds and so on, with a view to getting the first up and toddling and creating a prudential yet encouraging climate for investors, is worth doing in most sub-Saharan African states.

The key goals of a financial regulatory system are:
• to create greater transparency (to market actors and, especially, ordinary users as well as to regulators) and to reduce uncertainty (clear, published rules and guidelines);
• to deter and to punish fraud and reckless imprudence;
• to prevent, or at least limit, cartel imposition (on access, charges, deposit rates);
• to limit user risk by reducing fraud and reckless imprudence, by insurance funds and capital/liquid asset requirements and by institutional disclosure.

To be effective such a system requires an appropriate infrastructure of laws and regulations. However, these can only facilitate; a system is empowered (or disempowered) by its staff. Its results depend not so much on how draconian are the penalties, but on the probability of fraudulent or reckless practices being detected, and acted against, promptly, and of near insolvency being identified in time to avert massive costs.

7 Public utilities: Is the British experience a model for developing countries?

John F. McEldowney

BACKGROUND

Developing countries considering privatizating their public utilities could learn from the British experience. Britain was one of the first countries to embark on a full scale nationalization programme and one of the first to embark on privatization of the major utilities such as telecommunications, gas, water, electricity, coal and rail. Privatization has raised fundamental questions about the effective regulation of Company Act companies, a term used to describe the legal status of the companies newly-formed under privatization. Regulation is a crucial part of the structures put in place after privatization, underlined by the fact that many of the utilities in the United Kingdom remain virtual monopolies. Regulation through a variety of semi-independent agencies is primarily intended to protect the interests of consumers but is, increasingly, required to provide supervision of competition in the utility industries[1].

Any assessment of the UK's experience of privatization has to take account of the fact that regulation of the utilities is still at an early stage. At the outset the principles adopted in the privatization of water, gas, telecommunications and electricity have involved the setting of the prices the utilities may charge their customers through a price formula linked to the retail price index minus some 'x' factor designed to hold prices below inflation. The control of this price cap is in the hands of the regulator. However, the role of the regulators has increasingly proved controversial as the utilities have come under intense public criticism over excessive profits, dividends, share prices and executive salaries. This has led to a greater openness about regulation policy with the inevitable consequence that the debate has entered the political arena.

We will look at the variety of legal and economic powers available to regulators. To date the experience of regulation has highlighted an uncertainty over the extent of the regulators' powers, influenced by the political sensitivity which surrounds regulatory issues. Safeguarding the interests of the taxpayer, the consumer and the shareholder involves complex and often competing

---

1   See: Richard Green, Catherine Waddams Price, 'Liberalisation and Divestituture in the UK Energy Sector' Fiscal Studies Vol. 16/1 (1995) pp75-89.

demands. Political choices are involved in setting priorities and providing an agenda for the future development of the utilities. Regulation policy is therefore at the heart of good regulation. The British experience has been *ad hoc*; there is no coherent policymaking to achieve a consistent approach among regulators combining accountability with performance indicators.

The widespread public and political sensitivity surrounding regulation may seem surprising. The effectiveness of regulation is an important and politically sensitive issue. At the outset of privatization the political dimension of each regulator's role was concealed in discussions about ownership and debates about the efficiency and effectiveness of the nationalized industries. It is only now by clarifying the political dimension that a full picture of the privatization programme will emerge. Changes in the regulatory culture has significance for the way utility companies operate. The choice of individual regulator may also affect market sensitivity to regulation. The effectiveness of government policy towards regulation is dubious when conflicting interests such as consumer prices and shareholder dividends are considered. The effectiveness of the Government's privatization strategies is thrown into further doubt now that competition may require that the utility industries be restructured. Even breaking up natural monopolies may not provide a solution to the problem of competition. The monopoly operator may provide economies of scale not available to smaller operators. Smaller operators may not provide economic efficiency because of lack of expertise or sufficient bargaining power through the contracts each makes with larger units. They may also show a tendency to develop and undertake the various contracts on their own. A smaller operator may find it has to become a larger single unit to organize its external contracts more efficiently.[2]

The complex picture which emerges from the regulation of UK utilities may cast doubt on the value of the British experience as a model for the future.

INTRODUCTION

The UK post-war nationalization programme[3] included the major utilities water, gas, electricity, and transport including rail, bus and air. It also covered the British Steel Corporation, the Post Office and the United Kingdom Atomic Energy Authority. The movement in favour of nationalization was worldwide. Unquestionably nationalization had social, economic and ideological significance.[4]

---

2   See: C. Foster, *Privatisation, Public Ownership and the Regulation of Natural Monopoly* (Oxford: Blackwell, 1992).
3   See: Matthew Bishop, John Kay and Colin Mayer, *The Regulatory Challenge* (Oxford University Press,1995), John McEldowney, *Public Law* (Sweet and Maxwell, 1994) and John McEldowney,'Law and Regulation: Current Issues and Future Directions' in Bishop, Kay and Mayer, op. cit., pp408-422.

Since 1979 the privatization programme in the UK has entailed the sale of assets of the major nationalized industries in public ownership.[5] Craig has noted how eclectic reasons may be advanced for privatization:[6]

> ... improving efficiency, reducing government involvement in industrial decision-making, widening share ownership, encouraging share ownership by employees, alleviating problems of public sector pay determination, reducing the public sector borrowing requirement and the enhancement of economic freedom.

The success of privatization has been judged on three criteria. First, privatization has provided significant revenue sums for the Treasury; net receipts to the Treasury are in excess of £35 billion.[7] Second, privatization has proved to be diverse in application and popular with the electorate, seen as providing a wider share ownership than hitherto. Third, privatization has provided for a radical restructuring of the internal management and organization of major industries including the introduction of new technologies and more efficient staffing. It has had an impact on trade union membership and has radically changed the culture of industry through demands for increased efficiency.

Early privatization sales included companies as diverse as British Petroleum, Amersham International (a radio-chemical company) and Cable and Wireless. Once privatized these industries gained from competitiveness by increasing their market share. No special regulatory system was put in place to regulate their behaviour as privatized companies. Later, privatizations have included the main public utilities such as the sale of British Telecom[8] in 1984. This was followed by British Gas[9] in 1986, the electricity industry[10] in 1989, the water industry[11] in 1989, British Coal[12] in 1994 and British Rail[13] in 1995. Plans to privatize the Post Office announced in the Queen's speech in 1994 have been indefinitely postponed. The four major utilities – telecommunications, gas, electricity and

---

4   See: T. Prosser, *Nationalised Industries and Public Control* (Oxford University Press, 1986) and T. Prosser, 'Privatisation,Regulation and Public Services' Juridical Review Vol. 3 (1994) pp3-17. Also A. I. Ogus, *Regulation, Legal Form and Economic Theory* (Oxford: Clarendon Press, 1994).
5   See: Ron Hodges and Mike Wright, 'Audit and Accountability in the Privatisation Process: The Role of the National Audit Office' Journal of Business Finance and Accounting Vol. 22,/2 (March 1995) pp153-170.
6   Paul Craig, *Administrative Law* (Sweet and Maxwell 1994) p101.
7   This is an estimate drawn from the House of Commons Research Paper 93/85. I am very grateful to Priscilla Baines, from the House of Commons Library, for help and advice in the preparation of this part of this paper. See: John McEldowney,'The National Audit Office and Privatisation' Modern Law Review (1991) p933.
8   Telecommunications Act 1984.
9   Gas Act 1986.
10 The Electricity Act 1989.
11 The Water Act 1989 now consolidated in the Water Industry Act 1991 and amended by the Environment Act 1995.
12 British Coal Act 1994.
13 Railways Act 1993.

water – have been privatized as a virtual monopoly or with limited competition. This raises the question of how such significant market power in the hands of a monopoly may best be addressed.[14] Few will consider private monopoly power any less problematic than a public monopoly. The problems of private monopoly were not addressed when UK privatization got underway. The subsequent introduction of competition into monopolies has proved difficult. Two approaches can be considered: the creation of greater competition through regulation may encourage the monopoly to behave in a less predatory way; through restructuring, the utility may be broken up into smaller units to encourage competition.

Privatization has provided an important agenda for developing innovative and creative legislation concerning the regulation and day-to-day running of the newly-privatized enterprises. Privatization policies are fashionable in Europe,[15] North America and Japan and also among developing and newly-industrialized countries. The starting point of this paper is to consider the variety and complexity of regulation introduced in the UK. This is followed by a discussion on how competition may be promoted through regulation. Finally, the shortcomings of the existing regulatory arrangements will be considered, with a look at how future regulation could be improved upon.

REGULATION AND PRIVATIZATION: GENERAL CONSIDERATIONS

Nationalization and privatization share at least one common underlying principle.[16] Both strategies are drawn from strong ideological preferences[17] about the way in which ownership may operate. In the case of nationalization, public ownership is seen as essential to provide full employment and to distribute profits for the general benefit of society. In the case of privatization, ownership is regarded as falling under market forces and profit may be encouraged as a means of achieving greater economic prosperity with benefits to shareholders, taxpayers and consumers. The debate involving arguments for

---

14 See: C. Foster, *Privatisation, Public Ownership and the Regulation of Natural Monopoly* (Oxford: Blackwell, 1992).

15 See: Istvan Pogany, 'Privatisation and Regulatory Change in Hungary' in M. Moran and T. Prosser, *Privatization and Regulatory Change in Europe* (Open University Press, 1994). Also see: Jacques Pelkmans and Norbert Wagner, *Privatization and Deregulation in Asean and EC* (Institute of Southeast Asia Studies, 1990) and L. Gray Cowan, *Privatization in the Developing World* (Prager, 1990).

16 Cento Veljanovski, *Selling the State: Privatisation in Britain* (London, 1988), L. Hancher, M. Moran, *Capitalism, Culture and Economic Regulation* (Oxford University Press, 1989) p22 M. E. Beesley, *Liberalisation of the Use of the British Telecommunications Network* (London: HMSO, 1981), Deloitte, Haskins and Sells, *British Gas Efficiency Study* (1983), Vickers and Yarrow, *Privatisation, An Economic Analysis* (Cambridge, Mass, London: MIT Press, 1988) p248.

17 See for a comparative analysis: J. Luis Gusach and Pablo T. Spiller, 'Regulation and Private Sector Development in Latin America', unpublished paper at the 'Conference on Private Sector Development:Issues in Latin America and the Caribbean Marbella', Chile, 13-14 October 1994.

and against privatization or nationalization rarely raises questions of what is the most suitable or potentially successful strategy to be adopted for a particular industry. The ideological nature of the debate renders clear objectives or a non-ideological based diagnosis of existing problems almost impossible. The striking feature of privatization is that the elements critical to its success depend largely on competition and efficiency within the privatized industry as well as the use of regulatory powers to oversee consumer protection and quality control. Arguably, similar considerations exist for nationalized industries. Privatization should not be seen as a panacea – rather it may make transparent complex issues about how best to provide regulation. If this challenge is not met then privatization could become an electoral liability for the government that introduces it.

There are also important constitutional issues about how accountability may best be provided.[18] Reliance on a regulator may devolve politically sensitive and complex policy issues to government-appointed officials. Reliance on government decision-making may mean that party politics intervenes too much in the development of regulatory policy. Shifts in party political support either within government itself or through a change in government may have adverse effects on long-term planning. Striking a balance between regulator and government may require consideration of how to achieve successful accountability when industry and vested interests may engage in overt lobbying activities.[19] The complexity of regulation, its technical and legal mechanisms[20] for control may make policy creation beyond the grasp of day-to-day party politics.

Resolving regulatory problems through competition policy or consumer protection must be set in the context of the UK's approach to regulation. In most instances regulation of the utilities was considered as an afterthought rather than as a central part of a carefully worked out strategy. The main focus at the time of privatization was to achieve a successful flotation of the newly-formed companies and the sale of shares. Thus, individualized structures for regulation were created for each of the utilities telecommunications, water, gas, electricity, and rail,[21] on an *ad hoc* basis. It was assumed that consumer protection should be the main focus of regulation. A slow learning curve developed from the early experience of telecommunications in 1984 to the more sophisticated regulatory

---

18 See: T. Daintith, 'Political Programmes and the Content of the Constitution' in W. Finnie, C. Himsworth, N. Walker (eds.) *Edinburgh Essays in Public Law* (Edinburgh University Press, 1991) pp41-55.
19 One model of regulation that may be compared and contrasted to the utility regulators is the Civil Aviation Authority. See: R. Baldwin and C. McCrudden, *Regulation and Public Law* (London: Weidenfeld and Nicolson, 1987). Also see: Laker Airways v Department of Trade [1977] Q.B. 643.
20 See for example the views of the courts in Panel on Take-overs and Mergers ex parte Datafin plc (1987) Q.B. 815.
21 Rail is currently undergoing privatization, the Railways Act 1993 .See: 'The Treasury and Civil Service Select Committee: The Future of the railways in the Light of the Government's White paper Proposals' (2nd Report) HC 246-i (1992-93) p364.

system put in place for electricity and water in 1989. Even then the question of competition was not properly addressed by government strategy. This deficiency in strategy has left a legacy of inadequate regulation and arguably one which in the UK may return to cast doubt on the efficacy of the original strategy adopted for privatization. The role of the regulators and their future strategy is uncertain. There is lack of clarity as to how the regulators should develop policy and more importantly there is vagueness about the extent of policy considerations that should be in place to guide the regulators. The role of government remains an important part of any regulatory structure but the independence of the regulator leaves uncertainty over the influence of government policy. This is underlined by any party political differences which exist over the role of regulation policy.

REGULATION: POWERS AND DUTIES OF THE REGULATORS

An important issue that confronts the newly-privatized utilities is the question of the accountability of the regulators.[22]

Improving regulation: the Competition and Service (Utilities) Act 1992

While in the early stages of privatization regulation was perceived as largely a matter of consumer protection, it soon became apparent that in many cases the way in which privatization strategy was implemented resulted in maintaining the utilities as monopolies or virtual monopolies.[23] Reliance was placed on competition being introduced through the particular regulatory structures developed for each utility. The experience of British Telecom and British Gas was that the regulatory structures put in place under respectively the Telecommunications Act 1984 and the Gas Act 1986 were weaker[24] than the regulation provided for electricity under the Electricity Act 1989 or for water under the Water Act 1989 (now contained in a consolidation, the Water Industry Act 1991). The Government introduced legislation in 1992 to give additional powers to the regulators in the four major utilities – these are contained in the Competition and Service (Utilities) Act 1992. This has involved conferring additional powers and duties on the four regulators.

---

22 See: A. McHarg, 'Accountability in the electricity supply industry', Utilities Law Review (Spring 1995) p34-42, Cento Veljanovski, 'The Regulation Game' in Veljanovski (ed) *Regulators and the Market* (London: Institute of Economic Affairs, 1991).
23 General discussion of the Monopolies and Mergers Commission see: B. Collins and B. Wharton, 'Nationalised Industries: Responses to the Monopolies & Mergers Commission', Public Money, Vol. 4 (1984-85) pp30-32.
24 See the 'Report of the Gas Regulator, the Director general of Gas Supply: Report for 1988' (London: HMSO, Cm. 197, p9). Further reports highlighted various difficulties. See: 'Report for 1989' (London: London: HMSO, Cm. 142), 'Report for 1990' (London: HMSO, Cm. 158), 'Report for 1991' (London: HMSO Cm. 193).

The main functions of the regulators include[25] the following powers:
• to issue licences under delegated powers by the Secretary of State and grant exemptions from licence requirements;
• to set performance standards and settle levels of compensation between suppliers and customers;
• to exercise a discretion to investigate certain disputes between utilities and their customers such as the charges or the terms of certain agreements;
• to exercise powers to investigate and publish information about companies including information that allows for a comparison of the performance of different companies.

In addition to the above, regulators are responsible for monitoring compliance with the terms of the licence and to enforce licence conditions when appropriate. The regulators may agree changes to licence conditions with the utility operator. In the event of disagreement there are powers available to each regulator to ask the MMC to consider whether the terms of the licence should be amended in the public interest.

The principal duties of the regulators are to ensure that all reasonable demands for utility services are satisfied and that licence-holders have sufficient finance to carry on their regulated duties. Regulators have a duty to promote competition and to safeguard the interests of consumers in respect of prices and quality of service. Judicial review of the powers and duties of regulators is possible, but to date the opportunities for review have appeared to be limited.[26]

The question is: What policy concerns that should influence the regulators in the exercise of their powers? The answer depends on the aims and objectives that should be set for regulating what are in many cases, natural monopolies. This raises the question of how competition in the utilities can be achieved.

Competition in the utilities

The UK has experienced a slow learning curve in establishing the role of the regulator in a competitive market. Various examples illustrate this point. The first review of competition policy of the telecommunications industry, privatized in 1984, was not carried out until 1991. The 1984 Act had created a duopoly – British Telecom (BT) and Mercury. The latter was created as a small enterprise

---

25 The summary of legal powers may be found in sections 1-10 that apply to telecommunications, of the Competition and Service (Utilities) Act 1992, hereinafter the 1992 Act, sections 11-19 of the 1992 Act apply to gas, sections 20-25 of the 1992 Act that apply to electricity and sections 26-36 of the 1992 Act that apply to the water industry. Also see: Fiona Woolf and Stephen McCue, 'Who regulates the regulator? the great debate' Utilities Law Review [1993] p199-203.
26 See: C. Graham and T. Prosser, 'Privatising Nationalised Industries: Constitutional Issues and New Legal Techniques', Modern Law Review Vol. 50 (1987) p16. Also see: G. Borrie, 'The Regulation of Public and Private Power', Public Law [1989] p552.

to provide competition for BT. This restricted competition was the subject of the 1991 duopoly review[27] which recommended that the restriction should be ended and competition promoted through licence applications. It also recommended that cable operators should not be obliged to provide television in conjunction with BT or Mercury, that there should be equal access to any long distance operator and liberalization of private closed networks. The responsibility of implementing these recommendations has largely fallen to the regulator.

Then there is the case of the privatization of British Gas in 1986. This was accomplished through British Gas maintaining a vertically integrated monopoly; thus it owned, operated and maintained the transmission and distribution system and was the only supplier of gas to customers. Since privatization the regulator attempted to encourage competition in the contract customer sector, that is those using 25,000 therms plus per annum. In 1989, the lack of progress in competition and acrimony between the regulator and British Gas caused the regulator to refer[28] competition issues to the MMC to undertake an investigation into British Gas and its control of supply. The MMC Report[29] concluded that there was a need for greater transparency in the pricing policy of British Gas, a need for third party access to the pipelines owned by British Gas and for gas to be made available from other competitors by requiring that at least 10 per cent of all new deliveries of gas be to sources other than British Gas. Further steps were taken in 1991 following a referral by the Department of Trade and Industry to the Office of Fair Trading. The Report of the Office of Fair Trading[30] recommended that: British Gas make available to competitors a substantial supply of gas in the traditional contract market; the British Gas monopoly to supply tariff customers should be abolished; there should be the creation of an arm's length subsidiary of British Gas for the transmission and storage of gas on a more open and transparent basis; competitors be afforded the same opportunities as British Gas regarding planning permission to construct pipelines.

Implementation of these recommendations has been ongoing, supported by a threat by the Office of Fair Trading that if British Gas does not undertake such changes a further referral will be made to the MMC.

In the event the regulator was left to negotiate with British Gas the future development of the market. Agreement was finally reached after a threat of referral. These changes are expected to end the monopoly British Gas has over the market. Legislation concerning implementation of the necessary restructuring

---

27 See: *Competition and Choice: Telecommunications Policy in the 1990s* (London: HMSO, 1991, Cm. 1303).
28 See: Sections 47(1), 49(1) and 50(1) of the Fair Trading Act 1973. The MMC held that a monopoly did arise under section 6 (1a) of the 1973 Act.
29 See: 'MMC Report, 1988', (London: HMSO Cm. 500). See Tim Frazer 'Monopoly, Prohibition and Deterrence', <u>Modern Law Review</u> Vol. 58, (1995) pp846-860.
30 See: 'OFT Report, 1991', <u>The Gas Review</u> (London: HMSO, 1991).

of the industry is on the agenda. Separation of the transmission system from British Gas is likely to be undertaken shortly. By avoiding radical restructuring of the various industries, the Government has had to depend on the regulators to provide competition via granting new licences. Encouraging competition via this mechanism has raised issues about the powers of the regulator.

The functions of the MMC have had to be extended[31] to investigate not only mergers and their regulation, but also anti-competitive practices.[32] Regulating monopolies involves consideration of Articles 85 and 86 of the Treaty of Rome and the Government is considering how to amend existing monopoly legislation.[33]

The MMC works closely with the Director General of Fair Trading who may refer a case of a monopoly or any anti-competitive practice to the MMC.[34] In the context of the utilities, there are concerns that no single body has an oversight of all the competition issues. In general, utilities are unwilling to have a reference made to the MMC because of the costs and time delays involved and the lack of confidentiality involved in reaching its conclusions. There is also concern over the complexity of the issues that the MMC is required to judge, such as economic costs and benefits of regulation, the interests of workers and employment in the industry, the effect on consumers, industrial efficiency and the balance of payments. The question of employment is contentious since party political differences suggest that not all afford it the same priority.

The MMC may seek to give an objective and rigorous review[35] of many of these issues when considering a referral but few can doubt the political significance to its work. The weakness of the regulatory structure may be its inability to adjust to political realities. Party political considerations may unduly inhibit regulatory policy and ultimately be to blame for the lack of any coherent regulatory policy for example, in not promoting an energy policy for the utilities.

Some tentative conclusions may be advanced about the current state of regulating the utilities. A number of approaches are possible in the regulation of natural monopolies. Some favour the break-up of natural monopolies to encourage greater competition with little or no regulation.[36] This is seen by others as an

31 See the Monopolies and Mergers Act 1965 and extensions to its powers contained in the Competition Act 1980.
32 See: 'Review of Restrictive Trade Practices Policy', Cmnd. 7512 (London: HMSO, 1979).
33 'Opening Markets: New Policy on Restrictive Trade Practices' Cm 727 (London: HMSO, 1989) and 'Abuse of Market Power' Cm 2100 (London: HMSO, 1992). See: Tim Frazer 'Monopoly, Prohibition and Deterrence' Modern Law Review ((1995) pp846-859.
34 The MMC has powers under the Airports Act 1986 and the Broadcasting Act 1990 to investigate mergers and other matters referred to it by the Office of Fair Trading.
35 The MMC is subject to judicial review but this may be regarded as of limited use in this area. See: R. v MMC ex parte Mathew Brown plc (1987) 1 World Law Review 1235.
36 See for a discussion of these points: M. Bishop, John Kay and Colin Mayer, *The Regulatory Challenge* (Oxford University Press, 1995) pp2-17.

undesirable development[37] when all that is required is greater liberalization of the markets held by the monopoly operator. In the case of gas, for example, this might involve entry into the gas pipeline at a level that is not disadvantageous to competitors of British Gas. Still further some economists argue that there should be more rigorous regulation of the utilities with regulators prepared to implement an interventionist policy[38] to prevent predatory pricing, excessive monopoly profits and increased competition through tight regulatory policy. The debate as to the most suitable mode of regulation is likely to continue in Britain. Any change in the government or in government policy is likely to require a major re-think of the future regulation of the utilities. One issue which will be central for the future discussion of regulation is price regulation.

Price regulation: RPI-x price controls

An important part of the privatization structure put in place first in telecommunications in 1984 and later in the other major utilities such as gas, water and electricity is the method of price control expressed in the formula RPI-x.[39] This method of price control requires that the price index for a defined amount of the firm's regulated products should increase by no more than the rate of inflation (RPI) minus x per cent per annum. Fixing 'x' is the job of the regulator. Experience to date has shown that there is considerable discretion involved since the regulator can decide on 'x' with relatively little public debate and openness. Little information or reasoning is provided by regulators when making their decision, the British Gas case being a prime example.[40] Very often agreements are reached because of the threat of an MMC referral.

Rees and Vickers have shown[41] that RPI-x price control may be operated in two ways – passively or actively. Under the 'passive RPI-x' approach the regulator adopts a minimalist stance merely checking data and leaving the utility company with broad discretion over pricing policy. Under the active approach the regulator adopts an interventionist stance, seeks more information, applies criteria over standards and scrutinizes investment and profit as part of an overall

---

37 For a good discussion of the arguments about the break-up of monopoly powers see: C. Foster, *Privatisation, Public Ownership and the Regulation of Natural Monopoly* (Oxford: Blackwell, 1992).
38 See: C. M. Armstrong, S. Cowan and J. S. Vickers, *Regulatory Reform: Economic Analysis and British Experience* (Cambridge, Mass., London: MIT Press, 1994).
39 There is an important debate about the advantages and disadvantages of the rate-of-return regulation. See S. J. Brown and D. S. Sibley, *The Theory of Public Utility Pricing* (Cambridge University Press, 1986) and also the 'Rand Journal of Economics Symposium on Price-Cap regulation' Rand Journal of Economics Vol. 20 (1989) pp369-472.
40 See: OFGAS (1991), *New Gas Tariff Formula* (London: OFGAS, 1991). There are also a variety of OFTEL papers on this subject: (London: OFTEL, 1988) 'The Control of British Telecom's Prices' (London: OFTEL, 1992) 'The Regulation of BT's Prices' (London: OFTEL, 1993).
41 See: Ray Rees and John Vickers, 'RPI-x Price Cap Regulation' in Bishop, Kay and Mayer, op. cit., pp381-3.

regulatory strategy. The experience of electricity is instructive of the sensitivity of the price cap. The electricity regulator has reconsidered the RPI-x formula in the light of new information on the profits available to the regional electricity companies.[42] The consequences of the regulator's decision were particularly price sensitive: share prices in the electricity sector fell sharply, a takeover bid by Trafalgar House for Northern Electric was abandoned, the Government was embarrassed that the regulator's announcement coincided with the sale of further government shares in National Power and Power Gen, and doubts arose over the intended stock market flotation of National Grid Holdings.

The RPI-x formula has proved controversial and complex in its operation. It is likely to be a main focus of industrial policy for future regulation of UK utilities.

SETTING STANDARDS: THE CITIZEN'S CHARTER AND THE USE OF CONTRACT

Contract and consumer protection

The British experience of post-privatization has raised questions about consumer protection. An enduring feature of the development of the common law is its capacity to evolve and change. Gap filling is a necessity as well as a strategy. In essence this pragmatic approach to problem-solving permits change without any apparent major rethink or radical break with the past. Consistent with privatization policies the Government has adopted a more managerial approach to the public sector than in the past. This has included the more radical approach, such as contracting out public sector services, to the less interventionist approach, such as market testing,[43] for example, by local government for the provision of goods and services . A striking feature of such approaches is the increasing reliance on the market and commercial judgement in the public sector. Efficiency and value for money indicators and reliance on public audit are evidence of the extension of the 'market approach' to the public sector.

The Citizen's Charter

The Citizen's Charter[44] initiative was introduced in July 1991 with four objectives for consumer protection: to improve the quality of public services; to provide choice to consumers between competing standards of service; to provide citizens with information about the quality and standard of service; to provide value for money in the quality and delivery of services. The Citizen's Charter is part of the development of regulation in the public sector through contract.

---

42 See: 'Have the utility regulators run out of control?' Leader article in *The Independent* 12 March 1995.
43 See: John F. McEldowney, *Public Law* (Sweet and Maxwell, 1994).
44 See: *Citizen's Charter* Cmnd. 1599 (London: HMSO, 1991).

Contract law is increasingly useful as an explanation of the relationship between the citizen and the state. This approach to the public sector is more widely drawn and all embracing than privatization[45] of the nationalized industries. It has been characterized as a new style of public sector managerialism. Instead of public bodies providing goods and services as benefits to the public, such goods and services are provided through contract. Public bodies such as local government are increasingly seen as regulators, rather than providers of goods and services.[46]

This new approach encourages changes in the culture of the public sector and, through value for money auditing[47], a more economical use of public money.[48] The consumer is cast in the role of complainant; it is hoped that the making of complaints will stimulate better standards.[49] The Citizen's Charter raises high expectations that may only be addressed through government policy and Parliamentary control. As an innovative tool the Charter highlights consumer rights through empowering citizens to take action to remedy their grievances. If the Charter is taken to its logical conclusion it should stimulate more open government and better information to the consumer. This is consistent with the requirement of a more open debate on regulatory policy discussed above.

The Government has also embarked on new procedures to simplify existing regulations and unnecessary rules. The Deregulation and Contracting Out Act 1994 provides that amending orders, called deregulation orders, may be introduced to amend delegated legislation or where necessary primary legislation.[50] This is a novel way to lift the burden of unnecessary regulation from industry.[51]

CONCLUSIONS

Lessons from the British experience of privatization

In the developing world[52] the process of privatization is one of experimentation and learning.[53] We need to consider a country's institutional and administrative arrangements to assess whether the British experience can contribute to this process. According to Levy and Spiller[54] there are five institutional issues to be

---

45 See: Nigel Lawson, *The Frontiers of Privatisation* (London: Adam Smith Institute, 1988).
46 See: John F. McEldowney, 'Managing the Police', Local Authority Law (1993) pp5-6. Also see: Sir Robin Butler, 'The Evolution of the Civil Service – A Progress Report' Public Administration Vol. 71 (1993) pp395-406.
47 See: John F. McEldowney, 'The National Audit Office and privatisation' Modern Law Review (1991) p933.
48 See: John F. McEldowney, 'The Control of Public Expenditure' in Jowell and Oliver (eds.), *The Changing Constitution* (Oxford University Press, 1994) pp175-207.
49 See: John F. McEldowney, 'Contract Compliance and Public Audit' chapter 4 in C. Willett (ed.), *The Citizen's Charter* (Edward Elgar Press, 1995). Also see: John Stewart, 'The limitations of Government by Contract' Public Money and Management (1993) pp7-9. Mark Freedland, 'Government by Contract and Public Law' Public Law (Winter 1994) pp86-104.
50 See: Michael Ryle, 'The Deregulation and Contracting Out Bill 1994 – A Blueprint for reform of the Legislative Process?' Statute Law Review Vol. 15 (1994) pp170-181.

considered in any privatization process: a country's legislative, executive and judicial institutions, how the citizen is given rights and how those rights are enforced, and the character of the prevailing ideology of the state. In evaluating the British contribution in these terms there are a number of general lessons that can be gained. Market forces cannot be left to their own devices.[55] The decision whether or not to maintain natural monopolies or to break up such monopolies into smaller enterprises appears, from the British experience, to have been badly considered and poorly devised.[56] At the time of privatization the main preoccupation seems to have been to float the newly-privatized companies on the stock market rather than to adopt a careful and technical review of the best options for subsequent commercial operations. A well-developed plan or future strategy was not part of the British approach to privatization.

Once privatized the question arises as to how best to regulate the newly-privatized industries. Regulation through the RPI-x formula is likely to continue to prove politically sensitive and to call into question the judgement of regulators. The accountability of regulators in these matters is likely to be a factor in determining the success of privatization in Britain.

Regulating the utilities involves complex licensing, contractual and statutory powers. The British system of regulation depends on the ability of the regulator to gain the confidence of a wide range of interested groups from consumers, and shareholders, to the industry and the government. Regulatory decisions are not clearly articulated and regulatory policy appears to be vague and this has implications for the value of shares of regulated companies. Possessing such market sensitive information and decision-making power requires sound judgement and good communication skills. A more open culture of regulation in Britain is needed for this power to be used to best effect. There is considerable uncertainty as to how future governments may change regulatory policy. Such uncertainty is bound to increase at a time of a general election or where government majorities are reduced through by-election results.

The British system appears to suffer from the worst of both worlds. Regulatory policy is implicitly in the hands of individual regulators. As a result policy is not

51 The Deregulation and Contracting Out Act 1994 follows the recommendations of the Hansard Society in its report 'Making the Law' (Hansard Society, 1993).
52 See: Werner Baer and Michael E. Conroy, *Latin America: Privatization, Property Right and Deregulation 2 (Proceedings of the First Conference of Latin America 2000)*, (JAI Press Inc., 1994).
53 L. Gray Cowan, *Privatization in the Developing World* (Praeger, 1990) p102.
54 Brian Levy and P. T. Spiller, 'Regulation, Institutions and Commitment in Telecommunications: A Comparative Analysis of Five Country Studies' in *Proceedings of the World Bank Annual Conference on Development Economics* (Washington DC: The World Bank, 1993).
55 This is well explained in Luigi Manzetti, 'The Politics of Privatisation and Deregulation in Latin America' The Quarterly Review of Economics and Finance Vol. 34 special issue (1994) pp43-75.
56 See the controversy over British Rail privatization. See: Jeffrey Goh, 'The railways, the privatisation and the derailment' Utilities Law Review [1994] pp157-8.

articulated in any coherent forum and is left to be devised on an *ad hoc* basis. Arbitration of disputes between regulators and companies through the MMC appears too time-consuming, expensive and unduly complicated.

Learning through experience is a common inheritance from many of the privatization policies adopted in the 1980s. While transplanting one system of law or regulation from one country to another is not desirable, learning from the experience of past mistakes in Britain may provide lessons for developing countries in the development of regulatory practice and procedure.

Future directions of accountability

Initially UK privatization has been considered a political success for the Government because of its electoral popularity. Privatization has allowed the implementation of a radical strategy for resolving complex industrial and trade union issues. Thus, outmoded industries such as coal have been effectively reorganized through privatization strategies despite obvious political controversy. However, such successes appear to be too simplistic from the analysis offered above. Any complete incorporation of the British experience of regulation in a developing country would be dangerous since there are important questions about privatization unresolved. The first is how to combine policy with regulation in a way that is accountable. There is a great irony in asking this question in that way. The question of accountability and efficiency raised by the nationalized industries in their relationship with the government of the day led to the development of a range of techniques to allow competitive industries to become consistent with political ideology.

The experience, to date, of privatization has indicated that the difficulties experienced in nationalization, of providing a satisfactory basis for both the various privatized utility industries and government to operate under, remain. We have seen that in the case of telecommunications and gas a weak regulatory framework has had little impact on the essential requirement of competition. Supplementing weak regulation requires careful consideration of the policy issues involved. There are also important political and constitutional issues to be considered.[57] Constitutional lawyers have recognized that the regulatory bodies constructed under the major privatizations lack clearly defined objectives and the means to achieve them. There are three elements involved in addressing these deficiencies: the various regulators (including the MMC) should have adequate powers to oversee the industry and be transparent in the formulation of the policies required to regulate their industries; the courts and the power of judicial review should be fully considered in setting out the various powers of the regulators; the role of the Secretary of State in terms of ministerial responsibility to Parliament should be clearly defined.

At the heart of the problem of accountability is the question of how to devise an adequate policy or sets of principles to guide regulators. There is also a need for a coherent set of objectives for privatized industry to act efficiently and at the same time reconcile consumer demands for a good quality service at a reasonable price with shareholders' desire for high returns on their investments.

There is no single solution that appears adequate. The courts are expensive, unduly technical and pragmatic in operation. Historically, ministerial responsibility has proved ineffective in providing an objective standard with which to check policy decision-taking. Under its guise ministers remain remarkably free to act within the overall policy objectives often set by the political demands of the day.

Changes are possible to the role of regulatory bodies and the development of inter-regulation agencies in the style of the United States Federal Administrative Procedure Act[58]. Setting up such procedurse might provide a more satisfactory solution to the problems outlined above, allowing data, analysis and rules to be co-related. The past lessons of UK nationalization point to the difficulty of a government setting targets, strategies and financial planning for the nationalized industries. The experience of privatization has shown that the lessons of the nationalized industries have not been learned. The questions of accountability and efficiency in respect to the newly-privatized industries remain largely unresolved in the same way as for the nationalized industries.

There are considerable challenges ahead. The legal requirements of licences and regulatory controls apply techniques from private law to public law. New techniques of analysis[59] and greater consistency of approach are required from regulators. A regulatory commission[60] may be required to build a confident and more open system of regulation. Britain may have to draw on the regulatory experience of other countries before deciding what direction to take for the future.[61] There are therefore lessons in the dangers of copying ideas without assessing their worth.

---

57 See: T. Daintith and B. Sah, 'Privatisation and the Economic neutrality of the Constitution' Public Law (1993) p465.
58 See: P. P. Craig, *Public Law and Democracy in the U.K and U.S.A.* (Oxford University Press, 1991).
59 See: 'The European Community dimension to competition policy' in Tim Frazer, 'Competition Policy after 1992: the Next Step' Modern Law Review Vol. 53 (1990) p609.
60 This idea has been proposed in some of the literature on utilities in the United Kingdom.
61 See: M. Moran and T. Prosser, *Privatization and Regulatory Change in Europe* (Open University Press, 1994).

COMMENT

Malcolm D. Rowat

REGULATORY FRAMEWORKS AND PRIVATIZATION

Attention should be given to the conceptual framework to be adopted to analyse a regulatory system[1]. This framework must encompass a methodology and must take account of the problems that regulation is seeking to address. Account must be taken of the nature of a country's institutional and organizational endowment. There is no ideal regulatory model. A regulatory system must therefore become country specific. Regulation is a problem of conflict involving contracting problems between government and firms, customers, consumers and interest groups. Interest groups within society may act as a catalyst for change which may have a positive or negative influence on regulatory policy.

Regulatory frameworks may be divided into 'basic' and 'detailed' engineering. 'Basic' engineering can be defined as the mechanisms by which societies create substantive or procedural constraints on regulatory discretion and resolve disputes that arise within those constraints. 'Detailed' engineering covers the specific rules concerning utility pricing, cross-subsidies, interconnection arrangements and the like. Various goals may be achieved through a variety of compliance mechanisms. These include the provision of substantive restraints on regulatory discretion; formal or informal constraints on the executive to change the regulatory framework, and the use of institutions to enforce both substantive and procedural constraints.

Country specific arrangements[2] to be taken into account include the institutional and organizational structures that are systemic to the country. Six areas, in particular, may be identified: the legislative and executive branches of government, the judiciary, informal norms, administrative capacity, the character of society's contending special interests and the role of ideology in society. The range of regulatory instruments available include specific and specialized legislation, presidential decree, contracts, including franchising and concessions, and administrative procedures to ensure degrees of transparency and accountability, such as the use of the United States Federal Administrative Procedure Act.

---

1   See: J. Luis Guasch and Pablo T. Spiller, 'Regulation and Private Sector Development in Latin America' unpublished paper, November 1994.
2   See: Ricardo Paredes, *Privatization and regulation in a Less Developed Economy: The Chilean Case* (Santiago, Chile: Universidad de Chile, 1994).

A balance needs to be struck regarding the choice of regulatory instrument. On the one hand it may be desirable to reduce the choice of regulatory instrument and any undue influence from outside the regulatory agency. On the other hand it is necessary to provide incentives for efficient utility operation and to allow the flexibility to adjust to changing market circumstances. At the same time there must be the additional dimension of flexibility to allow for renegotiation as circumstances change. This is particularly true of technological change which proceeds at a rapid pace. It does not follow, however, that independent self-financed agencies or separate regulatory agencies for each sector are definitely required. Multi-tasked agencies may operate more effectively when organized in a regulatory panel.

LESSONS FROM THE UNITED KINGDOM AND DEVELOPING COUNTRIES

The United Kingdom was one of the first countries to nationalize, it was also the first to privatize. The UK experience of privatization offers some tentative lessons that may be considered by developing countries. Regulatory frameworks need to be established prior to privatization. It is important that the unbundling of physical assets takes place prior to privatization sales. This will assist in the structuring of competition after privatization. Setting accountability and performance standards is also an optimum first stage in the various privatization strategies and stages towards competition. Often, nationalized companies are monopolies and setting competition strategies in place before privatization needs careful consideration.

Regulatory structures set up prior to privatization should include providing regulators with sufficient powers and guidance as to their future policy and objectives. Uncertainty should be reduced to a minimum to provide some level of predictability and security for private investors. The importance of inter-regulatory activity needs to be addressed. This may favour the adoption of a commission or a number of regulators to oversee privatization and competition strategy. Forward-planning includes addressing the question of consumer protection which includes achieving this via the adoption of legislative strategies such as the Competition and Service (Utilities Act) 1992 and the Citizen's Charter.

8 Competition policy in Latin America: Legal and institutional issues

Malcolm D. Rowat*

INTRODUCTION

Latin America has emerged from the 'lost decade' of the 1980s with substantially transformed economies characterized by sounder fiscal policies (cuts in expenditures, increases in revenues through better tax administration and from the one-time proceeds of privatization), substantial deregulation and decentralization of economic activity, outward-looking trade and investment policies, and greater domestic savings. While progress has been uneven across the region, in virtually all countries a more prominent role is envisaged for the private sector as the future engine of growth.

Unlike earlier decades in Latin America where macro-economic instability and import protection coincided with a domestic 'competition policy' characterized by price and exchange controls as well as capacity licensing, the 'new' Latin America has called forth the need for an entirely different approach to fostering a competitive environment for private sector development. This is particularly important in a region where there have historically been very high concentrations in the manufacturing sector which could be exacerbated through uncontrolled privatization. Infrastructure privatization has largely been handled through separate utility regulation statutes.

Competition policy (or antitrust policy in the USA) can be defined narrowly in accordance with the practice of the majority of OECD countries "as the body of laws and regulations governing business practices (horizontal or vertical agreements between enterprises, abuses of dominant positions, monopolization, mergers and acquisitions)".[1] However, it is often viewed in a broader context to include the myriad of government policies that impact competition at both the local and national level including trade liberalization (import competition), foreign investment regulation, protection of property rights (including intellectual property) and consumer protection to name a few. The core objective of competition policy in nearly all jurisdictions is to preserve and protect the

---

* The views in this chapter are those of the author in his personal capacity and are not necessarily those of the World Bank where he is employed.
1 Organization for Economic Co-operation and Development (OECD) Interim Report on 'Conference of Competition Policies', (June 1994) Annex, p8.

process of competition not competitors with a view to maximizing economic efficiency (both allocative and dynamic) by achieving efficient market outcomes in the form of lower consumer prices and better quality products. Some countries or jurisdictions also include broader 'public interest' objectives (regional development, promotion of small businesses, export promotion, decentralization of decision-making) which often tend to undercut the fundamental efficiency objectives of competition policy.

This paper examines recent Latin American experiences (legislative, institutional and enforcement) with the establishment of competition policies at the national level, using the narrower definition of competition policy. It also examines the nexus of competition policy and the broader framework of trade liberalization, consumer protection, foreign investment regulation, and intellectual property protection. Finally, the paper looks at competition policy from a sub-regional and regional integration context (MERCOSUR, Andean Pact and NAFTA), and the prospects for international convergence. The paper does not purport to explain why competition policy is important but rather evaluates how it has been implemented to date in Latin America and to suggest some areas for further reform.

SCOPE OF COMPETITION POLICY

Ideally, competition policy (laws and regulations and enforcement capacity) should cover all business practices, whether public or private, with exemptions limited to certain aspects of activities already regulated under other statutes (such as natural monopolies). Where public enterprises operate in markets in competition with private firms, they should be subject to the same competition restrictions as private firms in the market.

While some variations exist across countries, most competition laws can be broken down into components dealing with enterprise conduct and market structure. Either of these may be subject to civil and/or occasionally criminal procedures. Conduct restraints can be divided into horizontal and vertical.

In the case of horizontal agreements among enterprises, these are normally considered *per se*[2] illegal when they represent 'naked restraints' such as agreements involving bid-rigging, price-fixing, output restraints, market segmentation and customer allocation. The enforcement of these *per se* laws can

---

2   Under common law jurisdictions regardless of the facts and circumstances, such conduct is illegal; opposite of rule of reason requiring case-by-case analysis. Under civil law systems, legislation tends to be more specific to provide more certainty to private parties (less reliance on court interpretation) such as through block exemptions in the European Union with the possible drawback that the law will not 'evolve' in the light of changing external market circumstances.

be difficult in the absence of concrete evidence, particularly where the collusion transcends national borders. However, there may be other types of agreements that have potential pro-competitive effects such as research and development cartels that benefit from risk and information sharing as well as scale economies or joint purchasing arrangements. These usually fall under a 'rule of reason' analysis or may benefit from certain 'block exemptions' as under the European Union's know-how licensing, patent licensing, exclusive distribution agreements, and so on. In the latter case, block exemptions under Article 85(3) of the Treaty of Rome eliminate the notification requirement to the Commission in areas that would otherwise constitute a *per se* violation.

In the case of vertical restraints (contractual agreements between supplier and purchaser/retailer in both upstream and downstream markets), experience has varied widely across developed countries. In the EU, for example, vertical restraints are more forcefully prohibited particularly when there is an underlying regional integration objective or concern with the freedom of economic action. In the USA, enforcement has been much more uneven.

It is useful, however, to distinguish between vertical price restraints and non-price type restraints. In the former case, resale price maintenance (where a supplier conditions sale on controlling the distributor's price) has been the subject of considerable debate in different jurisdictions since in some cases it may be efficiency enhancing (in many OECD countries, for example, it is prohibited *per se*).

Others have argued that "while more conceptual and empirical research is needed in this area, there appears to be a consensus that vertical restraints can only play a facilitating role in making collusion easier than otherwise, and will be ineffective unless market conditions already are favorable for horizontal agreements".[3] However, in Latin America as elsewhere, some empirical evidence suggests that since a significant differential still exists between domestic and international prices in a number of markets after trade liberalization, violating the law of one price (LOP), certain anticompetitive forces (such as upstream/downstream concentration of market power) may be at work in 'capturing' the lower domestic prices for themselves rather than passing them on to consumers. While many factors (such as differential product standards, information asymmetrics and large differences in transportation costs) may together be at work to explain this phenomenon, it should be the subject of further research.[4]

---

3   Shyan Khemani and Sathaput Dutz, 'The Instruments of Competition Policy and their Relevance for Economic Development' in Claudio Frischtak (ed.), *Regulatory Policies and Reforms in Industrializing Countries*, (The World Bank, forthcoming).
4   Dutz and Suthiwart-Narueput 'Competition Issues Beyond Trade Liberalization: Distribution and Domestic Market Access' (unpublished, November 1994).

In the case of non-price vertical restraints (such as exclusive dealing where the distributor cannot purchase the competitor's products, refusal to deal, exclusive territory, tying, and full line forcing where supplier requires dealer to carry all of the supplier's products), the impact on competition will depend on the facts and circumstances of each case necessitating a rule of reason analysis.

A special category of the conduct portion of competition policy is the abuse of dominant position (AOD) doctrine, whereby relatively large firms engage in anticompetitive conduct by preventing entry or forcing exit of competitors through various kinds of monopolistic conduct including predatory pricing and market foreclosure as described above. However, in these cases, it is not always apparent whether the large firm is simply more efficient than its competitors and/or enjoys the benefits of sunk costs as opposed to engaging in non-competitive behaviour to raise rivals' costs. Further, it is also debatable as to what constitutes a 'large' firm, and by deduction, market power. This may, of course, be of greater relevance to developing countries where levels of economic concentration are much higher than in developed countries.

With respect to issues of market structure, competition authorities have naturally taken an interest in the potential impact of inter-corporate transactions involving horizontal or vertical mergers, takeovers, joint ventures or asset transfers and conglomerate transactions involving firms in unrelated businesses since these can lead to a reduction in the independence of competing suppliers or increased concentration of the market. A variety of merger guidelines have been used in developed countries, along with pre-notification procedures to assess such things as the efficiency claims of mergers, as against the likely rise of excessive concentration. In the context of developing countries, such considerations take on heightened importance where particular industries tend to be already highly concentrated and where economies of scale become an important consideration in developing export potential in the absence of a large domestic market.

From a developing country perspective, conduct violations are difficult to enforce in the absence of experienced investigatory capacity to bring provable cases. On the other hand, market structure violations generally assume the availability of good quality economic and market data in order to be able to analyse the costs and benefits of complex transactions. Setting competition policy priorities will have to be a factor in these institutional constraints on a case-by-case basis.

---

5 Argentina (1919 and revised through 1980); Mexico (1934); Colombia (1959), and Chile (1959 and revised in 1973).
6 This law was passed by the military government that entirely supported a private-sector orientated strategy through privatization, deregulation and trade liberalization.

ORIGIN OF COMPETITION POLICY IN LATIN AMERICA

Until the 1990s, there were few competition laws on the books in the Latin American region other than through broad general references in constitutions. Of the few that did exist[5] only the Chile law revised in 1973[6] enjoyed effective enforcement. In Argentina and particularly Colombia, a combination of vested interests, gaps in the legislative coverage, weak implementation and enforcement capacity drastically undermined the impact of such legislation.

With the advent of large-scale privatization of both infrastructure and manufacturing facilities, deregulation, trade liberalization, economic stabilization and even steps towards regional or global integration, the need to have a framework for competition policy became apparent across the region. Specifically, in the rush to privatize public assets – many of which were losing money – governments initially gave priority to improving their own fiscal position. During the past few years, however, five countries have passed new competition laws: Peru – 1991; Venezuela – 1992; Colombia – revised 1992; Mexico effectiveness – 1993; and Brazil – 1994. Costa Rica enacted a new law in January 1995 while Argentina, Panama, El Salvador, Paraguay and Ecuador are in various stages of finalization of new competition legislation. This proliferation of new legislation (and related institutions) raises a number of interesting issues in that the scope and provisions of the newly enacted laws and those proposed display a wide variation. However, the real test is in the implementation. While this is not necessarily surprising or unusual given the diversity of the countries involved, prima facie one can distinguish distinct levels of legislative quality which could be of particular importance as the impetus for regional integration grows and the need for policy harmonization becomes more desirable (see below).

ASSESSING THE SUBSTANTIVE LEGISLATIVE SCOPE

All the Latin American countries that have either passed or are contemplating passing new competition laws operate under the civil law system. Not surprisingly, then, the competition laws (and accompanying regulations) passed or proposed are typically extremely detailed to provide sufficient guidance to firms, lawyers and judges in their interpretation since there is not so much weight given to the notion that courts should not interfere with principles announced in former decisions (*stare decisis*).

Globally, there is a wide variation in the coverage and analytical tools of competition laws, even among OECD countries such as the USA and those in the EU. Furthermore, a wide range of agencies both bilateral (especially the USA, Canada, Germany and the UK) and multilateral (OECD, UNCTAD, which has developed a general model competition law, and the World Bank) have provided advice and training in drafting legislation and setting up institutions for developing countries resulting in a range of outcomes (some developing countries also produce home-grown varieties).

Mexico

The Government of Mexico enacted the Ley Federal de Competencia Economica (Economic Competition Law) in December 1992 which became effective in June 1993.[7] This forms part of a broader set of legislative reforms (including foreign investment regulation, intellectual property protection, antidumping and consumer protection) geared to enhancing private sector investment particularly in the context of the recent NAFTA treaty with the USA and Canada which includes a provision wherein "each Party recognizes the importance of co-operation and co-ordination among their authorities to further effective competition law enforcement in the free trade area".[8]

With respect to the substantive principles, the law provides detailed provisions relating to conduct and market structure considerations. However, the absence of long promised accompanying regulations has created some uncertainty on the part of private firms and their attorneys. The law also provides exceptions to the antitrust statute to include labour unions, co-operative export associations, as well as strategic areas reserved exclusively for the state. However, significantly, Mexico does not exclude public enterprises from the statute where they engage in non-strategic (for example, commercial) activities. One example is that of PEMEX, the state oil company which owns and operates retail gas outlets.

In the case of conduct violations, the law provides a typical distinction between 'absolute' (*per se*) and 'relative' (rule of reason) monopolistic practices categorizing the distinctive practices largely in the breakdown described earlier (Articles 9 and 10, respectively; see footnote 2 and accompanying text). With respect to the 'relative' practices (such as vertical price and non-price restraints), Article 11 provides that for a violation to occur, the violator must have significant market power in the relevant market and the activity must have an anticompetitive effect on the market. Articles 12 and 13 provide typical elaborations of what constitute the market (such as barriers to entry, degree of substitutability) and market power (such as market share, power of the firm's competitors). There is no provision for price discrimination as a conduct violation, which has often become a contentious issue in other countries, such as the USA.

---

7   For a detailed evaluation of Mexico's new Economic Competition Law see Joshua Newberg, 'Mexico's New Economic Competition Law: Toward the Development of a Mexican Law of Antitrust' Columbia Journal of Transnational Law Vol. 31 (1994) p587.
8   The North American Free Trade Agreement (NAFTA), Vol. I, Part Five, chapter 15, Article 1501 (1992).

With respect to structure or concentrations, the law contains detailed provisions for pre-notification of mergers and acquisitions that meet one or more of three tests[9] based on the size of the transaction, size of the target and size of the parties. These thresholds, which are set in terms of multiples of the minimum wage, appear somewhat cumbersome particularly in light of the volatility of the peso/dollar exchange rate which could significantly impact foreign transactions. The parties must submit the appropriate degree of documentation to the antitrust authorities who have 20 days to seek additional information and thereafter 45 days to make a decision (or a further 60 days under exceptional circumstances for complex cases).[10]

The standard of review is provided in Article 17, which generally prohibits transactions that provide market power (using Article 12 criteria) to the post-transaction entity to facilitate predatory conduct or exclude competitors or encourage anticompetitive practices by the parties. Nevertheless, as explained below, the absence of regulations, particularly in this area, has contributed to the initial uncertainty as to how the statutes should be implemented.

There is also a question as to how the statute would apply to transactions that were consummated prior to the passage of the Economic Competition Law. Moreover, no provision is made for the review of privatization transactions particularly involving concession agreements, although in practice, some procedures have developed in this area.

Chile

Chile revised its competition law in 1973 (Decree Law [D.L.] 211/1973) at a time of major market reforms in the country. It also produced separate legislation on consumer and intellectual property protection.

Not surprisingly, Chile's law, predating that of Mexico by 20 years, is much more general in scope; Article 1 deems as a restrictive practice any conduct that hampers competition while Article 2 provides some broad examples of anticompetitive conduct for both horizontal and vertical restraints. No regulations have ever been issued under the law. As a result, in the absence of a clear demarcation between *per se* and rule of reason violations, the administrative rulings and the case law, even in a civil law system, have become a determining though non-binding factor in the interpretation of the law. While some particularly unredeeming conduct such as price-fixing or territorial or customer divisions by

---

9 If the value of the transaction exceeds 12 million times the daily minimum wage for the Federal District of Mexico; if the transaction involves the acquisition of 35 per cent or more of the assets of capital stock of an agent whose assets or sales exceed 12 million times the daily minimum wage for the Federal District of Mexico; or if two or more parties to the transaction have assets or annual sales that exceed 48 million times the daily minimum wage for the Federal District of Mexico (Article 20).

10 In the absence of formal notification, the transaction is approved.

competitors will require little if any showing of anticompetitive effect, most cases of competitively questionable conduct will require some showing of an adverse effect on competition in order to establish a violation. "This has been characteristic of a more recent antitrust case law, which has developed a market-effects standard, whereas the earlier case laws tended more toward using *per se* approach to illegality." [11]

In terms of coverage, the law exempts state-owned businesses or public institutions that have been granted monopolies under statute (Article 4) from specific legislation that predates D.L. 211/1993 that restricts competition for valid reasons at that time (Article 3) or have been granted specific exemptions by the antitrust authorities. There is no provision for pre-merger review, with the result that merger and acquisition transactions may be evaluated on an *ex post* basis (either *ex officio* or stemming from a third-party complaint) thereby making 'unscrambling' costly.

Venezuela

Aside from the general provisions in the Venezuela Constitution (Articles 96 and 97) which refer to the competition objective, Venezuela did not have a competition statute until the Law to Promote and Protect Free Competition was enacted in December 1992. It is broad in scope covering individuals or groups, public or private, non-profit as well as profit entities that are engaged in economic activity in Venezuela.

Article 5 of the law provides for a general prohibition against anticompetitive conduct, while Article 6 specifically prohibits a wide range of activities that do not distinguish *per se* and rule of reason standards (except for abuse of dominant position situations where a variety of factors would be used to determine the level of effective competition). This implies an onerous role for the implementing agency where special exemptions need to be authorized. [12] Perhaps in recognition of this fact, a decree (No. 2775) was issued on 21 January 1993 that provided greater clarity as to when exemptions could be granted and greater precision on what constitutes the relevant market and factors that inhibit competition.

Peru

Peru has probably been the most active country, along with Mexico, in passing new legislation in recent years which deals with private sector development.

Specifically, in November 1991, Peru enacted an antitrust law (D.L. 701) in addition to a Consumer Protection Law (D.L. 716) and an Unfair Competition

---

11 J. Garrett (ed.), *World Antitrust Law* (1995) chapter 34, p10.
12 Under Partial Regulation 1 of the Law to Promote and Protect Free Competition, approved by the President of the Republic, conduct that does not affect more than 10 per cent of the relevant market will not be covered under the statute.

Law (D.L. 26122) in December 1971.[13] There is some overlap between the unfair competition law and the antitrust law and there is some question as to whether the former is even needed.

The antitrust law covers both individuals and corporations, public and private, that engage in economic activity in Peru. However, it does not apply in the international market unless there is direct effect on the Peruvian market.

The substantive provisions are restricted to violations that abuse a dominant position (although no objective criteria are provided as to what constitutes a dominant position such as market shares, and so on) and a long list of factors are offered as to what constitutes abuse (refusal to deal, tying clauses, price-fixing). Restraints of trade are also violations under the law with *per se* standards (output and market regulation, tying clauses, and so on). There is no treatment of structural issues involving mergers and acquisitions.

Colombia

Colombia has had a competition law (Law 155) since 1959 but it was never really enforced due to lack of political will in an economy characterized by a high degree of concentration of industry and ownership. As part of a broader set of measures designed to promote private sector development through privatization, deregulation, liberalization of trade and foreign investment, the government passed a Decree (D.L. 2153) on 30 December 1992 (no law was passed to avoid opposition from Congress) to modernize but not replace the old competition law.

Unlike Law 155, which provided for *per se* violations such as price-fixing but with generous exceptions due to overall economic interest, the new Decree explicitly lists a ban on a wide range of agreements under a *per se* formulation (price-fixing, restrictions on outputs, geographic markets) with some exceptions including ones related to research and development objectives and common facilities provided they are not anticompetitive (Articles 46 – 48). However, the Decree does not contain any provisions on vertical restraints since these are subsumed under a clause (Article 50) on abuse of dominant position (such as predatory pricing) although no structural criteria for dominance are included.

With respect to market structure, the Decree contains only one general clause (Article 51) that permits mergers and acquisitions provided the increased concentration can be justified on economic efficiency grounds. Nevertheless, the absence of any details in the form of regulations and guidelines on levels of concentration, size of transaction, market power, or efficiency measurements makes this whole section rather vague. Colombia has also recently passed related laws dealing with consumer protection, intellectual property and antidumping.

---

13 For a more detailed description of both the laws and the institutional framework see *Peru – Establishing a Competitive Market Environment* (The World Bank, 22 July 1993) pp22-27.

Brazil

Brazil's Constitution and a number of laws beginning in 1962 together provide for a competition law framework. Most recently, Brazil's Congress passed the Act for the Prevention and Repression of Infringements against Economic Order (Law No. 8.884 of 11 June 1994) which became effective two days later as Brazil's antitrust statute. Prior to this, Brazil had a long history of protection, regulation, public sector dominance, high concentrations of industry and utilization of price control as a means of controlling both competition and inflation.

The new law is comprehensive in that detailed category prohibitions are provided for both conduct and structure violations, although no *per se* restrictions are given. However, Article 20 provides for conduct violations even where there is no effect on competition but market power is assumed where market share exceeds 30 per cent.

Other unusual features of the law include a conduct violation without specific guidance on when a bar on the use of industrial or intellectual property rights or technology can be enforced (Article 21, XVI) or what constitutes the imposition of abusive prices (Article 21, XXIV), both reflecting policy legacies of the past.

Argentina

Argentina has had an antitrust law since 1919 although this has been amended several times, most recently in 1980. While the most recent law (Law No. 22.262) represented a substantial improvement on previous versions, it suffered from major deficiencies including ignoring structural issues (mergers and acquisitions) while giving attention to conduct violations, limited penalties and a weak institutional enforcement framework.

For these and other reasons, Argentina has been considering a variety of alternative legislative reforms in this area during the past several years, culminating in a new draft law which has passed the lower house of the Argentine Congress and is now pending before the Argentine Senate. While the new draft law addresses many of the weaknesses of the existing statute, there are still areas where improvements could be made. Shortcomings include the exclusion of individuals and Government institutions (Article 1); the inclusion of abuse of dominant position provisions without any definition of market power; no pre-notification for mergers and acquisition analysis; inclusion of a public interest exception as well as a concentration exemption for scale economies in markets facing import competition; and the criminalization of abuse of dominant position violations, an excessively harsh remedy (Article 36).

INSTITUTIONAL ARRANGEMENTS

A number of principles can be said to apply to the administrative arrangements for the implementation – as opposed to the enforcement – of competition laws, irrespective of the country-specific environment:
• the competition authority should be independent and insulated from political interference;
• the investigation, prosecution and adjudication functions in the enforcement of competition law should act separately;
• a system of checks and balances should be in place with appropriate rights of appeal and review of decisions and facts on legal and economic grounds;
• the proceedings should be transparent while safeguarding sensitive business information of a competitive nature;
• cases and related matters must be resolved expeditiously;
• the proceedings should be accessible to all affected parties with provisions for introducing expert testimony and evidence;
• the competition authority should have an advocacy function, particularly as it relates to the formulation of economic regulatory policies to put alternative best practices of competition in the market;
• the competition authority should also be accorded a wider role in government economic policy decision-making including those on international trade, foreign investment, consumer protection, and intellectual property.[14]

The Latin American Region has displayed a range of institutional arrangements under which to administer these new laws, often departing from the maxims mentioned above. The institutional and enforcement arrangements are more significant than the legislative framework in measuring the effectiveness of the policy. As throughout the public sector, competition authorities suffer from the lack of civil service reform on salary levels and career development potential.

Mexico
To implement its objectives, the Mexican statute provides for the establishment of a five-member Federal Competition Commission which operates as an autonomous body within the Secretariat of Commerce and Industrial Development (SECOFI). The Commissioners are appointed by the Federal Executive for 10-year renewable terms (the initial members are appointed for different staggered intervals to ensure staggered future rotation) and cannot be removed except for cause. The Commission is dependent on the executive branch for its budget which is potentially a means of curbing its autonomy.[15] The Commission has an

---

14 Khemani and Dutz, ibid. pp20-21.
15 One suggestion of the Commission is to keep a certain percentage of the fines collected as a means of self-financing which, of course, creates its own incentive problems.

Executive Director and a staff of about 40 (equally mixed between lawyers and economists) many of whom are relatively inexperienced.

In terms of responsibilities, the Commission is authorized to: investigate at the request of interested parties or on its own initiative anticompetitive violations under the direction of its Executive Secretary; adjudicate cases through the decision of the Commissioners and impose sanctions; provide advisory opinions to other government agencies whose actions and/or proposals for laws and regulations may impact competition; participate with other government agencies in the negotiation of treaties that affect competition. In terms of sanctioning power, the Commission can grant injunctive relief or assess fines on businesses for *per se* violations of up to 375,000 times the minimum wage of the Federal District (roughly US$1 million); up to US$600,000 for rule of reason violations and up to US$270,000 for failure to file a required pre-merger notification.[16]

Interestingly there is a distinction made between rule of reason for merger cases where only an injured party (or the Commission) may bring a case (Article 38) and *per se* violations, where any private party can bring suit. This distinction is designed to discourage frivolous suits. The Commission need not go to court to impose a fine and in a real sense functions both as investigator and adjudicator. Alleged violators can appeal the decision of the Commission which must be decided by the full Commission within 60 days.

Chile

Chile's institutional arrangements to administer its 1973 statutes are unique in that they provide for a two-tier system. This includes Preventive Commissions of four members for each region of the country as well as a Central Preventive Commission with five members[17] that handles cases in more than one region, in addition to cases from Santiago. The Resolutive Commission handles all appeals from Preventive Commissions and is empowered to order the National Prosecutor, from the separate Office of the Prosecutor, to bring criminal charges for violations of the law (Article 18).

Investigations can be enacted by the Prosecutor's Office including at the request of an interested party, a claim may be lodged before one of the Commissions by any interested party against a firm or individual over an alleged anticompetitive practice and advisory requests can be submitted to any Commission for an advanced ruling. Private suits can also be brought in general jurisdiction courts once one of the Commissions has found fault, but only compensatory damages are available.

---

16 Provision is also included for fines of up to US$20,000 against individuals who engage in anticompetitive practices on behalf of corporations.
17 Including government officials, academics and judicial representatives.

With respect to sanctions, only the Preventive Commissions have the power to stop conduct or agreements for a period not exceeding 30 days although they can request the Prosecutor's Office to suggest that the Resolutive Commission imposes fines or changes in contracts.[18] The Resolutive Commission can terminate or modify conduct or agreements that restrain competition without any subsequent judicial review. It can also impose other sanctions including fines (up to roughly US$400,000) and can order criminal prosecution (to be heard by the Justice of the Court of Appeals) although this is rare and there have been no successful prosecutions of competition criminal cases in Chile.[19]

Venezuela

Venezuela's competition law is implemented by the Superintendency for the Promotion and Protection of Free Competition, an ostensibly autonomous administrative agency under the Ministry of Development. It has a staff of about 20 professionals. It has broad powers to investigate, and request information from, all individuals or firms, whether public or private, local or foreign that do business in Venezuela. This can be done at the request of an affected party or by the agency itself. When violations occur, the Superintendency can impose fines (up to 20 per cent of the violator's sales or up to 40 per cent for repeat offenders), issue desist orders or impose extra conditions on the violator. There are no criminal penalties. All decisions are appealable to an Administrative Court following a decision by the Superintendency where the latter acts within 30 days of receiving complete documentation from the parties. Once the Superintendency has reached a final decision, persons or businesses injured by anticompetitive practices can seek "simple" damages through the courts and the prevailing party can usually expect attorney's fees.[20]

Peru

Among the most unique organizational set-ups for implementation of a competition law is that of Peru, specifically the National Institute for the Defense of Competition and Protection of Intellectual Property (INDECOPI) created under Decree Law 25868 on 24 November 1992.

It is considered an autonomous body with a Board of Directors (three government members), and an unpaid nine-member Advisory Council made up of public and private sector representatives, under seven Commissions and

---

18 "In any event, the reason for the simultaneous operation of two commissions, involving unnecessary duplication of effort and work, is still not evident." Ricardo Paredes, *Jurisprudence of the Antitrust Commissions in Chile*.

19 J. Garrett, ibid. chapter 34, pp14-15.

20 J. Garrett, ibid. chapter 34, p23.

Technical Secretariats (competition, dumping and subsidies, consumer protection, advertising, unfair competition, technical standards and non-tariff barriers, and entry and exit barriers).

This organizational structure, although beneficial in terms of providing opportunities for synergy particularly between competition, dumping and intellectual property protection may at the same time be too fragmented with three Commissions – unfair competition, consumer protection and advertising – overlapping to a considerable extent. Recently, INDECOPI has sought to consolidate these Commissions into a smaller number in an attempt to improve their efficiency.

INDECOPI has the power to conduct investigations, make recommendations (via the Secretariats) and hold hearings and pass judgment (via the Commissions). A special tribunal is available within INDECOPI to hear appeals, reflecting the lack of confidence in the Peruvian judiciary; but this also conveys extraordinary power on one institution and it remains to be seen how effectively it will be discharged. INDECOPI's tribunals include part-time judges (lawyers in private practice) who adjudicate cases involving firms for whom they counsel in private practice thereby creating a flagrant conflict of interest.

INDECOPI's budgetary resources are not defined by the law thereby creating some uncertainty, although it does collect one-third of its required revenues from the copyright and the patent office. Prestigious and experienced persons have been appointed to the Commission and the special Tribunal, although enforcement capacity is limited by the excessively low maximum sanctions (US$35,000) and the fact that there is no provision for private suits.

Colombia

As in other Andean countries, Colombia has consolidated extensive powers into the agency responsible for implementation of the Competition Decree, the Superintendency of Industry and Commerce, located as an autonomous body with its own budgetary and financial controls under the Ministry of Economic Development. Similar to Peru, the Superintendency also includes a special office for intellectual property protection and consumer protection, while a separate agency (INCOMEX – Institute of Foreign Trade) handles the implementation of the antidumping law.

Under Article 2 of the Decree, the Superintendent has the power to investigate competition cases, prosecute partly through power to collect information from the parties, and pass judgment through the office of an Administrative Tribunal within the Superintendency. The Superintendent has the power to impose fines, issue injunctions and modify transactions. There is also a non-binding Advisory Council made up of representatives of the public and private sectors. Decisions of the Superintendent can only be appealed on legal grounds. Given the newness of the organization, the Superintendent is building up a staff of about 20 relatively young lawyers and economists.

Brazil

With the passage of the new competition law in 1994, Brazil created a new organizational structure by virtue of keeping the Economic Law Office (SDE) as the investigatory arm of the Ministry of Justice (which will also file administrative proceedings) while transforming the Economic Protection Administration Council (CADE) into an independent federal adjudicative government entity under the Ministry of Justice. The Ministry of Finance also plays a role in reviewing merger and acquisition matters. SDE decisions are not appealable to a higher executive level while CADE decisions taken by majority vote (with a quorum of three) are not subject to executive branch review with decisions promptly executable through the office of the Attorney General in the courts. CADE has the power to issue various preventive measures[21] including cease and desist orders and consent decrees as well as fines ranging from 30 per cent of gross billings (and an additional 10 to 15 per cent of such a fine if corporate individuals are also found liable) or if not calculable, a range from US$3,000 to roughly US$3 million.

Argentina

Subject to passage of a new law, Argentina's enforcement capacity of its existing law rests with the National Commission in Defense of Competition (CDC) which is organized under the authority of the Secretary of Commerce. It has a President who is also one of the Undersecretaries of Commerce and four members appointed by the Ministry of Economy, of whom two should be lawyers and two economists, with four-year tenures. The President alone has the power to make the decisions which most likely blurs the independence of the Commission itself.[22]

The Commission can initiate investigations on its own or based on a complaint by a third party. It has full subpoena powers. Barring a settlement or a dismissal, the Commission can impose fines (up to 20 per cent more than the gain from the conduct), and issue cease and desist orders. Fines and orders of the Commission are appealable to the courts. The law also provides for criminal penalties for conduct that causes injury not in the general economic interest.

---

21 Including the rather novel concept of granting compulsory licences for patents held by the violator.
22 For a detailed analysis of the present Argentine administrative arrangements for implementing the Competition Law, see 'Report of the Advisory Team on Competition Policy and Consumer Protection in Argentina', 10 August 1992 prepared by Economist Inc. and reprinted by the World Bank in 'Competition Policy Seminar', Vol. I (World Bank, 1993).

ENFORCEMENT

For most Latin American countries, the passage of new competition laws and the establishment of institutional frameworks as well as staffing is very recent. It is therefore premature to draw too many conclusions from the pattern of case disposition to date. Even less can be said about the experience of cases appealed through the courts, since in most countries these have been infrequent. This is partly explainable by the fact that court systems in Latin America, with the possible exception of Chile, suffer from long delays, cumbersome administrative procedures, judges with insufficient training particularly in fields such as competition policy, and unpredictable and non-transparent results in the absence of deciding like cases in a like manner. Nevertheless, a summary analysis of the experience to date does provide some useful insights.

In the case of Chile, which has the longest active record of enforcement from 1973, the various Commissions have concentrated on conduct violations, particularly the vertical kind, reflecting a general problem throughout the region of being able to come up with sufficient evidence to make a horizontal cartel arrangement a provable violation. As a result, Chilean enforcement agencies have concentrated on price discrimination cases. Between 1976-1993, for example, 16 claims were submitted to the Resolutive Commission of which five were appealed to the Supreme Court with one dismissal; 18 resale price maintenance cases of which 10 were found guilty; and 12 cases of exclusive distribution in a non-agent setting of which two were appealed to the Supreme Court which found sanctionable violations. The Resolutive Commission handled 31 cases of price agreements of which five were appealed to the Supreme Court and three were sanctioned.

In Venezuela, other than a substantial number of consultations, the Superintendency handled 13 conduct cases in its first two years including price agreements (two out of three convictions), exclusive distributions and boycotts. Six merger cases were decided including one denial which was subsequently appealed and approved but with strict conditions attached. Judging by the Superintendency's draft Annual Report for 1994, there has been a reduction in the number of cases brought. This partly reflects the change in government and the related economic crises that led to temporary exchange and price controls (only three new merger cases were reviewed of which one was not approved).

Examining the first year of Mexico's operation through June 1994 is quite instructive. Not surprisingly, the bulk of the Commission's activity has been devoted to merger cases based partly on the fact that the pre-notification requirement provides an effective way of generating cases.[23] By contrast, conduct

---

23 'Comision Federal de Competencia' (Mexico: 1993-94) p17.

cases, particularly with an inexperienced staff are more difficult to bring and win. As a result, 52 merger cases were reviewed (37 industrial, 4 telecommunication, and 11 financial) of which 39 were approved, and the remainder either modified or rejected, a rate of modification/rejection considerably higher than the merger task force of the EU but where advanced consultations are probably less. This was accomplished well within the 45 -day stipulated time interval. In an unusual situation, the Commission also acted as an adviser to the Ministry of Finance and Public Credit on the suitability from a competition perspective of 34 buyers in privatization auctions. This area was not covered by the Economic Competition Law and as a result the Commission has felt that despite this participation the competitive dimension of privatization (including concession agreements) has not been given sufficient attention.

The other interesting development in the first year was that out of the 22 private suits brought for conduct violations, 16 were dismissed for not meeting the minimum threshold requirements for proceeding, reflecting the inexperience of plaintiffs. Of the Commission's own 15 *ex officio* investigations completed, six resulted in fines, and two in consent decrees. However, in the first half of the fiscal year through December 1994 activity has picked up substantially with 43 new merger cases and 70 new private actions which are better prepared than those from the first year. This reflects the Commission's effort to 'educate' the public about competition policy (public speeches, published documents) to counteract the 'protected' culture which still exists in the industrial community.

All seven of Peru's Commissions have been active in the first year of operation, with the Commission on competition concentrating on price-fixing and abuse of dominant position cases. Similarly, in Colombia, 25 investigations were launched during the period 1993/94, three of which have already led to significant fines. The case of Brazil is too recent to offer any insights.

The Argentina case is also unique in that its amended 1980 law does not include any 'structure' provisions. This is in addition to the other shortcomings noted earlier which should be rectified if the new law is passed by the Senate. However, during the period 1980 to 1992, 285 anticompetitive investigations (an average of 24 per year) were handled by the Commission, and of the 199 concluded, 70 were dismissed by the Commission and only 49 led to findings of guilt before the Secretary of Commerce. This reflects the fact that the Commission has been relatively weak and has concentrated its attention on the smaller firm cases who did not have the political clout of the well-connected larger private firms. This lack of overall effectiveness was particularly unfortunate at a time when major privatizations took place without due regard for the competition dimension (for example, in the steel sector despite efforts to inject competition criteria into the bidding process).

Harmonization

Not surprisingly, the substantial increase in foreign investment, transitional mergers, joint-ventures, international licensing arrangements, and strategic alliances has magnified the problem of difference in both substance and procedure between national (and in some cases supranational) competition laws which creates uncertainty, since private parties need to seek authorizations from multiple jurisdictions, and raises transaction costs. Use of extraterritorial jurisdiction based on the 'effects' doctrine, particularly by the USA, has created a backlash from other countries resulting in statutes being blocked. While proposals have been made to harmonize national competition laws (by the publication of a draft International Antitrust Code in 1993 by the Max Plank Institute, and the proposed competition initiative under the World Trade Organization which may result in competition policy being on the agenda of the Ministerial Conference scheduled in November 1996 in Singapore) it remains to be seen how much will happen in this area in the foreseeable future. Most likely, efforts will be made to co-ordinate and co-operate across jurisdictions to the extent feasible particularly with respect to procedural standards, or perhaps with universal 'floors'.

For example, in the past year, the USA and Canada together successfully brought two criminal international cartel cases[24] using a mutual legal assistance treaty[25] while the USA and EU successfully co-operated, with the active consent of the target Microsoft, to issue a consent decree (an undertaking from the EU) restricting Microsoft's software licensing practices. The consent decree has since been rejected in US Federal Court but this was overturned on appeal.

In the OECD's 'Interim Report on Convergence of Competition Policies' (June 1994), the following recommendations for the harmonization of merger guidelines were proposed:

> • development of more specific guidelines for the application of the 1986 OECD Recommendation in connection with merger investigations, including suggestions to: (i) notify at an earlier stage; (ii) establish contact directly between the competition authorities, and, (iii) notify every other competition authority known or understood to be investigating, or likely to investigate, the transaction;
>
> • development of one or alternate models of a protocol for parties to a merger to waive confidentiality protection in order to permit the sharing of confidential information among reviewing authorities;

---

24 See C. Goldman and J. Kissack, 'Joint Sovereign Criminal Investigations, US and Foreign Governments – Can They Really Do That? – A Canadian Perspective' paper presented at Criminal Antitrust Law and Procedure Workshop on 23-24 February 1995 sponsored by the Section of Antitrust Law of the American Bar Association.
25 The US Congress recently passed the International Enforcement Assistance Act of 1994 which will provide for exchange of confidential information between competition authorities provided there is an existing Mutual Legal Assistance Treaty (MLAT).

- collection and dissemination to other member countries of each member's guidelines on the application and interpretation of their confidentiality laws as applied to merger investigations;
- development of a model formulation that member countries could incorporate into their merger notification forms to elicit information about notifications to, and inquiries by, competition authorities of other jurisdictions;
- measures to encourage competition authorities when requested to identify for foreign counterparts publicly available information relevant to the investigation at hand and, as far as practicable, assist in obtaining such information;
- authorities examining consideration of the feasibility of model filing forms for those questions that are likely to be common to the same transaction.[26]

In the case of Latin America, the emergence of a number of regional integration agreements at a time when competition policy is being accentuated naturally raises the issue of regional or sub-regional harmonization. This can apply to the substantive provision of respective laws for both conduct and structure violations. Of particular importance is the critical determination of what constitutes the 'market' for purposes of concentration analysis which, with the reduction of internal trade barriers within regional trade blocs, could include the entire region for certain products. Co-ordination of process enforcement and procedures, dispute resolution mechanisms and related issues such as antidumping in a regional market context would also be important.

In the case of the NAFTA agreement (between Mexico, the USA and Canada), competition policy was explicitly mentioned in a 'trade' agreement[27] based on a set of general principles or objectives. However, the NAFTA agreement also included the establishment of a Working Group (Article 1504) on Trade and Competition in NAFTA, and in July 1994, a report on the 'Competition Dimension of NAFTA' was issued by the American Bar Association Section of Antitrust Law that contains, in almost 200 pages, specific recommendations on harmonization particularly with respect to process, procedure and enforcement (for example, streamlining of the filing and information requirements for multinational mergers and joint ventures). This is particularly relevant for Mexico in that both the USA and Canada together have more than 100 years' experience of implementing antitrust policy, more recently in co-operation with each other. The medium-term possibility of a Western Hemisphere Free Trade Area should also provide some incentive for harmonization throughout the rest of the region.

In the case of the Andean Pact countries (Colombia, Bolivia, Ecuador, Peru and Venezuela) whose objective is to create a regional common market under the Cartagena Agreement, a multilateral agency – the Cartagena Commission created under the Agreement – has the authority to promulgate rules applicable

---

26 'Interim Report on Convergence of Competition Policies', (OECD, June 1994) p15.
27 North American Free Trade Agreement, ibid., chapter 15.

to member countries. Decision No. 285 in March 1991 established standards for preventing market distortions arising from anticompetitive practices that are similar to Venezuela's law. The jurisdiction extends to conduct by a firm doing business in more than one member country or in one or more member countries and a firm outside the regional market. These rules can be enforced through the national competition authorities[28] but countries or private firms can submit claims of violation to the Board of the Cartagena Agreement which can hear and decide cases that restrict free competition.[29] It remains to be seen how effective this mechanism will be given the inherent constraints of building up institutional capacity at either the national or supranational level. It is interesting to note that, in the case of the EU where supranational authority on competition matters (coexisting with national authority) has been established for decades and despite a recent emphasis on subsidiarity, "competition law until now has been developed overwhelmingly through Commission decisions in Brussels and appeals against Commission decisions brought before the European Court of Justice and Court of First Instance; breakthroughs before National Courts are relatively infrequent."[30]

In the case of MERCOSUR (Brazil, Argentina, Paraguay and Uruguay), which officially came into effect on 1 January 1995 with a common external tariff and set of comprehensive internal tariff reductions (with some exemptions particularly for the smaller countries), discussions are under way on the adoption of a protocol on competition policy. Decision No. 21/94 of the Common Market Council provides general draft guidelines prepared by the Committee of Competition Policy of Subgroup No. 10 which was to be finalized by 30 June 1995. The draft, to which is attached a three-page Annex on substantive provisions, provides a fairly broad set of objectives and practices relating to conduct and structure to which member countries should adhere. Specifically, the draft protocol covers both goods and services and appears to imply *per se* violation in the typical areas of price-fixing and geographic market segmentation as well as in areas of abuse of dominant position (resale price maintenance, refusals to deal, and even unjustified restraints on technology development). A separate section provides for 'structure' reviews where concentrations exceed 20 per cent of the relevant market but without defining how the relevant market will be determined within MERCOSUR. The draft protocol also states that member countries will establish coordination mechanisms among corresponding national competition authorities, while the Trade Commission will look after enforcement of competition policy within MERCOSUR. Considerable

---

28 Bolivia and Ecuador have yet to establish effective national authorities in this area.
29 J. Garrett, ibid. chapter 34, p18.
30 Ian Forrester, 'Competition Structures for the 21st Century' presented at the 21st Annual Conference on International Antitrust Law and Policy, Fordham Corporate Law Institute.

clarification is still required both in terms of the scope of the protocol and the institutional arrangements for enforcement. This is compounded by the fact that Brazil has recently passed new legislation in this area, while Argentina's new proposed law is pending in the Senate.

NEXUS WITH OTHER POLICY INSTRUMENTS

While the flurry of activity in the Latin American region to develop or modernize the competition law framework is to be commended, particularly as the prospects for a Western Hemisphere Free Trade Area become brighter, other policy instruments can also have a significant impact on domestic competition. The more important of these include the trade policy regime, consumer protection, intellectual property protection and foreign investment regulation.

In the case of trade policy, it is not accidental that as trade was liberalized throughout the region countries (including Mexico, Brazil, Argentina and Colombia) developed or strengthened antidumping legislation which in theory and practice could be used to diminish import competition.[31] Where such instruments are captured by domestic interests, they can seriously undermine the efforts of competition authorities. Of note is the fact that in the USA and EU, the agencies dealing with competition and antidumping are kept quite separate and independent, and a country such as Mexico has followed this practice. On the other hand, regional trading bloc partners such as Australia and New Zealand have eliminated antidumping suits within the trading bloc, and this appears to be the pattern in the Andean Pact countries as well. In essence, competition policy could replace the antidumping regimes within a trading bloc, and when it exists externally, policymakers should co-ordinate their responses in the two areas (for example, Canada sometimes attaches import liberalization conditions to the approval of a merger transaction).

A second closely related policy objective of competition policy, that of consumer protection, is only just beginning to emerge as an area of concern and emphasis in the Latin American region. Nonetheless, it is not surprising that many of the countries that have recently enacted new competition legislation have also legislated in the consumer protection area. This is particularly true of the Andean Pact countries that have often included a separate consumer protection unit or secretariat within the competition authority. There is no doubt that consumer protection issues – such as false advertising, mislabelling of

---

31 For a detailed discussion of this phenomenon, see Luis Guasch and Sanath Rajapatirana, *The Interface of Trade, Investment and Competition Policies: Selected Issues and Challenges for Latin America* (World Bank, 5 October 1994) pp21-23.

products, quality standards – are closely linked to the broader concern of competition policy. These therefore need to be addressed simultaneously to ensure maximum effectiveness.

A third important area has been that of foreign investment regulation where historical restrictions on foreign investment in Latin America hindered the domestic competitive environment. As capital inflows have become an increasingly important source of funds for Latin America, not surprisingly countries have simultaneously sought to modernize their foreign investment laws (for example, Mexico) to make them more hospitable to foreign investors, by removing restrictions on eligible sectors for foreign investment, repatriation rights, compensation for expropriation and provisions for dispute resolution.

Many countries in Latin America (Chile, Bolivia, Argentina) have entered into bilateral investment treaties primarily with developed countries. A good example is the 1993 US-Argentina Treaty, the first to be concluded by the USA with a Latin American country since the announcement of the Enterprise for the Americas Initiative in June 1990. By providing for international arbitration of investment disputes included under the International Center for the Settlement of Investment Disputes (ICSID), the Treaty repudiated the Calvo Doctrine (of Argentinian origin) which requires that aliens submit disputes arising in a country to local jurisdiction; 21 Latin American and Caribbean countries have now signed the ICSID Convention. Other features of the treaty include provision for national treatment, freedom from 'performance' requirements, and the freedom to hire top managers of their choice regardless of nationality. During the past three and a half years, Latin American countries have become parties to 30 bilateral investment treaties, a sharp increase from earlier years which will serve to lock in many of the reforms that have had an effect on the investment climate.

The fourth policy prong normally grouped with competition policy is intellectual property protection. There is an obvious link between the policy for licensing and sale of patents, for example, and the degree of competition, particularly when the patent represents a 'bottleneck' in a network, for example in telecommunications or software development. The USA and EU have long linked intellectual property and competition policy to fashion an integrated view of competition policy with the former for the first time in 1995 issuing elaborate guidelines on how to analyse intellectual property arrangements from a competition perspective. In the case of Latin America, effective legally-based intellectual property protection is a relatively recent phenomenon.[32] New laws

---

32 For a detailed assessment of intellectual property protection in Latin America, see Malcolm Rowat, 'An Assessment of Intellectual Property in LDCs from Both a Legal and Economic Perspective – Case Studies of Mexico, Chile and Argentina' Denver Journal of International Law and Policy, Vol. 21, No. 2 (Winter 1993) p401.

have recently been passed in countries such as Mexico and Peru, and their effectiveness as extra dimensions of competition policy will depend on their scope and enforcement capacity. Up until now, intellectual property and competition law have been seen as entirely separate legal reform initiatives although some countries, particularly those in the Andean Pact, have placed the responsibility for both competition policy and intellectual property protection under one agency. Although Brazil's new law attempts to link the two, it remains to be seen how it will be implemented. Countries contemplating reform in these areas would do well to consider the issues together.

CONCLUSIONS AND RECOMMENDATIONS

The rapid transformation of Latin America economies through trade liberalization, deregulation, decentralization and privatization sparked, among other things, an examination of the need for a new policy framework for competition affecting both the public and private sectors. The recent proliferation of new and/or proposed new laws throughout the region is testament to that. Despite this level of activity, in each of these countries the political economy of reform needs to be examined carefully, since vested interests that enjoyed the highly protectionist environments of the past are usually averse to succumbing to a new competitive regime (the backtracking in the case of Venezuela is an example of this). Competition authorities need to make a special effort to 'educate' the public about the merits of a sensible competition policy.

Each of the jurisdictions, with the possible exception of Mexico, has shown fundamental flaws in the implementation of its legislation and/or institutional and enforcement arrangements. Even in the case of Mexico, certain ambiguities remain with respect to historically excessive concentrations, bidding criteria for privatization, and the absence of detailed regulations to guide private parties. Thus, the variety of *ad hoc* technical assistance from bilateral and multilateral sources has either not been sought or not been effective or effectively used. Further, more effort could be made at cross-fertilization within the region.

With respect to institutions, the tendency has been to consolidate excessive investigatory and judicatory power in one institution (particularly in the Andean Pact countries) which partly reflects the poor state of the judicial system. Given the complexity of competition law, there may be a case for establishing specialized competition courts where judges would be trained to specialize in this particular field. In some countries, greater leeway should be given for private suits to supplement the investigative capacity of fledgling government agencies that are, for the most part, staffed with young, inexperienced practitioners locked into a civil service system in need of reform. Not surprisingly, merger rather than conduct cases are given priority because of the greater ease with which competition institutions can review them.

The need for better legislation, institutions and enforcement capacity will become even greater as the move towards greater regional integration becomes more pronounced. The fact that the three major groupings in the region (NAFTA, MERCOSUR and Andean Pact) are focusing on competition policy harmonization is a welcome development that needs to be strongly supported by outside agencies.

In addition, policymakers need to integrate the other major policy instruments that affect competition policy (antidumping, consumer protection, foreign investment regulation and intellectual property protection) into the formulation of competition policy. Even some OECD countries have been unable to do this effectively. However, Latin America has a better chance of achieving this in the present more hospitable climate of legal reform.

COMMENT

Luis José Diez-Canseco Núñez

Malcolm Rowat's paper is full of information which deserves deeper analysis and provokes many more discussions than I can possibly cover here.

My comments will be structured around five questions:
- What value must be given to competition legislation, and must it be developed independently from other legal disciplines?
- What kind of legislative model must be followed?
- What kind of institutional framework is needed for enforcement purposes?
- What other activities have to be carried out?
- What can we do?

Before attempting to answer these questions, I will try to identify the framework within which competition policy has emerged in Latin America to complement the observations expounded by Rowat. Similar considerations might also be relevant for other developing countries.

ECONOMIC DEVELOPMENT MODEL

Competition legislation appears as a recent necessity in the region. This is due, in part, to the fact that for the first time in history Latin American countries have adopted market-orientated economies. In other words, they have chosen a development model or system based on competition.

Not too long ago the economies of most of the Latin American countries were of an agricultural and mining profile, based on exports. However, especially since the 1950s, national industry has emerged. It flourished under protectionist schemes known as 'import substitution' which compelled Latin American and other developing countries to adopt a series of macro-economic measures rather remote from the principles of competition. Examples include the high level of tariff protection (including importation prohibition) for products in competition with national industry, nationalizations, and the proliferation of state enterprises and monopolies; restrictive exchange controls mechanisms in relation to foreign investment; subsidized exports; duty-free treatment for the import of certain capital goods; importation quotas for basic inputs and commodities; price controls. It was a scheme in which the state held the reins of the market.

This situation coexisted with what might be called the 'economy of apparent market', that is, an economic system where the private sector was free to develop certain economic activities which the state did not consider 'priority' or 'strategic' operations – those endeavours which the state did not reserve for itself or, alternatively, those which economic power groups had managed to keep outside of state control.

Ironically, the prevailing economic policy in Latin America was contrary to that enshrined in most of the countries' constitutions. Following the principles which arose during the French Revolution, which were then adopted later by Spain at Cadiz and projected thereafter on its former colonies, the majority of their constitutions claimed that their economic systems revolve around the principle of free trade and industry[1]. Simultaneously, general prohibitions were established concerning monopolies. Such a tradition would lead one to suppose that competition was the inspiring principle behind the economic policies of the countries of Latin America.

History would have it otherwise. The mercantilism that encouraged economic (and political) power groups in the past and through most of this century did not favour competition. Simultaneously, the populist governments that had flourished in recent years could not adopt an economic system founded on the expansion of the market, since public intervention was the rule. Moreover, populism evolved into socialism and for the latter competition has clearly been anathema. Additionally, and to complicate things even more, the principle of free trade and industry, which was part of the Constitution, was subordinated to statutes of revolutionary governments and of governments of national reconstruction or any other expression that would legitimize to the military dictatorships which emerged during that period.

The rest of the story is well known: an increasing deficit in the balance of payments; the creation of a gigantic state apparatus; the crisis of the external debt; problems of monopoly and speculation regarding prices of goods and services owing to price controls, and the inflationary spirals. These were among the factors that triggered a clear process of restoration of political democracy, and which led to the adoption of economic policies which were contrary to the extant policies. This is how liberal governments, now so common in the region, came to be.

---

1 There is a vast body of literature dealing with the contents and evolution of the principle of free trade and industry under the French and Spanish legal traditions. Good examples are: Gérard Farjat and Bernard Remiche, *Liberté et droit économique* (Liberty and economic law), (Brussels: De Boeck Université, 1992); Martín Bassols Coma, *Constitución y Sistema Económico* (Constitution and the Economic System), (Madrid: Tecnos, 1985); Santos Pastor, *Sistema Jurídico y Economía* Legal System and the Economy), (Madrid: Tecnos, 1989).

2 For a detailed explanation of the meaning and extent of this concept, see Winfried Jung (ed.), *Social Market Economy. An Economic System for Developing Counties*, (Sankt Augustin: Academia Verlag Richarz AV, 1990). Concerning its relationship with competition legislation: Busdesministerium für Wirtschaft, *Wettbewerbspolitik in der Sozialen Marktwirtschaft* (Competition Policy in a Social Market Economy), (Berlin: 1992); Juan Ignacio Font Galán, *Constitución Económica y Derecho de la Competencia* (Economic Constitution and Competition Law), (Madrid: Tecnos, 1987).

COMPETITION AND THE CONSTITUTIONAL MANDATE

As mentioned above, most constitutions in Latin America embody a precept upholding freedom of trade and industry as the inspiring principle of their economies (often known as a 'Social Market Economy').[2] One might as a consequence believe that this principle implies the need for a legal structure to apply such a mandate. I am referring to the three sets of legislation whose purpose it is to protect the components of the market system: the repression of unfair competition (business guardianship), the protection of the consumer (consumer and users guardianship), and, above all, freedom of competition (guardianship of the economic system as an abstraction).

This last ramification, the guardianship of the economic system as an abstraction, constitutes the key ingredient for guaranteeing free access to market operators and preventing these operators from establishing agreements among themselves which would result in restricting competition, or taking advantage of a dominant position, as well as controlling mergers and business concentration.[3]

Neither mercantilism, nor populism, and even less so socialism, could make a legal structure based on free competition relevant (sometimes I even wonder whether they grasped the importance of competition). Indeed, the wind was blowing in the opposite direction to that which privileges market forces as the vital breath for development. Supply and demand, as well as competition, were not mechanisms for development. Quite the contrary; during a certain period it was common to think of the constitutional mandate which guaranteed freedom of trade and industry as being not only disturbing but also undesirable.

Despite the fact that national constitutions in Latin America paid lip-service to certain paradigms, reality was different. Venezuela is an example of how upsetting the principle of freedom of commerce and industry could be. In the early 1960s, and soon after proclaiming its new Constitution, Venezuela suspended the economic liberties enshrined in that very Constitution. The suspension lasted almost 30 years.

The conclusion that might be drawn here is that there is little or no need for regulations on free competition and related areas[4] when the economic model is hostile to them. Nevertheless, during recent decades, some countries (such as Argentina, Brazil and Colombia) have adopted regulatory structures that remain unapplied or, in exceptional cases, that have been applied intermittently or in very specific fashion. With the exception of Chile, which after 1973 chose an economic model diametrically opposite to those adopted by the majority of

---

3 Wolfgang Fikentscher, 'Las tres funciones del control de la economía' (The three purposes of economic control), *Revista de Derecho Mercantil* (1984) pp172-73.
4 Repression of unfair competition legislation scarcely existed and consumer protection regulations were linked to price controls.

countries in the Latin American region, the other countries dropped from their priorities such concerns as the development of an adequate legal structure to promote free competition.

Since the beginning of the 1990s, the constant policy has been towards democratization. Similarly, discussions revolve around such notions as 'internationalization',[5] 'liberalization',[6] 'privatization',[7] 'industrial restructuring',[8] 'deregulation',[9] 'downsizing of the State',[10] 'tributary reform',[11] 'elimination of subsidies'.[12] All of these 'ations' of the 1990s[13] have competition as their binding element.

I will now turn to the questions.

WHAT IMPORTANCE MUST BE ATTRIBUTED TO COMPETITION LEGISLATION? DOES COMPETITION LAW NEED TO BE DEVELOPED INDEPENDENTLY FROM OTHER LEGAL DISCIPLINES?

The greatest importance must be given to competition legislation and it should advance in co-ordination with other legislative developments.

Legislation concerning competition is of utmost importance because its purpose is to preserve the system enshrined in the constitution. It is especially essential in those countries of Latin America where freedom of trade and industry has been officially declared the inspiring principle of their economies.

However, it is important to note that guaranteeing the existence of a market-orientated economy goes beyond simply having a constitutional text. Certain exercises are necessary to implement such a mandate. This is particularly true in the case of Latin America where, following the tradition of Continental Law, constitutional precepts are, in principle, not self-executing.

The first exercise lies more in the domain of a decision than an activity. It consists of the government's will to design and implement a competition policy. Then, attention must be given to the legislative act or acts required to develop such a policy. This is the proclamation of a 'General Law' or 'Organic Law'[14]

---

5 In Spanish: 'internacionalización' or 'apertura'.
6 In Spanish: 'liberalización'.
7 In Spanish: 'privatización'.
8 In Spanish: 'reconversión'.
9 In Spanish: 'desregulación'.
10 In Spanish: 'readecuación del tamaño del Estado'.
11 In Spanish: 'reordenación tributaria'.
12 In Spanish: 'eliminación de subsidios'.
13 '-tions' is the English equivalent of the Spanish plural ending 'ciones'. The operative nouns in the previous footnotes – all of which represent various economic policies – have the same ending.
14 'General laws' or 'organic laws' are, following the Spanish legal tradition, those laws that develop an explicit constitutional provision. This is the case of competition legislation which embodies freedom of trade and commerce.

that could also be termed 'antimonopoly',[15] 'promotion of free competition',[16] 'safeguarding competition',[17] 'control of restrictive business practices',[18] or even, 'antitrust' (although this last term is conceptually alien to the continental legal tradition of Latin America). Alongisde this, a law enforcement organization or agency must be created and, last but not least, human and financial resources must be assigned to that organization so that it can accomplish the set objectives.

In limiting my comments to the legislative act, it must be emphasized that adopting adequate regulations is by itself an extremely significant effort. Experience tells us that such an effort runs in parallel with the adoption or reform of various juridical disciplines that in the hispanoamerican doctrine constitutes what is called 'market law'.[19] These provide for consumer protection and the repression of unfair competition.[20] To them one must add intellectual property law,[21] anti-dumping regulations, provisions relating to geographic indications, and advertising legislation.

The goal of market law (the key element being free competition regulations) is the juridical, both joint and balanced, guardianship of the market components or actors who are entrepreneurs, consumers and, as stated before, the free market system as an abstraction. Seen in this perspective, the statutes for the repression of unfair competition have the purpose of protecting directly the interests of entrepreneurs, and indirectly, the consumer and the free market economic system. At the same time, the provisions regarding consumers attempt to protect them while simultaneously protecting entrepreneurs and the economic system. Finally, the precepts on free competition attempt to avoid distortions in the competitive process, thus protecting consumers and promoting a free market economy and the development of the private sector.

---

15 For example, in Chile, India, Pakistan, Poland, Republic of Korea, Russian Federation.

16 For example, in Colombia, Costa Rica, France, Peru, South Africa, Venezuela.

17 For example, in Belgium, Bulgaria, Czech Republic, Italy, Portugal, Spain.

18 For example in Germany, Kenya, United Kingdom.

19 In Spanish: 'Derecho del mercado', 'Derecho de la ordenación del mercado' or 'Derecho del tráfico económico'.

20 In Spanish: 'Represión de la competencia desleal'. The best conceptual approach on this language is that of Aurelio Menéndez, *La competencia desleal* (Unfair Competition), (Madrid: Civitas, 1988). Also see: Gustavo Ghidini, *Slealtà della Concorrenza e Constituzione Economica* (Fair competition and Economic Constitution), (Milan: Padova, 1978); Juan José Otamendi, *Comentarios a la Ley de Competencia Desleal* (Comments on the Unfair Competition Law), (Arazandi: Pamplona, 1994).

21 Intellectual property law refers to the categories that are the subject of the Agreement on Trade-Related Aspects of Intellectual Property Rights (TRIPS): copyright and related rights; trademarks, geographical indications, industrial designs, patents, layout-designs (topographies) of integrated circuits, protection of undisclosed information, industrial property and copyright. Annex 1C of the Marrakesh Agreement Establishing the World Trade Organization, sections 1 to 7 of part II. Note that the same Annex, section 8 of part II contains specific provisions on the control of anticompetitive practices in contractual licences. Other agreements to be considered include: 'Agreement establishing the World Intellectual Property Organization', the 'Paris Convention for the Protection of Industrial Property' and the 'Berne Convention for the Protection of Literary and Artistic Works'.

There are clear linkages among and between these legal bodies. Therefore, it is significant to note the importance of each; otherwise, the development of legislation aimed at putting order in the market could be partial and result in imbalances among the different components of the system.

In addition to recommending the adoption of competition law, I would suggest the development of a similar parallel exercise: the protection of the consumer, the repression of unfair competition, and other related legal issues.

WHAT IS THE MODEL TO FOLLOW?

The United Nations Conference on Trade and Development (UNCTAD), has the universal mandate to promote policymaking and legislation on competition. This is based on General Assembly Resolution 35/63 approving the "Set of Multilaterally Agreed Equitable Principles and Rules for the Control of Restrictive Business Practices".[22]

In developing the mandate, UNCTAD implements multiple activities of co-operation and technical assistance. Through UNCTAD conferences, workshops and diverse seminars are organized; countries receive help with the drafting of legal texts and supporting laws, as well as extensive training for competent authorities.[23]

By the same token, UNCTAD has been developing and promoting a model law on competition.[24] This consists of a skeleton of the law setting out diverse elements that should be considered in such legislation together with comments and references to comparative law. This instrument attempts to serve as an orientation to those countries that are considering the adoption or the reform of existing legislation. The text includes suggestions on how to deal with such matters as the protection of the consumer,[25] and such areas as repression of unfair competition and intellectual property protection.

Yet despite being responsible for the development of the model law, I cannot recommend its adoption by any given country without a previous study of that country's legal tradition. This does pose a problem because authors, and especially those of legislative texts, tend to consider their work a panacea of juridical technique, and are therefore, tempted to propose their application as a

---

22 Resolution 35/63 adopted by the United Nations General Assembly at its thirty-fifth session, on 5 December 1980.

23 Philippe Brusick, 'United Nations Control of Restrictive Business Practices', Journal of World Trade, Vol. 17 (1983) p337.

24 Draft commentaries to possible elements for articles of a model-law or laws on restrictive business practices. UNCTAD TD/B/RBP/81/Rev.3 (2 August 1994).

25 Especially following the recommendations of the United Nations on consumer protection (General Assembly Resolution 39/248 of 9 April 1985).

sort of magic solution. Such an approach would be irresponsible. It might be useful to recall one of the principles of good government: the importance of consent and concordance between what the government proposes, and what the citizens believe to be adequate. The legitimacy of regulations on free competition would lie in the capacity of the government to recognize the singularities of the country's legal tradition.

There may be the temptation to take advantage of the fact that many countries do not have specific legislation, and hence a common text could be promoted and some sort of legislative harmonization reached. However, experience has shown that despite the fact that in Latin America a common legal tradition exists from colonial times, it is still necessary to adjust any text to each country's reality. In effect, each country has certain particularities that are especially evident in the field of procedural law.[26]

If one accepts the existence – worldwide – of different legal systems and traditions, it will be difficult to promote harmonization (the Set of Principles and Rules on Restrictive Business Practices adopted by the UN General Assembly in 1980 and UNCTAD's Competition Model-Law could be an attempt). Coincidentally, in competition law two clearly differentiated models prevail. The North American model or 'antitrust'; and the European model, of German inspiration, as followed by the European Communities. Both models have the same goal, and they present similarities. However, there are subjects which these models treat differently, sometimes in a quite contrary fashion.[27] Thus, it would be difficult to say which is better.

In my opinion, the 'antitrust' system should not be considered for Latin American countries. This is not because it is inappropriate (and it is important to note that the North American legislation has been in use for more than a century), but because it responds to mechanisms and to institutions that are remote from Latin American juridical traditions. For practical reasons, I would tend to recommend a model of European inspiration, formulated, for example, after Spanish legislation,[28] taking into account key elements as proposed in UNCTAD's model law, and certainly not neglecting the peculiarities of the particular country. In the case of the relationship between Spain and Latin America, not only do these countries share the same language, but they also speak the same juridical language.

---

26 Manuel Lozano Higuero y Pinto, *La protección procesal de los intereses difusos* (Procedural protection of diffuse interests), (Madrid: García Blanco, 1983).
27 For example, the prohibition principle on agreements, the 'rule of reason', the notification system in co-operative arrangements, the block exemption rules on various kinds of agreements and so on.
28 For example, technicalities in the drafting of judicial resolutions, access to decisions by the competent authorities and courts, availability of doctrine, law review articles, economic journals and so on, makes it easier to follow the Spanish approach.

Relationships similar to the one between Latin America and Spain should be considered for the rest of the world. In this way, countries such as France and the United Kingdom, for example, could serve as sources of inspiration for many countries in the Caribbean region, Africa and Asia. Legislation could assimilate the shared juridical structures, techniques and traditions. This is not simply a hypothetical argument because it is so in reality. A careful analysis of legislation adopted in recent years in Latin America reveals a clear Spanish influence with the exception of cases such as Costa Rica and Mexico. The latter are interesting, as they have creatively adapted the 'antitrust' model, while the remaining countries have competition legislation that closely follows the European approach.

WHAT INSTITUTIONAL STRUCTURE SHOULD BE CREATED TO ENFORCE THIS LEGISLATION?

Institutional structure is one of the most important aspects of competition law. It is not enough to have a constitutional mandate. Nor is it sufficient to promulgate the respective law. A suitable administrative structure is needed o apply the law. Otherwise, despite regulations there are no mechanisms to enforce them.

I will not deal with how to constitute the administering authority or agency – what was said in relation to the type of legislation that should be adopted as a model also applies to the question of the institutional structure that should be promoted. Each country has to create a structure linked to its reality. Careful attention needs to be paid to such concerns because not all the countries have the capacity – due to budgetary constraints or to the lack of human resources – to put these institutions in place. What is really needed is a 'custom-made suit'.

There is, however, one element that should be highlighted and that should be common to all of these institutions: autonomy of this administering authority. Success depends on it. It is a well-known fact that political powers continuously intervene in the decision-making of the bodies in charge of overseeing the enforcement of regulations. Similarly, there is continuous 'pressure' from certain groups interested in the decision-making process (sometimes called corruption). For a technically adequate administration of legislation, it is important to avoid interference of any sort.

It is imperative that the authority not only has formal autonomy, but also functional autonomy. To reach this objective the authority must be provided with, *inter alia*, a particular labour regime in relation to other administrative bodies. Also, it must be furnished with the resources required to accomplish its tasks and to recruit – as well as maintain – human resources of a high professional calibre. Such considerations may sound foreign to an audience of people from developed countries. However, it is important to note that in many countries of Latin America the public service career is not the best paid nor the most prestigious professionally speaking. The ridiculously low salaries paid to civil servants result in technical deficiencies and in the possibility that they could be influenced by external factors. While resources alone will not guarantee autonomy they are a factor.

Autonomy would also result in a climate conducive to what the experts in the area of good government call 'accountability'. The authorities would have a greater degree of control in the use of resources if they were not part of the administrative tangle of central government. Moreover, the authority's performance could be assessed more precisely. These are factors which would promote greater transparency.

I would like to highlight two interesting Latin American experiences: the Superintendency of Industry and Commerce of Colombia,[29] and the National Institute for the Defense of Competition and the Promotion of Intellectual Property (INDECOPI)[30] of Peru. Both bodies are the result of the merger of the administration of competition regulations with legislation on consumer protection, repression of unfair competition, and intellectual property. What is relevant is that they have achieved better co-ordination in the application of legislation, and that the respective budgets are supported with resources provided by the registration fees of their intellectual property offices. This allows for budgetary autonomy.

WHAT OTHER ACTIVITIES SHOULD BE PROMOTED?

The other activities that we will look at relate to the significant effort that goes beyond legal and institutional considerations, and which we may call 'creation and development of a competition culture'.

The interventionist and mercantilist tradition of the Latin American countries has generated a passive attitude on the part of the private sector concerning the mechanisms of market access and participation. This feature, known as 'economic paternalism', leads important economic sectors to believe that the state has responsibility for resolving specific problems, that it is called to provide

---

29 Decree 2153 of 30 December 1992. The Superintendency of Industry and Commerce is also responsible for the administration of the following legislation: patents, trademarks, consumer protection, chambers of commerce, technical standards and metrology.

30 Decree Law N° 25868 of 6 November 1992, as amended by Legislative Decree N°788 of 29 December 1994. INDECOPI is also responsible for the administration of the following legislation: anti-dumping and subsidies, consumer protection, advertising, repression of unfair competition, quality control and non-custom barriers, bankruptcy procedures, trademarks, patents, plant varieties, geographical indications and transfer of technology.

alternatives and to facilitate the development of any activity. Likewise, the Latin American consumer is not accustomed to looking after his or her own interests, believing that the state should provide solutions.

Such attitudes need to be examined in the framework of a market-orientated economy. Legislation on free competition and related subjects sets out the parameters or rules of the games for the performance of economic operators. These should recognize that development has been opened to free private initiative, and that regulations and an authority exist to control *ex post* abuses, as well as to impose sanctions against irregularities or the misuse of the freedom of trade and industries.

In creating a competition culture operators must know the scope and relevance of this kind of legislation, as well as their rights and responsibilities therein. They should be aware of the fact that they are immersed in a market economy, with its precise rules, and that these rules can be diametrically opposed to those existing previously. At this level, resolving the inherent problems would also promote respect for the principle by which the economy should be governed by competition principles and rules and not by *ad hoc* decisions of politicians, government officials or interest groups (thus adhering to the good government principle known as 'rule of law').

The development of a competition culture is a gigantic effort that will take years to achieve and in which many actors will participate – probably fewer in those countries where an important 'informal economy' existed and where competition is the rule.

It is indispensable to divulge what the market really is, to define the role of its components, to explain what competition is and what it means to compete; to reveal the contents of legislation and to make clear its enforcement mechanisms. This knowledge is particularly relevant in the case of small and medium-sized entrepreneurs as well as for consumers, since they can often be the most harmed by restrictive business practices.

The dissemination of information about the market process should be extended to legislators, civil servants and especially judges who in a particular case might generate interpretations as well as judgments that would impair the spirit of competition legislation. In this respect, it is important to stress that one of the principles of good government is that there must be an adequate administration of justice, and this cannot be attained simply by avoiding corruption, but must be pursued also through training of those persons who have decision-making power. In this context, an erroneous judgment in the field of competition has an impact that goes beyond the parties to a dispute. It has consequences for the entire economy of a particular country. Law practitioners, economists, and business managers, as well as centres of learning, because they are, or will be, the responsible parties in the making of decisions, should also be made aware of this. Finally, but no less important, it should also be extended to organized civil society in the form of consumers' associations.

As a Latin American, I may affirm that decades of mercantilism and interventionism have distorted (or obscured) my view of competition. It is useful to focus on its spirit so that we use it as a plan of action in our economic development. Similarly, we have responsibility to support the institutions that have been created to guarantee a free market, because thereby we will be promoting a model for development while at the same time assuring its maintenance. It was Karl Marx who observed that capitalism contained the germ of its own destruction. His statement is true because if the free market economy is allowed to function without any rules of the game, if we do not have regulations that will guarantee and promote free competition, probably the pendulum of history will swing back to economic concentrations, and the arguments that generated many of the revolutions of this century will gain new strength, resulting in the destruction not only of economic democracy but also of political democracy. Following the principles of good government, we must promote a competition culture which gives due recognition to adequate legislation and those institutions that encourage democracy.

WHAT CAN BE DONE?

Much of our daily work at UNCTAD consists of providing assistance and responding to the requests of Governments and non-governmental organizations in developing countries, least-developed countries and countries in transition. It is our responsibility to be up-to-date on the economic and legal developments internationally. This is precisely what allows us to assign and distribute our human and financial resources reasonably well as we attend to the increasing needs of the international community.

However, I have observed a phenomenon related to the growing importance that governments assign to the issue of competition at the national and international levels. I am referring to the lack of co-ordination and co-operation among the different international agencies which for various reasons have assumed or are assuming responsibility for promoting policy and legislation. As already mentioned, UNCTAD has the universal mandate, stemming from a resolution of the United Nations General Assembly. In parallel to UNCTAD's efforts, the Organization for Economic Cooperation and Development (OECD) and the World Bank are active in this matter. Also the Inter-American Development Bank (IADB), within the framework of its activities on the Modernization of the State, will soon promote projects in this field.

These efforts are laudable, but it is important that we all work towards the same goal. Where there is a lack of co-ordination among our agencies, this is at odds with proper administration of available economic resources. Similarly, where there is duplication of efforts, overlapping of assistance missions, repetition of similar events, contradictory opinions on what should or should not be done, lack of promotion of complementary legislation (the most distressing case being consumer protection), and, occasionally, the promotion of legislative models far from a particular tradition, these are all less than optimal uses of scarce resources.

International co-operation is not a matter of who gets what first or who did something best; it is a matter of doing the job well, no matter who does it. For this, co-ordination among international agencies is essential.

CONCLUSIONS

My conclusions match the five questions formulated at the beginning: there is a need to emphasize the importance of free competition legislation as the best instrument to promote economic democracy, and to recognize the necessity of having complementary legislations, particularly consumer protection and repression of unfair competition; the legislative model chosen should be close to the legal traditions of the country concerned; the enforcement agency should be autonomous; strong efforts should be directed towards encouraging a competition culture; and lastly, there must be close co-ordination of whatever co-operation efforts are made to implement these activities.

This in my opinion is good government in the field of competition law.

9 Land rights and agrarian reform: Latin American and South African perspectives

Joseph R. Thome

INTRODUCTION

Not enough attention has been given to the important role the law has to play in the process of development and social change. It may receive passing interest or malignment from scholars and policymakers, but little effort has been spent on examining closely the contribution it has to make.

Comparative studies on this subject can serve a useful function. They can help to de-mystify the power of law in social relations, a perspective much too prevalent in contemporary law and development programmes.[1] This, in turn, can contribute to a more realistic understanding of law's potential contributions as well as its limits in promoting a process of development which achieves a relatively equitable distribution of its fruits.

I will begin with a general discussion of property rights concepts and institutions and their effect on land tenure systems. I will then look at two seemingly disparate but yet parallel case studies, Chile and South Africa,[2] to examine the impact of these concepts, institutions and processes in the development of land tenure systems and in the introduction of agrarian reform programmes in these two countries.

The question may be asked: why focus on two experiences which on the surface appear so different, in place, time and peoples? I have long worked on these issues as they have played out in Latin America and, more specifically, in Chile. Only since 1992 have I begun to immerse myself in the complexity of South African land tenure systems and evolution. Yet this exposure has led to my perception of some striking parallels in the genesis of land tenure problems and the reform responses initially devised in both countries. In each case, land

---

1 See, for example, de Soto, 1991. For an excellent review of law and development scholarship, see Tamanaha, 1995.
2 While I will be making reference to various Latin American experiences, my focus will be on Chile, where agrarian reform developed slowly, gathered momentum under Allende (1970-1973), and finally unravelled after the 1973 *coup*. As regards Africa, there my sole focus will be on South Africa, where the pressure for agrarian reform has been building up at least since 1913 and is only now, under Mandela, beginning to take shape.

concentration and its social and political manifestations developed over a centuries-long colonization and post-independence process, where essentially racist and exploitative programmes and institutions were masked by adherence to 'legalistic' formulas which supposedly reflected economically rational modernization policies.

Ultimately, the resulting inequitable social and economic structures also produced similar agrarian reform responses, as both nations took similar paths towards 'negotiated' and legally constituted processes, in each case requiring fundamental reforms in their basic legal and institutional frameworks.[3]

LAND RIGHTS, LAND TENURE SYSTEMS AND AGRARIAN REFORM

Since land rights will be discussed in reference to agrarian reform, let us start at the end: What does 'agrarian reform' mean? Not the type of 'indirect' measures exemplified by land taxation and titling of public or other 'unoccupied' land, such as homesteading and settlement or colonization schemes in frontier areas, and land market schemes. These processes can be crucial for development purposes or for resolving potential or existing land conflicts. Nevertheless, they do not involve the direct restoration or redistribution of resources (wealth, power, autonomy), which represent the essence of agrarian reform.

Agrarian reform involves a dramatic or substantial change in the rural power structure and a redistribution of rights and a reformation of institutions so as to benefit the landless or rural poor. In the process, agrarian reform can also produce a forced modernization of the agricultural sector, as happened in Chile (de Janvry, 1981). In essence, this process involves change, access, and security (Thome, 1968:14):

> 1) Changing legal, social and economic institutions and processes that perpetuate inequitable or inefficient land tenure systems, labor relations and make difficult any redistributive measures.
>
> 2) Providing the landless/rural poor with effective access to productive land with adequate infrastructure and to other essential goods and services;
>
> 3) Providing security over the newly gained land and other resources, through title deeds, the official recognition of customary or indigenous rights, or through "voice"; ie., effective participation in political or policy process by grass-root organizations and the like.

This reshuffling of land rights is political in nature, determining who wields power within rural society. In many if not all societies, dominant groups will attempt to legitimize their status and actions by acting within or manipulating the

---

3   Hopefully, South Africa's current journey toward more equitable and productive rural structures will not in the future parallel Pinochet's neo-liberal counter-reforms; these may have accelerated the process of modernization in agriculture, but at a very high social cost as well. See Kay and Silva (1992) pp289-299.

prevailing legal framework. Once in place, however, legal institutions tend to acquire an autonomy of their own, to some extent limiting arbitrary public and private behaviour. Land rights and other legal concepts and institutions can play crucial supportive roles in limiting or making possible the enactment of the reform, in defining its boundaries, and in determining or channelling the process. Of particular historical importance are issues concerning the valid exercise of eminent domain powers and the right of compensation for state interference with private property rights.[4]

In this context, it becomes clearer that agrarian structures and legal frameworks affect each other and that both reflect, influence, and are part of their respective societies. Officially, the legal framework, through its property laws, determines the use and allocation of resources within society. In reality, the process is much more complex and dynamic. Property is also a social construct. Its meaning is not constant; rather, it changes over time in relation to the purposes which the dominant or influential sectors in society expect the institution to serve (Macpherson,1983:1.) In modern western societies, private property is generally conceived as a bundle of legal rights which confer control over resources; the most essential elements in this bundle are the absolute rights of an owner to exclude others from the use and enjoyment of the thing 'owned', and to dispose of it at his or her discretion (Macpherson,1983:10). Though conventionally conceived as a 'private' right, the public nature of private property rights becomes apparent upon observation of their enforcement. In effect, property rights are treated as 'entitlements'; state agencies, such as the police or other official agencies, intervene in order to preserve the private control and allocation of resources, thereby lending the landowner substantial power and control over those non-owners whose livelihood or even survival may depend on access to these resources (Macpherson,1983: 3).

As societies evolve and develop, legal concepts, such as property rights, also change, albeit more slowly than other institutions. Property rights are particularly resistant to change. The institution of 'private property' seems to be endowed with certain 'mythical' qualities, allowing historically determined rights and concepts to retain power long after they have outlived their initial economic and political justifications. "But the myth of property is pernicious because it hides a structure of power and insulates it from democratic debate." (Nedelsky, 1990: 260; Christman, 1994: 3)

Nevertheless, the 'myth of property' can be a double-edged sword; it can be an instrument for change as the landless and the poor also want a share of its

---

4   Given the complexity of the topic, little if any attention will be paid in this paper to problems in the actual implementation of agrarian reform, though these may represent the key factors in the process.

magical power. In Latin America, this pressure for land has been a key component of revolutionary struggles, as in Mexico (1910), Bolivia (1952), Cuba (1959), and more recently, Nicaragua and El Salvador (1979). This pressure, however, can be channelled into institutional and negotiated processes, as was the case in Venezuela (1960), Chile (1964-73) and South Africa (1994 –).

Political transitions and the property rights issue

At least since the 16th century, western-influenced legal systems have emphasized the protection of private and individual property rights. In the United States, as in other countries, the legal concept of property was a symbol of stability and security. While the framers of the American constitution were cognizant that private property rights would lead to unequal distribution, their preoccupation with the 'tyranny of majority' was paramount. Thus, while they tried to balance individual rights and collective rights, in the end they favoured property as a symbol of the limits to legitimate governmental power (Elster, 1988: 245-247). Despite significant changes in the past 50 years, property still retains a symbolic force as the foundation of American freedoms (Nedelsky, 1988: 241).

Property not only plays a symbolic role but also a crucial political role; that of limiting majority rights in a democracy. Even 'leftist' politicians involved in transitions to democracy have at times accepted the view that the rich would never accept democracy unless they had a constitutional guarantee against 'confiscation' by the propertyless majority. Given the veto power the 'haves' tend to have over what political regimes are adopted, then it may be in the interest of the propertyless to concede them such guarantees (Elster, 1988:14).

A South African observer has recently suggested that this accommodation was necessary to achieve the negotiated transition in South Africa:

> ...Basically the Grand Bargain in South Africa was: blacks get the vote, whites keep the money. Whites in South Africa, now some 13% of the population, own roughly 85% of the country's land and, along with foreign investors, at least 90% of commerce and industry.

> "Freezing this great gap was the price of having democratic elections. This yawning difference in wealth is partly locked in place by the country's interim Constitution, which will make even the most modest land reform painfully difficult. And partly it is locked in place by pressures outside the agreement, which would make any other bargain impossible. Any real distribution of wealth would mean economically catastrophic white flight and a cold shoulder from aid donors like the United States, the World Bank, the International Monetary Fund and the foreign investors Mr. Mandela is wooing. (Hochschild, 1995: 6)

However, as argued in the case study below, it isn't all that clear that the current legal framework in South Africa is so pro-private property as to make any meaningful agrarian reform impossible. Moreover, Hochschild may too easily assume that the South African transition is a controlled, top-down approach, with little if any role for pressure from below.

Nevertheless, in the western legal tradition property rights have generally received constitutional protection through such devices as limiting 'takings' to those necessary for the public good, and only with full and prior compensation. Complete adherence to these safeguards would make it nearly impossible to enact and implement any effective agrarian reform processes. However, the 'full' story is much more complex, indicating a more open legal universe than is commonly believed. In this paper I argue that property rights do not have to be conceived as narrowly individualistic and absolute, thereby opening the legal door to agrarian reform processes. There are other, more reasonable and equitable concepts that justify limitations on private property rights. Moreover, these are not merely abstract notions; western nations have applied these alternative private property rights concepts in order to carry out social reforms.

Traditional absolutist private property rights were reconfirmed by influential legal instruments of the emergent 'liberal' societies of the 19th century in Latin America and other nations falling within the civil law tradition, the French Civil Code of 1804 being one example. However, the absolute nature of individual property rights did not go unchallenged. Leon Duguit, a prominent French legal scholar of the 19th century, was particularly critical of the doctrine of unrestricted private rights. He used the concept of the 'social function' of property to articulate what he thought was not only a more reasonable and equitable definition of property rights, but one which was already supplanting the absolute, individualistic concept:

> Every individual is under an obligation to perform a certain function in the community, determined directly by the station which he occupies in it. The possessor of wealth, by reason simply of his possession, is enabled thereby to accomplish a certain work where others cannot. He alone can increase the general stock of wealth by putting his capital to use. For social reasons he is under a duty, therefore, to perform this work and society will protect his acts only if he accomplishes it and in the measure in which he accomplishes it. Property is no longer a subjective right of the owner; it is the social function of the possessor of wealth... (1918: 130-136, as cited in Karst and Rosenn, 1975: 312)

In the common law world, influential scholars such as Tawney, Cohen, and Ely also analysed the social effects of absolute private property rights, coming to similar conclusions as Duguit (Karst and Rosenn, 1975: 313-319).[5]

Social developments since the First World War provided a further impetus for the adoption of social controls over property rights. The seminal German Constitution of Weimar (1919) probably represents the first legal enactment of the principle that 'property obligates', and this was reproduced in the German

---

5 These concerns were not merely academic: the 1851 Constitution of the State of Ohio states that "Private property shall ever be held inviolate but subservient to the public welfare..." (ibid., p317.)

Constitution of 1949. Since that time, many other nations have enacted similar principles in their constitutions. The Irish Constitution of 1937, for example, stated that property rights should be regulated in accordance with the principles of social justice, and should be limited in order to meet the demands of the general well-being. The Japanese Constitution of 1946 declared that the law shall define property rights in accordance with the public well-being. In Italy, the Constitution of 1947 established that the law can limit and impose obligations on private property, so that the nation may benefit from the land, and in order that equitable social relations may be created. It can limit the extension of property and bring about changes on *latifundia*[6] (Italy and Japan subsequently carried out significant land reforms, aided by their defeat in the Second World War.)

These and other examples indicate that a new concept of property rights, based on the principle of 'social function', has evolved in many western nations. A decision by the Supreme Court of Colombia demonstrates the application of this more limited concept of property rights, as well as a modern 'bundle-of-rights' type of rationale for resolving property rights conflicts. In affirming the constitutionality of the Colombian Agrarian Reform Law of 1961, the court found that the social function of property can manifest itself only through precise obligations or burdens. These are to be defined by the legislature and relate to all the attributes of property (such as its use, enjoyment and abuse), any one or all of which can be affected at any given moment. Among these legislatively defined 'burdens' is that of "...working the lands economically under the threat of losing them". The court took pains in elaborating the conceptual basis of this "social function" limitation on traditional property rights:

> The Framers of the 1936 amendment made the fundamental right of ownership relative, accentuating its subordination to the interests of the community, and also accentuating limitations on the free choice of the owner...
>
> "The Framers founded individual ownership on the social function that involves obligations, in accordance with the views of modern social function theorists who reject the fixed and ever identical form attributed to that institution by the [classical] economic schools, recognizing that, since ownership has taken very different forms throughout history and is susceptible to very great modifications, it is fully guaranteed ...only to the degree that it responds to the collective necessities of economic life. (Colombian Supreme Court of Justice, 1965, in Karst and Rosenn, 1975: 348-349)

Lesser interferences with private property rights are also common throughout the western world. As Christman points out, even "(I)n a basically capitalist society such as the United States....there are any number of restrictions on individuals' prerogatives regarding the way they can use, change, destroy, and charge for the use of their possessions....The notion of private property, then,

---

6   Much of this material is taken from Frei and Trivelli (1967).

begins too look rather fuzzy". (1994: 4) Land-use planning, zoning, the use of 'police powers' to safeguard public health, landlord-tenant laws and other regulations on the use and enjoyment of private property are seldom challenged as unconstitutional, although they often represent uncompensated limitations on property rights (Plager, 1970). Usually, only the factual basis or specific application of these limitations are disputed. This gives rise to litigation over whether they constitute a 'taking' rather than a mere regulation, thereby raising the question of compensation.[7]

The legal framework and negotiated agrarian reform processes

A negotiated land reform process requires an appropriate legal framework. However, this is most difficult to achieve, for agrarian reform is an intensely political and conflictive process (Dorner, 1987: 4). Existing institutional arrangements and long-held legal concepts must be replaced. Political pressure, particularly from below, and the corresponding determination and power of the state is essential. At this point, however, the legal arena may become the preferred site for the struggle against the reform process, with political or ideological motivations disguised under the mantle of inherent, ethical, or social values, cultural traits, or of 'technical' or 'scientific' legal or economic doctrines.

A negotiated and legal process of land reform may require constitutional amendments and other substantive legal changes. As noted above, substantive land redistribution cannot be achieved if this process is subject to constitutionally required and rigidly interpreted 'public use' and 'just compensation' criteria. In situations where they no longer dominate the political process, the privileged sectors of society may resort to 'lego-political' rhetoric in an attempt to maintain legal structures which provide undue protection to private property rights. Hallowed arguments on individual rights, freedom, economic efficiency and the like will be used. Should they prevail, token distributions would be the only viable or affordable alternative, thereby frustrating any redistributive goals and perhaps pushing the process out of the negotiating arena and into a militant or violent process.

We will now look at how property rights affected land tenure structures and the enactment of agrarian reform legislation and programmes in both Chile and South Africa.

---

7 In recent years, however, the American proponents for expanding the scope of 'takings' to include State regulations have been gaining ground. A recent example is Bill H.R 9 recently passed in the US House of Representatives and sent to the Senate for its consideration. Among its various measures, this bill provides that Government regulation which prevents land development in order to preserve wetlands or endangered species, constitutes a taking, requiring full market value compensation when the land declines in value by at least 20 per cent due to the action taken by the State (Cushman, *New York Times*, 1995: 1, 6).

Latin American and South African Perspsectives

Chile

Imposition of western property regimes and resulting land tenure structures

As in the rest of Hispanic Latin America, the basic legal framework for the current land tenure system in Chile was set during the three century-plus Spanish colonial rule (1500-1810) and reinforced after independence, particularly by the 'liberal' reforms of the mid-19th century.

The Spanish colonization of Latin America was carried out within a highly legalistic framework. Even the initial conquest itself was 'legalized' through a Papal Bull which in effect divided the New World between Spain and Portugal (The Treaty of Tordesillas). Indeed, before assuming jurisdiction and control over Indian peoples and lands, the invading armies were required to read a statement to the Indians explaining the Papal authorization for Spanish assumption of sovereignty over their domain (the *requerimento*).

This concern for legality extended to the property and individual rights of the indigenous peoples of the New World. A few years after the *conquistadores* initiated their often brutal excursions in the New World, the Spanish Crown promulgated laws and regulations in an attempt to curtail unauthorized land grabbings and extractions of labour and other tribute from the conquered peoples. At the same time, Indian land rights over substantial tracts were granted legal protection through the establishment of reserves and the recognition of *ejido* or communal village lands (Bartra, 1993: 81; Morse, 1964: 139-141). Nevertheless, while the Castillian monarch held absolute legal control over the 'Kingdom of the Indies', he was unable or unwilling to curb the rapacious instincts of the Spanish colonizers and settlers. The usurpation of Indian lands continued and an increasing number of land conflicts were resolved in favour of the Spanish settlers, often through payment of fees to the financially strapped Spanish crown, known as *recomposiciones*. The results were a landscape dominated by large estates, which housed many tenants (Bauer, 1992: 22) and the formation of a mostly White landed élite which in some form has generally persevered throughout Latin America even to this day (Morse, 1964: 147).

When independence finally arrived in the early 19th century, it was not as a result of a social revolution from below but rather a substitution of local *criollo* rule for European rule. However, prevalent European concepts of liberalism were adopted, including legal norms which guaranteed private property rights. Thus, Article 582 of the 19th century Chilean Civil Code mirrors the corresponding provision in the Napoleonic Code, in providing that "Ownership is the real right in a corporeal thing to enjoy it and dispose of it arbitrarily, provided no other law is violated." (Thome, 1971: 83)

Throughout the 19th and well into the 20th century, the landed élites in Chile, as in other Latin nations continued to dominate political life. Their position allowed them to use or manipulate the legal system as an instrument for extending their land holdings. This was the case with liberal 'modernizing' legislation whose goal was to liquidate what were conceived as feudal or pre-capitalist land tenure arrangements. Lands possessed by the 'dead hands' of the Catholic Church (often the largest landowner) were expropriated and sold to the highest bidder. At the same time, other laws also ordered the distribution of abandoned communal land or ordered that the lands of indigenous villages be divided into parcels and converted into private freehold property. In the end, these 'liberal' land reforms completed the process of virtual elimination of communal indigenous property and consolidated the dominant economic and political position of the latifundia throughout rural Latin America (Bartra, 1993: 83).

Towards a reformulation of land rights; legitimizing and enabling agrarian reform in Chile

The power of the landed élites began to erode in the 20th century. Pressures from a growing middle class and the demands of newly-emerging labour organizations and socialist inspired political parties began to be reflected in the legal framework. In 1925 a new constitution was promulgated, making possible the moderate social legislation of the following years. Influenced by the concepts of Leon Duguit, President Alessandri insisted on some constitutional limitations on the absolute character of private property rights, introducing the concept of the 'social function' of property.[8] While the requirement of prior compensation was retained from the 1833 Constitution, the new constitution opened the way for modest land redistribution and settlement projects in virgin lands through the Caja de Colonización Agrícola (Agricultural Colonization Board). The results were unimpressive; by 1962, when the Caja ceased its activities, it had managed to settle only 4,206 families throughout the country (Thome, 1971: 85-86).

By 1962, *campesino* demands and international pressure through the Alliance for Progress led the Conservative government of Jorge Alessandri to enact Land Reform Law No. 15020 of 1962. Under this law, the Caja was eliminated and two new agencies created: the Corporación de Reforma Agraria (CORA) and the Instituto de Desarrollo Agropecuario (INDAP), both of which remained as the

---

8   The relevant section of the 1925 Constitution reads as follows:
"No one shall be deprived of his property, or any part of it, or any right he might have to it, except by judgment of a court of law or by expropriation by reason of public utility as declared by law. In such a case, the owner shall be previously indemnified either by agreement or by judgment of a court of law. The exercise of the right of property is subject to the limitations or regulations required for the maintenance and progress of the social order and, furthermore, the law may impose obligations or servitudes of public utility in favor of the general interests of the State, the welfare of the people, and public health." (O'Connor, 1968: 27)

key agrarian reform institutions until 1973. As with the Caja's projects, however, the results were meagre. Constitutional provisions, as interpreted by the Courts, continued to demand prior compensation based on market value. In addition, the elaborate provisions of the law made it exceedingly difficult to expropriate any significant amounts of privately owned land. Thus, by the end of the Alessandri administration in 1964, CORA had carried out a mere 1,354 land divisions totaling 51,442 hectares (Thome, 1971: 86-87).

However, the pressures for agrarian reform had not diminished. As of 1964, the prevailing socio-economic structure in the Chilean countryside was still characterized by a concentration of land and water resources in a few hands, creating serious economic and social problems.[9] This state of affairs led the new Christian Democratic Government of Eduardo Frei to introduce in November 1965 an agrarian reform bill to Congress. The principal objectives of this bill were to provide thousands of families with their own land, fulfilling their ancient desire to be owners of the land they worked, to improve agricultural productivity and the conditions of the rural population (Frei and Trivelli, 1967: 12-14).

The concepts underpinning these objectives were derived from the theory of the 'social function' of ownership as well as from the more progressive teachings of the Catholic Church. Within this framework, property rights were to be extended and perfected by providing them with a 'social sense' which would permit this full exercise. As stated by President Frei:

> Property should be maintained and respected. However, it should be socially regulated. No property rights should be allowed to exist which, in their implementation, damage the common well-being and rights of the community. When this happens it means that the basic principle of the primacy of the general wellbeing over the rights of the individual is not being adhered to, impelling the State to reorganize, regulate, and redistribute those rights, in order to prevent their abuse.
>
> "The agrarian reform will guarantee and respect the property rights of those persons who meet the social functions these rights demand. The social functions are: not to have accumulated vast properties, to have adhered to the existing social legislation, to have included the peasants in the benefits acquired from the land, and to have created conditions of stability, justice, and well-being. (Frei and Trivelli, 1967: 13)

In the congressional arena the agrarian reform bill and its constitutional authorization – an amendment to Article 10 of the Constitution – became subject

---

9 Large estates, each more than 2,000 acres, constituted only 2.2 per cent of the total number of farm units but 68.8 per cent of the total area of agricultural land. At the other extreme, 117,000 tiny minifundia plots represented 78 per cent of all farms but only five per cent of the agricultural land. Indeed, 185,000 rural families owned or possessed no land whatsoever. This structure had contributed to inefficiency and low productivity in the agricultural sector, such as increasingly unfavourable balances of trade in agricultural products. Social conditions in the rural areas were no better, including a 36 per cent rate of illiteracy versus 11 per cent in urban areas. These conditions were pushing peasants into the cities, creating difficult urban development problems; between 1940 and 1960 approximately one million peasants moved to urban centres, out of a total population which hovered at 9 million (Frei and Trivelli, 1967:7-11).

to intense and protracted debates lasting almost two years (Chile-Senado, 1966: 32). Several amendments were adopted, watering down some of the provisions of the original bill, as a result of this pressure from some Christian Democrats, Conservative congress members, and the National Agricultural Society, a powerful landowner association. These altered the system of payments for expropriations, increased the amounts of land left to the expropriated owners as 'reserves', and exempted certain vineyards from expropriation (Kaufman, 1972: 97). Nevertheless, the law which was finally enacted in 1967 was basically the same Bill that was introduced in November 1965. President Frei threw the weight of his prestige and authority behind the Bill and the Constitutional amendments, making it difficult for party members to break rank, and the Radical, Communist and Socialist parties gave their support to both measures, guaranteeing an ample majority in both chambers of Congress (Kaufman, 1972: 94, 106).

In January 1967 the Congress amended Article 10, Section 10 of the 1925 Constitution, thus opening the door for translating the controversial agrarian reform policy of the Christian Democratic Party into law. The 1967 amendment removed the 1925 Constitution limitations on takings and compensation and, by stipulating that new expropriation procedures and norms could be established through legislation, also made possible a quicker and more extensive process of expropriation.[10] Several months later, Agrarian reform law No. 16.640 was passed by Congress and promulgated on July 29, 1967 (Thome,1971: 499-500).

Land rights and implementation of reform

Aside from expanding the justifications for 'takings' or expropriations so as to include 'social interest' as defined by the legislature, the newly-amended Article 10 also broadened the compensation formulas for such 'takings'. It authorized the legislature to determine the conditions for such compensation, thereby

---

10 Relevant sections of Article 10 as amended follow:

"When the interests of the national community should require, the law shall be empowered to reserve in the State the exclusive dominion of natural resources, productive goods, or others which might be declared of preeminent importance for the economic, social, or cultural life of the country. It will also favor the proper distribution of property and the establishment of family property.

"No one shall be deprived of his property except by virtue of the general or special law which authorizes expropriation for the cause of public utility or social interest declared by the Legislator. He who is expropriated shall have a right to indemnization which amount and condition of payment shall be determined by taking into consideration both the social interests and those of the individual. The law shall determine the norms for fixing the indemnity, the court which shall have jurisdiction of appeals as to the amount fixed, which in every case shall pass judgment according to the law, form of extinguishing the obligation, and the conditions and means by which the expropriator shall take physical possession of the expropriated property.

"As to the expropriation of landed estates, the indemnity shall be equivalent to the current assessment for the territorial tax, plus the value of improvements not included in the assessment, and may be paid in the form and condition determined by the law." (Translation by O'Connor, 1968: 19-30)

making possible a much more expanded reform programme.[11] Accordingly, Articles 42 et.seq. of Law 16640 (Ley 16.640, 1967: pp24-25) provided that the basis for compensation would be the tax appraisal value plus cash payments for improvements not included in the appraisal. Moreover, the law provided that the actual payments could be deferred or amortized for up to 30 years. Lands expropriated because they were abandoned or poorly used would receive only five per cent of the appraised value in cash at the time of expropriation, with the balance payable over a 30 year period, through bonds only partially adjusted for inflation. On the other hand, lands expropriated for excess size (larger than the equivalent of 80 irrigated hectares in the Central Valley of Chile, as determined by a table in Law 16640), regardless of the quality of their use, would receive a 10 per cent cash payment and the balance in 20 year bonds (Articles 45 and 46).

The Constitution also allowed the legislature to decide which courts would have jurisdiction to resolve land reform conflicts, for which purpose it established a special Agrarian Tribunal system, with limited appeal rights (Articles 136-154).[12]

Conflicts of all types were quick to follow the initiation of the reform process, providing many examples of how available legal instruments were utilized by the proponents and opponents of agrarian reform.[13] It is not my intention to analyze fully the legal and other issues that surfaced during the Frei (Christian Democratic, 1964-1970) or the Allende (Socialist, 1970-1973) agrarian reform processes, nor during the neo-liberal 'counter-reform' initiated by General Pinochet after the 1973 *coup*.[14] Instead, my purpose was more modest. My intention was to examine the instrumental role of legal concepts, institutions and

---

11 ibid.

12 The Supreme Court of Chile did assume appellate jurisdiction over these conflicts through the *Recursos de Queja* (a writ based on the assertion that a trial court has abused its discretion). See Thome, 1989: 198.

13 More often than not, the legal battles were over compensation schemes, both in the Frei and particularly in the Allende agrarian reforms. This is not really surprising. For one thing, the grounds for expropriation most commonly applied – excess size – were based on objective criteria set out in great detail by Article 172 of Law 16640, where the entire country, with the exception of the southernmost provinces, was divided into physical and geographical categories. Within each category, a specific area (in hectares) was identified as the equivalent of 80 Basic Irrigated Hectares (BIH) in the Central Valley of Chile, the benchmark for excess size expropriations. It was thus not difficult to establish whether any given farm exceeded or not the minimum 80 BIH so as to make it eligible for or exempt from expropriation. On the other hand, the appraisals of improvements not included in the property tax assessments were subjective in nature, and reasonable people or expert witness could produce widely divergent figures. Moreover, as all post-November 1964 improvements had to be compensated for in toto and in cash, substantial amounts of money were often involved. In fact, many landowners didn't appear that concerned over being expropriated but rather seemed more interested in the total amount of cash compensation they could obtain. Given the poor land market at the time, perhaps expropriation and a high appraisal for improvements on the land was the best way to convert what had become non-marketable assets into cold cash, easily transferrable into foreign currency or converted into more productive investments.

14 For analyses of these processes, see Thome, 1989; Kay and Silva, 1992; and Thiesenhusen, 1995.

processes by both defenders and critics of absolute private property, at particular junctions of the political life of Chile when agrarian reform became a crucial social issue.

South Africa
Imposition of western property regimes and resulting land tenure structures
European colonization in southern Africa parallelled the process in Latin America, at least as regards its impact on land rights and land tenure structures. From early on, colonial legislation regimes placed many restrictions on indigenous land rights, a process that has continued until recently.[15] Acting under this legislation, government officials began the process of forcing the native Black African population into reserves much too small for their needs. By the late 19th century, for example, reserves for the Black Africans in the Transvaal and Natal totalled only 0.76 million out of 69 million hectares and 0.84 million out of five million hectares, respectively[16] (Binswanger and Deininger, 1993: p14).

As a result of this legislation and policies, tenant farming (among White farmers, tenants were known as 'squatters') became the predominant mode of production available to Black Africans. As of 1882, 55 per cent of the native population in Natal worked as tenants, 35 per cent 'owned' their land while 20 per cent were allowed to live and work in crown land. In the Transvaal, tenancy was even more prevalent; by 1904, out of a total Black African population of 900,000, 50 per cent lived and worked in European owned land. Other laws and regulations were enacted over the coming years, further restricting the land rights, including tenancy, of the Black Africans. By 1892, for instance, all tenants living on White farms had to be registered and had to pay a poll tax (Binswanger and Deininger, 1993: 14).

The 1890s marked a watershed in the legal onslaught against Black African farmers (Binswanger and Deininger, 1993: 14). Increasingly concerned with competition from the smaller but more productive African family farms and the increasing ability of African farmers to purchase agricultural land, European farmers began to pressure for more restrictive policies on Black African farming. Official responses were not long in coming; the Glen Grey Act of 1894 restricted family land ownership or usufruct in the Reserves to one parcel of some three hectares. This Act also imposed a labour tax on all non-owner men who were living in the reserves and banned the sale, rental or sub-division of land.

---

15 A recent study estimates that 130 different statutes affect land law in South Africa, providing further evidence of the fragmentation of indigenous land rights through apartheid policies and programmes (Klug,1995 [b]: p5).
16 One hectare is equivalent to 2.54 acres.

Even more draconian restrictions followed fast upon the organization of South Africa as a virtual independent State in 1910. The key legal provision was the Native Lands Act of 1913 (confirmed in 1936). The implementation of this Act ultimately resulted in the allocation of 87 per cent of the country's best land to whites who constituted less than 18 per cent of the population (Skweyiya, 1990: 197). At the same time, Black Africans' access to land was restricted to the reserves, which constituted no more than 7.9 per cent of the country's area (Binswanger and Deininger, 1993: 14-15). The Act prohibited land transactions by Black Africans outside the reserve areas, unless prior ministerial approval was obtained. As a consequence, Blacks who held land in the rest of the country did so only by virtue of exceptions to this fundamental restriction. Finally, the Act prohibited Black Africans from working as sharecroppers or tenants, though this provision was often ignored (Budlender and Latsky, 1990: 156, 157).

Formerly independent Black African family farmers were forced into a wage labour status on the mines, in the process ending Black African farming above subsistence level and degrading the reserves to the status of 'dormitories' for mine workers. Indeed, Binswanger and Deininger argue that the 1913 Act constitutes the original legal basis for subsequent apartheid policies (1993: 15).

Other legal restrictions on Black African tenure systems followed apace. Beginning with the Glen Grey Act of 1894, for instance, the State began to interfere with the natural evolution of a formerly flexible and responsive communal tenure system. Through rigid codifications and dubious judicial precedents,[17] it imposed a supposedly 'traditional' system which restricted developing democratic institutions, giving Chiefs (most of whom were collaborators of the colonial regimes) the sole power to allocate or transfer communal lands, even to outsiders (Binswanger and Deininger, 1993: 15-16).

In more recent times, the 1936 Development Trust and Land Act introduced PTO (permission to occupy) rights for Black Africans, to be exercised on mostly 'released' or 'trust' lands; that is, lands formerly out of limits to Blacks, which were set aside for acquisition by the South African Development Trust, or SADT (de Wet, 1994: 362; Klug, 1995 [b]: 5-6). Under this Act, the SADT become the owner of all state-owned land within the scheduled and released areas (Budlender and Latsky, 1990: 164). On the surface this policy appeared to make land available to Black African farmers; in reality, this Act was the basic instrument

---

17 See Klug,1995(a) for an insightful analysis of 'Official' indigenous or customary land rights as they emerged from the 1906 case, Hermansberg Mission Society v Commissioner of Native Affairs and Darius Mogale 1906 T.S. 135. Klug persuasively argues that the presiding Judge misinterpreted indigenous customary law by ruling that under it, only the King or Chief of the tribe owned the land (as trustee of the tribe) and that his subjects only had usufruct rights. This became a precedent and basis for future determinations by English colonial powers of indigenous land rights throughout the continent (7; 9).

for the removal of Black Farmers from the so-called 'Black Spots', that is, from more valuable areas exclusively reserved for White farmers. Documented and poignant stories abound of forced removals of Black farm families from lands they had owned under freehold title for various generations (de Wet,1 994: 363). These removals were still taking place well into the 1970s.

Other apartheid legislation regulating land settlement included: Prevention of Illegal Squatting Act 52 of 1951; Trespass Act 6 of 1959; Prohibition of Interdicts Act 64 of 1956; Slums Act 76 of 1979; Proscription of Labour Tenancies Act of 1973; Republic of South Africa Constitution Act 110 of 1983; Group Areas Act 36 of 1966 (amending the Group Areas Act of 1950), and Abolition of Passes and Co-ordination of Documents Act 67 of 1952 (Skweyiya, 1990: 198).

From this tangle of some 130 statutes affecting land rights in South Africa, three primary forms of Black African land tenure rights emerge: communal tenure on 'scheduled land' or reserve lands, as defined by Act 27 of 1913; freehold tenure, some of which managed to survive in some areas; and; PTO (permission to occupy) rights on 'released' or 'trust' lands (Klug, 1995: 5).

The end result of this apartheid-based legal structure was not hard to predict: White Europeans settled on the lands from which Black Africans were excluded or removed, so that by 1991 they controlled 87 per cent of the land, mostly under duly recorded freehold title, even though Whites represent barely 13 to 15 per cent of the population of South Africa. In contrast, Black Africans, representing some 85 per cent of the population, held only 13 per cent of the land, mostly in non-freehold and inadequately recorded tenure forms (Klug, 1995: 7).

In the process White farmers also received substantial amounts of government financial and technical assistance to facilitate their expansion (Skweyiya, 1990: p198). Black African farmers did not fare nearly as well. Given the insufficient amount of land allocated to the Black African rural population, most were either crowded into inadequately small farms (often with poor quality land) or had no access to land whatsoever. As of 1990, for instance, there were approximately 1.3 million Black farm workers in South Africa; less than half a million of them lived permanently on White-owned farms. Well over half of the agricultural workforce, were transformed into an itinerant work-force, finding employment only when White farmers needed extra labour. However, some retained direct access to land as peasants or small producers. As few as a hundred or so were commercial agricultural producers but they were generally subject to the domination of White farmers in terms of policy development, marketing and distribution (Marcus, 1990: 179).

Throughout the 20th century, there still remained significant pockets of land owned in freehold by Black communities within areas generally reserved for

Whites, the so-called 'Black spots'. In most cases this land was acquired before the enactment of the 1913 Land Act. Most of these properties were 'expropriated' under the terms of the 1936 Act and the families moved to the reserves or homelands (de Wet, 1994: 362). Some communities managed to resist the evictions; others have struggled over the years to regain their lost lands, including the invasion or reoccupation of their former properties. In some cases, the former owners have managed to come to a settlement with the new White owners (AFRA, 1991, 1992 (a), (b), (c), (d),1992; Davidson, 1994: A1, A8). These post-1913 evictions and the subsequent struggles and claims for land restoration have become the basis for the Restitution of Land Rights Act, as analysed below.

Reformulation of land rights; legitimizing and enabling agrarian reform in South Africa

In response to increasing domestic and international pressure, in 1991 the South African Government issued a policy *White Paper*, whose basic policy goal was to re-establish social stability through moderate reforms that would retain existing security and community structures and be carried out within the framework of a market-orientated economy.[18] Under this scheme, private ownership of land under freehold titles would continue to receive priority, but supposedly would be made accessible to all through the abolition of racist laws and the promulgation of modern, non-racist land laws (Republic of South Africa, 1991: p1). However, the Government rejected as unfeasible proposals to initiate wide-scale programmes of land restoration in favour of those individuals and communities who had lost their land due to past policies and programmes. "An attempt to return to the previous order will only disrupt the country's pace of development to the detriment of all" (Republic of South Africa, 1991: 6).

To these ends, the Government enacted several laws, including The Abolition of Racially Based Land Measures Act and The Upgrading of Land Tenure Rights Act (Republic of South Africa, 1991: 17-18). The Abolition of Racially Based Land Measures Act (Act 108 of 1991) repealed the Land Acts of 1913 and 1936, and all other provisions regulating access to land, based on race or population group membership. The Upgrading of Land Tenure Rights Act was aimed at providing land tenure security through extending freehold titles to most

---

18 Again, this process bears a striking resemblance to the land reform and other 'progressive' legislation enacted throughout most of Latin America after the 1961 'Declaration of Punta Del Este', a key Alliance for Progress initiative pushed by Washington as a response to the Cuban Revolution. Most of this legislation was mostly symbolic in nature; some, such as, Venezuela did produce some land redistribution. Chilean law 15520 of 1961 fell under the former category, though it did help to legitimize the concept of land reform and set some institutional bases for the subsequent more successful legislation and process.

landholders. It conferred the capacity to acquire land and land title to tribes and provided for an upgrading of 'lower order' land tenure rights to full ownership, but would not interfere with traditional systems of land tenure (communal tribal lands held in trust), unless the tribes requested titling. The Act also prohibited the tribe from selling its land to persons other than its members during the first ten years after its transfer to the tribe unless the tribe obtained a prior court order authorizing the sale.[19]

The Black/ANC response to this *White Paper* was far from enthusiastic (AFRA Newsletters, 1992). Peasant communities judged the Government's policy ineffective and launched the National Land Restoration Campaign to reassert their claims to their lost lands. In response, in 1991 the Government established an Advisory Commission on Land Allocation (ACLA). The Commission basic function was to make recommendations to the Government on the best use and allocation of undeveloped state-owned land, most of which had been acquired through the racially-based land legislation. However, the Commission was widely criticized as having little power to address the demands for land restoration and to being subject to the discretionary power of the National Government (Klug, 1995 [b]: p9). Again, the Government was forced to respond and in 1993 it amended ACLA's terms of reference to give it wider jurisdiction and powers. However, the Commission's new grants of power were still severely limited and subject to ministerial control. For instance, its orders were not directly binding on the Deeds Registrar but subject to ministerial intervention. Even more serious, its orders could not bind the State until full payment of compensation for extinguished rights was satisfied; this would allow the State to delay the processing of land claims, arguing insufficient funds. As a consequence, the Commission still lacked sufficient power to deal effectively with the restitution claims of those forcibly removed from their land by apartheid laws and policies (Klug, 1995 [b]: 14-15). Acting under the new 1994 constitution and with a new president, Nelson Mandela, the current Government replaced ACLA with a new investigatory commission and established a new Land Claims Court to resolve restoration claims (Klug, 1995 [d]).

Land rights and the initiation of the reform
After a protracted political struggle and the imposition of international pressures, a long and mostly secret process of negotiations between the African National Congress and the South African Government finally produced an agreement for an orderly transition to full democracy. For the first time in the history of South

---

19 Klug points out a basic problem with this upgrading or privatization scheme: it can consume available institutional resources to the neglect of the recording needs of other widely used forms of tenure, such as collective and indigenous rights (Klug, 1995 [b]: 7).

Africa a full free election was held, culminating in the election of Nelson Mandela and a new, interim Constitution (Hochschild, 1995: 6).

Though enacted in 1993,[20] the new interim Constitution did not come into effect until the eve of the election on 27 April 1994 (Klug, 1995 [c]: 1). It puts into place a new constitutional and legal framework, crucially affecting property rights and future land tenure systems well into the future, since many of its provisions are likely to remain in the final constitution (Klug, 1995 [b]: 21).

Section 28 of the Constitution, the property clause, is of particular importance for the future of land reform.[21] Its text raises several issues:

> a) How much protection will courts give to this constitutionally protected property right? Too much can lead to conflicts with a democratically elected legislature. Does it unduly limit State's eminent domain power? That is, what is "public purpose"? If the Court adopts a restricted reading (as has happened in some countries), it may frustrate the Government's efforts to reallocate land.

> b) How much and under what circumstances will compensation be paid to the landowners who lose part or all of their rights? Under Sec. 28, the Constitutional Court will determine what compensation would be just and equitable, considering inter alia, the past use of the property, its population, the history of its acquisition, its market value, and the interests of those affected. (Klug, 1995(b): 24-25)

Klug argues that the presence of these 'balancing' criteria prevent a narrow reading of 'public purpose' (1995 [b]: 25). Hochschild, however, fears that the property right clause "...will make even the most modest land reform painfully difficult" (1995 [b]: 6). However, as already noted in other agrarian reform experiences, courts have often interpreted similar clauses so as to further the legislative intent and facilitate a more effective process.

Once or even while the above Constitutional issues are being resolved, South Africa still has to face the task of enacting an enabling agrarian reform law, something akin to Chile's Law 16640 of 1967, as well as other complementary legislation and regulations. This land legislation will have the difficult tasks of nationalizing the land law to provide a national framework which would prevent the complete fragmentation of land rights while also taking into account different forms of tenure as well as ensuring some form of local or regional control. The State will also have to acquire new lands in order to increase Black

---

20 Constitution of the Republic of South Africa Act 200 of 1993, Section 73(1); see Klug,1995(c).
21 Article 28. Property.- (1) Every person shall have the right to acquire and hold rights in property and, to the extent that the nature of the rights permit, to dispose of such rights. (2) No deprivation of any rights in property shall be permitted otherwise than in accordance with a law. (3) Where any rights in property are expropriated pursuant to a law referred to in subsection (2), such expropriation shall be permissible for public purposes only and shall be subject to the payment of agreed compensation or, failing agreement, to the payment of such compensation and within such period as may be determined by a court of law as just and equitable, taking into account all relevant factors, including, in the case of determination of compensation, the use to which the property is being put, the history of its acquisition, its market value, the value of the investments in it and the interests of those affected (Constitution, Republic of South Africa, Act 200 of 1993.)

landholdings beyond the 13 per cent stipulated in the racially based land acts of old. For this purpose, the State will have to resort to such mechanisms as foreclosures of debt-ridden White-owned farms, land purchases and expropriation processes (Klug,1995 [b]: 41-42).

The promulgation of a land acquisition or land reform act is essential. It must cover the three essential issues of any land reform programme. These are to identify the land subject to reform, to establish what compensation will be due to expropriated owners, and to determine who will be the beneficiaries. All three require clear criteria which are easy to apply and interpret (Thome, 1968; Klug,1995 [b]: 43).[22]

The 1993 Interim Constitution also addresses the land restoration issue in Articles 121, 122 and 123.[23] While the Government has not yet promulgated any statutes to carry out a more controversial land reform process, involving substantial expropriation and re-distribution of land, in 1994 it did enact a Restitution of Land Rights Act.[24] In introducing the Bill to the National Assembly, the Select Committee on Land Affairs explained that it provides for the restitution of land rights in accordance to the constitutional objective of restoring land to those persons or communities who were dispossessed of their land under or for the purpose of furthering the objects of racially-based discriminatory legislation. For such purposes, it provides for the establishment of a Commission on Restitution on Land Rights, which shall function independently and with the necessary support structures on a national and regional level. In a move which parallels the special Agrarian Tribunals established in Chile to adjudicate disputes arising from the implementation of its agrarian reform (*supra*), the Bill

---

22 The following are among these necessary criteria:
- establishing the goals of the reform: Can equity or distributive concerns be balanced with productivity and other economic needs? How much land and how many beneficiaries should be targeted? What forms of tenure should be adopted?;
- establishing criteria for acquiring or expropriating land for redistribution: Should the grounds for expropriation be limited to abandoned or poorly used land, or should excess size, regardless of productivity, be included? In either case, what should be the criteria for determining adequacy of use or excess size? Should prior owners be allowed to retain any portion of the land?;
- extent of complementary programmes; should limited resources be dedicated to credit, technical and other assistance, or to infrastructure?;
- administration of the reform; should the process be centralized within one autonomous super-agency, or spread out throughout various ministries or regional agencies? Should there be any participation in the process by peasants or other representatives of the rural sector?;
- compensation aspects: should the expropriated land be paid according to its market value, or according to some other criteria, such as tax appraisals? Should payment be made in cash, or in long-term bonds, or in some other commodity?;
- responsibilities of the beneficiaries: should reform beneficiaries pay part or all of the land they receive? Of the improvements made in the land? If so, on what terms?;
- financing the reform process;
- review and evaluation of the reform: should there be a review process of the agrarian reform programme? If so, by whom? The regular court system? A special tribunal?

also establishes a special Land Court even though this is not expressly provided for in the Constitution. This option was found to be necessary so that claims could be dealt with effectively without the delays associated with normal court procedures (Republic of South Africa,1994: 1-2).

At this early stage in South Africa's agrarian reform process, it is too early to tell how effectively its existing enabling statutes, such as the Restitution Act, will be implemented, or whether any meaningful agrarian reform legislation and programmes will be enacted and implemented. Nevertheless, the 1993 Constitution and the Restitution Act do provide a clear framework for the recognition and adjudication of land claims. This right is incorporated within the equality clause of the Bill of Rights and thus linked to the constitutional mandate to address the legacy of apartheid (Klug, 1995 [d]: 6).

The Act limits claims to documented claims involving land rights lost after 19 June 1913 (Klug,1995 [d]: 9). This limitation may in effect exclude the claims of perhaps millions of Black African farmers, many of whom continue to work as tenants in White-owned farms, but who claim a 'birthright' to the land where they work or similar lands (Davidson,1994: 1). Their demands must be met either through negotiated purchases, the grant to state owned lands, or will have to wait until a comprehensive agrarian reform law is promulgated.

---

23 The more relevant sections of the Constitution regarding restoration follow (Constitution of the Republic of South Africa, Act 200 of 1993):

Restitution of Land Rights

121. Claims.-(1) An Act of Parliament shall provide for matters relating to restitution of land rights as envisaged in this section and in sections 122 and 123.

(2) A person or a community shall be entitled to claim restitution of a right in land from the state if -

(a) such a person or community was dispossessed of such right at any time after a date to be fixed by the Act referred to in subsection (1); and

(b) such dispossession was effected under or for the purpose of furthering the object of a law which would have been inconsistent with the prohibition of racial discrimination contained in section 8 (2), had that section been in operation at the time of such dispossession........

122. Commission.- (1)The Act contemplated in section 121(1) shall establish a Commission on Restitution of Land Rights, which shall be competent to-

(a) investigate the merits of any claims;

(b) mediate and settle disputes arising from such claims;

(c) draw up reports on unsettled claims for submission as evidence to a court of law and to present any other relevant evidence to the court; and

(d) exercise and perform any such other powers and functions as may be provided for in said act........

123. Court orders. -(1) Where a claim contemplated in section 121 (2) is lodged with a court of law and the land in question is-

(a) in the possession of the state and the state certifies that the restoration of the right in question is feasible, the court may, subject to subsection (4), order the state o restore the relevant right to the claimant; or

(b) in the possession of a private owner and the state certifies tat the acquisition of such land by the state is feasible, the court may, subject to subsection (4), order the state to purchase or expropriate such land and restore the relevant right to the claimant...

(The remaining sub-sections of 123 deal with the criteria for deciding whether or not to order restoration or is equivalent, and the amount of compensation due the prior owner, in terms very similar as those used for the property clause, Article 28.)

However, even well-documented claims of the improper deprivation of land rights may not result in full restitution. Under the Act, if the land in question is in the possession of a private owner, the Land Court must "find that it is just and equitable to restore the right taking into consideration all relevant factors". These include hardship caused, use to which the property is being put, interests of the owners, and the interests of the dispossessed. A finding of "just and equitable" restoration in such a case still requires a process of expropriation subject to compensation (Klug, 1995 [d]: 11). Since the extent of the compensation obligation is yet to be defined, the risk remains that limited fiscal resources will restrict the number of successful resolutions of restitution claims.

As Klug argues:

> (F)ailure to grant a right to restoration and particularly the power given the state to certify whether restoration is suitable in particular cases pose the greatest challenges to the legitimacy of this framework. If in.... addressing land claims the state repeatedly fails to allow the courts to grant restoration, it is likely to be confronted with an increasing pattern of land invasions.... (Klug, 1995 [d]: 12)

These and other complex provisions of the Act, amply documented by Klug (1995 [d]), are reminiscent of similar problems in the Mexican Agrarian Reform process. In that process, the agrarian laws established two procedures for acquiring land for meeting its goals: restitution and expropriation. Because of its procedural complexities, particularly in proving past ownership, restitution did not prove an effective means for land redistribution; only six per cent of the total land distributed through 1944 was acquired through restitution (Karst and Rosenn, 1975: 284-285). The slack was filled by a very comprehensive expropriation process, not yet in place in South Africa.

It is clear that the land claims process is closely intertwined with the broader process of land reform; both will feed off each other. Unless effective and accessible means to either or both processes are made available, the issue of the meaning and limitations of 'property rights' may once again 'bedevil' the permanent constitution-making process in South Africa (Klug, 1995 [d]: 35).

CONCLUSIONS

We have looked at Chile and South Africa because of the striking parallels that exist between the two in the evolution of the legal frameworks for land tenure structures and agrarian reform policies. There are, however, many other legal

---

24 Restitution of Land Rights Act, Act No.22 of 1994. In accordance to its preamble, the purpose of this Act is: "To provide for the restitution of rights in land in respect of which person or communities were dispossessed under or for the purposes of furthering the objects of any racially based discriminatory law; to establish a Commission on Restitution of Land Rights and a Land Claims Court and to provide for matters connected therewith".

issues that are not covered by the scope of this paper, as well as social, political and other factors.

As South Africa is barely initiating its own agrarian reform process, it remains to be seen how far it will go and what problems it will encounter in, to cite Hirschman, its 'journey toward progress.' The Chilean experience can be useful, however, in pointing out some potentially useful legal instrumentalities, as well as the problems they also create.

I have argued that property rights need not be conceived as mythical and inviolate pronouncements enshrining absolute individual rights. Alternative jurisprudential principles exist in the legal firmament to justify reasonable and equitable limitations on private property rights. These principles have been put into practice, restricting private property rights through such mechanisms as police powers, land use controls, zoning and eminent domain.

The 'social function' of property concept has been of particular importance to the developing nations, allowing many to justify and carry out significant agrarian reform programmes. Nevertheless, the concept of private property rights still has a certain 'mythical' aura, representing a formidable obstacle to change and equitable development. Private ownership of land is a powerful instrument, endowing its holders with incentives and freedoms. However, too much of a good thing is a bad thing. Unlimited private property rights tend to result in a concentration of property in a few hands leading to a not uncommon monopolization by the privileged over these resources, to the detriment of the rest. It is the purpose of agrarian reform to distribute the power of property among the many, making for a more just, productive and stable society.

In Chile, agrarian reform ran its course up to the coup of 1973, to be followed by a neo-liberal 'counter-reform'. However, the aftermath was not a return to the structures of old; the traditional latifundia disappeared, replaced by more compact and efficient commercial farms. The end result was a modernized and more productive agricultural sector, much along the lines suggested by de Janvry (1981), but which still faces serious equity problems.[25]

South Africa has not yet pushed through a thorough agrarian reform, although it has embarked on it through the land restitution process and various pilot projects. The necessary legal and institutional framework is beginning to take shape; unless the process is totally rejected by domestic and international players essential to South Africa's political and economic welfare, it can eventually enable the implementation of an agrarian reform that would not only lead to more equitable land distribution, but a more productive and efficient agricultural sector as well.

---

25 For a full analysis of the current situation in the Chilean countryside, see Kay and Silva, 1992.

REFERENCES

AFRA Newsletter, No. 8, (Pietermaritzburg, South Africa: Association for Rural Advancement, December 1990).

AFRA Newsletter, No. 9, (ibid., February 1991[a]).

AFRA Newsletter, No. 11, (ibid., April 1991[b]).

AFRA Newsletter, No. 13, (ibid., November 1991[c]).

AFRA Newsletter, No. 13, (ibid., December 1991[d]).

AFRA Newsletter, No. 15, (ibid., May 1992).

Bauer, Arnold J, 'Rural Society and Politics in Comparative Perspective' in Kay, Cristóbal and Silva, Patricio, eds., *Development and Social Change in the Chilean Countryside*, (Amsterdam: Centre for Latin American Research and Documentation [CEDLA], 1992) pp.19-32.

Bartra, Roger, *Agrarian Structure and Political power in Mexico* (translated by Ault, Stephen K.) (Baltimore: The Johns Hopkins Press, 1993).

Binswanger, Hans P. and Deininger, Klaus, *South African Land Policy: The Legacy of History and Current Options* (The World Bank and University of Minnesota, unpublished report, 37 pp, document in possession of author, 1993).

Budlender, Geoff and Latsky, Johan, 'Unravelling Rights to Land and to Agricultural Activity in Rural Race Zones', South Africa Journal on Human Rights (1990).

Budlender, Geoff, Claasens, A, et al., 'Statement on the White Paper on Land Reform and the Accompanying Bills', *Land Reform: Current Documents*, (Johannesburg: Centre for Applied Legal Studies, University of Witwatersrand, 1991).

Chile Senate 'Informe de la Comisión de Constitución, Legislación, Justicia y Reglamento' Boletín No. 22,021, (Santiago: Instituto Geográfico, 1966).

Christman, John, *The Myth of Property: Toward an Egalitarian Theory of Property,* (New York: Oxford University Press, 1994).

Colombia, Supreme Court of Justice 'Case of Constitutionality of Law 135 (Plenary Session 1964', Bogotá: VII Derecho Colombiano (1965), quoted in Karst and Rosenn (1975) pp 346-351.

Cushman, John, 'Houses Passes Bill That Would Limit Many Regulations', *New York Times*, (4 March 1995) p1 and p6.

Davidson, Joe, 'South Africa Ponders Its Next Controversy: Who Owns the Land?' *Wall Street Journal*, Vol. LXXV, No. 142, (May 4, 1994) pA-1 and pA-8.

de Janvry, Alain, *The Agrarian Question and Reformism in Latin America*, (Baltimore: Johns Hopkins University Press, 1981).

de Soto, Hernando, 'El Otro Sendero', Editorial Diana, Mexico (1991).

de Wet, Chris, 'Resettlement and Land Reform in South Africa', Review of African Political Economy, (Johannesburg: ROAPE Publications, 1994) pp359-373.

Dorner, Peter, *Latin American Land Reforms in Theory and Practice: A Retrospective Analysis*. (Madison: University of Wisconsin Press, 1992).

Duguit, Leon, 'Les Transformations Generales Du Droit Prive', (Register transl.), in The Progress of *Continental Law in the 19th Century,* (1918) pp130-136, as cited in Karst and Rosenn (1975) pp310-31.

Elster, Jon, 'Introduction', in Elster, Jon, and Slagstad, Rune, eds., *Constitutionalism and Democracy,* (Cambridge: Cambridge University Press, 1988) pp1-17.

Frei, Eduardo and Trivelli, Hugo, 'Mensaje del Ejecutivo al Congreso Proponiendo la Aprobación del Proyecto de Ley de Reforma Agraria', in Vodavonic, Antonio, *Ley de Reforma Agraria*, (Santiago: Editorial Nascimento, 1967; excerpts translated by Philip Hazelton).

Gardner, James, *Legal Imperialism*, (Madison: University of Wisconsin Press, 1980).

Garrido, Juan, Guerrero, Cristián, and Valdés, María Soledad, eds., *Historia de la Reforma Agraria en Chile*, (Santiago: Editorial Universitaria, 1988).

Hocschild, Adam, 'A Match Made in Secret', *New York Times*, (5 March 1995) p6; book review of Spark, Alister, *Tomorrow is Another Country: The inside story of South Africa's Road to Change* (New York: Hill and Wang, 1995).

Huerta, Maria Antonieta, *Otro Agro Para Chile: La historia de la reforma agraria en el proceso social y político*, (Santiago [Chile]: CISEC-CESOC, 1989).

Karst, Kenneth and Rosenn, Keith, *Law and Development in Latin America*, (Los Angeles: University of California Press 1975).

Kaufman, Robert R., *The politics of land reform in Chile*, 1950-1970, (Cambridge, Mass.: Harvard University Press, 1972).

Kay, Cristóbal and Silva, Patricio, eds., *Development and Social Change in the Chilean Countryside*, (Amsterdam: CEDLA, 1992),

Klug, Heinz, 'Defining the Property Rights of Others: Political Power, Indigeneous Tenure and the Construction of Customary law', (unpublished Draft Chapter, Dissertation for S.J.D., University of Wisconsin; Madison, WI., 1995(a), 48 pp; cited with permission; document in my possession.)

Klug, Heinz, 'Bedeviling Agrarian Reform: The Impact of Past, Present and Future Legal Frameworks', (unpublished Draft Chapter, Dissertation for S.J.D., University of Wisconsin; Madison, WI., 1995(b), 62 pp; cited with permission – document in my possession.)

Klug, Heinz, 'South Africa's New Constitution: The Challenges of Diversity and Identity', unpublished Draft Chapter, Dissertation for S.J.D., University of Wisconsin; Madison, WI., 1995(c), 48 pp; cited with permission – document in my possession.)

Klug, Heinz, 'Historical Claims and the Right to Restitution', unpublished Draft Chapter, Dissertation for S.J.D., University of Wisconsin; Madison, WI., 1995(d), 38 pp; cited with permission – document in my possession.)

MacPherson, C.B., *Property: Mainstream and Critical Positions* (Toronto: University of Toronto Press, 1983).

Marcus, Tessa, 'Land Reform – Considering National, Class and Gender Issues', South Africa Journal on Human Rights (1990).

McAuslan, Patrick, 'Law, Governance And The Development Of The Market: Practical Problems And Possible Solutions', paper presented at the 'Seminar On Good Government And Law', London, 27–28 March 1995).

Moral Lopez, Pedro, *Sistemas Jurídicos de la Reforma Agraria y del Desarrollo*, (Santiago: ICIRA. 1968).

Morse, Richard.1964. 'The Heritage of Latin America' in Hartz, Louis, ed., *The Founding of New Societies*, (New York: Harcourt, Brace and World, 1964) p124.

Nedelsky, Jennifer, *Private Property and the Limits of American Constitutionalism*, (Chicago: University of Chicago Press, 1990).

Nedelsky, Jennifer, 'American constitutionalism and the paradox of private property' in Elster, Jon and Slagstad, Rune, eds., *Constitutionalism and Democracy*, (Cambridge: Cambridge University Press, 1993) pp241-273.

O'Connor, Theron, 'Some Aspects of the Development and Erosion of the Right of Private Ownership in the Civil Law System' (Madison: unpublished seminar paper, 1968; in my possession.)

Petras, James F., and Laporte, Robert E.,*Cultivating Revolution: The United States and Agrarian Reform in Latin America*, (New York: Vintage Books, 1973).

Plager, Sheldon, *Social Justice Through Law: New Approaches in the Law of Property*, (Mineola, New York: Foundation Press, 1970).

Republic of South Africa, 'White Paper on Land Reform', (Pretoria: Government Printer, 1991).

Republic of South Africa, 'General Notice; Notice 1090 of 1994; Select Committee on Land Affairs; Restitution of Lands Rights Bill', Government Gazette, Vol. 351, No. 16002, (Pretoria: 30 September 1994) pp1-2.

Skweyiya, Zola, 'Towards a Solution to the Land Question in Post-Apartheid South Africa: Problems and Models', South Africa Journal on Human Rights (1990).

Tamanaha, Brian Z., 'The Lessons of Law-and-Development Studies' American Journal of International Law Vol. 89 (1995) review article, p470.

Thiesenhusen, William, ed., *Broken Promises*, (Boulder, Westview Press, 1995).

Thome, Joseph R., 'The Process of Land Reform in Latin America', Wisconsin Law Review (1968) pp9-22.

Thome, Joseph R., 'Agrarian Reform Legislation: Chile' in Dorner, Peter, ed., *Land Reform in Latin America: Issues and Cases*, Land Economics Monograph Series, no.3, (Madison: 1971) pp81-102.

Thome, Joseph R., 'Law, Conflict and Change: Frei's Law and Allende's Agrarian Reform', in Thiesenhusen, William C., ed., *Searching for Agrarian Reform in Latin America*, (Boston: Unwyn Hyman1989) pp188-215.

World Bank, 'Options for Land Reform and Rural Restructuring in South Africa', report prepared for Land and Agricultural Policy Centre, 'Conference on Land Redistribution Options', 12-15 October 1993, Johannesburg, South Africa, 75pp plus annex.

COMMENT

Lawrence Tshuma

LAW AND DEVELOPMENT

Thome's paper addresses the interface between two very controversial issues: the role of law in the process of development on the one hand, and agrarian reform on the other. As often as not, law is presumed uncritically to play a positive and facilitative role in the process of development and social change. More often than not, development and social change are conceived as societal modernization. Despite more than three decades of unsuccessful modernization programmes in the developing world, faith in modernization remains high as evidenced by structural adjustment programmes of the 1980s and 1990s. According to Habermas (1987:2) 'modernization' was introduced as a technical term only in the 1950s and is the mark of a theoretical approach that takes up Weber's problem of European cultural and societal rationalization but elaborates it with tools of social-scientific functionalism.

In the sphere of law, as Thome observes, modernization theory is generally associated with the 'Law and Development' movement of the 1960s and 1970s. In the spirit of social-scientific functionalism that characterized modernization theory, the law and development movement's approach was premised on the assumption that law was context-neutral and therefore above problems of a historical and geographical nature. In other words, law as a neutral institution transcended time and space. In relation to society, law was viewed in instrumental terms as capable of bringing about change, problem-solving, and policy implementation (Fitzpatrick 1992:6). The approach abstracted law from society and presupposed their separation. According to the approach, law, in its autonomy and untainted purity, is always available to be used by disinterested rulers to resolve problems and contradictions within society (Tshuma 1995:19). For Fitzpatrick (1992) this is one of the enduring mythologies of law.

The same instrumental approach underpins structural adjustment programmes, the dominant development paradigm of the 1980s and 1990s in the developing world, and the transitions to capitalist systems in the former state socialist systems of Eastern Europe. However, as Thome observes, legal frameworks reflect, influence, and are part of their respective societies. Law reflects, mediates and expresses power relations in society and the contradictions they engender. The problematic and contradictory role of law in, and its potential contributions and limits to, the process of development should be appreciated. While dominant classes and groups may use law to protect their interests and undemocratic social relations, marginalized classes and groups may see it as a framework for furthering their own interests and transforming undemocratic social relations. Law is therefore a site of social struggles. Thome's paper addresses what are arguably some of the most contentious and controversial sites of law and social struggles in the developing world: property rights in land and agrarian reform.

PROPERTY RIGHTS IN LAND AND AGRARIAN REFORM

Thome discusses the role of law in the redistribution of property rights in land simultaneously to benefit the landless or rural poor and to undermine the power of the landowning class in the course of agrarian reform. Law plays a contradictory role in the process of agrarian reform because it is always part of the problem and may be part of the solution. It is part of the problem in the sense that the land rights and tenure systems that underpin domination and exploitation are partly constructed by, and institutionalized in, law. It may be part of the solution in that the construction of alternative and more democratic land rights and tenure systems may be mediated in part by law. For the dominant classes and groups, law is a symbol of stability and protects the *status quo*, or at least mediates changes that do not lead to radical transformations in the *status quo*. For the marginalized and poor, while existing legal institutions and land rights are symbols of domination and exploitation, their struggle is for more democratic legal institutions and land rights. As Thome argues, land rights and other legal institutions can play crucial and supportive roles in limiting or making possible the enactment of agrarian reform, in defining its boundaries, and in determining or channelling the process.

Critical to agrarian reform is the appreciation that property rights in general and land rights in particular are social constructions that are determined by and determine power relations. Thome's brief historical analysis of the colonization of both Latin America and South Africa and the consequent creation of private property rights in land for European settlers on the one hand, and the destruction of the land entitlements of indigenous people and the restructuring of their tenure systems on the other, amply demonstrates the point that property rights are social constructs. Once constructed, however, private property rights are instutionalized and protected by the state through its coercive apparatus, while in law and ideology they assume the form of an inherent individual human right that is entrenched in the constitution. As a constitutional category, private property rights are protected and can only be interfered with subject to safeguards such as compulsory acquisition for public purposes only and the prior payment of full compensation. In the former colonies the protection of private property rights in land, acts as a hindrance to programmes of agrarian reform and thus limits majority rights.

The significance of Thome's paper is that it offers an alternative approach to conceptualizing property rights in a way that would facilitate agrarian reform and democracy instead of frustrating them. Rather than view property rights as unrestricted and exclusive individual rights, Thome argues for a 'social function' of property concept which emphasizes social control over private property rights in order to facilitate programmes for the achievement of social justice. He shows that the 'social function' principle has been recognised and entrenched in a number of existing constitutions.

There are, however, alternative conceptualizations of the social function of property rights. Throughout history property rights have frequently been justified on the basis of one or other social function. Pre-liberal natural rights theories constructed exclusive property rights in order to justify social inequality (Macpherson 1978:203). For Aquinas, the world was God's property and had been given to the collective stewardship of human beings as a community of goods (Hont and Ignatieff 1983:26-7). Private possession was, however, legitimate because "each person takes more trouble to care for something that is his sole responsibility than what is held in common by many" (Aquinas quoted in Hont and Ignatieff 1983:27). The exclusive character of property was suspended in times of need when the poor were entitled to claim their original share in the community of goods. While Grotius historicized Aquinas' theory, he still maintained that in times of necessity private rights were superseded by the natural rights of the propertyless to the means of survival. In Grotian natural law jurisprudence, distributive justice, such as the supersession of private property rights, was theorized as an exception rather than as a rule, while expletive justice, which in the main comprised private property rights, was theorized as the rule. In the words of Hont and Ignatieff (1983: 27-8), "A man had a right only to what was his own. He had no right to what was his due. His imperfect right to be treated with humanity only hardened into a perfect right under conditions of gravest necessity". In Pufendorf's theory, in times of need the poor were not entitled to rights in the private property of the rich. Rather the rich were under legally unenforceable obligations to help the poor (Hont and Ignatieff 1983).

According to Locke's theory of property rights, in times of necessity those without property were entitled to the property of others to the extent of their needs. The obligation on the part of the rich was an individual matter, "a side constraint, rather than a structuring condition on whatever property arrangements happened to be in force" (Hont and Ignatieff 1983:37). The needy could only appeal to the rich for assistance on condition that they had performed labour in a calling. In Locke's theory, the basis of property is labour (Locke 1978). Once the industrious have acquired property rights through their labour and a situation of scarcity in the supply of land develops, government and positive laws of property become a necessity. The laws of property provide that those without property should not temper with the property of those who have acquired it through their labour. The role of government is to secure private property. Locke also argued that exclusive property rights created the incentives necessary to increase the productivity of the soil and push back the limits of scarcity (Hont and Ignatieff 1983:41). In addition, the division of labour encouraged productivity.

Hont and Ignatieff argue that Pufendorf and Locke's theories laid the foundation for Adam Smith's market solution to the problem of how to enjoy the benefits of exclusive dominion without excluding the propertyless wage-earners from the means of subsistence (1983:42). The argument that high prices and the division of labour would stimulate the productivity of land, shifted the natural law problem of adjudicating the need claims of the poor and the property claims of the rich beyond a juridical plane into non-zero sum market solutions. Smith saw property rights as a historically specific social construction in the process of human development. His theory sought to show how markets in subsistence goods and labour could provide for the needs of the propertyless. In the tradition of natural jurisprudence, he made a distinction between 'strict' and 'distributive' justice. The function of government was to ensure strict justice by protecting private property rights (Hont and Ignatieff 1983:43). Distributive justice lay outside the province of government. For the utilitarians, Bentham and the Mills, property rights derived from labour. As Macpherson (1978:203-4) argues, "Security of enjoyment of the fruits of one's labour was the reason for property: without property in the fruits and in the means of labour no one would have an incentive to labour, and utility could not be maximized".

The principle of social function is as old as the concept and institution of private property. It therefore goes back in history beyond the instances to which Thome refers. To natural law theorists, property had a social function even though this gradually became a residual rather than an integral element. Given their fundamental premise that the earth was initially given to humankind in common, it was inevitable that they would justify private property on the basis of some social function. That social function was ultimately assumed by the market in the theories of Adam Smith and some of those who came after him.

Unfortunately Thome's conception of the social function of property which is predicated on the state's regulatory role in promoting distributive justice is not the only one. Indeed at this historical juncture, it is not the dominant one. The dominant paradigm sees the market rather than the state as performing the social function. Unlike the social function that Thome analyses, which is predicated on the restriction of property rights, the dominant paradigm sees the unrestricted enjoyment of private property rights as underpinning the market. The role of the state is to protect private property rights in order to facilitate the workings of markets. In agrarian reform, as in other spheres of life, the role of the state is limited to protecting property rights in order to facilitate the workings of the market. Only in situations where the market fails can state interference be justified. However, even then, once the conditions for the proper functioning of the market have been restored, the state should retreat to its usual role of policing. Chile's agrarian reforms under Pinochet epitomize faith in the market as the best institution for safeguarding and promoting the social function through unrestricted private property rights.

In the heyday of the welfare state Macpherson (1978:205-7) argued for a broader conception of property rights than the narrow exclusive one associated with liberalism. He argued for a right not to be excluded from the use or benefit of the achievements of the whole of society, including access to society's accumulated means of labour, that is, the accumulated capital of society and its natural resources and the consequent right to an income from one's work on them. In addition or alternatively, the right not to be excluded included a right to an income from the whole produce of society, an income related not to the work but to what is needed for a full human life. With respect to agrarian reform, Thiesenhusen (1989:1) argues in similar vein. He sees the redistribution of land which is a major source of employment in agrarian societies as some kind of affirmative action. But in the 1980s and the 1990s the market has asserted itself with a vengeance and the welfare state has been forced into a retreat. In the developing world, structural adjustment programmes are predicated on the rolling back of the state and consequently the release of the market and its supposed efficacious role in the allocation of resources including land. The market is in turn predicated on the protection of private property rights. In other words, the market is supposed to allocate resources and serve the social function of distributive justice.

Ultimately, as Thome's discussion of agrarian reform in Chile demonstrates, the construction of the social function principle of property rights and its institutionalization in, and implementation by, land laws is determined by and determines power relations in society. The social function of property principle is as much a social construct as the exclusive property rights and is therefore a contested domain. Thus in agrarian reforms which are undertaken by dominant groups under pressure from below and in an attempt to resolve economic and political contradictions without transforming dominant social relations, the social function principle of property may be invoked as a defensive mechanism rather than one intended to foster far-reaching social changes. This appears to have been the case in most Latin American agrarian reforms. The social function principle of property may therefore be invoked by dominant groups which are only committed to limited rather than far-reaching reforms as seems to have been the case in Chile between 1925 and 1962.

In negotiated political transitions, such as the South African one, the nature of the changes in power relations is determined largely by the compromises that are made with the old ruling regime on the one hand, and the pressures for change from below on the other. These changes are important for as Sobhan (1993:4) observes, agrarian reforms originate in a change in the balance of power in society and the nature of the adjustment in relations of power has a profound effect on the outcome of the reforms.

It is still too early to judge the nature of the change in the balance of power relations in South Africa. If history is anything to go by, successful agrarian reforms have been undertaken in situations where the old order has been completely overthrown either from below or from outside as in Japan, North and South Korea, Taiwan, China, Vietnam and Cuba (Sobhan 1993).

The construction of new property entitlements and tenure systems has thus occurred in circumstances where the new forces are unfettered by the previous ruling regime and the structures and institutions that supported it. Other reforms have effected social transitions without transforming effectively the social relations of production and domination. As Thome shows, this is what the apartheid regime sought to do in 1991 when it was clear that change was on the way in South Africa. The regime attempted to introduce cosmetic agrarian changes which would not have transformed the status quo. It is important to ensure that dominant interests do not limit agrarian reform to cosmetic changes once contemplated by the regime.

While it is appreciated that the political transition in South Africa is historically specific and therefore different from others in Africa, there is a danger of not learning from the mistakes of African countries which have embarked on agrarian reform.

In the context of former Southern African settler colonies, South Africa would do better not to follow the over-cautious route taken by Zimbabwe which has failed to transform the colonial agrarian structure more than fifteen years after independence (Moyo 1995, Tshuma 1995).

Over-sensitivity to the concerns of capital and the North on the sanctity of private property rights may limit agrarian reform. Moreover, South Africa should be careful not to retain colonial agrarian policies regarding customary entitlements and tenure as has been the case in most of sub-Saharan Africa (Oketh-Ogendo 1993).

REFERENCES

Fitzpatrick, Peter, *The Mythology of Law* (London: Routledge, 1992).

Habermas, Jurgen, *Philosophical Discourse on Modernity* (Oxford: Polity Press, 1987).

Hont, Istvan and Ignatieff, Michael, 'Needs and Justice in the Wealth of Nations: An Introductory Essay', in Hont, Istvan and Ignatieff, Michael eds. *Wealth and Virtue* (Cambridge: Cambridge University Press, 1983) p1.

Locke, John, 'Of Property' in Macpherson, C.B. ed. *Property: Mainstream and Critical Positions* (Oxford: Basil Blackwell, 1978) p17.

Macpherson, C.B., 'Liberal Democracy and Property' in Macpherson, C.B. ed. *Property: Mainstream and Critical Positions* (Oxford: Basil Blackwell, 1978) p199.

Moyo, Sam, *The Land Question In Zimbabwe* (Harare: Sapes Books, 1995).

Oketh-Ogendo, H.W.O., 'Agrarian Reform in Sub-Saharan Africa: An Assessment of State Responses to the African Agrarian Crisis and Their Implications for Agricultural Development' in Bassett, T.J. and Crummey, D.E. ed. *Land in African Agrarian Systems* (Madison: The University of Wisconsin Press,1993).

Sobhan, Rehman, *Agrarian Reform and Social Transformation: Preconditions for Development* (London and New Jersey: Zed Books, 1993).

Thiesenhusen, William, 'Introduction' in Thiesenhusen, William. ed. *Searching for Agrarian Reform in Latin America* (Boston: Unwin Hyman, 1989) p1.

Tshuma, Lawrence, *Law, State and Agrarian Reform In Zimbabwe* (unpublished PhD thesis, University of Warwick, England: 1995).

10 Access to justice in South and South-east Asia

Ross Cranston*

Regrettably, access jurisprudence is the Cinderella of the Indian Justice System. Ubi jus, ibi remedium is basic to the credibility in the law. But when a person goes to court in search of relief and has a case to substantiate the wrong done to him, prompt remedy must issue. Unfortunately, our Procedural Codes, Civil and Criminal, are beset with baffling steps that it is more accurate to describe our system as a government of lawyers and not a government of laws.[1]

A legal and regulatory framework which protects property and contractual rights, ensures a fair and quick settlement of disputes and establishes a fair and stable labor/management relationship is a fundamental element in the stability and flexibility needed for the investment environment.[2]

INTRODUCTION

Access to justice reforms have been characterized as falling into three distinct waves.[3] The first wave began in the early 1960s and involved the extension of legal aid; this meant that the profession had to forgo the important tenet: independence from the state. The second wave focused upon the representation of diffuse or collective interests such as consumers and environmentalists, and involved standing rules, multi-party actions and the like. The first and second waves are incorporated in the third, but the third goes beyond them to expand legal representation and improve adjudicative procedures to accommodate different types of litigants and issues. Each of these waves in the access to justice movement is concerned with what can be called 'social access': making individuals and in some cases groups of individuals aware of their legal rights and then enabling them to obtain legal services to invoke these rights.

While the development of access to justice in South and South-east Asia does contain elements of these 'waves', their focus is askew. This is especially so if we wish to bring into the picture the most notable development in access to justice in the region of the last decade – the concern with economic access, by providing economic institutions, especially banks and other financial institutions,

---

* As ever, I am indebted to my research assistant Sonali Akeyratne for her assistance with this chapter.
1 Justice V.R. Krishna Iyer, *Justice and Beyond* (New Delhi: 1980) pp68-69.
2 Ibrahim Shihata, *The World Bank in a Changing World* (Nighoff, 1991) p234.
3 M. Cappelletti and B. Garth, 'Access to Justice: the worldwide movement to make rights effective', in *Access to Justice* (Milan: 1978) v.1.

with a mechanism for redress to judicial remedies. There has been no recent counterpart in Europe or North America to the notion of furthering economic access to justice, although it is not unfair to say that economic institutions in these countries are already well served by existing arrangements.

The justifications for facilitating social access are familiar. There is an unacceptable incongruence between the rights recognised by the legal order and the experiences of individuals. The reasons are well known and need not detain us long.[4] Access to justice makes rights effective. In broad terms this furthers the rule of law. As the Supreme Court of India put it in a leading decision on public interest litigation, if no one can maintain an action for redress of a public wrong, "it would be disastrous for the rule of law, for it would be open to the state or a public authority to act with impunity...".[5] Similarly with private wrongs, especially if the landlord, employer or money-lender has legal help. Furthermore, access to justice underpins the legitimacy of the state. Not only does it demonstrate a state's concern for the individual's plight but it can act as a channel for frustration and serve to dampen conflict. Finally, there is the important point that economic development might actually reduce access to justice to the less well-off. As Barry Metzger has put it:

> The price of legal services has been bid up substantially as a result of the increased demand by government and upper income groups. The legal profession tends to gravitate toward the most lucrative work – in a developing society, the rapidly growing commercial work – with a resultant decrease in legal services available for purchase at the lower margin. The extent to which economic development results in a contraction of services at the lower margin depends upon the ease and rapidity of entrance into the legal profession.[6]

Economic access to justice has a quite different basis. In broad terms it is founded on the notion of "improving the efficacy or competence of judicial systems to reduce the costs of economic transactions".[7] It is part of a favourable investment environment and is thus premised on the assumption that economic development has an important legal component. While this is problematic as a universal truth, in particular cases a causal link between legal innovation and development can be identified.[8] Delays encountered in litigation before the courts of the region create one of the barriers to economic access. In 1987 the Supreme Court of India noted that even if no new cases were subsequently filed,

---

4 For one western analysis see Ross Cranston, *Legal Foundations of the Welfare State* (London: 1985) p51ff.
5 S.P. Gupta v Union of India, AIR 1982 SC 149, 190.
6 Barry Metzger 'Legal services to the poor and national development objectives', in *Committee on Legal Services to the Poor in Developing Countries, Legal Aid and World Poverty* (New York: International Legal Centre, 1974) p9.
7 World Bank, *Governance and Development* (Washington: 1992) p32.
8 P. von Mehren and T. Sawers, 'Revitalizing the law and development movement: a case study of title in Thailand' Harvard Int.L.J. Vol. 33 (1992) p67.
9 P. N. Kumar v Municipal Corporation of Delhi (1987) 4 SCC 609, 610.

it would take 15 years to dispose of all pending cases.[9] In 1993 it was taking between 12 and 15 years for a case to be tried before the Bombay High Court, with an additional period of 10 to 12 years before all appeals would be exhausted. Few countries can match India in the size of the problem, although it would be wrong to think it was unique.[10]

The reasons for the crisis in access to justice in the region are not central to our concerns. Instead we will concentrate on the governmental measures taken to foster access to justice. The paper will focus largely on the Indian sub-continent, with references to Malaysia and Indonesia, hereafter referred to as the region. Given the enormity and diversity of the region, the paucity of information about some jurisdictions and my lack of familiarity, this paper will merely provide a sketch of the issues involved.

SOCIAL ACCESS

Mirroring the waves to promote access to justice in developed countries is a comparable emphasis on legal aid, public interest actions and innovative court structures. However, because law and legal institutions are moulded by their economic and social context, facilitating social access to justice in these ways often has a different character in different jurisdictions. As in countries outside the region, there has also been a move to encourage the extra-judicial settlement of disputes, although alternative dispute resolution (ADR) takes a particular turn when it draws on traditional institutions. The following discussion focuses on these selective areas.

Yet this is far from being the complete story of social access to justice. The nature and operation of the legal profession, which can block access to justice is another issue. The profession does this if lawyers do not think the poor have many legal problems, if they are geographically concentrated in the major cities, have commercial (rather than individual) clients, and require a down-payment on fees before taking action.[11] The Indian Law Commission has said that the profession itself has an obligation to ensure equal access to justice for all.[12] Para-legals might in some respects compensate for these professional impediments:

---

10 See, for example, F. Morgan, 'Country Report for Indonesia' in 'Symposium on Legal Issues in Debt Recovery, Credit and Security' (Manila, 1993, unpublished) p180; 'National Center for State Courts, Report to the Asia Foundation on trip to the Philippines ...', (Williamsburg: 1989) p3.
11 See K. G. Machado and Rahim Said, 'The Malaysian legal profession in transition', in Dias, C.J. et al., *Lawyers in the Third World: Comparative and Developmental Perspectives* (Uppsala, 1981) pp256, 260, 262.
12 Law Commission of India, 'One Hundred and Thirty-First Report on Role of the Legal Profession in the Administration of Justice' (Delhi, 1988) pp13, 20.

Malaysia has its petition writers, India its pleaders and Indonesia its 'pokrol bambu'; all make the law more comprehensible and accessible to the less well-off, although not all provide the degree of competence expected of lawyers.[13]

Legal aid: individual and structural

Typically legal aid has a dual character: it can be individually based, but it can also be structural.[14] The former tends to be the norm: civil legal aid is given to individuals by way of advice, assistance or representation for family matters, disputes over property (especially housing), accident compensation claims and the like. The focus is on assisting poorer individuals to cope with routine legal problems through lawyers acting in the ordinary way as advisers and advocates. While essential, individually based legal aid relies on lawyer expertise at the expense of client empowerment. Moreover it also has the disadvantage that:

> ... usually the legal service ends when the client's rights are successfully asserted in the court following which neither the lawyer nor the court takes any steps to prevent the same wrong from being committed against other members of the community.[15]

Structural legal aid envisages using legal services to assist groups as well as individuals in the pursuit of legal rights and social change. A solution is sought to a structure or practice which causes individual injustice. Human rights issues are high on the agenda. Particular cases are conceived of as test cases; law is seen as a resource for applying pressure, especially when political institutions are unresponsive; and even if cases are unsuccessful in a legal sense they might work as part of a total strategy of publicizing an abuse and educating the populace. Structural legal aid also encompasses the education and mobilization of those who are the victims of a particular injustice.

Individually-based legal aid schemes operate throughout the region, run both by the state but also on a voluntary basis by bar councils, law faculties and social and religious groups. Everywhere, state legal aid schemes are under fiscal pressure; this is also the case in the region. Even in a wealthy country such as Singapore the focus on national economic growth has been at the expense of legal aid. The official legal aid scheme has been underfunded, it has lacked

---

13 See K.G. Machado & Rahim Said, op.cit., pp262-3; C. Morrison, 'Clerks and clients: paraprofessional roles and cultural identities in Indian litigation' in Law & Soc. R. 1 Vol. 9 (1974); D. Lev, 'Bush-lawyers in Indonesia' in Y. Ghai, et al., *The Political Economy of Law* (Delhi: 1987).

14 The distinction is widely recognised, if not exactly in these terms. See, for example, M. Cappelletti, J. Gordley & E. Johnson, *Toward Equal Justice: A Comparative Study of Legal Aid in Modern Societies*, (Milan: 1975) pp.85, 109; M. Galanter, *Law and Society in Modern India* (New Delhi: Oxford University Press, 1989) p287.

15 A Valera, et al., 'An integrated approach in providing legal services to the rural poor and other disadvantaged groups' in International Commission of Jurists, Report of Seminars on Legal Services for the Rural Poor and other Disadvantaged Groups (Geneva: 1988) p47.

publicity, and scant attention has been given to innovations in other comparable jurisdictions in matters such as the range of provision and the mode of delivery.[16]

Take India as another example. An obligation to provide legal aid is one of the Directive Principles of the Indian Constitution (Article 39A), which the Supreme Court has interpreted as being addressed primarily to the legislature and executive.[17] The legal aid movement in India can be traced back to Bombay Legal Aid Society, which has operated since 1925. As in many countries, however, there is a gap in India between aspiration and reality. That is not through any absence of thought about the matter: in 1949 committees in both Bombay and West Bengal were appointed to report on legal aid; in 1957 a law ministers' conference concluded that each state should formulate a scheme for legal aid; the fourteenth report of the Law Commission recommended the immediate provision of legal aid to the poor; an expert committee on legal aid under Mr Justice Krishna Iyer reported in 1973; the constitution was amended in 1976 by the insertion of Article 39A; and the Bhagwati Committee's Report on *National Judicare; Equal Justice – Social Justice* was published in 1977.[18] Indeed the Committee for Implementing Legal Aid Scheme, constituted in 1980, has achieved much, for example, a model legal aid scheme adopted by almost all jurisdictions, para-legal training, grants in aid to particular legal aid programmes and legal aid teaching materials.

Yet the funds allocated have been inadequate; when allocated they have been under-utilized; and until a decade ago the supply for this need was minuscule.[19] The Legal Services Authorities Act 1987 provides for a comprehensive, nation-wide scheme of publicly funded legal services, but it has not yet been brought into force. Objections were raised that it eroded the autonomy of the judiciary and that the boundaries between the executive and judiciary were not clear. Successive governments have sought to amend it, but since legal aid has a low priority on the national agenda these attempts have so far come to nothing.[20]

Structural legal aid in the region has had some noticeable, if isolated, successes. Proponents include the Indonesian Legal Aid Foundation, the Free Legal Assistance Group in the Philippines, the Union of Civil Liberties in

16 H.Y. Yeo, 'Assessing the state of civil legal aid in Singapore' International and Comparative Law Quarterly Vol. 41 (1992) p875.
17 Rajan Dwivedi v UOI, AIR 1983 SC 624.
18 See also S. Sharma, *Legal Aid to the Poor*, (New Delhi, 1993); L. Singhvi & D. Friedman, 'Free legal services in Delhi and Bombay, India' in *Legal Aid and World Poverty*, (New York, 1974).
19 See the report on Himachal Pradesh in M. Chitkara & P. Mehta, *Law and the Poor*, (New Delhi, 1991) pp106-122.
20 I. Jaising, 'India's Legal Services Authorities Act 1987' in Legal Action Group, Shaping the Future. New Directions for Legal Services, Seminar 1 (unpublished, 1994); Rajeev Dhavan, 'Law as Struggle: Notes on Public Interest Law in India' (Madison, Wisconsin: Institute for Legal Studies, Working Paper,1993) pp37-9.

Thailand, and the legal resources centre of the Consumers' Association of Penang (Malaysia). In India, the Supreme Court has recognised structural legal aid by holding that Article 39A of the Constitution obliges a state to encourage and support social action groups in their legal aid programmes.[21] Structural legal aid is also recognised in the as yet unproclaimed Legal Services Authorities Act 1987: the National Legal Services Authority must, among other things, support public interest litigation with regard to consumer protection, environmental protection or other matters of special concern to the weaker sections of society. A number of social action groups have been responsible for the public interest litigation already instituted before Indian courts.

Some of the legal aid organizations in Indonesia have been notable for their structural approach . To an extent they are moulded by their history. Concrete steps to establish legal aid organizations began in 1967-1968 as a reaction to a wave of preventive detentions and arrests; thus the movement for structural legal aid in Indonesia grew out of a struggle for constitutionalism and the rule of law.[22] Later on the process of implementing the national plan of development brought about the forcible eviction of people from their homes with building works and this led to a legal reaction which had to be attuned to the political and economic context. A national legal aid workshop agreed in 1980 that 'conscientisiasation' – making people aware of their rights – should be the aim of structural legal aid which, accompanied by organizational efforts, would gradually change the unjust social structure. Daniel Lev has described the approach in his excellent account of the legal aid movement in Indonesia:

> If the disabilities of the majority poor were understood to result from social and economic inequality, protected by an authoritarian and repressive state, legal aid narrowly conceived was obviously inadequate. Even in legal terms it was limited by bureaucratic and judicial corruption, inefficiency, and lack of independence – and, further, by the reality that neither state nor society took law and legal process all that seriously. In these circumstances, offering nothing more than legal counsel to the needy was hopelessly beside the point. It might even lend legitimacy to the political order that sustained the conditions of the poor.[23]

Not surprisingly, the Indonesian government has criticized structural legal aid as 'politicization' and has sought alternatively to confine it to individual service provision, co-opt it and also to prohibit it. The Government has denied legal aid workers permission to engage in relevant research, and district heads around Jakarta have refused to allow legal aid posts to be established.[24]

---

21 Centre for Legal Research v State of Kerala, AIR 1986 SC 2195.
22 B. Nasution, 'The legal aid movement in Indonesia: towards the implementation of the structural legal aid concept' in H. Scoble & L. Wiseberg, *Access to Justice* (London: 1985) p34.
23 D. Lev, *Legal Aid in Indonesia* (Melbourne: 1987) p20.
24 T. Mulya Lubis, 'Legal aid: some reflections' in H. Scoble & L. Wiseberg, op. cit., p44. See also D. Lev, *Lawyers as Outsiders: Advocacy versus the State in Indonesia* (London: 1992) pp31-32.

There are many obstacles to an adequate system of legal aid in the region. Countries, especially developing countries, have many calls on national resources and in the main legal aid (indeed, the law generally) ranks low in the list of priorities. Even when resources are available these might not be effectively employed because of ignorance within the community or poor infrastructure for delivery of the service.

Government-organized legal aid has been perceived, at certain times and in certain places, as a 'gimmick of the government'.[25] (Legal aid channelled through voluntary groups, bar associations and law schools does not have the same complexion.) If legal aid goes beyond its traditional confines of being orientated to the individual, to challenge the societal framework, government opposition is likely. As a Filipino legal aid lawyer puts it: "To talk of human rights, or structural change, will already raise eyebrows, and might be construed as subversive or seditious."[26] The experience of the Indonesian Legal Aid Foundation in this regard has already been referred to. In India, tax law has been used.[27] In Malaysia, lawyers of the Consumers' Association of Penang were fined for contempt of court when they criticized a Supreme Court decision made in the course of a campaign for enhancing tenant farmers' rights.[28] Writing in 1988, one commentator saw a variety of laws springing up all over Asia to threaten or impede the activities of rural-based and social action groups.[29]

Public interest litigation

One of the most dramatic examples of the courts themselves furthering social access is through public interest litigation. Public interest litigation provides collective access to justice: although it can indirectly protect individual interests, the focus is on seeking a remedy which can apply to all such cases of that wrongdoing. There are elements of collective access to justice in many countries in the region, in some instances statute based.[30] By common consent, public interest litigation in India is the most dramatic example; its procedural aspects

---

25 S. Sharma, op. cit., p80.
26 H. Soliman, 'A critical analysis of legal services for the rural poor and other disadvantaged groups' in International Commission of Jurists *Report of Seminars on Legal Services for the Rural Poor and Other Disadvantaged Groups* (Geneva: 1988) p47.
27 Rajeev Dhavan, op. cit., p41.
28 A. Harding, 'Public interest groups, public interest law and development in Malaysia' Third World Legal Studies Vol. 231 (1992) pp232-3.
29 C. Dias, 'Obstacles to using law as a resource for the poor: the recapturing of law by the poor' in International Commission of Jurists, op. cit., p40. See also C. Dias, 'Problems and challenges faced by legal resource groups in south Asian region' Journal of Indian Law Institute Vol. 30 (1988) p63.
30 As well as references cited elsewhere in this chapter see D. Harland, 'Collective access to justice – some perspectives from Asia and the Pacific' in Chulalongkorn Law Review Vol. 6 (1989-1990) p126.

are the focus of the following discussion.[31] Procedurally, Indian public interest litigation represents a dramatic break with traditional common law model although in broad terms it can be thought of as the Indian equivalent to the class action or multi-party suit. In terms of access to justice it can be initiated by a simple letter addressed to the court, rather than by filing a written plaint; hence the term the 'epistolary jurisdiction'. Public interest litigation has swept away the doctrine of standing, which demands that a litigant have a direct interest in the proceedings being instituted. Any member of the public who is not a "busybody" is able to assert "diffuse, collective and meta-individual rights" such as that to a healthy environment.[32] Petitioners are permitted to represent those who are not free to approach the court directly "by reason of poverty, helplessness or disability or socially or economically disadvantaged position".[33] Public interest groups, academics and journalists have been among the petitioners recognised by the court.[34]

A third procedural innovation has been in the conduct and outcome of litigation. The Supreme Court has emphasized the need to depart from an adversarial procedure "which will make it possible for the poor and weak to bring the necessary material before the Court for the purpose of securing enforcement of their fundamental rights".[35] Special commissions have been appointed by the court to collect and determine facts and to propose and monitor remedies.[36] Interim remedies have been granted pending a decision on the factual and legal issues. Final remedies have been in the nature of legislative instruments with detailed proscriptions and penalties.[37]

Public interest litigation in India has not been without its critics. While the Supreme Court has acknowledged the need for judicial deference to executive and parliamentary government, its orders have sometimes demanded a reallocation

---

31 Substantively there must be a violation of a fundamental right, since public interest litigation (PIL) is founded in the constitution. There is a great deal of writing about Indian PIL. for example G. Peiris, 'Public interest litigation in the Indian subcontinent: current dimensions' in International and Comparative Law Quarterly Vol. 40(1991) p66; Rajeev Dhavan, op. cit., pp14-22; S. Sorabjee, 'Obliging government to control itself: recent developments in Indian administrative law' in Public Law (1994) p39; K. Bhatia, *Judicial Activism and Social Change* (New Delhi: 1990); C.D. Cunningham, 'Public interest litigation in Indian Supreme Courts: a study in the light of American experience' in Journal of Indian Law Institte Vol. 29 (1987) p494. (I am grateful to my colleague Dr. Werner Menski for his assistance on this.)
32 S. P. Gupta v Union of India, AIR 1982 SC 149, 192.
33 ibid.; Forward Construction Company v Prabahat Mandal, AIR 1986 SC 391, 393.
34 For example, Upendra Baxi v State of UP (1983) 2 SCC 308; Sheela Barse v. State of Maharashtra, AIR 1983 SC 378. See Mool Chand Sharma, 'Court as an Institution for the Delivery of Socio-Economic Justice in India' in Ram Autar Sharma (ed.), *Justice and Social Order in India* (New Delhi: 1984) pp37-8.
35 Bandhua Mukti Morcha v Union of India, AIR 1984 SC 802, 815.
36 For example, M. C. Mehta v Union of India, AIR 1987 SC 965 (the Sri Ram Fertilizers Gas Leak case); Olga Tellis v Bombay Municipal Corp., AIR 1986 SC 180 (the Bombay Pavement Dwellers case); Vishal Jeet v Union of India, AIR 1990 SC 1412.
37 Lakshmi Kant Pandey v Union of India, AIR 1984 SC 469.

of budgetary priorities.[38] Critics have contended that the Supreme Court lacks jurisdiction to frame such orders, indeed that in doing so the court impermissibly trenches on the role of government.[39] On the other hand public interest lawyers have criticized the delay in getting cases on and the dismissive way that some judges have handled matters when they have reached the top of the queue. Even when successful, public interest lawyers point to the barriers placed in the way of implementing the resulting orders.[40] However, from the outside whatever its practical limitations in particular cases, public interest litigation seems to have raised the profile of the importance of access to justice for the general population.

Informal justice

Informal justice, that is justice removed from the panpoly of state courts and similar dispute-resolving mechanisms, exists in all societies. It can constitute both unofficial and state law. Unofficial law ranges from the folk law of, say, an Indonesian village;[41] through the caste ('jati') panchayats of India, which might have considerable territorial scope;[42] to the rules and sanctions operated by the trade associations or chambers of commerce. Unofficial law facilitates access to justice. As Reginald Green notes, depending on the power configurations, folk law might be much more user-friendly and accessible than the official machinery of justice, which is light years away from the experiences of ordinary people.[43]

State-sponsored informal justice has obvious attractions to policymakers: relative cheapness; wide geographic dispersal, and a lack of technicality in the procedures and orders. However, access to justice pursued through more informal settings than the courts throws up immediate problems. What is the relationship with the formal system, and to what extent is it a mask for an extension of state or other power? How informal is the informal system and is the informality a trap for the citizen who finds that more assistance is required than anticipated? Does informal justice compromise the individual's rights either because it is inferior in quality or because the nature of its decision-making overrides legal rights?[44]

---

38 For example, State of Himachal Pradesh v V. R. Sharma, AIR 1986 SC 847.

39 See, for example, Bakhshish Singh, 'Law in India and Weaker Sections – A Judicial Perspective' in Ram Autar Sharma (ed.), op. cit.

40 Madu Kishmar, 'Public interest litigation' in Manushi no.81 (March-April 1994) p11.

41 K. von Benda-Beckmann, *The Broken Stairways to Consensus* (Dordrecht: 1984).

42 U. Baxi, 'People's law in India – the Hindu society' in Masaji Chiba, *Asian Indigenous Law* (London: 1986) p235ff.

43 Reginald Green, 'Bureaucracy and law and order have something to be said about and for them', infra, Julio Faundez (ed.) *Law and good government* (Macmillan, 1996) p?? As Green recognises, folk law might also be an instrument of oppression.

44 For example, R. Abel, 'The contradictions of informal justice' in R. Abel (ed.), *The Politics of Informal Justice* (New York: 1982); H. Genn, 'Tribunals and informal justice' Modern Law Review Vol. 56 (1993) p393.

There are many examples of state-sponsored informal justice in the region. Let us briefly examine one jurisdiction, India. There the British formed panchayats as units of local government and as simple judicial tribunals. Development varied between provinces and overall did not fulfil expectations. However, in some places the panchayats handled considerable volumes of civil disputes.[45] For this reason some writers have said they were based on traditional dispute-resolving mechanisms by village elders. Article 40 of the Indian Constitution obliges the states to organize village panchayats and in the immediate post-Independence period there was a great burst of activity. However, factionalism and corruption led to a significant loss of faith in the panchayats as organs of local government, but the Seventy-Third Amendment to the constitution in 1992 has led to a revival in their fortunes.

In the post-Independence period nyaya panchayats were constituted as distinct bodies on the judicial side as a consequence of the separation of powers demanded by Article 50 of the new Constitution. Nyaya panchayats were established for a group of villages, were staffed by lay elected members, adopted an informal procedure and forbade legal representation (although in civil matters representation by an agent was sometimes permitted). Like the courts, fees were imposed (albeit minor) and execution could be levied. The volume of cases was considerable and there were delays. Poor resourcing was at the root of many of the nyaya panchayats' problems. Despite support for them in the Bhagwati Committee's Report on *National Judicare: Equal Justice – Social Justice* (1977), states in which they were established gradually wound them up.[46]

Yet the pressure on the formal court system in India has demanded a functional equivalent to the nyaya panchayats. One informal mechanism has been the Lok Adalat (people's court). Lok Adalats have been operating in some areas over a long period: for example between 1949 and 1971, the Lok Adalat at Rangpur settled some 17,156 disputes, of which 10,165 involved family matters.[47] In his fascinating accounts of the Rangpur Lok Adalat, Upendra Baxi describes its considerable caseload and the wide, popular support it enjoyed. He also outlines its multifunctional character: in addition to conflict management it acted as an ombudsman, performed invigilatory functions with regard to the behaviour of public officials, provided a focal point for mobilization against injustice, assisted people to prepare representations to, and obtain benefits from,

45 H. Tinker, *Foundations of Local Self-government in India, Pakistan and Burma*(London: 1954) p197 ff.
46 P. C. Mathur, 'Re-modelling Panchayati Raj institutions in India', in R. B. Jain (ed.), *Panchayati Raj* (New Delhi: 1981) p178. See generally, U. Baxi, 'Nyaya Panchayats: experimentation in legal access for village population' in U. Baxi, *The Crisis of the Indian Legal System* (New Delhi: 1982). (This paper, written with Marc Galanter, has appeared in various other collections.) Cf. Bangladesh's Village Courts Ordinance, Ord. LXI of 1976.
47 U. Baxi, 'From Takrar to Karar: the lok adalat at Rangpur – a preliminary study' J. Const'l. & Parl. Studies Vol. 10 (1976) p52.

the authorities, guided people with regard to their rights over land and revenue records and performed a record-keeping role.[48]

More recently the establishment of Lok Adalats has been fostered by bodies such as the Committee for Implementing Legal Aid Schemes (which is chaired by a sitting judge of the Supreme Court). The Lok Adalats, ordinarily comprising a retired judge, a lawyer and a social worker, mediate disputes in a non-technical manner. If there is no settlement, cases can revert to the formal system. The Lok Adalats have generally been organized by state or district legal aid or advice committees. Mr Justice A M Ahmadi describes their role as follows:

> The date and place of holding a Lok Adalat are fixed about a month or so in advance. The date so fixed is, generally, a Saturday or a Sunday or some other holiday so that normal court work is not disrupted. Information about the holding of a Lok Adalat is given wide publicity through press, posters and, where possible, through radio, TV and cinema slides. Before a Lok Adalat is held, its organizers request the presiding officers of the various local courts to scrutinize cases pending in their courts which, in their opinion, are eminently fit for a negotiated settlement. Once the cases are identified, parties to the dispute are motivated by law students, para-legals and social workers to settle their disputes through Lok Adalats. By way of encouragement, the motivators are given transportation and other out of pocket expenses, food packets on the day of the Lok Adalat and also letters of appreciation but no remuneration, since the emphasis is on the system being service-oriented.[49]

As of 1992, the 5,634 Lok Adalats in operation had disposed of some 3.25 million cases over the previous decade. They have been most successful with motor accident claims, revenue matters and minor criminal matters, but less so with family disputes. Lok Adalats have also handled disputes consequential on economic change, for example land claims:

> In one Lok Adalat at Visakhapatnam, claims for additional compensation of about 25,000 villagers whose lands were acquired for a steel plant, were settled. Similarly, about 40,000 land acquisition cases arising out of three irrigation projects were settled in Andhra Pradesh recently. Claims of 9046 small cane growers and 1186 workmen of sick sugar factories taken over by the State Government were settled at a single Lok Adalat and payment to the tune of Rs. 12.33 million was made.[50]

The Lok Adalats are to be formally constituted under the Legal Services Authorities Act 1987 (not yet in force). Under the Act, each state must organize Lok Adalats, which will have jurisdiction to decide on a compromise in civil, criminal or revenue disputes. In any pending suit, the presiding officer may refer the case to the Lok Adalat for settlement if the parties make a joint application.

---

48 U. Baxi, 'Popular justice, participatory development and power politics: The Lok Adalat in turmoil' in A. Allott & G. Woodman (eds.), *People's Law and State Law* (1985) p184.

49 Mr. Justice A.M. Ahmadi, 'Arbitration and alternative forms of justice', <u>Indo-British Legal Forum</u>, Vol. 2 (London: 1992) p84.

50 ibid., p86.

The award of the Lok Adalat will operate as a decree if a settlement is arrived at after a joint reference. Whether the greater institutionalization envisaged by the Act will undercut the work of the Lok Adalats remains to be seen.

Alternative dispute resolution

Alternative (sometimes called 'appropriate') dispute resolution has been the flavour of the decade. If by ADR is meant 'alternative' to the courts, then this form of resolution has a considerable history. In the region, tribunals have long been established, even in colonial times, to handle industrial and labour matters. Arbitration also has a long pedigree, although it has been little used in some countries, being seen as western domination.[51] However, arbitration has become increasingly popular. Malaysia is one example. Here arbitration clauses are often inserted in insurance policies, building and construction contracts and joint venture agreements, although not in loan and credit agreements. Apart from the speedier resolution of disputes which arbitration might bring, the inclusion of arbitration clauses has been boosted by the establishment of the Regional Arbitration Centre in Malaysia.[52] Malaysia (and Singapore) has also legislated for a small claims court for matters such as defective goods, repayment of money lent and small debts. Legal representation is forbidden and costs cannot generally be awarded to a successful party (the normal rule in those jurisdictions).[53]

When ADR is discussed these days, however, mediation rather than tribunals or arbitration is taken as its archetypal form. In the region, mediation procedures have been recommended by the Law Commission of India and the High Court Arrears Committee and have been introduced in some parts of the country. The procedures have disposed of a significant number of cases, notably accident compensation claims.[54] There has been an attempt to use mediation in Malaysia and Indonesia. Perhaps the most concerted efforts have been in Sri Lanka, where mediation has been a prerequisite to litigation. In brief the Conciliation Boards Act No.10 of 1958 was intended for the amicable settlement of village disputes. Its main proponent, Neelan Tiruchelvam, summarized their purpose as follows:

> The willingness of the rural disputants to rush into the courts for even the most frivolous causes, and the corresponding inability of the court system to cope with the flood of litigation, bred public contempt for the judicial process. One way of protecting the courts from such pressures was to establish a screening mechanism

---

51 But the Indian Council of Arbitration was founded in 1965, jointly funded by the government and Federation of Indian Chambers of Commerce and Industry.
52 Chen Kah Leng, 'Country Report for Malaysia', *Symposium on Legal Issues in Debt Recovery, Credit and Security* (Manila: unpublished, 1993) pp31-2; Homayoon Arfazadeh, 'New perspectives in South East Asia and delocalised arbitration in Kuala Lumpur' Journal of International Arbitration Vol. 8 (1991) p102.
53 Ho Peng Kee, 'Small claims process: the Singapore experience' Civil Justice Quarterly Vol. 7 (1988) p329.
54 Mr. Justice A. M. Ahmadi, op.cit., pp88, 89-90, 104-7.

which would shut out those controversies amenable to amicable resolution. What
was uppermost in [his] mind was the need for an efficient conflict-resolving mechanism
to subdue the spirit of litigiousness which seemed to haunt the rural populace.[55]

The Conciliation Boards Act's success in the rural context meant it was
extended five years later to the island as a whole.[56] Unless a certificate was obtained
from the chair of the local conciliation board to say that there was no possibility
of a settlement, a court had no jurisdiction to entertain a matter. Membership of
the boards became political, the legal profession resented its exclusion from
them, and delays in the issue of certificates and the inappropriateness of some
disputes for conciliation led to the discrediting of the system.[57] Its eventual
abandonment came with a change in government. Soon after, however, a
prominent committee of judges and lawyers in Sri Lanka called for the
reintroduction of conciliation in a specified list of matters "to considerably
curtail the law's delays".[58] The Mediation Boards Act No. 72 of 1988 answers
that call: under it mediators consider certain criminal offences and civil disputes
(with some exceptions, for example if one of the parties is the state). Panels of
mediators have been appointed throughout Sri Lanka, many mediators have
received training and a considerable volume of disputes handled.

Yet mediation in the specific area of debt recovery has continued to operate
in Sri Lanka since the 1930s. Widespread distress caused to agriculturalists then
led to the establishment of the Debt Conciliation Board.[59] Debtors in difficulty can
apply to the Board to effect a settlement of debts owed. The legislation defines
'debtor' as a person who has created a mortgage or charge over immovable property
whose debts in respect of such property exceed the prescribed amount. As a result
of a legislative amendment a 'debtor' includes a transferee of a right of redemption
of a conditional transfer of land.[60] 'Debt' is defined to include all liabilities
owing to a creditor in cash or kind, secured or unsecured, whether mature or not.
Consequently, although the Board does not have general authority in the case of
debts which are not secured on immovable property, it can deal with applications
in respect of debts generally if incurred along with secured debts.

The procedure is that the Board ascertains whether it has jurisdiction, and if
so, notifies the Land Registry and the creditor. The position is then frozen until
the final hearing when the Board proposes a settlement, for example, repayment

55 N. Tiruchelvam, 'Competing ideologies of conflict resolution in Sri Lanka, a multi-religious society'
in Masaji Chiba, op.cit., p179.
56 cf. Bangladesh's Conciliation of Disputes (Municipal Areas) Ordinance No.V of 1969.
57 J. Canaga Retna, "The legal system of Sri Lanka", in K. Redden (ed.), Modern Legal Systems,
Buffalo, 1985, v.9, pp.770-771.
58 Seminar on the Administration of Justice, Colombo, 1984, p.21.
59 Debt Conciliation Ordinance, ch.91, s.19(i). A substantial increase in work after 1983 was due to a
propaganda campaign carried out with the help of the Agrarian Services Department to popularise the
activities of the Board at the rural level; most applicants appear to be farmers and agriculturalists.
60 s.64, as amended by Act No.20 of 1983.

by instalments, extension of repayment period, reduction of interest. In three-quarters of cases the parties accept the Board's settlement proposals. If a creditor refuses to accept the Board's proposals, the Board issues a certificate to the debtor. If the creditor then takes legal proceedings, the debtor can produce the certificate, and the court is then empowered to grant a period of up to ten years for the debtor to settle the debt, to reduce the interest, and to refuse the creditor any costs. The courts apply the Board's proposals in the great majority of cases.

There are serious limitations on the Board's jurisdiction. For example, it does not have any jurisdiction over government-sponsored banks or institutions operating as lending or financing agencies. The justification is that the law was enacted to protect debtors from unconscionable money lenders and state institutions are not in this category.[61] There seems no reason now to exclude any lending institutions from its remit. Moreover, there is the important limitation that there be a mortgage or conditional transfer of immoveables. The jurisdiction of the Board was set at a time when the problem of small debtors was confined largely to agriculturalists. Now, many consumer debtors incur financial difficulties in relation to moveables such as vehicles. There seems to be a strong argument that these, too, should be able to invoke the assistance of the Board.

An important argument in favour of ADR is that it reduces the costs and delays of court-based litigation.[62] ADR works more quickly and more cheaply, and if significant numbers of cases are diverted to ADR the courts ought to be able to process those remaining more quickly. Certainly in India, in relation to road traffic accident compensation, ADR appears to have had a positive effect. ADR might also widen access to justice: those who would probably never approach lawyers or the courts might be prepared to use ADR. The experience of mediation and debt conciliation in Sri Lanka seems to provide an example. Just what makes successful ADR, however, needs careful thought – the type of cases, at which point they should be mediated and whether, as in the Sri Lanka debt conciliation case, mediation should be backed by an adjudicative capacity.

ECONOMIC ACCESS

Economic access is designed to facilitate legal remedies for business. It has been prompted largely by the same barriers to access faced by individuals, although a concern with judicial hostility to business interests has also been articulated. At its core have been the problems faced by banks and other financial institutions

---

61 *Report of the Bank of Ceylon Commission*, Session Paper No. xxvii, 1968, p36.
62 There is an enormous literature. Professor Frank Sander of Harvard Law School has been a leading proponent. For example, F. Sander, 'Alternative dispute resolution in the United States: an overview' in *Justice for a Generation* (St. Paul, Minn.: 1985).

in having credit repaid. With so many bad loans on their books a cloud has hung over the solvency of many banks in the region. The rationale for speedy debt recovery has been stated by the Sri Lankan Supreme Court:

> Expeditious debt recovery is, in the long term, beneficial to borrowers in general for at least two reasons. Firstly, expeditious repayment or recovery of debts enhances the ability of lending institutions to lend to other borrowers. Secondly, the Law's delays in respect of debt recovery, howsoever and by whomsoever caused, tend to make lending institutions much more cautious and slow in lending; by refusing some applications, by requiring higher security from some borrowers, and by insisting on more stringent terms as to interest from other borrowers. Expeditious debt recovery will thus tend to make credit available more readily and on easier terms, and will maximize the flow of money into the economy. Undoubtedly, there is a legitimate national interest in expediting the recovery of debts by lending institutions engaged in the business of providing credit, and thereby stimulating the national economy and national development.[63]

We will now examine two aspects of how states in the region have furthered economic access. The first is relatively straightforward, the establishment of special courts. The second is in its infancy and involves state sanctioning of self-help by banks and other financial institutions to recover against the security (collateral) they have taken from borrowers for the credit advanced.

Special debt recovery courts

India has now followed Pakistan and Bangladesh in constituting special debt recovery courts. The courts are designed to further economic access. Their final adoption can be attributed in part to pressure from outside these countries, notably from the World Bank. These special courts enable claimants to bypass the great delays of the ordinary courts and they offer an expedited form of relief to those seeking the recovery of credit advanced. Economic justifications for these courts are to improve the balance sheets of local banks and financial institutions and to release unproductive financial assets for reinvestment. These courts are seen to create an environment more favourable to foreign investment.

The Indian debt recovery legislation of 1993 had a long gestation. Concern stretches back several decades over the infection of the portfolios of banks and other financial institutions by so-called sick industries. The Sick Industries Industrial Companies (Special Provisions) Act 1985 constituted the Board for Industrial and Financial Rehabilitation, was set up with the mandate of reviving sick industries. At the same time as recommending this legislation the Tiwari Committee spoke of the need for special courts to avoid the law's delays:

> Large amounts advanced by the banks and financial institutions to defaulting industrial units and other defaulting borrowers are locked up due to the delays under the existing legal procedure and process for recovery.

---

63 Supreme Court Special Determination No. 1/90, 4 January 1990.

The Civil Courts are burdened with diverse types of cases. Recovery of dues by the banks and financial institutions is not given any priority by the Civil Courts... The progress more often gets bogged down through interlocutory petitions and stay orders from higher courts. Due to the delays involved in such elaborate process the interests of the banks and financial institutions are very often adversely affected. Attempts will, therefore, have to be made to reduce the impact of the arduous procedures presently obtaining for the recovery of dues insofar as the banks and financial institutions are concerned...

In the light of what is stated above, it is recommended that the Central Government may set up a class of tribunals which would in a summary way but following the principles of natural justice, adjudicate finally, within a time-bound schedule, all matters in relation to recovery of dues of the banks and financial institutions. These tribunals should be manned by persons having specialized knowledge in the functioning of banks, financial institutions and industry.[64]

Draft legislation was prepared by the Vesuvalla Committee in 1986, further impetus was given by the Narasimham and Hedge Committees, and finally the legislation was adopted in 1993.

The Recovery of Debts Due to Banks and Financial Institutions Act 1993 – to give it its full title – constitutes special tribunals with the sole jurisdiction over all actions to recover debts due to banks and financial institutions. Cases of this nature pending before the ordinary courts, of which there are believed to be some ten million, are to be transferred to the tribunals.[65] Presided over by lawyers, the tribunals can make a determination by expedited procedure that a debt is owing. Thereupon the recovery officers appointed under the Act are empowered to attach and sell any property of the debtor, to arrest and detain debtors and to appoint receivers over a debtor's property (pending sale).[66] Appeals to a special appellate tribunal are possible and constitutionally it is not possible to exclude judicial review by the High Courts. Implementation of the legislation has been delayed by what appears to be a constitutional challenge.

Pakistan and Bangladesh already have special debt recovery courts operating. The Pakistani legislation on one report seems to have been successful.[67] There are apparently technical problems with the Bangladeshi court.[68] In Sri Lanka the Presidential Banking Commission has recommended a new commercial court which would have jurisdiction over matters of a commercial nature and over actions under the debt recovery laws.[69] This is a half-way house to a special court.

---

64 *Report of the Committee to Examine the Legal and other Difficulties Faced by Banks and Financial Institutions in Rehabilitation of Sick Industrial Undertakings* (Bombay: 1984) pp77, 79.
65 s.31; V. Shroff, 'The Indian Debt Recovery Act' Journal of International Banking Law Vol. 1 (1995) p29.
66 s.25.
67 K. Kabraji, 'Country Report on Pakistan', *Symposium on Debt Recovery in Asia and the Pacific* (Manila: unpublished, 1993) pp70-74.
68 A. Husain, 'Country Report on Bangladesh', ibid., unpublished, pp.28-29.
69 *Third Interim Report of the Presidential Commission on Finance and Banking on Debt Recovery Legislation* (Colombo: 1992) pp24-5. This recommendation has a long history. In 1985 the Debt Recovery Committee recommended the establishment of a separate District Court in Colombo to be

Clearly, then, special courts facilitate access to justice. They might also have had an important psychological effect on borrowers, inducing the recalcitrant to repay more diligently. However, in considering whether they contribute to good government we must start with the proposition that there is nothing objectionable to special courts or special lists *per se*. They have been established in many jurisdictions for many purposes. Such arrangements permit specialization by judges, promote greater consistency and expertise of decision-making in particular areas, allow more authoritative decisions on certain questions of law, and allow certain types of issues to be progressed with greater speed. The decision to establish a special tribunal should turn on a detailed consideration of the benefits and costs. Special tribunals have costs, for example the extra resources needed to administer them. The major cost is that of equity – some litigants gain over others. Ought not the benefits gained, such as reduced delay for the cases handled, to accrue to other cases as well? Might not the establishment of special courts for powerful interests such as banks lessen the pressure which they would otherwise bring to bear on reform of the system as a whole? These issues would appear not to have been properly argued in relation to the establishment of special debt recovery courts in the sub-continent.

Self-help and security (collateral)

Professor Sally Falk Moore identifies three important qualities of self-help: it is undertaken in the name of right and is not simply for naked advantage; it is the intransigent side of conciliation, in that societies in which self-help is widely used normally have well-established conciliation procedures and ideological framework, and it will usually permit the mobilization of others in the individual's cause – thus she writes of the expansibility of certain disputes and the containment of others.[70] Moore reminds us that self-help is not unregulated by society. In many societies its use is sanctioned by the formal legal system, not least because it can facilitate access to justice which would otherwise be hampered by the delay or cost of invoking legal process.

In many cases, lenders will not advance credit without security (collateral), so that in the event of default they can recoup from the debtor's assets. Typically, security will be taken over a debtor's land (including the buildings on it, and any

---

designated the Commercial Credit Court. It would be available to approved credit agencies, and its procedures would enable recovery of debts within six months (*Report of the Committee appointed by the Hon. the Minister of Justice Dr. Nissanka Wijeyeratne*, 1985). The proposal attracted a great deal of opposition, especially from the bar. Subsequently, a special committee recommended the establishment of an additional court in Colombo to hear matters of a commercial nature: *Final Report of the Committee Appointed to Examine the Establishment of a Special Court for Commercial Matters* (Chairman: S.J. Kadirgamar Q.C.). The District Judge of Colombo would refer to that court all 'commercial' matters. Then after several other twists and turns – including pressure from the World Bank – the Presidential Banking Commission reported.

70 Sally Falk Moore, *Law as Process* (London: 1978) p.99.

plant and machinery) and over other business assets such as work in progress, stock in trade, receivables and intellectual property. A crucial issue is whether on default the law permits lenders to proceed against the assets over which security has been taken without having to obtain a court order. If lenders can resort to self-help in this way it short-circuits any delay and expense involved in litigation and also curtails the opportunities for the debtor who would wrongfully dissipate assets.

In the common law, self-help for creditors and others seeking money payments has always had a place although it has been more frowned on by civil law systems. Self-help in relation to security is the most important example. Common law courts have responded with varying degrees of enthusiasm to some of the self-help remedies and many have been diminished in scope by judicial attrition and legislative policy.[71] This has been the case in common law jurisdictions of the region in relation to security, it seems, because of a sympathy for debtors over creditors, but also because of a fear that self-help might not be socially containable.[72] The story is more conveniently told by illustrating the legal and social limitations on lenders exercising self-help against security.

Legal limitations on exercising security

A typical feature of common law mortgages over land is a power to sell without intervention of the court on default by the mortgagor. Yet India rejected this approach in its Transfer of Property Act 1882. Generally speaking to sell the property, or foreclose, a mortgagee must obtain a court decree.[73] Only in certain limited situations does a mortgagee have a power to sell the mortgaged property in default of payment of the mortgage money without the intervention of the court. The most important of these exceptions are: when the mortgagee is the government; where an English mortgage[74] is involved and the persons are not Hindus, Muslims, Buddhists or another gazetted sect; when the property is in Calcutta, Madras, Bombay or other such notified areas. The origin of the restriction on self-help by mortgagees derived from a concern to protect Indians from unscrupulous money-lenders who were the main purveyors of credit to non-Europeans at the time this law was enacted.[75]

---

71 R. Pennington, 'Receiverships and extrajudicial remedies', in Ross Cranston (ed.), *Banks and Remedies* (London: 1992) p101.
72 See Ross Cranston, 'Credit, security and debt recovery: law's role in Asia and the Pacific', U.St. Louis L.J. (1995).
73 s.67.
74 The legislation divides mortgages into simple mortgages, mortgages by conditional sale, usufructuary mortgages and English mortgages. See *Rashbehary Ghose on the Law of Mortgage*, 6th ed., (Calcutta: 1988) p293 ff.
75 "There are parts of India in which such a power would be abused by Native mortgagees...": W. Stokes, *The Anglo-Indian Codes*, Vol. 1 (Oxford: 1887) p733. See generally M. P. Jain, *Outlines of Indian Legal History* (Bombay: 1990) pp533-5.

Malaysia, too, has limited self-help for those taking security over land. Its National Land Code of 1965 sets out the procedures if chargees (mortgagees) wish to sell land in the event of a breach by a chargor of any agreement. On breach of an agreement, a chargee must serve a notice of default, and if this has not been remedied within the period specified (at least a month), the chargee may apply for an order for sale.[76] For land held under land office title, the chargee applies to the court, which must order the sale of the land unless it is satisfied of the existence of a cause to the contrary.[77] Despite these provisions, a decision in Malaysia in the 1980s extended the scope of self-help in relation to charges over land. In United Malayan Banking Corporation Berhad v. Official Receiver & Liquidator of Soon Hup Seng Sdn. Bhd. (in liquidation),[78] the bank had a first and second fixed charge on land with a shop to secure a loan to the borrower. The borrower also executed a floating charge, which gave the bank a power of attorney. The fixed charges were registered under both the National Land Code 1965 and the Companies Act 1965, and the debenture was registered under the latter. One effect of the decision is to give a bank in this situation, when it also has a floating charge, the power to sell the land without going to court, despite the provisions of the National Land Code.[79] The case attracted strong criticism for undermining the purposes of the National Land Code.

Social limits on exercising security

Even when the law on the books permits self-help by creditors holding security, impediments might operate in practice. The situation in South Asia in relation to hire purchase and a floating charge over a company's assets illustrates this.

Hire purchase was developed in England in the late nineteenth century as the preferred method of instalment credit. Its use spread to many other parts of the common law world such as India, Sri Lanka and Malaysia.[80] It became an especially popular method for financing the purchase of consumer goods, notably motor vehicles. A closely related legal technique is equipment leasing, which is widely used by businesses for acquiring equipment and machinery on credit in jurisdictions where lease payments are tax deductible.

---

76 s.254.
77 National Land code s.256 (3). For land office title or a related qualified title, the application is made to an official, who after holding an inquiry must order the sale unless satisfied of the existence of a cause to the contrary (s.263[1]).
78 Malaysian Law Journal Vol. 1 (1986) s.75.
79 Michael Lim, 'An ASEAN overview: Malaysia' in *Current Developments in International Banking and Corporate Financial Operations* (Singapore: 1989) pp389-397; J. Sihombing, *National Land Code*, 2nd ed., (Kuala Lumpur: 1992) pp546-551.
80 Hire Purchase Act 1982 (Sri Lanka); Hire Purchase Act 1967 (Malaysia). In India the Hire Purchase Act 1972 has not been brought into force, apparently because of opposition from the transport lobby: hire purchase (and lease) are regulated by the relevant agreement and common law, in particular, the rules about bailment in the Indian Contract Act.

Functionally, hire purchase and equipment leasing are a form of security. Legally, the goods are hired or leased for the period of the agreement, at an agreed rental. With hire purchase the agreement will give the hirer an option to purchase the goods at the end of the period. Because the bank, finance house or dealer hiring or leasing the goods remains the owner during the period of the agreement, there is no legal objection to it retaining the right to retake possession on breach of the agreement. The right of the owner to repossess the goods is restricted, however, by consumer protection provisions in some jurisdictions: for example, the owner cannot repossess without notice or after two successive defaults, or once the hirer has paid a certain percentage of the hire purchase price.[81] There are also the limits imposed by the general law on entering property to retake goods and on causing a breach of the peace.

Although hire purchase (and equipment leasing) permits self-help by repossession[82] there has been a considerable reluctance to use it in the Indian sub-continent. Those hiring or leasing goods tend not to repossess without first going to court. There might of course be a problem in repossessing property which has somehow become part of a factory, for example. With motor vehicles and other standalone property, however, the real obstacle seems to be the behaviour, or anticipated behaviour, of the debtor.[83] Not only might the debtor conceal or wrongfully dispose of the property, but any attempt at repossession might be physically resisted. Labour on the sub-continent is cheap so that it is relatively easy to have, say, a motor vehicle constantly attended by a driver or caretaker. There do not appear to be the same obstacles to repossession in Malaysia.

The floating charge is another creature of late nineteenth century English law. It is now recognised in the law of many countries as a flexible device whereby banks and other financial institutions can take security over a company's assets.[84] Unlike a fixed charge or mortgage, the floating charge does not attach to any particular property. Rather, it is a charge on the assets for the time being of a company, both present and future. The floating charge is appropriate in the case of the stock in trade or receivables of a company, which are changing from

---

81 For example, Hire Purchase Act 1967, s.16 (Malaysia); Hire Purchase Act 1982, s.20 (Sri Lanka) respectively. See Gan Ching Chuan & Nik Ramlah Mahmood, 'Two decades of the law relating to sale of goods, hire purchase and equipment leasing' in *Developments in Malaysian Law* (Kuala Lumpur: 1992) pp212, 217, 229.

82 Although there is some authority in India that this right to repossess can be effected only by court action, the better view is to the contrary provided this is done non-violently: see especially K.L. Johar & Co. v Deputy Commercial Tax Officer Coimbatore III AIR 1965 SC 1082. See also V. Kothari, *Lease Financing and Hire Purchase*, 2nd ed. (Nagpur: 1986) p182.

83 In Sri Lanka there has been the added problem that the Commissioner of Motor Vehicles has refused to register the bank or finance company as the absolute owner on repossession without the borrower having a right to object. This has defeated the object of repossession, to allow the lender to sell the vehicle quickly.

84 For example, Indian Companies Act 1956, s.124; A. Ramaiya, *Guide to the Companies Act*, 12th ed. (Agra: 1992) p641 ff; Companies Act 1965, s.108 (Malaysia); Companies Act 1982 (Sri Lanka), s.91.

time to time in the course of business. There is no reason that the agreement creating a floating charge should not provide for automatic crystallization into a fixed charge as soon as default occurs. The person in whose favour the floating charge is created may assume the power under the agreement to appoint a receiver to take over the business in the event of default. The receiver will have the power to run the business and to sell its assets so as to recoup the chargee. Legislation provides that a floating charge is void against the liquidator and any creditor of the company, unless it is registered with the registrar of companies within a certain number of days of its creation. (The company must still repay the money even if the charge is not registered.) The idea of the registration requirement is to give other company creditors notice that the assets have been charged.

A crucial point about floating charges is that the instrument can provide for the appointment of a receiver without resort to the court. Any prohibition on enforcing security by self-help does not apply in the case of floating charges. Yet the assumption among many banks and lawyers on the Indian sub-continent seems to be that to appoint a receiver, an application to the court is necessary. Even if this is not the case there is a marked reluctance to proceed without a court order because of the problems which might be encountered. A leading commercial lawyer writes of the situation in India:

> In an agreement of hypothecation of tangible moveable property (including raw materials, finished goods and goods in process), there is usually a specific power to take possession and to sell without intervention of court on the happening of certain events. Exercise of this power without court intervention is difficult in practice since goods are in the possession of the borrower and actual possession is first to be taken before the sale is effected. If possession is not given voluntarily, it is not otherwise lawful for the lender to forcibly assume possession despite existence of such a power in the document. There is a view that this may amount to breach of peace, wrongful entry, wrongful restraint, trespass etc., for which the borrower can file criminal proceedings against the bank. Even assuming the possession is taken, there is the further practical question of lawfully keeping possession of the goods within the borrower's premises pending realisations, short of removal and storage elsewhere. Frequently, hypothecated goods are not demarcated and taking possession by locking up the entire premises is also not feasible.[85]

Perhaps the greatest problem in India is the resistance which it is feared receivers would face from workers if they went into a business without a court order.

Reviving self-help
Furthering economic access to justice has led to a revival of the self-help idea. The Banking Laws Committee appointed by the Indian Government recommended that banks and public financing institutions should have the power to enforce security extra-judicially. Its argument was that the general law

---

85 C. Shroff, 'India Country Report', *Symposium on Legal Issues in Debt Recovery, Credit and Security* (Manila: unpublished, 1993) p29.

relating to real property security was developed at a time when unscrupulous money-lenders were the main suppliers of credit but that it had ceased to be appropriate when banks and other public finance institutions were providing credit for development purposes. Money-lenders were quite rightly prohibited from exercising the right of private sale without the intervention of the court, but the continuation of this restriction with reference to banks and other public financing institutions "affects adversely the flow of credit and encourages protracted and vexatious litigation which comes in the way of expeditious recovery...". The Committee concluded:

> The power of sale without the intervention of the court should be allowed to all banks and certain notified financing institutions and this should be available to them with reference to all types of advances other than those made against the security of agricultural land and should be available independent of the form of the mortgage in their favour.[86]

The Committee confined its recommendations to banks and certain financial institutions on grounds of simplicity, but also because it felt that these bodies could be trusted not to abuse the power. Borrowers should be given suitable notice before the secured party, entitled to sell the property without recourse to the court.

While nothing has been done in this regard in India, Sri Lanka has quite radically changed its laws with the Debt Recovery (Special Provisions) Act No.2 of 1990, which empowers banks to enforce security outside the courts. I have told the story of the background to the Act elsewhere.[87] As might be expected the Act did not transform practice overnight. One local commercial bank invoked the power immediately, but other local commercial banks, and certainly the foreign banks, were more hesitant. Possibly this was not without cause because there were early examples of the courts blocking enforcement by use of injunction. (Apparently, injunctions were issued on technical grounds, for example, that the interest statements proffered by lenders were not completely accurate.) Even with these hesitations and though not invoked by all banks, the Act's presence on the statute book seems to have had an important radiating effect on borrowers.

---

86 Indian Government Banking Laws Committee, 'Report on Real Property Security Law' (New Delhi: 1977) p34.

87 Ross Cranston, 'The transplant of commercial law: security law in Sri Lanka' Canadian Bus.L.J. Vol. 19 (1991) p296. The Act is mentioned in the World Bank document, *Governance and Development* (World Bank, 1992) p34 as establishing "a better balance between the rights and obligations of debtors and creditors".

CONCLUSIONS

Access to justice is one aspect of good governance. While many disputes in modern societies are resolved extra-judicially, courts and court-like bodies exercising state power must be there as a backstop when this does not occur. To varying extents courts also have the function of determining norms so that disputes can then be settled 'in the shadow of the law'. Further, rights proclaimed by modern states must ultimately be enforceable, in some cases through judicial mechanisms if they are not to be conceived of by the populace as illusory. So in various ways access to justice not only contributes to a peaceful society but to economic development and the rule of law.

Yet access to justice is a protean concept. Professor Lawrence Friedman has observed that when people talk about 'access to justice' they mean many different things, but "every discussion assumes a goal called 'justice', and assumes further that some group or person living in a society finds the door closed...".[88] This chapter has drawn an admittedly imprecise distinction between social and economic access. Both are necessary, it can be argued, to achieve the goals mentioned. In many societies the focus is quite rightly on social access, since the delays and expense of litigation are an obstacle to many individuals pursuing legal rights. Economic access has not been a pressing problem, since typically wealth and its correlates guarantee access to legal services and the courts. In the sub-continent of Asia and in parts of South-east Asia, however, both social and economic access have not been achieved. The delays have been so great in India, and the courts so discouraging, as in Indonesia, that even banks and financial institutions find the path to the courts barred.

This chapter sketches some dimensions of the response to these access to justice problems. The attempted solutions for social access will be familiar; less so the measures addressing blockages to economic access. Yet it has been on the latter that bodies such as the World Bank have focused in recent years, some would say at the expense of the total justice system and access for all.[89] The discussion in this chapter is by no means exhaustive of state measures addressing access to justice problems. For example, other public institutions such as ombudsmen can further access to justice: they can provide a relatively inexpensive remedy to individuals and groups not only in relation to public administration but also against banks, insurance companies and other financial institutions.

---

88 'Access to justice: social and historical context' in M. Cappelletti & J. Weisner (eds), *Access to Justice* Vol. 2 (Milan: 1978) pp3, 5.
89 P. McAuslan, 'Law, governance and the development of the market: practical problems and possible solutions', in Julio Faundez (ed.), *Good government and law* (Macmillan, 1996) chapter 1, pp.?? cf. for example, Ibraham Shihata, "Judicial reform in developing countries and the role of the World Bank' in *Inter-American Development Bank, Justice and Development in Latin America and the Caribbean* (Washington: 1993).

COMMENT

Maria Luiza Vianna Pessoa de Mendonca

Professor Cranston's paper offers an interesting and stimulating introduction to the issue of access to justice. In this short comment I will offer a brief outline of some aspects of the access to justice debate in Brazil today.

The reform of the judiciary is currently under discussion in the context of the wider national debate on constitutional reform. Judicial reform is an urgent and delicate political issue. There is broad agreement that the judiciary needs to become more efficient. However, the debate on how this should be achieved has only just begun. The urgency of this debate is underscored by recent public opinion surveys which have shown that the system of justice in Brazil does not enjoy the legitimacy it should have in a properly constituted democratic society. According to one such public opinion survey – conducted by JB-Vox Populi during the first semester of 1995 – only just over 25 per cent of the people in Brazil trust Brazilian justice. While the widespread popular distrust of the system of justice in Brazil cannot be blamed exclusively on the judiciary, its low public esteem is a matter of serious concern.

The Brazilian judiciary is plagued by problems which are familiar to other countries of the region: the shortage of personnel; their lack of adequate training, and the increasingly large workload of courts. The shortage of personnel stems largely from the difficulties involved in filling vacancies because of lack of suitable candidates. For example, statistics for the period 1991-1995 show that 40 per cent of the vacancies in the judiciary were not filled. The poor quality of many law courses is one reason for the poor performance of candidates for posts to the judiciary. There is also much room for improvement in the tests used to select personnel for the judiciary since these often concentrate on areas of knowledge and skills which are not directly relevant to the daily tasks of a judge.

The workload of courts is constantly increasing; as a consequence the backlog of cases now stands at a staggering figure of 50 million. This means that each Brazilian judge has a backlog of roughly 6,000 cases. It is not surprising that courts do not perform their tasks efficiently.

However, it would be misleading to assume that the shortcomings of the Brazilian judiciary are only related to lack of resources. The inefficiency of the system is related to the excessive formalism of legal procedures. Oral proceedings are rare. Moreover, although in theory there are only two judicial instances, in practice, the Superior Courts often act as a third instance, thus slowing down the judicial process and, indirectly, undermining the authority of lower courts.

Brazilian scholars studying Civil and Criminal Procedure are well aware of modern doctrinal and theoretical developments and these perspectives are reflected in the legislation enacted during the last twenty years. However, these theories and doctrines have not been fully implemented, thus increasing the gap between the law of the textbooks and reality. Until the legal profession, the government and the members of the judiciary make a determined effort to achieve meaningful change, the judiciary will continue to be held in low esteem. While additional resources will go a long way towards improving the role of the judiciary, the intellectual and practical challenges required to achieve meaningful changes must come from within. Computers and other forms of support offered by multilateral and bilateral donors are welcomed, but only if they are part of a broader strategy which is seriously designed to improve access to justice to all Brazilians, particularly to the very poor in the city and countryside. The current debate on Constitutional reform offers an invaluable opportunity to begin moving in the right direction.

11 Women, representation and good government: Perspectives on India and Chile

Shirin M. Rai

INTRODUCTION

Good government as a concept is taking root in the imaginations, discourses, and policies of world aid agencies. This has taken place in the period characterised by the crumbling polarities in the world political system as a consequence of the fall of the Soviet Union and the regimes of Eastern Europe. However, the idea seems, as yet, tentative and at times even confused. Democracy seems a key element in good government for example, but we are as yet unclear whether it is a precondition for good government, or whether good government is a consequence of democratic pluralism (Burnell, 1994). An engagement with democracy is incomplete without examining levels and forms of participation in politics, as well as the translation of participatory movements into institutions, organizations and practices of governance. In this context, accountability and consent are essential elements of good and therefore legitimate government (Fierlbeck, 1995).

The two elements of gender and good government that this paper will explore are the transparency and democracy of political institutions in the way that they address the issue of representation of women and their various interests, and the capacity of organizations, set up to translate the demands of the women's movements into policies, to do so in a way that will challenge the status quo. I will examine these two issues through two case studies – the National Commission for Women in India, and the Servicio Nacional de la Mujer (SERNAM – National Women's Office)[1] in Chile.

Both India and Chile are and have been strong multi-party political systems. There have been periods of dictatorship in both countries – in Chile during the Pinochet regime (1973-90) and in India for a much shorter period (1975-77) during the National Emergency declared by Mrs. Gandhi. However, political parties have continued to play an important role in articulating interests and representing these in the political sphere. Such strong party systems tend to

---

1 The material on SERNAM presented in this chapter has been taken from Ann Matear and Georgina Waylen's work on this organization.

marginalize issue-based politics, or to co-opt movements that are based on single issues. In both the countries the women's movements have had to confront this practice. The choice between retaining autonomy but being marginalized within the dominant political system, or being part of the mainstream political organizations but losing autonomy and risking expropriation is a painful but real one for most social movements. The dilemma this choice poses is a difficult one to resolve and the women's movements in both countries have struggled with it.

Another feature of this multi-party system is that while the parties have dominated politics, they have remained organizationally weak and dependent on local élites (Bjorkman, 1987; Faundez, 1988). As a result the parties have suffered because of their transparency when mediating their interests within the organizations, as well as reducing their capacity to implement policies. Local élites in both countries have been able to influence policy formulations and to subvert the implementation of policies adverse to their interests. These factors have affected the way women's issues have been addressed by the two states.

A discussion of the way in which the party systems have responded to the growing mobilization of women will allow us to examine the two central issues of transparency and capacity, in the context of good governance. I will argue that: the party-based institutional politics constrain women from organizing their own interests; social and political institutions can create choice barriers for women representatives; institutional politics (in this case the representation of interests via women-centred organizations) can form only one of the many strategies that women need to use in their struggle to see their interests represented and translated into policies.

WOMEN'S MOVEMENTS, AND WOMEN IN INSTITUTIONS: LESSONS FROM CHILE AND INDIA

Women have always been active in Indian and Chilean political life, although their visibility and autonomy have varied from one historical phase to another. Women have participated at all levels of public life, from local to national level, and have engaged in struggles both non-violent and violent (Liddle and Joshi, 1986: 5). Once entering public life they have received acceptance because of the iconography of motherhood– Bharat Mata in India and Madres in Chile – and because their participation in all forms of public life, from social services for people with disabilities or the under-privileged to more conventional political activism, has been described as a 'woman's role' and somehow in tune with their maternal character. However, the number of women taking a public role has been minimal. Gender has not been the only variable affecting women's participation in politics; their access to the public sphere has depended on many factors, class, religion, and caste being the most important. However, in no social category have women been more able to participate in political life than men. Further, participation in public life has not necessarily correlated with the representation of women by women in public institutions. While women have provided legitimacy to these movements and organizations, their gains have been less obvious.

Historical development

In both India and Chile women's movements have made significant gains through the 1970s and 1980s. With the growth of women's movements, issues of self-definition and long-term strategy have become important. One issue of self-definition hinges on the relationship between the women's movement and feminist discourses. Women activists and feminist theorists have not always had a comfortable relationship with each other in these countries. In an article called 'Why I do not call myself a Feminist', Madhu Kishwar wrote:

> The definitions, even the issues, the forms of struggle and institutions are exported from west to east, and too often we are expected to be the echo of what are assumed to be more advanced women's movements in the west. (*Manushi*, 1986; also Chuchryk, 1989)

Another element of discordance between women activists and feminist theorists and academics has been class. The feminist movement in Latin America, for example, has been characterized by the involvement of a large sector of the female middle class, disproportionately intellectuals (Vargas, 1993; Matear, 1995). Women's movements (and feminist discourses) have been linked to the project of modernism and modernisation which has had a particular but significant impact upon public policies and the institutions and political rhetoric of many Third World countries. One of the central modernist projects has been individuation in society, accompanied by a political rhetoric which has used the universalist language of equality and citizenship. This tension between individuation and universalism has been carried into the women's movement – they have fought for full citizenship rights, but have been seen as women with particular interests, thus weakening their clout and leading to a more ambivalent positioning of women in politics (Phillips, 1992; Rai, 1994).

In post-colonial India the women's movement developed in the 1960s and 1970s and spanned a whole range of issues – civil liberties, consumer action, corruption, and workplace rights. Most of the groups involved were urban-based, and their members were drawn from the educated middle class, and from the left of the political spectrum (Kumar, 1989). These groups differed on questions of strategy – some wanting to join the mainstream economic and political organizations such as trade unions and parties, others arguing for a more spontaneous position. The latter were the first feminist groups. These early women's organizations remained loosely aligned. A second wave of women's movement grew in the 1980s, again around specific socio-economic and political issues, from dowry murders, to police rape, to unionizing women workers, and establishing women's co-operatives to generate independent income for women. Throughout this period, feminist groups maintained a presence within the women's movement and they gradually developed links with each other, as well as with international feminist movements.

In Chile, the women's movement started on issues of civil and human rights in the 1970s. Women campaigned against the abuses of power by the military regime. The Agrupacion de Familiares de Detenidos y Desaparecidos (Association of Families of Detained-Disappeared Persons), as mothers and as the conscience-keepers of society, challenged and effectively subverted the gender roles for women that the military regime had promoted. As in India, the 1980s saw the rise of urban women's groups focusing on issues such as consumer rights, and welfare organization in poorer areas. This included communal soup pots (*ollas comunes*) as well as crafts workshops that helped women generate some income to support their families (Waylen, 1995; Matear, 1995). Simultaneously, feminist groups made up largely of left-wing, middle-class educated and often professional women campaigned for women's rights and equality. The Circulo de Estudios de la Mujer set up in 1977 is one example. These feminist groups have been able to organize and network not only within Chile but regionally more effectively than the Indian feminist groups, because of initiatives such as the setting up of the feminist umbrella group Mujer Por la Vida (Women for Life) in Chile, and the Feminist Encounters organized by various feminist groups in Latin America (Chuchryk, 1989 and Vargas, 1993). The sense of isolation was thus reduced for these women, though the divisions within the women's movement in Chile remain.

The feminist movements in Chile and India also gained from the international initiatives such as the UN Decade for Women which provided a focus for women's groups and prompted a response from national governments, and continuing programmes such as the World Conference on Women (Beijing, September 1995). Multi-lateral banks, bilateral aid agencies, and non-governmental organizations have since the 1980s also raised issues of gender in development programmes. Women's movements have at times been able to affect and use the changing perceptions of these agencies to their advantage.

Institutions and representation

While the women's movements in India and Chile have been active, this has not translated into a significant increase in the number of women representatives in political institutions. India is a bicameral parliamentary democracy. The lower house is called the Lok Sabha (People's Assembly) and the upper house Rajya Sabha (State Assembly). The government of independent India introduced universal adult franchise, and the right to stand for election in 1950. In 1984 (later figures not available at the time of going to press), 58.6 per cent of the voters turning out were women (DWCD, 1988: 54). In 1991, women formed 5.2 per cent of the membership of the Lok Sabha and 9.8 per cent of the membership of the Rajya Sabha (Swarup et al, 1994: 362). This was lower than the preceding parliament, formed in 1989. Considering women make up 50 per cent of the population their representation in parliament is grossly disproportionate. The women representatives in the Indian parliament are mostly middle-class, professional women, with few or no links with the women's movement. A significant number of them have accessed politics through family links, some through various student and civil rights movements, and some because of state initiatives in increasing representation from the lower castes (Rai, 1995). Chile is also a bicameral political system with a Senate and a Chamber of Deputies. Women won the right to vote in 1949 and have since voted on separate electoral registers. Women constituted only 5.8 per cent of the Diputados and 6.4 per cent of the Senators, and except for the director of SERNAM none has ministerial status (Matear, 1995: 6). There has been a marginal increase in the representation of women in the Senate and the Chamber of Deputies between 1990 and 1994 (Matear, 1995: 6) The Chilean political system, like the Indian one, is dominated by 'political families' and women in political life tend to be part of these families, reinforcing their élite status (Waylen, 1995).

While under-represented in national legislative assemblies, women's movements have succeeded in putting the 'woman question' on the political agenda of most political parties in both India and Chile. In both countries "gender has become politicized" (Alvarez, 1990). This has posed similar issues for the Chilean and Indian women's movement – choices between autonomy or marginalization, expropriation or isolation, and the possibility of constraining political argument within the intellectual parameters of political parties.

In both India and Chile the more radical women's groups that have effectively opposed the state over employment, the environment, and human rights, have been marginalized in institutional politics. Those women who have achieved limited success in this area are the middle-class feminist professionals and academics who have put forward demands of a 'strategic' nature – equality with men in work and political institutions. This selective inclusion has tended to maintain the existing divisions within the women's movement. This in turn has posed difficult questions relating to the representation of and by women between feminist professionals and activists, and between women members of different political parties.

Institutional politics and problems of integration

In both India and Chile the 'politicization of gender' has brought about state-led initiatives aimed specifically at women. The Indian political system is debating whether women should have quotas in political institutions. A provision has been made for women to have a 33 per cent quota at the village council (panchayat) level, but some women parliamentarians are arguing for such a quota at all levels of representative institutions (Rai, 1995). This has not yet been raised as an issue in the Chilean political system. However, both states have set up women-led institutions that have an input into governmental policy making. In India, the National Commission for Women was set up in 1990. A comparable institution was set up in the same year in Chile – Servicio Nacional de la Mujer (SERNAM).

Both institutions were created through legislation and include women who have been active in the women's movement or are 'committed to the cause of women' or both. In Chile the Chair of SERNAM is also in the Cabinet, but this is not the case in India. Both bodies have a consultative status and the National Commission for Women also has the powers of a civil court. Both are inadequately financed, resulting in their continued dependence on their respective national government with consequences for their political muscle as well as effectiveness.

The National Commission for Women in India is a cross-party consultative body on women's interests. Its functions include: investigating matters pertaining to legal safeguards provided for women and recommending to the Government measures for effective implementation; periodically reviewing existing legal provisions affecting women and recommending amendments; taking up with the appropriate authorities cases involving violation of the legal provisions relating to women; participating in the planning process of socio-economic development of women and evaluating the progress made. Within three years of its establishment, however, women's organizations on the left, and a member of the executive who is also a member of the Communist Party of India (Marxist), have distanced themselves from this organization because of its political agenda and the dominance of women from the ruling Congress Party.

The case of SERNAM in Chile shows similar issues at stake. SERNAM was established in 1988 as a result of pressure on centre and left political parties by the Concertacion de Mujeres por la Democracia (Women's Movement for Democracy) which was inspired by the Mujer Por la Vida (Women for Life) experiment to provide an umbrella organization for women's groups. As a result, the leading posts within SERNAM have been filled by members of the political parties that form the governmental coalition (Matear, 1995: 2). The Concertacion had three aims: to raise women's issues in the national political arena, to work in the presidential and parliamentary campaigns on its own behalf, and to formulate a programme on women for future democratic government. SERNAM was established to put the last of these aims into force by enforcing women's rights in view of their new role in society, overcoming any form of discrimination by proposing policy measures and overseeing their implementation (Waylen, 1995).

Due to the influence of right-wing parties, and the growing retrenchment of the social and educational programmes of the Catholic Church and its emphasis on evangelisation, SERNAM has been most effective on the least controversial social issues: women's training, poverty alleviation, and income generation. This success has added to the growing suspicion among the more radical feminist groups that SERNAM cannot be effective in the cause of women because it has been 'integrated' into the state structures. These groups have accused SERNAM of colluding in the individuation of the state's approach to the gender issue, diluting their collective struggle which might otherwise have had more power to challenge gender relations in society (Waylen, 1995).

By setting up women specific institutions in response to the strength of the women's movements, both the Indian and the Chilean states have marginalized certain important sectors of the women's movement. This in turn has led to scepticism about the effectiveness of these two bodies, undermining their legitimacy to reflect women's "strategic interests" (Molyneux, 1985).

REPRESENTATION AND ACCOUNTABILITY

A study of the National Commission for Women and SERNAM raises important questions for the women's movement, particularly concerning its demand to increase the levels of participation of women in politics. These questions are also important for the debate on good government because they affect both the transparency and capacity of institutions to deliver on gender issues. We have seen how the two organizations arose from the respective governments' response to the women's movements' concern over representation. We have also seen how the institutionalisation of gender interests resulted in the co-option of these agendas by the respective dominant political parties, circumscribing the role of the National Commission and SERNAM in their political spheres. These constraints have in turn led to a weakening of the legitimacy of these organizations, making them more dependant on the political system, and less able to challenge the status quo. In this context a difficult question arises: 'What value representation?' Given the class, education, and institutional constraints imposed by a system of representative politics, is there any point in focusing on political institutions as targets for empowering women? Is there not a danger that institutionalisation will lead to the expropriation of the women's movements, which will render the representation of women's interests through the political system meaningless? I will explore issues of representation to address these questions.

Interests and representation

Representation is an important issue for the articulation of interests in the public sphere. The construction of interests itself is, however, problematic. Despite the fact that women have long taken issue with the concept of 'women's interests' on grounds of class, race, and sexuality, it still has currency within feminist thinking. In their study of Women and Politics Worldwide (1994: 10-14) Chowdhary and Nelson isolate four areas of women's interests: violence, safety and security; reproductive rights, abortion, and maternal and child health; equalising strategies including improved access to education, employment, healthcare, credit and other resource opportunities; redefining the political and legal rules of the game through increased access to political institutions and legal initiatives. While these issues are important to women worldwide, policies arising from their debate are likely to vary enormously across cultures, nations and political systems, even if these were somehow controlled and carried out by women. The cohesion suggested by the initial formulation of 'women's interests' would then be greatly diluted.

The history of both national, political and social movements in India and Chile (and indeed other countries) would suggest that intersecting interests that are built around nationality, ethnicity, class or caste destabilize not only the concept of 'women's interests' but also that of representation. Are we to conclude from our critique of assumptions about 'women's interests' that the category is a false one? Feminists such as Braidotti have argued against taking such a position. Instead they emphasise the importance of constructing interests through a conscious attempt that would recognise at the same time an essential feature of women's existence – their marginality in the political sphere, together with the differences that disturb that unity. While alliances formed on the basis of this "essentialism with a difference" (Braidotti, 1989: 102) would allow for interest representation to be sensitive to issues of class, ethnicity and race among women, in itself it does not address the question of the parameters of the state institutions within which these interests are to be represented. To be able to 'play the state' from within and from the outside is what would allow us that empowering latitude. I will return to this strategic issue later in the chapter.

Representation of interests

The importance of increasing the representation of women in legislative bodies has long been recognised by feminists and others. The debates on 'women's interests' have not taken away from the issue of participation of women in representative politics of the democratic states. The fact that in both India and Chile women representatives make up less than seven per cent of the total is a cause for concern. However, representative correlation seems to imply that only women can represent 'women's interests'. In the English constitutional debates of the 18th and 19th centuries, for example, Burke advocated the idea of 'virtual representation' which emphasised that a person could represent a group if he (*sic*) was a typical member of the group, sharing its characteristics, even if he was not elected by it. Accountability was therefore less important than representation of interests by one of the group. This would make sense in the case of women's representatives too, if we do not argue for all women electorates for women representatives, or for Women's Parties. If women representatives are representing mixed constituencies then how are they to be held accountable to women, and women's interests? The articulation and representation of women's interests will have to be left to women representatives who choose to articulate and represent them, without holding them responsible in any way. If this was not acceptable, if accountability was deemed necessary, then women's electorates would have to be considered.

Group representation and interest formulation

The question of accountability and interest has been addressed in a less radical, more pragmatic way by Marion Iris Young's analysis of group representation. She argues that oppressed groups in society should have a guaranteed role in policy formation on the grounds that access to public life is very difficult for these groups. She wants to see group representation work at three different, connected levels. First, that groups meet as groups, supported by public resources. Without this coming together, group identity will not be a democratically achieved position. Second, policymakers must show that the views of the group have been taken into account in any policy that they formulate. This would ensure that the interests of an oppressed or under-represented group are routinely taken into account. An example of how this works is the way political parties in many European countries are having to explain policy agendas with reference to their impact on the environment. Third, Young argues that group representation should involve the group having a "veto power regarding specific policies that affect a group directly, for example, reproductive rights for women..." (Young, 1989: 262)

Phillips points out that this last provision will run into difficulty on the ground that, "None of the groups we might think of is homogenous, and each will contain within itself a wide variety of competing views." (Phillips, 1991: 77) However, does not the first condition that Young sets for group representation to work address the question of crafting a consensus majority view? The difficulty perhaps lies in the element of 'public provision'. If the system of group representation is to be 'added on' to a party-based system of individual representation, then the input of the ruling party becomes critical. In a context where the differences between the parties on the right and left are not great (arguably the US), and where the limited political spectrum provides groups with largely focused policy formulation, Young's strategy might work. However, as the example of the Indian National Commission for Women discussed below will show, it is not easy to set up an institution of consultation backed by public resources without party politics destabilizing the project.

Party institutions and general interests

An important response to the question of interest representation has been on the grounds of 'general interest' as opposed to particular group interest. In the English constitutional debates, both Burke on the right and James Mill on the radical wing of the House of Commons were opposed to representation based on group interests as they believed that the proper task of the assembly was to identify and express a single national interest (Bobbio, 1984: 51). The party system is based on this argument. Parties seek to represent cross-class, -caste, -gender interests, and the representative members of parties are accountable to their electorate in representing these general interests. If the parties take a stand on particular issues to do with ethnicity, religion, class or sexuality, the representatives will articulate the party position. Even then, the representatives seem to have some autonomy in how, and to what extent, they choose to articulate various issues. Local area concerns, while not the primary focus of the representatives' attentions, do also play an important role in destabilizing this 'national interest' agenda. Accountability in this context is weak and variable, as is representation. As far as the impact on women's lives is concerned, is such representation acceptable to feminists if it is to be in the interests of women?

A further question in the context of representative democracy is whether accountability is also undermined when representative institutions are bypassed by organized interest groups. In such cases, the legislative body, and therefore its representatives, do not necessarily mediate between decision-makers and pressure groups organized for change. So what value is increased numbers of women representatives and the principle of accountability?

'Maternalism' and good government?

Interest representation is not the only functional basis upon which to argue for increased representation for women. A significant number of feminists have claimed that women bring special qualities to public political life. These qualities are rooted in their experience of their sex – as women and more particularly as mothers (Diamond and Harstock, 1981). There are obvious problems with such an analysis. Firstly, it is based on 'essentializing' women – something that the women's movement has fought against for good reasons for a long time. Secondly, it allows conservative male political theorists and politicians to defer the matter of women's representation on grounds of 'female culture' – that women are not (because of their maternal/sensitive natures) suited to the hurly-burly of political life. Third, this claim of 'female culture' in public life also undermines the public nature of politics. As Dietz comments:

> In so far as it [a democratic vision] derives its meaning from the collective and public engagement of peers, it sees citizens neither as wary strangers (as the liberal marketplace would have it) nor as 'loving intimates' (as the maternalist family imagines)... What this aim requires is not only a feminist determination to avoid 'womanism' while remaining attentive to women but also a commitment to the activity of citizenship, which includes and requires the participation of men. (1992: 75, 78)

Justice and legitimacy

It seems that the various views on why women's representation is important share a common core: the question of social justice and the issue of representative institutions. If there are impediments placed in the way of women (or any other group) to participate in public life – whether institutionalised or not – then there is an issue of denial of justice that needs to be addressed. Equally important, if institutions are seeking legitimacy on grounds of their representative character, then the vast underrepresentation of women (and other) groups is unacceptable. What women do when they do gain entry to political life can then be regarded as an entirely separate question. Studies have shown that once in a party political system most women representatives behave much the same as their male colleagues. However, we also have to take into account that levels of women's representation in most countries are so low that we do not have the context in which a self-confident women's group in political life might be seen to act.

Given the domination of the party political system by representative democracies, and the issues raised about accountable representation of groups, is there any reason to study women's representation yet again? I answer this question in the affirmative.

Why do we need more women representatives?

While we cannot argue that more women in public office would mean a better deal for women in general, there are still important reasons for exploring the issue of women's representation in political life. First, is the intuitive one: the greater the number of women in public office, articulating interests, and seen to be wielding power, the more disrupted the gender hierarchy in public life could become. Because these women are mainly élite women their impact on public consciousness could be more significant, though particular, than the small number of representatives would suggest.

Second, and more important, we could explore the strategies that women employ to access the public sphere in the context of a patriarchal socio-political system. These women have been successful in subverting the boundaries of gender, and in operating in an aggressive male-dominated sphere. Could other women learn from this cohort? The problem here is that these women are a minority élite. The class from which most of these successful women come is perhaps the most important factor in their successful inclusion into the political system. However, is this more true for a stable polity than it is for a polity that is witnessing mobilization on the basis of caste, region, religion and class? Do socio-political movements provide opportunities for women to use certain strategies that might be able to subvert the gender hierarchy in politics? If good government is about improving the access of marginalized groups such as women to political institutions it would be useful to explore successful strategies of access.

There is a third reason why it is important to examine women's representation in political institutions: we can explore the dynamic between institutional and grassroots politics. Two questions can be asked here: What has been the impact of the growing strength of the women's movement in putting the question of women's representation on the political agenda of political parties? and, in turn, has the women's movement been able to lobby the women representatives more effectively than men or has the form of party politics led to the expropriation of feminist voices?; How far have women in representative politics benefited from (without necessarily acknowledging it or even being aware of it) the growing confidence of the women's movement?

WHAT VALUE WOMEN REPRESENTATIVES?

The problem of representation highlighted in this paper is important in understanding women's role in institutional politics. If good government is democratic government then we need to consider the issues raised by the practice of formal democratic institutions, and their relation to the participatory politics of new social movements, such as the women's movement. Together with competing social loyalties, party-based institutional politics impose significant constraints upon women. Social and political institutions can (and do) form formidable choice-barriers for women representatives. Should we therefore skirt around formal institutions that are embedded in the dominant political discourses, and concentrate on mobilizing outside organizations?

There has been an ongoing debate within the feminist movement about the expropriatory power of institutions (Brown, 1992; Rai, 1995; Ehrenreich and Piven, 1982). The various positions have covered the entire spectrum from rejecting 'dealing' with state institutions entirely, to suggesting a 'in and against' the state approach, to examining the benefits of working with and through state institutions. I have argued that for women the state and civil society are both complex terrains – fractured, oppressive, threatening and also providing spaces for struggles and negotiations. These struggles and negotiations are grounded in the situation where various groups of women have to articulate their short- and long-term interests in the context of the multiplex power relations that form the state in any country. In turn, the state and its institutions are also 'shaped' by the forms and outcomes of these struggles. While denying this is the state's intention, or that struggles against states cause alliances to form, there are particular characteristics of Third World states such as India and Chile that need to be examined to form a judgement about the possible spaces for mobilization by women in their interests.

In both of these two countries the state and dominant political parties have taken up the cause of women's representation as part of the generalised discourse of modernity which they promote. This discourse, while not unified in itself, allows sections of the state to take initiatives to respond to the struggles of women for equality as well as for empowerment. This results in intra state conflict which allows further possibilities of negotiations and struggles by, and in the interests of women's organizations. The capacity of both of these states to implement its respective policies and enforce its laws is undermined by the weakness of the economy and political infrastructure, and by widespread corruption which leads to the delegitimization of government and the political system. This lack of capacity further enhances intra-state conflict.

Struggles also allow issues to be brought into the public sphere. Once this has happened it becomes difficult for governments not to address these issues and carry out a consultation and education process, however half-hearted. However, state institutions cannot be the sole focus of these struggles. Civil society while providing a space for mobilization also constrains the construction and organization of interests that challenge the dominant discourses of gendered power. Civil society is not an uncoerced space of free associations for women and other marginalized groups; it is deeply ambivalent about, if not hostile to, the reordering of gender relations. In this context the relationship between the state and civil society becomes an important arena for negotiation and struggle. Both the Indian and Chilean states can be said to be deeply 'embedded' in civil society and 'the peak interest groups' within it. As a result of this embeddedness, state institutions are constrained from proposing policies that would be disapproved of by peak interest groups. However, the modernist project that they ascribe to, especially when operating representative democratic political systems, does not allow them to be entirely neglectful of issues arising from women's struggles. It also forces them to take issue with some of the dominant interest groups. The result is a policy framework and the implementation of this which is at best patchy, allowing for further struggles provoked by the expansion of the domain of reform as well as by the increased capacity of the state to effectively implement existing policies. Both spaces – the informal and formalised networks of power – need to be negotiated by the women's movement to best serve 'women's interests.' (Rai, 1995a). Women's organizations such as the National Commission for Women and SERNAM can be effective in articulating and representing women's interests only in the context of such continuing negotiation.

This negotiation by its nature has to be complex, overlaid, and full of tension. As there is no one women's movement that we can point to, organizations such as SERNAM in Chile and the National Commission for Women in India would need to 'speak to' different groups of women organized around different issues. The interests that the organizations choose to privilege in negotiating with state organizations will vary, and of necessity will create hierarchies of interests around which new negotiations will be carried out. Conversely, these organizations will also need to negotiate with state organizations. These negotiations might be affected by: the coherence (or not) of particular state institutions and of their policy initiatives; the ability (or not) of state institutions to implement policies, and even the relations between state institutions, non-governmental organizations, and world monetary and aid agencies. This is a big agenda for women's organizations which cross boundaries between movements and institutions; it is an agenda that needs imagination, commitment, resources, and an understanding of the issues at stake. The outcomes of such investment of time, effort and resources are not certain, clear, or even necessarily always benign. If, however, the issues of accountability, democracy and capacity raised in this paper have to be addressed, then the continuing negotiation of boundaries between institutional and 'movement' politics needs to remain at the heart of the work of organizations such as the National Commission for Women and SERNAM.

REFERENCES

Alvarez, Sonia, *Engendering Democracy in Brazil: Women's Movements in Transition Politics* (New Jersey: Princeton University Press, 1990).

Bobbio, Noberto, *The Future of Democracy: A Defence of the Rules of the Game* (Cambridge: Polity Press, 1984).

Braidotti, Rosi, 'The politics of Ontological Difference' in T. Brennan (ed.) *Between Feminism and Psychoanalysis* (London: Routledge, 1989).

Brown, Wendy, 'Finding the Man in the State' Feminist Studies Vol. 18/1 (Spring 1992).

Burnell, Peter, *'Good Government' and Foreign Aid* (Working Paper No. 115, Department of Politics and International Studies, University of Warwick, Coventry, 1993).

Chuchryk, Patricia M., 'Feminist Anti-Authoritarian Politics: The Role of Women's Organizations in the Chilean Transition to Democracy' in Jaquette, Jean (ed.), *The Women's Movement in Latin America* (Boston: Unwin Hyman, 1989).

Diamond, Irene and Harstock, Nancy, 'Beyond interests in politics: a comment on Virginia Sapiro's "When are interests interesting?"', American Political Science Review, Vol. 75/3 (1981).

Dietz, Mary, 'Context is All: Feminism and Theories of Citizenship' in Mouffe, C. (ed.), *Dimensions of Radical Democracy* (London: Verso, 1991).

DWCD (Department of Women and Child Development), *National Perspective Plan for Women 1988-2000* (Delhi: Government of India, 1988).

Fierlbeck, Katherine, 'Getting Representation Right for Women in Development: Accountability, Consent, and the Articulation of Women's Interests' in IDS Bulletin Vol. 26/3 (1995).

Kishwar, Madhu, 'Why I do not call myself a feminist?', *Manushi* (1986).

Kumar, Radha, 'Contemporary Indian Feminism' in Feminist Review, No. 3 (Autumn 1989) pp20-9.

Liddle, Joanna, and Joshi, Rama, *Daughters of Independence* (New Delhi: Kali for Women, 1986).

Matear, Ann, 'The Servico Nacional de la Mujer (SERNAM): Equal Opportunities in Chile' Paper presented at Women, Law and Culture Conference at Warwick University, March 1995.

Nelson, Barbara, and Chowdhary, Najma (eds.), *Women and Politics Worldwide* (Yale University Press, 1994).

Outshoorn, Jane, 'Parity Democracy: a critical look at a "new" strategy' Paper prepared for the Workshop 'Citizenship and Plurality' ECPR, Leyden 2-5 April 1993.

Phillips, Anne, *Engendering Democracy* (Cambridge: Polity Press, 1991).

Rai, Shirin, 'Women Negotiating Boundaries: Gender, Law, and the Indian State' in Social and Legal Studies (1995a).

Rai, Shirin, 'Women and Public Power: Women in the Indian Parliament' in IDS Bulletin Vol. 26/3 (1995).

Rai, Shirin, 'Gender and Democratisation Or What Does Democracy Mean for Women in the Third World' in Democratization, Vol. 1/2 (1994).

Swarup, Hem Lata et.al., 'Women's Political Engagement in India' in Nelson, Barbara, and Chowdhury, Najma (eds.), *Women and Politics Worldwide* (London: Yale University Press, 1994).

Vargas, Virginia, 'The Feminist Movement in Latin America: Between Hope and Disenchantment' Paper presented at the Women's Studies Network (UK) Conference, June 1993.

Waylen, Georgina, 'Women's Movements, the State and Democratization in Chile' IDS Bulletin, Vol. 26/3 (1995).

Young, Iris M., 'Polity and group difference: a critique of the idea of universal citizenship' Ethics, Vol. 99 (1989).

COMMENT

Ann Matear

In recent years, the processes of democratization which have occurred throughout Eastern Europe and Latin America have highlighted many of the shortcomings of formal democracy in terms of representation, participation and accountability. Through case studies from Latin America and Asia, Rai provides a refreshing and pertinent analysis of good government *vis-a-vis* the representation of gender issues and women's political participation.

In India and Chile social movements, and women's movements in particular, have successfully provided a counterweight to formal political institutions. In both countries in 1990, state institutions were created to promote the position of women in society and to incorporate gender issues into the democratic process. The relationship between the women's movement and state institutions created to promote women's interests is not without tension. Access to political power may be contingent on abandoning the movement for the political parties and the state. If they do so, women activists may be better placed to influence outcomes and promote political, economic and social changes which can benefit women. Conversely, by entering formal politics they may limit their ability to criticize, to lobby, to constitute an autonomous political force.

The countries selected for analysis are significant as much for their similarities as for their differences. Both India and Chile have experienced multi-party democracy and periods of military rule within the last twenty years. In both countries, politics has been traditionally dominated by élites, and until recently gender issues have been relatively marginalized from mainstream politics. While gender strongly influences women's participation in the public sphere, it interrelates with other social factors which facilitate or impede access to the political system. In developing countries, women who participate actively in the political parties and the state are frequently linked to the political élites, are predominantly of middle or upper-middle class origins, and are university educated. Family networks provide women with a point of entry into the political class and a role model they can aspire to. It is significant that many of the role models for politically active women are fathers and brothers, as this tends to reproduce dominant patriarchal values within the political system and women who stand for election often do so on male terms.

The relationship between social movements and the state needs to be analysed within a specific political and historical context, and many of the differences between the case studies stem from this.

In the period analysed by Rai, Chile was experiencing a return to democracy after 17 years of military rule, while India was not undergoing a radical political transition. In Chile, the social movements were virtually the only expression of opposition to the authoritarian state between 1973 and 1988, as the political parties were banned and the unions continued to suffer repression. The women's movement played an important role in the opposition movement. Significantly, it linked the return to democracy in the nation to ending the authoritarian and repressive relationships which women endured on a daily basis within their homes and within society.

However, the movement's gender-specific demands were only a part of the global demand for democracy. The unity of purpose and common objective of ending the dictatorship obscured fundamental divisions which existed within the movement based on social class, political ideologies and the different approaches to feminism. The future of the movement and its insertion in the political process did not become an issue until democracy was clearly returning. Only then were the essential debates on autonomy, integration, inter-class allegiances, the movement's relationship with the state and the political parties actually raised.

The women's movement in Chile was not campaigning only on behalf of women – it was an expression of political opposition. Therefore the transition to democracy may have been the end of a particular stage in its life cycle, and this may account for the fragmentation of the women's movement following the return to democracy.

The transition in Chile was characterized by the re-emergence of institutional politics, with consensus on the political and economic models. This was paralleled by the contraction of civil society and the demobilization of the social movements. The opposition had become the government, therefore its enthusiasm for social protest, social movements, alternative grassroots politics and popular mobilization quickly waned. The political élites rapidly perceived that the very mechanisms which had returned them to power could lead to civil unrest if they were not brought under the control of the political institutions.

The political situation in India was not one of transition from dictatorship to democracy, therefore the relationship between the women's movement and the state was different. This may explain the fewer links between the female politicians and the movement in India.

In Chile, female élites were able to transfer from movement politics to the state, because the opposition became the government and they simply flowed with the tide.

In this particular historical context, socio-political movements successfully subverted gender barriers and provided entry into political institutions.

Index